The Collected Essays of
J.V. Cunningham

The
Collected Essays
of
J.V. Cunningham

THE **SWALLOW PRESS** INC.

CHICAGO

First Edition
First Printing

Published by
The Swallow Press Incorporated
Chicago, Illinois 60613

This book is printed on recycled paper

ISBN 0-8040-0670-9
LIBRARY OF CONGRESS CATALOG CARD NUMBER 75-21800

Contents

~~~~~~

Introduction

~~~~~~

There is less to be said about literature than has been said, and this book adds a little more. What it adds is, or was when first published, new, though it would take a lifetime of bibliographical search to be sure. And it has the merit and defect of brevity, with an occasional repetitiveness that may at times redeem the brevity.

I have excluded from this collection the articles and reviews published between the ages nineteen and twenty-three. They can be found in the periodicals (see Charles Gullans, *A Bibliography of the Published Works of J. V. Cunningham*, Los Angeles, 1973). These were apprentice pieces, written for money, in the honorable tradition of literary journalism, a calling graced—to name only old friends, two now dead—by Allen Tate, Yvor Winters, Philip Rahv, and Irving Howe. What I have retained is later, and in a narrower tradition: the tradition, to speak broadly, of classical Classical Philology.

Hence many of the essays are concerned with various aspects of form, including style, prosody, and the different kinds of fiction and forms of experience. And with the historical interpretation of texts: that is, with experiencing a text on its own terms. The spirit killeth, but the letter giveth life.

The two concerns tend to coincide, for forms are realized in circumstance. In fact, the essays themselves were in part determined by length and occasion, for, to note the overlooked obvious, length is a major principle of form, and often stipulated by occasion. "Woe or Wonder," for example, is a dissertation stripped to a monograph, which is to the scholarly "book" as the novelette is to the novel, with like advantages and disadvantages. Again, eleven of the pieces were public lectures. These are, by tradition and scheduling, from fifty to sixty minutes: that is, from five to six thousand words, for the public lecture voice speaks a hundred words a minute. Five others were read at special conferences, and vary in length with the time allotted. I may add, one's colleagues do not always observe the limits. There are also three introductions to anthologies, a book review, and a brief biography, and in each case the context determined the form.

Forms may be given or discovered—this corresponds to the current distinction between closed and open form—and may be both. But if, to quote E. M. Forster, "All that is prearranged is false," one could not in good faith give a public lecture or read a paper at MLA. Or meet his classes, or cash his salary check.

Lecture, paper, and introduction are further determined by the anticipated audience. Topic and text are often given, and should, at any rate, be ones the audience is familiar with, or thinks it should be familiar with. There are also certain antecedent forms given in the tradition, not stipulated but available and comforting. For example, one may begin with "the state of the question." The point of departure, then, will be some classic statement of the position disputed, and the speaker will hope to transfer that classicality to his own statement. For, though the end of the paper as published will be to inform and persuade, the end as delivered is to impress. For this is the oratory of display, a kissing cousin of sophistic declamation, and what is said is said with voice and presence, and it is public.

The length of "The Quest of the Opal," on the other hand, was not given, and the occasion was private. Several friends were puzzled by some poems I had written, and so, "a heretic of paraphrase," I turned them into prose, as any Elizabethan schoolboy had learned to do with his texts. I continued the practice for a while, then put the notes away. Coming across them some years later, I sensed an inherent form. In this case, the length of the final piece was determined by the material and the felt form. Later I salvaged twelve unused paragraphs and called them "The Journal of John Cardan."

Verse and prose are different dialects of a common language, and to turn one into the other is to translate. If something is lost in translation, something is also gained. In fact, to experience the literature of the past, or even of an alien culture of one's own day, is in a sense to translate, though the translation need not be formulated. If formulated, it is historical interpretation. I have discussed the principles and claims of such interpretation in numerous passages, but, since the virtue and defect of my prose is brevity, I shall add a few more words, and a few more interpretations.

First, what it is not. It does not consist in ascertaining the spirit of an age, and then relating particular works to that construction. It was not an age of reason that produced poems in syllogistic form, but a common schooling in the Old Logic. Hence I am not concerned with such notions as Modernism, except insofar as the notion itself is operative in a work. I have, for instance, as a poet been urged "to confront the twentieth century." The phrase is instant history, a tangle of doctrinaire prescriptions, written in the halls of academe. It implies the necessity of that Modernism whose memorial services are now being held. If my poems are not of their times, they are nevertheless part of the evidence for what the times are.

Now what it is. Every utterance is historical, even this, but not every one calls for interpretation. To interpret is to answer the question, What did he mean by that? and this implies the perception of some difficulty, some relevant uncertainty or ignorance, together with an imputation of value; the question was worth asking. Sometimes the answer is gloss: it is in The Dictionary. But we do not always recognize that there is a question, or we accept a mistaken answer. To the many glosses scattered through these essays I add a few more.

There is the couplet from Donne's verse letter, written while the English expeditionary fleet was becalmed in the Channel:

No use of lanterns, and in one place lay
Feathers and dust, today and yesterday.

Commentators, who know that lanterns are lanterns, tell us they were hung out at night to keep the fleet together, and would not be needed in a calm. The explanation reassures us, but it is inapposite. For "lanterns" at that time also meant "ventilators" (O.E.D., *s.v.* 4), which would, of course, more obviously be of no use in a calm.

Sometimes a little more than gloss is needed. When Othello seconds his wife's request—it is their wedding night—to accompany him on the expedition to Cyprus:

> I therefore beg it not
> To please the palate of my appetite,
> Nor to comply with heat, the young affects
> In my defunct and proper satisfaction,
> But to be free and bounteous to her mind.

he disclaims lust as a motive. But he parenthetically affirms the satisfaction that belongs to marriage, and states also, what is of legal importance, that the marriage has been consummated: "my defunct . . . satisfaction." Under *defungor* in Lewis and Short we read: "to have done with, acquit oneself of, discharge, perform, finish." The word is used in its basic Latin sense. There is, consequently, no need to emend, and read, as is commonly done:

> Nor to comply with heat—the young affects
> In me defunct—and proper satisfaction

which spoils the rhythm, and has been read as a confession of impotence.

To sum up:

> As woods whose change appears
> Still in their leaves throughout the sliding years,
> The first born dying, so the aged state
> Of words decay, and phrases born but late
> Like tender buds shoot up and freshly grow.
> Ourselves and all that's ours to death we owe.

And not words only, but forms of experience and the forms by which we construe it. We have dreams, but not dream visions. We think, but seldom syllogistically. The House of Hamlet and the House of Polonius were not nuclear families in the Bronx. Election is a safe and adequate pension, and damnation is to live remote from Manhattan or Cambridge, Mass. To re-experience with some immediacy and on their own terms these lost literary, academic, social, and religious forms is to possess the past. If we are concerned with experience in our own forms, we can write our own poems.

J. V. CUNNINGHAM

I

Woe or Wonder

The Emotional Effect of
Shakespearean Tragedy

Ripeness is All

I am concerned here with understanding precisely what Shakespeare meant. It is true that "when we read Shakespeare's plays," as one scholar says, "we are always meeting our own experiences and are constantly surprised by some phrase which expresses what we thought to be our own secret or our own discovery."[1] But the danger is that the meaning we find may really be our own secret, our own discovery, rather than Shakespeare's, and the more precious and beguiling for being our own. The danger I have in mind can be illustrated by our attitude toward one of the most famous of Shakespearean phrases, "Ripeness is all." It is a favorite quotation of Mr. Eliot's. "It seems to me," he says in discussing the question of truth and belief in poetry, "to have profound emotional meaning, with, at least, no literal fallacy."[2] He does not specify what this meaning is, but I take it that it is something not strictly denotative though emotionally compelling.

The phrase, indeed, has seemed to many to represent a profound intuition into reality and to sum up the essence of Shakespearean, or even of human, tragedy. It speaks quite nearly to us. What it means to each will perhaps depend on his or her own experience and his or her own way of relating the texture of experience to the insights of literature. Yet all would agree that "Ripeness is all" gathers into a phrase something of the

1

ultimate value of this life; it reassures us that maturity of experience is a final good, and that there is a fulness of feeling, an inner and emotional completion in life that is attainable and that will resolve our tragedies. Such at least seems to be the interpretation of a recent critic. "After repeated disaster," he says of Gloucester in *King Lear*:

> he can assent, "And that's true too," to Edgar's "Ripeness is all." For man may ripen into fulness of being, which means, among other things, that one part of him does not rule all the rest and that one moment's mood does not close off all the perspectives available to him.[3]

In this way we discover in Shakespeare's phrase the secret morality of our own times. It is a meaning I can enter into quite as deeply as anyone, but it is not what Shakespeare meant.

Shakespeare meant something much more traditional. The phrase occurs in *King Lear*. In an earlier scene Edgar had prevented Gloucester from committing suicide, that act which consummates the sin of despair, and Gloucester had accepted the situation in the true spirit of Christian resignation:

> henceforth I'll bear
> Affliction till it do cry out itself
> "Enough, enough," and die.
> 4. 6. 75-77

But now Gloucester seems to relapse for a moment, saying:

> No further, sir; a man may rot even here.

And Edgar stiffens his resolution with these words:

> Men must endure
> Their going hence even as their coming hither:
> Ripeness is all.
> 5. 2. 9-11

The context is the desire for death. The conclusion is that as we were passive to the hour of our birth so we must be passive to the hour of our death. So far, surely, the speech is an affirmation of the spirit of resignation, and it would be reasonable to suppose that the summary clause at the end, "Ripeness is all," is but the final restatement of this attitude. It was certainly an available attitude. The experience of Christian resignation was dense with the history of the Western spirit, and that history was alive and present in Shakespeare's time; it spoke daily from the pulpit and in the private consolations of intimate friends. The theme, furthermore, was a favorite with Shakespeare. It had been fully explored in the Duke's great speech in *Measure for Measure*:

> Be absolute for death. Either death or life
> Will thereby be the sweeter. Reason thus with life:
> If I do lose thee I do lose a thing
> That none but fools would keep. A breath thou art,
> Servile to all the skyey influences
> That do this habitation where thou keep'st
> Hourly afflict. Merely thou art death's fool;
> For him thou labour'st by thy flight to shun,
> And yet runn'st toward him still....
>   Yet in this life
> Lie hid moe thousand deaths; yet death we fear
> That makes these odds all even.
>   3. 1. 5-13, 39-41

But the finest expression, other than in the passage from *Lear*, is Hamlet's speech to Horatio as he goes to the catastrophe:

> we defy augury: there's a special providence in the fall of a sparrow. If it be now, 'tis not to come; if it be not to come, it will be now; if it be not now, yet it will come: the readiness is all.
>
>   5. 2. 230-33

This is as much as to say that we must endure our going hence, be it when it may, since the hour of our death is in the care of Providence: *the readiness is all*.

It has been said that this is Stoic, and certainly "augury" hints toward Antiquity. But he who speaks of a special provi-

dence in the fall of a sparrow could trust an audience in the age
of Elizabeth to think of Christian theology and the New Testament:

> And fear not them which kill the body, but are not able
> to kill the soul: but rather fear him which is able to
> destroy both body and soul in hell. Are not two spar-
> rows sold for a farthing? *and one of them shall not fall
> on the ground without your Father.* But the very hairs
> of your head are all numbered. Fear ye not therefore,
> ye are of more value than many sparrows.
>
> Watch therefore: for ye know not what hour your Lord
> doth come. But know this, that if the goodman of the
> house had known in what watch the thief would come,
> he would have watched, and would not have suffered
> his house to be broken up. *Therefore be ye also ready:*
> for in such hour as ye think not the Son of man cometh.
>
> Matt. 10:28-31; 24:42-44

It was not only Seneca and his sons who could urge men to
meet death with equanimity. Bishop Latimer, the Protestant
martyr, in a sermon preached before King Edward VI speaks
the thought and almost the words of Hamlet:

> *Unusquisque enim certum tempus habet praedefinitum
> a Domino:* "For every man hath a certain time ap-
> pointed him of God, and God hideth that same time
> from us." For some die in young age, some in old age,
> according as it pleaseth him. He hath not manifested
> to us the time because he would have us at all times
> ready; else if I knew the time, I would presume upon
> it, and so should be worse. But he would have us ready
> at all times, and therefore he hideth the time of our
> death from us. . . . But of that we may be sure, there
> shall not fall one hair from our head without his will;
> and we shall not die before the time that God hath ap-
> pointed unto us: which is a comfortable thing, specially
> in time of sickness or wars. . . . There be some which

say, when their friends are slain in battle, "Oh, if he had tarried at home, he should not have lost his life." These sayings are naught: for God hath appointed every man his time. To go to war in presumptuousness, without an ordinary calling, such going to war I allow not: but when thou art called, go in the name of the Lord; and be well assured in thy heart that thou canst not shorten thy life with well-doing.[4]

The similarity of the phrase in *Hamlet* to the one in *Lear* is so close that the first may be taken as the model and prototype of the other. But in *Lear* the phrase has been transmuted, and with it the idea and attitude. The deliberate and developed rhetoric of *Measure for Measure* has served its purpose to explore the area of experience, and has been put aside. The riddling logicality of Hamlet's speech has been simplified to the bare utterance of:

> Men must endure
> Their going hence even as their coming hither

and the concept of the arbitrariness of birth has been introduced to reinforce the arbitrariness of death. Finally, Hamlet's precise and traditional statement, " the readiness is all," has been transformed into a metaphor.

What does the metaphor mean? There is no need for conjecture; it had already by the time of *Lear* become trite with use, and with use in contexts closely related to this. In Thomas Wilson's *Art of Rhetoric* (1560) we read:

> Among fruit we see some apples are soon ripe and fall from the tree in the midst of summer; other be still green and tarry till winter, and hereupon are commonly called winter fruit: even so it is with man, some die young, some die old, and some die in their middle age.[5]

Shakespeare has Richard in *Richard II* comment on the death of John of Gaunt:

> The ripest fruit first falls, and so doth he:
> His time is spent
>
> 2. 1. 153-54

That is, as fruit falls in the order of ripeness, so a man dies when his time is spent, at his due moment in the cosmic process. Again, Touchstone's dry summary of life and time in *As You Like It*:

> And so, from hour to hour, we ripe and ripe,
> And then, from hour to hour, we rot and rot
>
> 2. 7. 26-27

does not mean that we ripen to maturity and then decline, but that we ripen toward death, and then quite simply and with no metaphors rot.

But death is not incidental to Shakespearean tragedy; it is rather the defining characteristic. Just as a Shakespearean comedy is a play that has a clown or two and ends in marriages, so a tragedy involves characters of high estate and concludes with violent deaths. The principle of its being is death, and when this is achieved the play is ended. In this sense, then, "Ripeness is all" is the structural principle of Shakespearean tragedy. Thus in *Richard III* the Cassandra-like chorus, the old Queen Margaret, enters alone as the play draws rapidly on to the final catastrophe and says:

> So now prosperity begins to mellow
> And drop into the rotten mouth of death
>
> 4. 4. 1-2

And in *Macbeth*, Malcolm says toward the close:

> Macbeth
> Is ripe for shaking, and the pow'rs above
> Put on their instruments.
>
> 4. 3. 237-39

In this passage the powers above, who are the agents of Providence, are associated with the ripened time. Providence is destiny, and in tragedy destiny is death.

By "Ripeness is all," then, Shakespeare means that the fruit will fall in its time, and man dies when God is ready. The phrase gathers into the simplest of sentences, the most final of linguistic patterns, a whole history of attempted formulations, and by the rhetorical device of a traditional metaphor transposes a state into a process. Furthermore, the metaphor shifts our point of view from a man's attitude toward death, from the "readiness" of Hamlet and the "Men must endure" of the first part of Edgar's speech, to the absolutness of the external process of Providence on which the attitude depends.

But this is not what the phrase means to the uninstructed modern reader, and this poses a problem. The modern meaning is one that is dear to us and one that is rich and important in itself. It would be natural to ask, Need we give it up? I see no reason why we should give up the meaning: maturity of experience is certainly a good, and the phrase in a modern context is well enough fitted to convey this meaning. But it is our phrase now, and not Shakespeare's, and we should accept the responsibility for it. The difference in meaning is unmistakable: ours looks toward life and his toward death; ours finds its locus in modern psychology and his in Christian theology. If we are secure in our own feelings we will accept our own meanings as ours, and if we have any respect for the great we will penetrate and embrace Shakespeare's meaning as his. For our purpose in the study of literature, and particularly in the historical interpretation of texts, is not in the ordinary sense to further the understanding of ourselves. It is rather to enable us to see how we could think and feel otherwise than as we do. It is to erect a larger context of experience within which we may define and understand our own by attending to the disparity between it and the experience of others.

In fact, the problem that is here raised with respect to literature is really the problem of any human relationship: Shall we understand another on his terms or on ours? It is the problem of affection and truth, of appreciation and scholarship. Shakespeare has always been an object of affection and an object of study. Now, it is common experience that affection begins in misunderstanding. We see our own meanings in what we love and we misconstrue for our own purposes. But life will not leave us there, and not only because of external pressures. What concerns us is naturally an object of study. We sit across the room and trace the lineaments of experience on the face of concern, and we find it is not what we thought it was. We come to see that what Shakespeare is saying is not what we thought he was saying, and we come finally to appreciate it for what it is. Where before we had constructed the fact from our feeling, we now construct our feeling from the fact. The end of affection and concern is accuracy and truth, with an alteration but no dimunition of feeling.

Aught of Woe or Wonder

~~~~~~

Whatever emotion and whatever tragedy may be, it has always been said that tragedy, and especially the tragic catastrophe, evokes strong and specific emotions. The doctrine is common to Antiquity and the present day as well as to Shakespeare and the Renaissance. "In undertaking any piece of literature," Erasmus remarks in a little Renaissance treatise on how to teach, "it is advisable to show what kind of work it is, the nature of its subject-matter, and what especially is to be looked for in that kind of work. . . . In tragedy one looks especially for the emotional effects, which are quite strong, and then for the means by which these effects are excited."[1] The nature of the effects, however, alters from period to period as the nature of tragedy alters and as the quality and structure of the emotional life varies from society to society, for there is a history of the emotions as well as a history of ideas. The effects we are concerned with here are those of Shakespearean tragedy and those specifically intended by the author and supported by his tradition. The question is, What emotional effects did Shakespeare intend to be evoked by the catastrophe of his greater tragedies?

I

We are told explicitly at the end of *Hamlet* what the emotional

9

effect of the tragic catastrophe is: it is one of fear, sorrow, and wonder. The point is made in two passages, the first of which reads:

> I follow thee.
> I am dead, Horatio. Wretched queen, adieu!
> You that look pale and tremble at this chance,
> That are but mutes or audience to this act,
> Had I but time (as this fell sergeant, Death,
> Is strict in his arrest) O, I could tell you—
> But let it be. Horatio, I am dead;
> Thou liv'st; report me and my cause aright
> To the unsatisfied.
>
> 5. 2. 343-51

The scene is familiar to every reader: the King and Queen are dead, Laertes has uttered his last words. And now Hamlet, in a fashion conventional to the Elizabethan drama, addresses his remarks rapidly to one character after another—to the dying Laertes, to Horatio, to the Queen; and finally he turns to the other actors on the stage, to the "mutes" who serve as "audience to this act." These "look pale and tremble": it is their function to express the proper emotional attitude and so to convey that attitude directly to the larger audience who witness the play, for emotional effects are directly transferable; indeed, they are much more communicable than ideas.

The way in which this process was understood in Shakespeare's time is explained by his contemporary, Thomas Dekker, in the prologue to one of his plays:

> That man give me whose breast filled by the Muses
> With rapture into a second them infuses;
> Can give the actor sorrow, rage, joy, passion,
> Whilst he again by self-same agitation
> Commands the hearers, sometimes drawing out tears,
> Then smiles, and fills them both with hopes and fears.[2]

The dramatist derives emotions from his sources of inspiration, infuses them into the actor, who in turn communicates them to the audience. The scheme of thought here is Platonic. It is that which Socrates explains to the professional reciter of Homer in Plato's dialogue *Ion* under the figure of a magnetic chain of attraction (533C), and doubtless is borrowed from that model. The Muse inspires Homer as a magnet moves an iron ring, the reciter Ion is moved by Homer as another ring by the magnetized one, and the audience finally is moved by Ion, so that three rings hang like a chain from the magnet. Thus feeling runs directly from the sources of poetry to the audience through the medium of poet and actor, and the emotions which in this case Ion excites in his hearers—fear, sorrow, and wonder (535B-C)[3] —are curiously enough those which Shakespeare in *Hamlet* ascribes to the tragic catastrophe. They are also, of course, the emotional effects which Aristotle ascribes to Greek tragedy— pity and fear, certainly, and as we shall see, wonder, too.[4]

The particular emotion denominated in the first passage from *Hamlet* is the conventional tragic effect of fear or terror, for to "look pale and tremble" are the very marks and signs of this. Richard in *Richard III* queries Buckingham on his qualifications for the role of tragic villain:

> Come, cousin, can'st thou quake and change thy color . . .
> As if thou wert distraught and mad with terror?

And Buckingham reassures him:

> Tut. I can counterfeit the deep tragedian.
>   3. 5. 1, 4-5

The emotion of fear is evoked by "this chance," in men who are "mutes or audience to this act." What is the precise meaning of "this act" and "this chance," since it is with respect to these that the effect is predicated? *Act* in such contexts signifies the particular course of events under consideration. So the First Gentleman comments on the narration of those extraordinary events that untangle the knot of *The Winter's Tale*: "The dignity of this act was worth the audience of kings and princes, for by such was it acted." (5. 2. 86-88) And Prospero in the *Tempest*, referring to the whole business of his deposition and exile, says

to Alonso: "Thy brother was a furtherer in this act." (5. 1. 73)
But the closest parallel to the present passage is in the final
speech in *Othello* where Lodovico, the representative of the
Venetian state, closes the play thus:

> Myself will straight aboard, and to the state
> This heavy act with heavy heart relate.

This heavy act—that is, "The tragic loading of this bed," the
deaths of Desdemona and Othello. There is here an exact correspondence between the quality of the events and the quality
of the emotion they evoke, between the heaviness of act and
the heaviness of heart. Similarly the emotion of fear or terror
would naturally be provoked by such fearful and terrible events
as the deaths of the King, Queen, and Laertes, and the imminent
death of Hamlet himself.

"This chance" has a meaning similar to "this act." It is,
furthermore, a notion and a term intimately associated with the
central Elizabethan conception of tragedy, and especially of the
tragic catastrophe. It concentrates in a word the two main aspects of that event, aspects that had long been fused in the Latin
equivalent, *casus*. For that word may signify, as it does in the
late medieval collections of tragic stories, the fall and death of
a great figure which constitutes the catastrophe; and it may also
signify the external cause of such a fall, the operation of that
agency which to man seems Chance or Fortune, but which from
a true and theological point of view is to be regarded as the unfolding of Divine Providence. Indeed, nothing really happens by
Chance or Fortune with respect to an absolute God, but only with
respect to secondary causes: *nihil est a casu vel fortuna respectu
Dei, sed respectu ceterarum causarum.*[5] Hence the display on the
stage of the operation of Chance, which is but the inscrutable
ways of Divine Providence, strikes the witnesses with fear and
terror when the case is notable, for it illuminates the disparity
between the relative world of man and the absoluteness of the
Eternal Cause.

The bare word, of course, though shot through with the
larger meanings of that historic term, does not carry with it
such a full and explicit theory as has just been sketched. Yet

its use here does imply the prior existence of such a context. What the bare word means can be ascertained by glancing through a Shakespeare concordance: the meaning ranges from the relatively colorless significance of "ordinary happening or event," through the denominatian of such events as make up a narrative (*Cymb*. 5. 5. 391), to the strictly philosophical significance of "Chance or Fortune." But the phrase, "this chance," has also a special and restricted meaning. It means the fall and death of notable persons and has in it an element of suddenness and surprise, of the apparently fortuitous.

For example, in the *Tragedy of Locrine* (about 1591), a bad but representative play, the chorus promises us:

> the sequel shall declare
> What tragic chances fall out in this war.
> 2 Prol., 16-17[6]

And fall they do, one after another. So also King Henry in *3 Henry VI* speaks of the dead slain in battle:

> How will the country for these woful chances
> Misthink the king, and not be satisfied!
> 2. 5. 107-08

But the best example is in *Macbeth*, where Macbeth speaks of the murder of Duncan after its accomplishment:

> Had I but died an hour before this chance,
> I had liv'd a blessed time.
> 2. 3. 96-97

That is, "My life had ended in the state of grace (*I had liv'd a blessed time*) if I had died before resolving to murder my King (*an hour before this chance*)," for the fall from the state of grace was coincident with the moral decision. "This chance," then, is the murder of Duncan, a notable fall. In the passage from *Hamlet* it is the tragic catastrophe. And the immediate emotional effect of this on the audience is said to be fear.

But fear is not the only effect ascribed to the catastrophe.

In another passage the effects are designated as those of sorrow and astonishment, or woe and wonder. After the death of Hamlet, the young Fortinbras enters in the majesty of state, and as he enters asks:

> Where is this sight?

Horatio answers him:

> What is it you would see?
> If aught of woe or wonder, cease your search.
>   5. 2. 373-74

The tableau of destruction remains on the stage:

> O proud Death,
> What feast is toward in thine eternal cell
> That thou so many princes at a shot
> So bloodily hast struck?
>   5. 2. 375-78

And Horatio, who was privy to it all, defines this sight as one of woe and wonder, *doloris et admirationis*. It is interesting to note that in the First Quarto, the mangled stage version of *Hamlet*, the passage reads:

> *Enter Fortinbrasse with his traine*
> FORTINBRASSE: Where is this bloody sight?
> HORATIO: If aught of woe or wonder you'ld behold
> Then looke upon this tragicke spectacle.

In both texts the spectacle is characterized by its proper effects. One of these is *woe* or sorrow, which is the ground of pity, as it was to the Watch who discovered the bodies of Romeo and Juliet:

> We see the ground on which these woes do lie,
> But the true ground of all these piteous woes
> We cannot without circumstance descry.
>   5. 3. 179-81

Hence pity is evoked by the woes of the catastrophe of *Romeo*, the tragic deaths, by what the chorus-character, Friar Laurence, had already called in the same scene "this lamentable chance." (146) Nevertheless, woe is not precisely pity. It is the more general term, of which pity is a species. It is the English equivalent of that *dolor sive tristitia* which in the medieval tradition of literary criticism is noted, rather than pity (*misericordia sive commiseratio*), as the subject and effect of tragedy,[7] and which in the medieval tradition of psychological analysis (which is substantially the Renaissance tradition) is treated at length along with fear as one of the basic and most powerful passions of the soul. The others are joy and hope (St. Thomas, *ST*, 1-2. 25. 4). Pity, then, denotes precisely the relationship of the spectator to the catastrophe; but the nature of the catastrophe itself is woeful.

The relationship of the terms is that expounded by Edgar in *Lear*. To Gloucester's question:

Now, good sir, what are you?

he answers:

A most poor man, made tame to fortune's blows,
Who, by the art of known and feeling sorrows,
Am pregnant to good pity.
4. 6. 224-27

If we may apply this passage to the general notion of tragedy, we may say that Edgar is the ideal spectator. He has attained the moral effect of that excitation of feeling; he has been "made tame" by participating in "fortune's blows," which are the material of tragedy; he has penetrated into that experience consciously and has realized its significance in feeling, and so has attained to the habit of, the capacity for exercising, the virtue of pity.

The catastrophe is sorrowful and naturally begets pity. It is also sudden, surprising, on a large scale, and involves great persons; hence it evokes wonder. This is an emotion less discussed in connection with tragedy than either fear or sorrow, and one that the literary person today does not easily think of as

an emotion, but it is a commonplace in the Renaissance especially in connection with the deaths of notable persons and with
the effects of drama and fiction. Dekker, for instance, with reference to the death of Queen Elizabeth, speaks of "the sorrow
and amazement that like an earthquake began to shake the dis-
tempered body of this island (by reason of our late sovereign's
departure)." And Sidney characterizes tragedy as "stirring the
affects of admiration and commiseration."[8] *Admiration*, of
course, is simply the Latin term for "wonder," as *commiseration*
is for "pity." The emotion itself is that state of overpowering
surprise, the shocked limit of feeling, which represents either
the extreme of joy or, as in this case, the extreme of fear. Indeed,
in the medieval tradition of psychological analysis it is defined
as a species of fear (*ST*, 1-2. 41. 4), and thus the relation of wonder to fear is similar to that of pity to sorrow.

II

Fear, sorrow, and wonder are the explicit effects of the tragic
catastrophe of *Hamlet*, or so at least it is here argued. But even
if one grants that the effects are named in the particular passages
cited, they are not spoken by the author in his own person. They
are spoken by characters in a play. The remarks are in character,
no doubt, and have some bearing on the delineation of character, but they can hardly be taken as expressing the author's intention with regard to the play as a whole, for drama by its very
nature denies the author not only the right but even the possibility of speaking in his own person. Whatever a character
thinks, says, or does must be taken only as an expression of
character, and as an action in the sense that character and action
are but aspects of each other. Hence Hamlet's and Horatio's remarks are elements in the total effect of the play, functionally
related to all other elements, but not to be taken as explicit comments which furnish a guiding principle of order for the whole
and consequently represent the author's intention.

But the assumptions that lie behind this point of view do
not apply to Elizabethan drama though they do apply to a good
many modern works. The principal assumption is that the work
as a whole is an indissoluble unit that exists only in its total

effect. This is one aspect of the doctrine of organic form. The assumption operates in this way among others: whatever is said in a play is construed in the light of the critic's total impression of the work, or more often of the character who speaks since the delineation of character is usually taken to be the primary end of fiction. Hence a speech is first read as contributing to the whole, either of the play or of the character, and then reinterpreted so as to conform to the whole that the critic has constructed. Whatever is discordant with this must be reconciled, often by the invocation of "irony," a device as fertile as Stoic allegory for disposing of the difficulties which the original text puts in the way of an interpretation.

Now, if every speech of an effective character is dramatic, in the modern sense, then it never means what it says but is only an expression of what the critic thinks the character's character is. What this leads to in practice can be made clear by an example. A modern critic, and a scholar quite learned in Renaissance thought, sees in Iago's rejoinder to Roderigo's confession of moral helplessness (*Othello*, 1. 3. 319*ff.*) "a grand perversion of the theory that good is the end and purpose of reason."[9] Roderigo has confessed with a shameless determinism his love for Desdemona, even though she is Othello's wife:

> What should I do? I confess it is my shame to be so fond, but it is not in my virtue to amend it.

And Iago replies:

> Virtue, a fig! 'Tis in ourselves that we are thus or thus. Our bodies are our gardens, to the which our wills are gardeners; so that if we will plant nettles or sow lettuce, set hyssop and weed up thyme, supply it with one gender of herbs or distract it with many—either to have it sterile with idleness or manured with industry—why, the power and corrigible authority of this lies in our wills.

The critic notes, "This passage states the ethics, the infidelity, of selfishness."

Perhaps he is mislead by "Virtue, a fig!" (the punctuation is mine), overlooking the fact that in the context ("it is not in my virtue to amend it") "virtue" has quite obviously the common Elizabethan meaning of "power," and that Iago is consequently by no means making light of that virtue which is the opposite of vice. For what does Iago say? He picks up Roderigo's assertion that it is not in his power not to be a sinning fool, to go kill himself for love, and maintains that we do have the power to make ourselves one thing or the other, good or evil, to control or not to control our bodies, our lower natures, and that this power is our will. This, so far as I can see, is a notorious commonplace of the Christian tradition, as well as of the Aristotelian. It is plain and hoary orthodoxy, and there is no perversion in it. Of course, a theologian might object that Iago's position is too Pelagian, that it makes no provision for the Grace of God, but the statement is brief and is not theological in context; in fact, you will hardly restrain a man from killing himself for love by suggesting that the Grace of God may prevent his accomplishing his purpose.

The second objection that could be made against the orthodoxy of this passage is that it is, perhaps, too voluntaristic, that nothing is said of reason. But this objection fails if we quote the whole passage, for Iago continues:

> If the balance of our lives had not one scale of reason to poise another of sensuality, the blood and baseness of our natures would conduct us to most prepost'rous conclusions. But we have reason to cool our raging motions, our carnal stings, our unbitted lusts; whereof I take this that you call love to be a sect or scion.

That is, Iago identifies the power and corrigible authority that lies in our wills with reason. Hence, it is evident that it is the medieval and Christian concept of the reasonable will which he opposes to the deterministic sensuality of Roderigo. Finally, no one, I trust, will maintain that Iago slanders in this instance true Love by designating Roderigo's infection as lust, which it is.

Yet on this latter passage the critic remarks: "Iago understands the warfare between reason and sensuality, but his ethics are totally inverted; reason works in him not good, as it should according to natural law, but evil, which he has chosen for his good." This, as a remark on Iago's character and actions in general, is aptly and accurately put. But the remark purports to be on this particular passage, and as such it is precisely wrong.

The passage is one of the finest statements, especially in its rhythm, of the traditional and orthodox view of the relation of the reasonable will to the sensitive soul; it has, then, its own absolute value as "thought," as the accomplished saying of something very much worth saying. It has also its function in the plot and its relation to Iago's character, but this function and relationship is rather "mechanical" (in fact, hierarchical) than "organic" (that is, monistic). Yet the passage serves the larger purposes of the plot without losing and altering its own quality as such. In the plot, it is an argument to persuade Roderigo from suicide, and is such an argument as a divine might use. But Iago's purpose in persuasion is not to save Roderigo's soul but to save his person and his purse for the benefit of Iago's own designs. The evil lies in the end, the intention; the means and the accidental effects are in themselves good, nor do they lose that quality in being used for an evil end. It is good to prevent a man from killing himself. The argument employed is orthodox and true, and no less true for the circumstances. The devil quotes Scripture to his purpose, but you need not for this reason take Scripture as an expression of the devil's character.

A Shakespearean speech, then, takes its point in part from itself, especially if it goes beyond the bare gist of what is needed for the plot, and in part from its context, from who says it and under what circumstances. But the relation of context and speech is one that depends on relevant considerations, and relevance is construed in terms of what is appropriate. It is beside the point, then, in considering the last scene of *Hamlet*, that Hamlet occupies a privileged position among Shakespeare's heroes, that he is said to be of all those the most lovingly and sympathetically presented, so much so that many feel in this instance the author has been partial to his character. It is beside the point, even, that earlier in the play Hamlet has shown a critical interest in the discussion of drama. His remarks to the players are called forth by that situation and are appropriate to it, though they are also interesting in themselves and go quite beyond what is needed for the action.

It is somewhat in point that Hamlet is the hero, and especially that he is at the moment he speaks the sole surviving member of the royal family, and hence for that moment the head of the state; he has the right to speak authoritatively. Besides, he is dying, and one's last words are commonly supposed to be truthful. But the real point is that his remarks are addressed to the standers-by as to an audience. They are a comment on the reactions of an audience, and must be taken as expressing how an audience would and should react. His remarks simply put into words what the other actors on the stage are to express in gesture, and if the actual audience does not feel the like, the play has been a failure.

III

The character of Horatio, however, and the circumstances under which he speaks are, in this respect, a little more complicated. In the first place, he speaks at the request of Fortinbras. And what is the significance of Fortinbras? He is the principle of renewed order in the state. He is the indispensable character for concluding a Shakespearean play; for each play, with the notable exception of *Troilus and Cressida*, begins with disorder in the state and concludes only on the restoration of order. As the representative of order he is in virtue of his office conceived of as reason: for authority is order, and order is reason. This is common doctrine. He speaks the truth and the truth is spoken to him. Consequently, his presence is almost a necessary condition for Horatio's remarks.

But what is the position of Horatio himself? Horatio, as has often been noted, is a kind of chorus. He is a special character outside of the plot, except insofar as he is the confidant of and spokesman for Hamlet. But he is not the kind of chorus that is swayed now to this side and now to that as the tides of sympathy and fortune shift, as is the Greek chorus, or the chorus in Jonson's *Cataline*. Horatio is the well-tempered man. He is the man of whom Hamlet has said:

> Since my dear soul was mistress of her choice
> And could of men distinguish, her election
> Hath seal'd thee for herself. For thou hast been
> As one, in suff'ring all, that suffers nothing;
> A man that Fortune's buffets and rewards
> Hath ta'en with equal thanks; and blest are those
> Whose blood and judgment are so well commingled
> That they are not a pipe for Fortune's finger
> To sound what stop she please. Give me that man
> That is not passion's slave, and I will wear him
> In my heart's core, ay, in my heart of hearts,
> As I do thee.
>
> 3. 2. 68-79

This speech has its own function in the scene—it is the play scene—and it serves particularly as a contrast with the later bitter ragging of Rosencrantz and Guildenstern: "You would play upon me; you would seem to know my stops; you would pluck out the heart of my mystery . . . ," and so on (3. 2. 380*ff.*). It has its own function as a thought worthy of being expressed and not inappropriate to the circumstances. But it is also the speech that establishes in fairly full and explicit terms the relevance of Horatio to the play.

One of the key terms in the passage is "election." This is a technical term in the medieval tradition for the act of moral choice (*ST*, 1-2, 13, translating Aristotle's *proairesis*) with respect to choosing the means to an end. The end is happiness, or some aspect of it, and true friendship with a just man is the means:

> Horatio, thou art e'en as just a man
> As e'er my conversation cop'd withal.
> 3. 2. 59-60

Thus election chooses Horatio. But moral choice is a function of reason, of the soul, and is exercised as soon as one attains the "age of reason," but not before (*ST*, 1. 100. 2, and 1-2. 13. 2. *contra*). Finally, the metaphor of sealing derives from the common Aristotelian and scholastic figure of imposing a seal on wax, which represents the relationship of form and matter: the choice of means gives determinate form to the end desired (*ST*, 1-2. 13. 1. c., especially *ad fin.*). The meaning is illustrated in the following passage:

> NESTOR: ... It is suppos'd
> He that meets Hector issues from our choice;
> And choice, being mutual act of all our souls,
> Makes merit her election
>   *Troilus*, 1. 3. 346-49

Choice is an act of the soul; the particular act of choosing this or this as means is "election." Sometimes the choice is erroneous, the will is carried away by the sensitive appetite (*ST*, 1-2. 77):

> HECTOR: But value dwells not in particular will:
> It holds his estimate and dignity
> As well wherein 'tis precious of itself
> As in the prizer. 'Tis mad idolatry
> To make the service greater than the god;
> And the will dotes that is attributive
> To what infectiously itself affects
> Without some image of th' affected merit.
> TROILUS: I take to-day a wife, and my election
> Is led on in the conduct of my will,
> My will enkindled by mine eyes and ears,
> Two traded pilots 'twixt the dangerous shores,
> Of will and judgment. How may I avoid,
> Although my will distaste what it elected,
> The wife I chose?
>   *Troilus*, 2. 2. 53-67

Similarly in *Cymbeline*:

> SECOND LORD: If it be a sin to make a true election,
>   she is damn'd.
>   1. 2. 29-30

To return, Hamlet says that Horatio is the man whom Hamlet, when he came to the age of reason, selected by a reasonable choice as the fit co-respondent of his dear soul, which is in its essence reason. For Horatio is one who is open to all experience but who suffers by it no inner alteration of his reasonable form. He is impassive to all passions. He is indifferent to the external operations of fortune, for he is a man of perfected self-mastery, sealed by grace, in whom the irrational and the rational are in due relation, the one subordinated to the other; and thus the inner unalterable core of reasonable order is not subject to the irrational alterations produced by the impingement of external circumstances. Hence Horatio should be regarded as the ideal commentator, like the similar characters in Jonson's plays, Cordatus, Crites, and Horace: he is reason expressing reasonable judgment on the action.

The point perhaps calls for some elaboration. The ideal spokesman in Elizabethan literature is always spokesman by virtue of his reasonableness. He is never intended to be biographically identifiable with the author, though of course it would be impossible for authors so individual as Shakespeare and Jonson not to infuse some of their own qualities into a character. But the Elizabethan author had no intention of expressing his own personality, either in a character or in his work as a whole. In fact, he did not know that he had such a thing as a personality, for the concept of personality can hardly be said to have been formed. It was the reasonable soul that was the central psychological concept of the Renaissance, and a man was praiseworthy, as Horatio was, insofar as the reasonable soul spoke in him and was hearkened to. It is true that a man was considered to have certain individualizing properties derived from his sex, his time of life, and his position in society, but these were comprised in the concept of decorum. They were the differentiations of reasonableness in accordance with circumstance. Whatever traits he might have beyond these, as for instance, melancholy or foppery, were the result of a disturbance of reasonable balance and a deviation from the ideal norm, and they were vicious insofar as they deviated. All this is familiar to the student of the Renaissance, but the conclusion is that the character who is presented as conforming to the ideal norm is presented as a standard by which deviations from the norm may be charted, and when he speaks he speaks in the light of reason, and what he says represents the author's explicit intentions. For the author himself is reason.

IV

The question of under what circumstances Horatio speaks has now been answered in part. He speaks in reply to Fortinbras' request, and Fortinbras is the principle of reason and order in the state, who expounds and exacts the truth; and he himself is the reasonable commentator.

But the situation is more complicated than this. The situation at the end of *Hamlet* is the kind of final one which is customary in Shakespeare's plays. The loose ends, or most of them, are now tied up; the course of action is recapitulated and in part explained; and the representative of the state invites the principal remaining characters to "go hence, to have more talk of these sad things" (*Romeo*, 5. 3. 307), "where we may leisurely / Each one demand and answer to his part." (*The Winter's Tale*, 5. 3. 152-53) But in *Hamlet* this basic situation is given a curious expansion and development.

We have already seen how Hamlet treats the cast on the stage as spectators of the catastrophe, and have quoted the passage in which he turns to Horatio, and, as it were, deputizes him. He lays on Horatio the charge "to tell my story," a charge which Horatio accepts when he proposes later to "speak to th' yet unknowing world / How these things came about." Indeed Fortinbras accepts the proposal: "Let us haste to hear it," he says, "And call the noblest to the audience." (5. 2. 360, 390, 397-98)

The lines are so familiar that the reader may not notice what is happening. It is implied in a series of ambiguities, as was implied more openly in Hamlet's speech, that the minor characters who remain on the stage are to be regarded as an audience. Such a notion is involved in Fortinbras' pun, to "call the noblest to the audience," for they shall attend the audience of the new king, and they shall be an audience to whom the events will be related. In like fashion, Horatio asks, before he begins his resumé of the plot, that orders be given that the bodies of the main characters in the catastrophe "High on a stage be placed to the view"; these bodies, then, which are to be placed on a ceremonial stage become by virtue of an obvious pun the characters who will act on a theatrical stage. For the difference between Hamlet's relation to his quasi-audience and Horatio's is this: the other characters are treated by Hamlet as spectators of the events which just took place on the stage; they are treated by Horatio as spectators or auditors of the events that he is about to recount or present. Horatio, who has been deputized by Hamlet to tell his story, is treated in the end almost as if he were the author of the play of *Hamlet*. The events which we have just seen on the stage are treated according to the usual dramatic convention as if they had just now really happened. They are reality, and the play about this reality will only begin when the play we have seen is over.

Thus Horatio, who is about to give an account of these events, is the imitator and expounder of the reality we have seen. It is in keeping with this curious sleight-of-hand that, in preparation for the play that will follow the final bare stage, Horatio presents the argument of the events in a kind of prologue:

> give order that these bodies
> High on a stage be placed to the view;
> And let me speak to th' yet unknowing world
> How these things came about. So shall you hear
> Of carnal, bloody, and unnatural acts;
> Of accidental judgments, casual slaughters;
> Of deaths put on by cunning and forc'd cause,
> And, in this upshot, purposes mistook
> Fall'n on th' inventors' heads. All this can I
> Truly deliver.
>
> 5. 2. 388-97

The passage is in effect a summary of the preceding action. It is in form an argument of the relation which is supposed to follow, and it has the stylistic qualities of the conventional argument. But what is more—it is the truth: "All this can I truly deliver," for I am the repository of Hamlet's trust, I am the reasonable man and hence the ideal spokesman, I am the intention of the author.

Consequently, Horatio's *Hamlet* is also Shakespeare's *Hamlet*. Each is constituted by the plot, by what happens. Each is concerned with "carnal, bloody, and unnatural acts," and these are, respectively, the adultery, murder, and incest which precede and lay the foundation for the play. The accidental judgment which leads to the casual slaughter is Hamlet's mistaking Polonius for the King, a judgment based upon misconstrued signs and hence not a true or substantial judgment. This is clear to anyone who is familiar with the scholastic discussion of manslaughter, or casual homicide. To employ the Latin terminology which Shakespeare uses in its anglicized form, this judgment *per accidens* leads to a slaughter which is *praeter intentionem*, and so casual, not causal (*ST*, 2-2. 64. 8).

Perhaps the idea here deserves a short digression. It appears again in an extraordinary passage in *The Winter's Tale*. Florizel says, in reply to the question, "Have you thought on a place whereto you'll go?" after marrying Perdita:

> Not any yet;
> But as th' unthought-on accident is guilty
> To what we wildly do, so we profess
> Ourselves to be the slaves of chance and flies
> Of every wind that blows.
>   4. 4. 548-52

The philosophy, no doubt, is too great for the occasion, but there is no reason to assume that it is not pertinent. Nevertheless, this is surely an odd passage, and the oddness lies in the comparison, in the *as* clause. For, to profess oneself the slave of chance and fly of every wind that blows is a common notion and fairly easy to understand: it is an indulgence often granted to young lovers by those whom their actions are not liable to hurt. But the notion is qualified by the preceding clause: we are the slaves of chance, Florizel says, in the sense in which the unthought-on accident is guilty to what we wildly do. What does this mean?

It depends on the distinction in casuistry that is drawn in Horatio's phrase above—that between causal and casual actions. The distinction is especially clear in the discussions of actions which arise from drunkenness, or any similar state of "wildly doing." For example, if a man gets drunk and in that state "unintentionally" kills another, he is not directly guilty of homicide spiritually, whatever he may be legally, for the result is beyond his intention. But he does not on this account get off spiritually easily. He is guilty of such a degree of irrational drunkenness as rendered the homicide possible, or even probable. The substance of his sin, then, lay in the choice by which he came into the condition of "wildly doing." The example is St. Thomas'. Hooker in the *Laws of Ecclesiastical Polity* deals with an analogous case:

> Finally, that which we do being evil, is notwithstanding by so much more pardonable, by how much the exigence of so doing or the difficulty of doing otherwise is greater; unless this necessity or difficulty have originally arisen from ourselves. It is no excuse therefore unto him, who being drunk committeth incest, and allegeth that his wits were not his own; inasmuch as himself might have chosen whether his wits should by that mean have been taken from him.
>
> 1. 9. 1[10]

In brief, then, the initial choice is intentional; the precise consequences may be accidental and the result of chance. Such is the scheme of thought that lies behind the *as* clause. The initial choice of going off with Perdita is within Florizel's power, and he will make it, for he has embraced the condition of "wildly doing":

FLORIZEL: From my succession wipe me, father! I
 Am heir to my affection.
CAMILLO: Be advis'd.
FLORIZEL: I am, and by my fancy. If my reason;
 Will thereto be obedient, I have reason;
 If not, my sense, better pleas'd with madness,
 Do bid it welcome.
CAMILLO: This is desperate, sir.
 4. 4. 491-96

He is heir to his emotions; he is advised by imagination to which his reason must subscribe. Hence what follows, as particularly the place whereto they'll go, will be accidental and the result of chance. It will be, like the death of Polonius, casual.

But to return to Horatio's speech in *Hamlet*—the "deaths put on by cunning and forced cause" are, of course, the deaths of Rosencrantz and Guildenstern, and "this upshot" in which the intrigue with dramatic justice recoils on the intriguers is the final scene of the play.

There is obviously a point-for-point correspondence between the items of Horatio's list and the main events of the central plot of *Hamlet*. However, the items themselves are not particularized as in the traditional argument, but generalized.[11] No names are mentioned, no particular circumstances alluded to. And the generalization is pointed by the consistent use of the generalized plural: *acts, judgments, slaughters, deaths, purposes, inventors*; for, though some of these items may be considered to be proper plurals, it is significant that all are pluralized. The items listed are such classes of action as generally form the subject matter of tragedy. They do not precisely correspond to, but they are of the same nature as, the items in the Donatan tradition, or in, for example, Scaliger's list of the subject matters of tragedy: "The matters of tragedy are great and terrible, as commands of kings, slaughters, despair, suicides, exiles, bereavements, parricides, incests, conflagrations, battles, the putting out of eyes, weeping, wailing, bewailing, funerals, eulogies, and dirges." Nor are such lists simply to be found in critical treatises: they are the common property of the times. In his theological controversy with Bishop Jewel, Mr. Harding seizes the occasion of Jewel's mention of Sophocles to insert a summary description of tragedy. "A tragedy," he says, "setteth forth the overthrows of kingdoms, murder of noble personages, and other great troubles, and endeth in woful lamentations." And Jewel retorts with a full list of the terrible tragic events associated with the villainous Popes of Rome.[12]

In brief, Horatio promises his audience a tragedy. "So shall you hear," he says—and then follows a generalized list of items which every member of the audience recognized at once as equivalent to the single word—"tragedy." The implication is that

Hamlet is a tragedy because it presents such tragic actions. Furthermore, the effects of tragedy that Shakespeare mentions in this scene—pity, fear, astonishment—arise from the nature of the tragic actions themselves, for these actions are, as Scaliger says, great and terrible, and they evoke a corresponding response. They are terrible in that they are great, and pitiable and wonderful for the same reason. Such an equation between the greatness of the persons and the action and the greatness of the tragic response is explicitly formulated in the final comment of Octavius, the representative of the state at the conclusion of *Antony and Cleopatra*:

> High events as these
> Strike those that make them; and their story is
> No less in pity than his glory which
> Brought them to be lamented.
> 5. 2. 363-66

A tragedy, then, is defined by the kind of actions it presents, and the effect of tragedy is the direct result of the presentation of such actions, though the validity of the effect may depend upon other considerations. The effect, moreover, is one of fear, sorrow, and wonder. This is no doubt a relatively crude aesthetic, but it is substantially Aristotle's, and it is Shakespeare's. It is also true.

The Donatan Tradition

~~~~~~

Fear, sorrow, and wonder are the emotions explicitly associated with tragedy, not only in *Hamlet*, but generally in the tradition of literary criticism of Shakespeare's day. The tradition is well known. It derives from a few timeworn texts which were repeated with the singlemindedness with which one recites the penny catechism.[1]

I

The basic text for the theory of tragedy comes from a schoolbook of the late classical period, Donatus on Terence:

> There are many differences between tragedy and comedy, but the principal difference is that in comedies the characters are of moderate estate, the difficulties that arise are slight, and the outcome of it all is joyful; but the marks of tragedy are precisely the opposite; the characters are great, the actions fearful in the extreme, and the outcome is sad and involves deaths. Again, in comedy all is disturbed at the beginning and tranquil at the close; in tragedy the order of progression is exactly reversed. The moral of tragedy is that life should be rejected; of comedy, that it should be embraced. And,

30

finally, in comedy the story is always made-up; in tragedy, the story is commonly true and based on history.[2]

Tragedy and comedy are precise contraries; from this center
the particular marks of distinction are evolved and disposed.
Such a way of looking at things was quite congenial to the medieval mind, whose basic discipline was the logic of Aristotle
and the principles of identity, contradiction, and the law of the
excluded middle, and whose view of men was conditioned by
the doctrine of Heaven and Hell, good and evil, grace and sin,
and of the irreparable differences between them. There went
along with this the clarity of definition and discrimination which
this habit of mind encouraged. If the clarity broke down in practice, if in the hurly-burly of the stage comedy intruded on tragedy, this could only be ascribed, so long as the habit of mind persisted, to the imperfect nature of man, which it was the duty of
thought and intention to remedy. Hence tragicomedy, for example, did not pose a practical problem since it was actually in
existence, nor a problem of authority since it had the warrant
of Plautus, but a logical problem, and almost an insuperable
one, for the two elements were defined by their opposition.

The distinctions which Donatus establishes between the two
forms are firmly held throughout the tradition. They are distinctions of 1) character, 2) order of progression in the plot, 3)
source and kind of plot, 4) moral purpose, 5) kind of incident
and the accompanying emotional effect, 6) kind of conclusion and
the accompanying emotional effect, together with three additional principles stated in other texts than Donatus— 7) the
nature of the subject matter, 8) the principle which accounts
for the turn in the fortune of the characters, and 9) the nature
of the style. Several of these imply each other, and a few corollary distinctions enter in the later tradition, but on the whole
these principles, the first six of which are clearly stated in Donatus, sufficiently characterize the tradition and amply account
for the nature of tragedy on the Elizabethan stage. Indeed, if
these distinctions are taken seriously and regarded as principles
of order by which the dramatist writes as he does rather than
as rules external to the work, it will be seen that Elizabethan
tragedy, including *Hamlet*, is in large part given merely by the

acceptance of these principles. It follows that the historian of Elizabethan drama might more plausibly begin with the traditional definition than with the earliest examples of medieval drama. The latter are historical forerunners which only in small part account for the developed product; the definition is almost the Archetype itself, in which the seminal ideas, the principles of order, explicitly dwell.

The first distinction is that the tragic characters must be great, and this means of high rank. It is the modern feeling that this is an artificial stipulation, explicable only in light of the erroneous social ideas of our ancestors. But *The Death of a Salesman* is not a tragedy in the old sense, and so one might conjecture there is something else involved: there is involved a radical difference in the nature of the tragic effect. For the field of tragedy will be the state, since men of high rank are rulers of the state. Tragedy will then involve not private life and private feeling—this is the province of comedy—but public life and public feeling. But public feeling is different in kind from private.[3] A public calamity moves us in a different way than does a private one. The murder of John Doe is one thing; the assassination of Trotsky or of Admiral Darlan is another. Hence the tragic emotions in the older tradition will be predominantly communal and public, and we will find that a similar qualification is implied in the other principles of order which Donatus distinguishes.

The second distinction is that the direction of the action in tragedy is from order to disorder; in comedy the converse. How deeply this scheme had entered into Shakespeare's thought can be conjectured from the passage in *Lear* in which it forms the structural framework of the expression. Edgar soliloquizes on the heath:

> To be worst,
> The lowest and most dejected thing of fortune,
> Stands still in esperance, lives not in fear.
> The lamentable change is from the best;
> The worst returns to laughter.
>
> 4. 1. 2-6

The change appropriate to tragedy ("the lamentable change") is from the best; the change from the worst is comedy. Yet Shakespearean tragedy does not exhibit this progression in its simple form. The greater part of a Shakespearean tragedy does, it is true, consist of a progression toward deeper and deeper disorder, but a) the beginning is not tranquil since there is already some disorder (as in the opening scenes of *Romeo*, *Hamlet*, and *Othello*), and b) the end always involves (with the curious exception of *Troilus* whose literary form is still a matter of dispute) the restoration of order and tranquility. That is, the principle is clearly operative, but under certain limitations.

We can see, however, why the limitations are introduced: a) Since the play deals with disorder, it is simple craftsmanship to begin with at least the first motions of disorder, and if a traditional precept be needed, Horace is at hand with the admonition to begin in the middle of things, which Shakespeare himself invokes in the prologue to *Troilus*. b) As for the conclusion, the concept of order was of such importance to Shakespeare and his contemporaries, and politically of such importance, that we may assume that he neither cared to end a play in disorder (except for *Troilus*), nor perhaps would he have felt safe in so doing. But beyond this, order at the end of such harrowing experiences as constitute tragedy implies an intention to communicate to the spectators a commensurate order in feeling—by a tranquil close to dismiss them in calm of mind, all passion spent. But this calm of mind is correlative with order in the state: the aesthetic feeling is in part political in nature.[4]

The third distinction is that the plot of tragedy is commonly historical and true, not feigned. We can understand, then, the fusion of the historical chronicle play and tragedy in Elizabethan drama, for it has its critical justification in this tenet. But if tragedy is historical, it is not merely realistic as distinguished from being fanciful; it has rather the compelling absoluteness of accomplished fact. Hence its effect will be accompanied by the recognition that things could not be otherwise, since this is how in fact they were. It follows from this, as from the principles of high rank in personages and of concluding order in the state, that the emotional effects of tragedy will be of a kind consonant with these requirements. They will be more impersonal than personal. The experiences which the spectator will associate with these effects, the traces and memories which will give them substance, will be drawn not from the guarded and private world of his sensibility, but from the more communal world of his public self. The content of the effects will thus be different in kind from that which the uninstructed modern reader will experience, and a comparable difference in kind is implied in the next principle.

This, the fourth, is the moral purpose of tragedy. Donatus tells us that the lesson expressed in tragedy is the rejection of life (*fugienda vita*). Thus, in a Christian and political context tragedy will be regarded as a warning against pride and against trusting in worldly prosperity. Sidney, for example, maintains that tragedy "with stirring the affects of admiration and commiseration teacheth the uncertainty of this world and upon how weak foundations gilden roofs are builded";[5] and Jonson closes *Sejanus* with these massive reflections:

> Let this example move th' insolent man
> Not to grow proud and careless of the gods.
> It is an odious wisdom to blaspheme,
> Much more to slighten or deny their powers;
> For whom the morning saw so great and high,
> Thus low and little fore the even doth lie.

But if one takes into account the subsequent principles in Donatus' definition, the fifth, that the incidents of tragedy involve great fears, and the sixth, that the catastrophe involves deaths and is sorrowful (*exitus funesti*), it will be clear that resignation to death in the Christian sense is the natural moral to such tragedy. It is, in fact, the moral of *Hamlet*, expressed by the hero as he goes to the catastrophe, disturbed by forebodings of the tragic issue:

> we defy augury; there's a special providence in the fall of a sparrow. If it be now, 'tis not to come; if it be not to come; it will be now; if it be not now, yet it will come: the readiness is all.
>
> 5. 2. 230-33

Such acquiescence, if we should take the Donatan moral seriously, would constitute the catharsis of this kind of tragedy, the effect of the tragic effect. It would be one of logic and theology, whose instrument is teaching, and whose end is Christian resignation.

But what must be the nature of the emotional effects themselves if they are to conduce to such an end? They must be impersonal to a marked degree. For resignation is the subsumption, and almost the loss, of the individual under the general. One's own death cannot be a matter of frightened concern, since it is not peculiar but common, since it is inevitable and given. So Caesar:

> Of all the wonders that I yet have heard,
> It seems to me most strange that men should fear,
> Seeing that death, a necessary end,
> Will come when it will come.
>> *Julius Caesar*, 2. 2. 34-37

And Gertrude to Hamlet:

> Thou know'st 'tis common. All that lives must die,
> Passing through nature to eternity.
>> 1. 2. 72-73

Thus the emotional disturbance of tragic incident is resolved in resignation.

The process is traditional in Christianity. Thomas Aquinas, for example, tells us (*ST*, 1-2. 42. 2. ad 3) that death and other lapses of Nature have Universal Nature, or Eternal Law, as cause; but the nature of a particular being fights against such lapses as much as it can, and from this striving springs sorrow and anguish when death is seen as present, fear and terror when it looms in the future. These are the tragic emotions, and aroused by the tragic fact of death. Resignation in this tradition is nothing other than the acquiescence of Particular in Universal Nature. It is nothing other than an effective belief in logic, so that to perceive the subsumption of instance under rule is to be satisfied. If all men are mortal, then Hamlet, being a man, is also mortal.

But emotional effects that are ordered toward acquiescence, disturbances that are intended to subside, are different in kind from those that are exploitable and are intended to be enjoyed. The latter are sentimental and private; the former are in potency to the impersonal order of their envisaged end.

II

A tragedy is a succession of fearful incidents, enacted by persons of high rank, that progresses from initial calm into ever-deepening disaster, and concludes sadly in deaths. Fear and sorrow are its appropriate emotions, fear of the catastrophe and sorrow at its accomplishment. They are appropriate because they are the natural emotions with which men regard death in prospect and in fulfillment. They are, furthermore, emotions of a public and impersonal order.

The similarity of this definition to that of Aristotle's *Poetics* is obvious, and in all likelihood the tradition derives partly from Aristotle himself, if not from the *Poetics* (which seems to have been little known in Antiquity and to have been recovered in the West only in the thirteenth century), then from his lost dialogue *On Poets* and from his student Theophrastus and the Peripatetic School. From such sources the tradition descended to the Alexandrian and Roman scholars, and from them to the school texts of late Antiquity.[6] But the history is not important in this connection. What is important is that these notions entered into the texture of medieval thought and came to the Renaissance as commonplaces. Hence, I shall present now a few additional texts in which may be distinguished certain further and corollary principles of order, together with a text from the late Middle Ages and one from Shakespeare's day in which can be seen the consistency of the tradition and the liveliness of reapprehension with which it was entertained two thousand years after Aristotle.

Of equal importance with that of Donatus is the definition of Diomedes, a grammarian of the fourth century A.D.:

> Tragedy involves the full cycle of fortune turning to adversity in characters of the heroic age—this is Theo-

phrastus' definition. . . . Comedy—we render the Greek definition—involves a full cycle in the fortune of private citizens, but never the danger of death. . . . The fortunes involved in comedy are those of little streets and unimportant households, not as in tragedy of princes and men of state. . . . The distinctions between comedy and tragedy are these: the characters of tragedy are semidivine, leaders of the state, kings; those of comedy are unimportant and private persons. The subjects of tragedy are woes, exiles, deaths; of comedy, love affairs and seductions. Finally, the movement of events in tragedy is almost always from happy circumstances to bitter deaths, accompanied at the end with the perception that the fortunes of the house involved have gone to ruin. Hence comedy and tragedy are by definition distinct: the one a full cycle of harmless incident, the other a reversal of great fortunes. Sorrow, then, is characteristic of tragedy.

Ars Grammatica, 3[7]

To this may be added two passages from Isidore of Seville's encyclopedia, the *Britannica* of ten centuries. The first is from the section "On Poets":

The tragic writers have attained considerable fame, principally for the plots of their plays, which are fashioned in the image of truth. . . . The comic writers deal with the lives of private citizens; the tragic, however, with affairs of state and the histories of kings. Similarly, the plots of tragedies deal with woful material; of comedies, with happy.

Etymologiae, 8. 7. 5-6

The second passage is from the section "On Shows":

Tragedians are those who recite to an audience a lamentable poem about historical events and the crimes of wicked princes.

18. 45

As early as the tenth century this is contracted into the curt phrase: *tragoedia luctuosum carmen.* Tragedy is a lamentable tale, a woeful story. To these texts may be added the influential sentence from Boethius' *Consolation of Philosophy:* "*quid tragoediarum clamor aliud deflet nisi indiscreto ictu fortunam felicia regna vertentem?*" which Chaucer translates:

> What other thyng bywalen the cryinges of tragedyes but oonly the dedes of Fortune that with unwar strook overturneth the realmes of great nobleye? (*Glose. Tragedye is to seyn a dite of a prosperite for a tyme, that endeth in wrecchidness.*)
> 2. Prose 2

together with Ovid's remark, "Tragedy is weightier in style than any other genre." (*Tristia,* 2. 381)

From these texts we may distinguish some additional principles of order. The seventh defines the range of subject matter: woes, exiles, slaughter, the crimes and villainies of princes, the ruin of a noble house, the downfall of kingdoms. The eighth defines the organization of the plot, which describes a period, a full circle, so that the tragic character may say at the end as Edmund says in *Lear*:

> The wheel is come full circle; I am here.
> 5. 3. 174

The principle of alteration, the power that turns the circle of prosperity, is Fortune, whose indiscriminate blow overturns prosperous kingdoms. The importance of this principle is well known and generally conceded. It accounts for the dominant conception of tragedy in the late Middle Ages and the Renaissance, that tragedy is the fall from prosperity of a character of high estate.

A classic example is Marlowe's *Edward II,* where in the final scene the Queen says to Mortimer:

> Now, Mortimer, begins our tragedy.
> 2591

And the nature of the tragedy is defined a few lines later by Mortimer himself:

> Base Fortune, now I see that in thy wheel
> There is a point to which when men aspire
> They tumble headlong down. That point I touched,
> And, seeing there was no place to mount up higher,
> Why should I grieve at my declining fall?
> Farewell, fair Queen, weep not for Mortimer
> That scorns the world and, as a traveller,
> Goes to discover countries yet unknown.
>
> 2627-34

The fall in this case is followed by Mortimer's death, and in general the tragic fall is consumated by death, so that the principle of Fortune and the principle of death are identified. Nevertheless, it is probably significant to ascertain upon which of the two emphasis is laid: here the emphasis is clearly on the fall; in Shakespeare it is clearly on death. Furthermore, the fall is generally sudden and absolute: note Chaucer's mistranslation as "unwar strook," or unforeseen, of *indiscreto ictu*, which means "a random stroke." This introduces the element of surprise, which will in part account for the addition of the effect of wonder, and which will obviously serve to transfer the effect of fear from the incidents that precede the catastrophe to the catastrophe itself.

The ninth is the principle of style: tragedy requires the weighty or high style, a requirement which is implied by the principle of decorum:

> But to present a kingly troop withal,
> Give me a stately-written tragedy,
> *Tragoedia cothurnata*, fitting kings.
> Containing matter, and not common things.
>
> *Spanish Tragedy*, 4. 154-57

For only the high style in its aspect of gravity is fitted to deal with affairs of state, and only the high style in its aspect of forceful utterance, of passion and vividness, is fitted to deal with crimes and villainies, and to call forth the terror, the woe, and especially the wonder which it is the peculiar function of high rhetoric to produce.

These texts, with others which need not be cited here, were copied again and again throughout the Middle Ages, repeatedly glossed, and indeed became so trite and commonplace that they can scarcely be said to have a history, only a continued and recurrent existence. One example will suffice to illustrate the continuation. It is a passage from Lydgate's *Troy Book* (about 1420) in which he develops a remark by Guido delle Colonne to the effect that tragedies and comedies were said to have been first acted at Troy:

> And first also, I rede, that in Troye
> Wer song and rad lusty fresche comedies,
> And other dites, that called be tragedies.
> And to declare, schortly in sentence   845
> Of bothe two the final difference:
> A comedie hath in his gynning,
> At prime face, a maner compleyning,
> And afterward endeth in gladnes;
> And it the dedis only doth express   850
> Of swiche as ben in pouert plounged lowe;
> But tragidie, who so list to knowe,
> It begynneth in prosperite,
> And endeth euer in aduersity;
> And it also doth the conquest trete   855
> Of riche kynges and of lordys grete,
> Of mighty men and olde conquerou[ri]s,
> Whiche by fraude of Fortunys schowris
> Ben ouercast and whelmed from her glorie
> > *Of a Theatyre stondynge in the princypale*
> > *paleys of Troye, declarenge the falle of*
> > *Pryncys and others.*
> And whilon thus was halwed the memorie   860
> Of tragedies, as bokis make minde,
> Whan thei wer rad or songyn, as I fynde,
> In the theatre ther was a smal auter
> Amyddes set, that was half circuler,

Whiche in-to the Est of custom was directe;   865
Up-on the whiche a pulpit was erecte,
And ther-in stod an aw[n]cien poete,
For to reherese by rhetorikes swete
The noble dedis, that wer historial,
Of kynges, princes for a memorial,   870
And of thes olde, worthi Emperours,
The grete emprises eke of conquerours,
And how thei gat in Martis high honour
The laurer grene for fyn of her labour,
The palm of knyghthod disservid by [old] date,   875
Or Parchas mad hem passyn in-to fate.
And after that, with chere and face pale,
With stile enclyned gan to turne his tale,
And for to synge, after al her loos,
Ful mortally the stroke of Antropos,   880
And telle also, for al her worthihede,
The sodeyn brekyng of her lives threde:
How pitiously thei made her mortal ende
Thorugh fals Fortune, that al the world will schende,
And how the fyn of al her worthines   885
Endid in sorwe and in highe tristesse,
By compassyng of fraude or fals tresoun,
By sodeyn mordre or vengaunce of poysoun,
Or conspirynge of fretyng fals envye,
How unwarly that thei dide dye;   890
And how her renoun and her highe fame
Was of hatrede sodeynly made lame;
And how her honour drowe un-to decline;
And the meschef of her unhappy fyne;
And how Fortune was to hem unswete—   895
Al this was tolde and rad of the poete,
And whil that he in the pulpet stood,
With dedly face al devoide of blood,
Singinge his dites, with muses al to-rent,
Amydde the theatre schrowdid in a tent,   900
Ther cam out men gastful of her cheris,
Disfigurid her facis with viseris,
Pleying by signes in the peples sight,

That the poete songon hath on hight;
So that ther was no maner discordaunce   905
Atwen his dites and her contenaunce:
For lik as he aloft[e] dide expresse
Wordes of Ioye or of heuynes,
Meving and cher, bynethe of hem pleying,
From point to point was alwey answering—   910
Now trist, now glad, now hevy, and [now] light,
And face chaunged with a sodeyn sight,
So craftily thei koude hem transfigure,
Conformyng hem to the chaunt[e]plure,
Now to synge and sodeinly to wepe,   915
So wel thei koude her observaunces kepe.[8]

Here are all the elements of the tradition, though jumbled together and in no particular order. The concept of tragedy is essentially determined, as it is in Donatus and Diomedes, by contrast with the concept of comedy. (845-46) Tragedy begins happily and ends in adversity (852*ff.*); the external principle of the reversal is Fortune (858-59; 884; 895); the characters are rich kings and great lords (856); tragedy is rhetorical (868), that is, in high style—"stile enclyned" (878)—and in verse (844); the subject matter is historical (869); the narrator clearly displays fear (877) and this is associated with the rhetorical manner and with the subject of death (878*ff.*); in fact, the terror which the narrator displays "with dedly face al devoide of blood" as he tears the cat ("the muses al torente") in bombastic high style is mirrored in the pantomime of the dumb-show, and, in general, there is an exact correspondence between the fear, sorrow, emotional excitation ("meving"), and the joy of the text and of the illustrative action, together with a considerable range in the emotions called forth. (897-916) Furthermore, the catastrophe is piteous (883) and sorrowful (886); it is sudden (882), and is brought about by violence and deceit—fraud, false treason, sudden murder, the vengeance of poison, or the conspiracy of biting envy (887-89); in fact, the tragic catastrophe is precisely sudden and violent death. (880*ff.*).

But here are also most of the elements of Elizabethan tragedy, and some that, though corollaries to the principles enunciated in the earlier tradition, are not explicit there. For example: if Marlowe's *Tamburlaine* is a tragical discourse and its presentation a "tragic glass," as it is called on the title page and in the prologue to the original edition, this is because the play is in high syle and as Lydgate here says:

> doth the conquest trete
> Of riche kynges and of lordys grete,
> Of mighty men and olde conquerou[ri]s.

The introduction of the notion of the "conspiringe of fretyng fals envye" as engineering the tragic catastrophe will help account—to choose one example among many—for the curious circumstance that the debate between Comedy and Tragedy in the Induction to the popular Elizabethan play of *Mucedorus* is conducted by Comedy and by Envy, who speaks for tragedy. It accounts also for many an Elizabethan play, particularly for the motivation of *Othello* and of Jonson's *Sejanus*. The concern for the honor and reputation of the protagonist after his tragic death is peculiarly relevant to the last scene of *Hamlet*. The "vengaunce of poysoun" is *Hamlet* again. Finally, the confusion of high style with bombast—"the muses al to-rente"— is markedly Elizabethan; the first we hear of Shakespeare in London is that—as Greene querulously complains—he thinks he can bombast out a blank verse with the best of them, even as Hamlet later thinks he can swing it as well as Laertes— "Nay, an thou'lt mouth, / I'll rant as well as thou." (5. 1. 306-07) In brief, if the words of the narrator were distributed among the actòrs of the dumb-show and the Globe were erected in Troy, Lydgate's play could be the *Spanish Tragedy* or *Hamlet*.

The persistence of a critical awareness of these principles may be illustrated from a single text, the Prologue to *Henry VIII*, usually said to be by Shakespeare and Fletcher. Who wrote the Prologue is unknown, but it does not matter:

> I come no more to make you laugh. Things now
> That bear a weighty and a serious brow,
> Sad, high, and working, full of state and woe,
> Such noble scenes as draw the eye to flow,

We now present. Those that can pity, here   5
May (if they think it well) let fall a tear:
The subject will deserve it. Such as give
Their money out of hope they may believe,
May here find truth too. Those that come to see
Only a show or two and so agree   10
The play may pass—if they be still and willing,
I'll undertake may see away their shilling
Richly in two short hours. Only they
That come to hear a merry bawdy play,
A noise of targets, or to see a fellow   15
In a long motley coat guarded with yellow,
Will be deceiv'd. For, gentle hearers, know,
To rank our chosen truth with such a show
As fool and fight is, beside forfeiting
Our own brains and the opinion that we bring   20
To make that only true we now intend,
Will leave us never an understanding friend.
Therefore, for goodness sake, as you are known
The first and happiest hearers of the town,
Be sad, as we would make ye. Think ye see   25
The very persons of our noble story
As they were living. Think you see them great,
And follow'd with the general throng, and sweat
Of thousand friends. Then, in a moment, see
How soon this mightiness meets misery.   30
And if you can be merry then, I'll say
A man may weep upon his wedding day.

The basis for discussion is again the sharp distinction of **comedy**
from **tragedy**, which is expressed not only in the opening **lines**
(1-2), but also is introduced with a certain truculence **into the**
middle where the historical nature of tragedy is affirmed (13-22,
but especially 17-21), and lies behind the turn of thought in the
final lines: for it would be as proper to weep at the **weddings**
which are the external signs that a comedy has been concluded:

Our wooing doth not end like an old play:
Jack hath not Gill. These ladies' courtesy

Might well have made our sport a comedy.
Love's Labour's Lost, 5. 2. 883-85

as to be merry at the deaths which conclude a tragedy. For tragedy is woeful. Its subjects are grave and of serious aspect (2);
they are sad, lofty, and have a strong emotional effect ("working," 3); they are noble scenes which evoke tears and pity (3-7),
being full of affairs of state and at the same time of woe, with
the implication that the former qualifies the latter. Furthermore,
the height of the persons and the richness of the emotional effect
are, it is almost implied, proportional to each other; this is a
notion which we shall find made explicit at the conclusion of
Antony and Cleopatra:

> High events as these
> Strike those that make them; and their story is
> No less in pity than his glory which
> Brought them to be lamented.
> 5. 2. 363-66

In the final part of the Prologue the spectators are abjured
to achieve the full emotional effect intended; they are to be as
sad as the authors and actors wish them to be. (23-25) They can
attain this end (the process is clearly described) by vividly realizing the events on the stage as if they were real, or, indeed, by
imputing to them the reality which in fact they have because
of the warrant of their historical truth (23-27); in this way the
spectators are to achieve the emotional end of historical tragedy, woe or pity—"for sorrow is characteristic of tragedy," as
Diomedes says. This effect culminates in the tragic catastrophe,
the sudden and violent ("in a moment, see" 29) fall from mightiness to misery. (27-30)

III

So much for the tradition. But what does Shakespeare himself
mean by tragedy? What does the term denote in his works, and
with what notions is it associated in context? It denotes pri-

marily violent death, and the notions with which it is associated are the principles of the Donatan tradition. I give now a number of representative passages from Shakespeare's works in which the term *tragedy* or one of its derivatives appears.

A. Talbot in *1 Henry VI*:

> Speak, Salisbury; at least, if thou canst speak.
> How far'st thou, mirror of all martial men?
> One of thy eyes and thy cheek's side struck off?
> Accursed tower! Accursed fatal hand
> That hath contriv'd this woful tragedy!
> > 1. 4. 73-77

Tragedy is death in battle, the sudden and violent death of a notable person. It is woeful. It is brought about by circumstances ("Accursed tower!") and by a responsible agent ("Accursed fatal hand").

B. Gloucester in *2 Henry VI*:

> I know their complot is to have my life;
> And if my death might make this island happy
> And prove the period of their tyranny,
> I would expend it with all willingness.
> But mine is made the prologue to their play;
> For thousands more, that yet suspect no peril,
> Will not conclude their plotted tragedy.
> > 3. 1. 147-53

Tragedy is the consequence of political intrigue; it involves the destiny of the state; and it concludes with unexpected deaths. But the point of the prophecy in this instance is that here not even holocausts, or tragedy on tragedy, will conclude the plot.

C. Warwick and Queen Margaret over the dead body of Gloucester in *2 Henry VI*—The Queen speaks:

> Then you belike suspect these noblemen
> As guilty of Duke Humphrey's timeless death?

And Warwick:

> Who finds the heifer dead, and bleeding fresh,
> And sees fast-by a butcher with an axe,
> But will suspect 'twas he that made the slaughter?
> Who finds the partridge in the puttock's nest
> But may imagine how the bird was dead,
> Although the kite soar with unbloodied beak?
> Even so suspicious is this tragedy.
> > 3. 2. 186-94

Tragedy is "timeless death"; that is, untimely, violent, as in *Titus Andronicus* (E, below).

D. Henry VI to Richard in the Tower, *3 Henry VI*:

> Ah, kill me with thy weapon, not with words!
> My breast can better brook thy dagger's point
> Than can my ears that tragic history.
> > 5. 6. 26-28

The tragic history is an account of the death of the young Prince Edward.

E. *Titus Andronicus*, 2. 3. 265: "timeless tragedy" means murder, untimely death.

F. *Titus Andronicus*, 4. 1. 45-60: tragedy is rape and murder.

G. *Richard III*. "Enter Queen with her hair about her ears, Rivers and Dorset after her":

> QUEEN: Ah, who shall hinder me to wail and weep,
> > To chide my fortune, and torment myself?
> > I'll join with black despair against my soul
> > And to myself become an enemy.
> DUCHESS OF YORK: What means this scene of rude
> > impatience?
> QUEEN: To make an act of tragic violence.
> > Edward, my lord, thy son, our king, is dead!
> > > 2. 2. 34-40

The nature of the act of tragic violence is defined in the preceding speech as sin ("And to myself become an enemy"), and specifically as the sin of despair. The characteristic act of despair is suicide. The act of tragic violence, then, is suicide.

H. Hastings in *Richard III*:

>But I shall laugh at this a twelvemonth hence,
>That they which brought me in my master's hate,
>I live to look upon their tragedy.
>Well, Catesby, ere a fortnight make me older,
>I'll send some packing that yet think not on't.
>3. 2. 57-61

Tragedy is violent unexpected death.

I. *Richard III*. "Enter old Queen Margaret":

>So now prosperity begins to mellow
>And drop into the rotten mouth of death.
>Here in these confines slyly have I lurk'd
>To watch the waning of mine enemies.
>A dire induction am I witness to,
>And will to France, hoping the consequence
>Will prove as bitter, black, and tragical.
>4. 4. 1-7

The preliminaries are dire—that is, the tragic atmosphere is one of fear—and promise by the law of aesthetic congruity that the consequence will be bitter and black—that is, tragical. The principle of order that connects preliminaries and consequence is the waning of prosperity: the wheel of Fortune.

J. *Midsummer Night's Dream*:

>THESEUS: " ... very tragical mirth."
>   Merry and tragical? tedious and brief?
>   That is hot ice and wondrous strange snow....
>PHILOSTRATE: And tragical, my noble lord, it is;
>   For Pyramus therein doth kill himself....
>THESEUS: ... Marry, if he that writ it had played
>   Pyramus and hang'd himself in Thisby's garter,
>   it would have been a fine tragedy.
>5. 1. 57-59, 66-67, 365-67

Tragedy and comedy are precise contraries. The distinguishing mark of tragedy is violent death, suicide.

K.   The Archbishop of Canterbury in *Henry V*, 1. 2. 105-06, speaks of "Edward the Black Prince," whose warlike spirit "on the French ground play'd a tragedy" by slaughtering the French army.

L.   *Othello*, 5. 2. 363: the representative of the state speaks of the dead bodies of Desdemona and Othello as "the tragic loading of this bed."

M.   *The Phoenix and Turtle*, 52: "the tragic scene" is the death of the phoenix and the dove.

N.   Lucrece in the *Rape of Lucrece*:

> "O comfort-killing Night, image of hell!
> Dim register and notary of shame!
> Black stage for tragedies and murthers fell!
> Vast sin-concealing chaos! nurse of blame!
> Blind muffled bawd! dark harbour for defame!
>   Grim cave of death! whisp'ring conspirator
>   With close-tongu'd treason and the ravisher!"
>   764-70

This passage constitutes a congeries of the fundamental notions and attitudes associated with the concept of tragedy; its objective content is murder, death, whispering conspiracy, close-tongued treason, rape; it deals in sin—night, its symbol, is the image of Hell, where grace dies ("comfort-killing") and chaos spreads, for chaos is the issue of sin as order is of grace; tragedy is preoccupied with fame (cf. *Hamlet*, 5. 2. 355-60); its atmosphere is dim, vast (that is, "disordered"), black, blind (that is, "irrational"), dark, grim.

O.   The lover in *A Lover's Complaint* is portrayed as a master of insincere rhetoric and capable of expressing all the external signs of the appropriate emotions:

> To blush at speeches rank, to weep at woes,
> Or to turn white and sound at tragic shows.
>   307-08

The effect of tragedy is fear or terror.

In brief, the tragic atmosphere and the anticipation of the tragic catastrophe is fearful; the catastrophe woeful. The process by which the catastrophe comes about involves intrigue, hypocrisy, political conspiracy and treason, acts of sin, and is conducted by responsible agents. These are the connotations of *tragedy*. The denotation is violent, unexpected death—murder, death in battle, suicide. To these is added rape.

This denotation of *tragedy*, however, is not merely Shakespearean; it is generally Elizabethan, as indeed is well known. Death in *Soliman and Perseda*, speaking as a chorus at the beginning of the play, says: "And what are tragedies but acts of death?" (1. 1. 7). And, again, at the conclusion:

> Packe *Loue* and *Fortune*, play in comedies,
> For powerfull Death best fitteth Tragedies.[9]

In the Induction to *A Warning for Fair Women*, which was produced by Shakespeare's company, the characters are Tragedy, History, and Comedy. Tragedy is called "a common executioner," "murther's Beadle," "The common hangman unto Tyranny," and a little later it is remarked:

> Then we shall have a tragedy indeed;
> Pure purple buskin, blood and murther right.
>   Induction, 6, 19, 20, 61-62[10]

Finally, Fletcher in the preface to the *Faithful Shepherdess* distinguishes tragicomedy from tragedy "in respect it wants deaths, which is enough to make it no tragedy. . . ." Hence death is the essential mark (note the technical language of "in respect"), the defining characteristic.

The tragic fact is death. Even the most natural death has in it a radical violence, for it is a transition from this life to something by definition quite otherwise; and, however much it may be expected, it is in its moment of incidence sudden, for it comes as a thief in the night, you know not the day nor the hour. Hence the characteristics of suddenness and violence which are attached to death in tragedy may be viewed as only artistic heightenings of the essential character of death: the

unnaturalness of the tragic event is only pointed and emphasized by the unnatural precipitancy of its accomplishment. If
Elizabethan dramas often end in almost indiscriminate butchery,
the intention, even if mistaken, is only to make them the more
tragic.

That tragedy is death is a conception which will account
for a puzzling feature in the history of Elizabethan drama:
namely, that we have a number of interesting plays, particularly
those traditionally associated with Shakespeare's name, *Arden
of Feversham*, *A Warning for Fair Women*, and the *Yorkshire
Tragedy*, in which recent and actual murders are dramatized.
These were regarded as tragedies; indeed one of them has the
extensive Induction which was quoted from above, in which
Tragedy after an argument with History and Comedy introduces
the play. Nevertheless, in these plays the usual notion that tragedy involves a notable reversal of prosperity and the fall of a
person from high estate to low is little attended to, though not
unnoticed, and at the same time the corollary notion that the
chief characters should be of princely, or at least of noble, rank
is deliberately violated. These are domestic tragedies. The characters involved are usually of what we would call the middle
class—they are normally gentlemen. The situation is sordid, not
splendid.

It is obvious that such a play, if the principle of decorum
is to be observed, must forego the high style appropriate to traditional tragedy. It must forego at the same time the splendor
and universality of great events; it must temper its effect to the
meanness of its theme. The advantage which such tragedy claims
for itself in exchange for the advantages of traditional tragedy
is that of unadorned truth—truth in the literal historical sense,
and unadorned in the sense of unrhetorical, or lacking the high
style. So Tragedy in *A Warning for Fair Women* introduces the
sordid story of murder with these remarks:

> My scene is London, native and your own.
> I sigh to think my subject too well-known.
> I am not feigned.
>
> 1. 86-88

"I am not feigned." Again, the author of *Arden of Feversham*, invoking the age-old commonplace of simple truth as opposed to artful feigning, a commonplace that derives from the early Christian defense of the unliterary character of the New Testament and from the older classical commonplace of nature and art, concludes the play with these words:

> Gentlemen, we hope you'll pardon this naked Tragedy,
> Wherein no filed points are foisted in
> To make it gracious to the ear or eye;
> For simple truth is gracious enough,
> And needs no other points of glosing stuff.
> Epilogue, 14-18[11]

A "naked tragedy" is unrhetorical, lacking in ornament, a tragedy in other than high style. Perhaps one should remark that the play does have a good deal of Kydian ornament in it, but this is beside the point, being only another lamentable example of the gap between profession and practice.

To conclude: if violent death is the distinguishing mark of tragedy, and this seems to be Shakespeare's understanding of the term, it follows 1) that domestic tragedy is a legitimate species since it has the defining characteristic and the associated property of historical truth; 2) that high tragedy will by logical implication involve the fall of princes since the violent death of a high character is such a fall, but that this theme is not logically primitive, but derived; 3) that the tragic attitude will be the attitude toward death; 4) that the tragic effects will be those appropriate to violent death: fear, sorrow, and perhaps wonder at the suddenness and violence; and 5) that the effect of tragedy is consequently not infinitely subtle but quite obvious. On this account the tragedy of *Hamlet* is the holocaust which concludes it, and the tragedy of Hamlet himself is his death.

Wonder

~~~~~~

But is wonder a traditional effect of tragedy? Does it appear in the tradition so closely associated with tragic woe that Horatio's *aught of woe or wonder* could be taken as a designation of the tragic effect? Certainly it is not explicit, if present at all, in Donatus or Diomedes. Yet about twenty years before the publication of *Hamlet* Sir Philip Sidney had defined tragedy in the passage already quoted as "stirring the affects of admiration and commiseration."[1] The literal meaning of *admiration* in the Renaissance—it is the meaning of the Latin word *admiratio*—is "wonder." Hence Horatio's phrase is simply a translation from Latin to Germanic diction of Sidney's, with the substitution of the more general and more traditional notion of sorrow for the more special and more Aristotelian notion of pity. Of course, we need not picture Shakespeare as filching his phrase from Sidney, though this is not at all improbable. The question is rather, How did wonder, or admiration, come to be recognized as an effect proper to tragedy, and on what authority was it raised to an equal status with sorrow and fear? On what precedent did Sidney and Shakespeare speak? For surely neither intended to say anything novel on this subject.

I

The precedent is as old as Aristotle's *Poetics*.[2] It is true that in

53

the famous definition of tragedy (1449b24-28) Aristotle speaks only of "incidents arousing pity and fear, wherewith to accomplish its catharsis of such emotions." There is, however, another emotion explicitly associated elsewhere in the *Poetics* with tragic incident and with the tragic catastrophe, and this is wonder or astonishment (*ekplexis, to thaumaston*).

Three principal texts bear on this point. The first occurs toward the end of the *Poetics*, in the comparison of tragedy and epic:

> The marvellous is certainly required in tragedy. Epic, however, offers more opening for the improbable, the chief factor in the marvellous, because in it the agents are not visibly before us. The scene of the pursuit of Hector would be ridiculous on the stage—the Greeks halting instead of pursuing him, and Achilles shaking his head to stop them; but in the poem the absurdity is overlooked. The marvellous, however, is a cause of pleasure, as is shown by the fact that we all tell a story with additions, in the belief we are doing our hearers a pleasure.
>
> 1460a11-17[3]

The marvellous is certainly required in tragedy. Furthermore, from the example which Aristotle gives of telling a story with additions it is clear that the marvellous derives its value from the point of view of its effect on the audience: wonder, for like begets like.

The point is supported by a later passage, the second principal text, in which Aristotle is discussing the sort of criticisms one may make of the poet's art:

> As to the criticisms relating to the poet's art itself. Any impossibilities there may be in his descriptions of things are faults. But from another point of view they are justifiable, if they serve the end of poetry itself—if (to assume what we have said of that end) they make the effect of either that very portion of the work or some

other portion more astounding. The Pursuit of Hector
is an instance in point.

1460b23*ff*.

That is, impossibilities can be defended on the grounds that they
make some portion of the work more astounding. The astounding
has therefore a kind of absolute value. As such, it is not merely
permissible, but necessary. In fact, the implication of this passage, which occurs in the extended comparison of tragedy and
epic, is that epic surpasses tragedy in this respect: you can get
away with more of the marvellous in a narration than on the
stage, for what seems marvellous when told may seem ridiculous
when seen. What is presented on the stage and before our eyes
cannot "fly from all humanity." Thus, the element of wonder,
which rests upon the improbable, cannot bulk so large or be
handled so indiscreetly as in straight narrative, but it cannot
be dispensed with. So Aristotle arrives at his canon for the
stage: "a likely impossibility is always preferable to an unconvincing possibility." (1460a26-27)

Furthermore, Aristotle posits here that wonder is an end
—if it be not the end—of poetry, of which tragedy is a species.
Now the end in the Aristotelian scheme is that toward which
all things conspire and to which they are subordinated. It will
be worth our while, then, to reconcile if possible this passage
in which wonder is spoken of as the end of poetry with those
others in which is implied that a specific kind of pleasure (involving pity and fear) is the end of tragedy (1448b18; 53a36;
53b11 and 12; 62a16; and 62b13). This passage will furnish the
general solution; the third principal text, which will be noticed
later, will furnish the specific solution applicable to tragedy.

The relationship of wonder and pleasure is that wonder is
pleasurable. (1460a17) It is pleasurable in itself. It is pleasurable
also in that it is the occasion and motive for learning, as is clear
from the famous passage in the *Metaphysics*:

> For it is owing to their wonder that men both now begin
> and at first began to philosophize. . . . And a man who
> is puzzled and wonders thinks himself ignorant (whence

> even the lover of myth is in a sense a lover of Wisdom,
> for the myth is composed of wonders).
>
> 1. 2. 982b11-19

Furthermore, myth, which furnished the material for Greek
tragedy, is described as composed of wonders, and the lover of
myth is a lover of Wisdom in that he, too, seeks to know.

Wonder is the occasion and motive for learning; learning
is pleasurable: by this chain are wonder and pleasure connected.
This is explained in the *Rhetoric*:

> Again, since learning and wondering are pleasant, it fol-
> lows that such things as acts of imitation must be pleas-
> ant—for instance, painting, sculpture, poetry—and ev-
> ery product of skilful imitation; this latter, even if the
> object imitated is not itself pleasant; for it is not the
> object itself which here gives delight; the spectator
> draws inferences ("That is a so-and-so") and thus learns
> something fresh. Dramatic turns of fortune and hair-
> breadth escapes from perils are pleasant, because we
> feel all such things are wonderful.
>
> 1. 11. 1371b4-12

Wonder and pleasure are the principal effects of art, and
consequently of tragedy and the tragic catastrophe; they are
its end. The two are correlative, for one is the motive for inference, the other its natural accompaniment. Furthermore, what
we now call aesthetic experience is for Aristotle substantially
the experience of inferring. This is clear from the passage just
cited, and is reinforced by the well-known passage early in the
Poetics in which Aristotle analyzes the general origin of poetry.
He points out that men, and especially the young, are natural
copycats and prone to make-believe. This is how they learn. Secondly, he says, "it is natural for all to delight in works of imitation":

> The truth of this second point is shown by experience:
> though the objects themselves may be painful to see,
> we delight to view the most realistic representations

of them in art, the forms for example of the lowest animals and of dead bodies. The explanation is to be found
in a further fact: to be learning something is the greatest of pleasures not only to the philosopher but also
the rest of mankind, however small their capacity for
it; the reason of the delight in seeing the picture is that
one is at the same time learning—gathering the meaning of things, e.g. that the man there is so-and-so; for
if one has not seen the thing before, one's pleasure will
not be in the picture as an imitation of it, but will be
due to the execution or colouring or some similar cause.

4. 1448b4-19

Wonder, then, is associated with pleasure as the end of poetry,
and it is also posited as required in tragedy. But is it specifically
associated, as it is in *Hamlet*, with the proper tragic effects of
pity and fear? It is, as one would expect, since Aristotle tells us
that through pity and fear tragedy attains its proper pleasure
(1453b10-11), and pleasure involves wonder. The text, which is
the third of the principal texts, reads:

Tragedy, however, is an imitation not only of a complete action, but also of incidents arousing pity and fear.
Such incidents have the very greatest effect on the mind
when they occur unexpectedly and at the same time in
consequence of one another; there is more of the marvellous in them then than if they happened of themselves or by mere chance. Even matters of chance seem
most marvellous if there is an appearance of design as
it were in them; as for instance the statue of Mitys at
Argos killed the author of Mitys's death by falling down
on him when a looker-on at a public spectacle; for incidents like that we think to be not without a meaning.
A Plot, therefore, of this sort is necessarily finer than
others.

9. 1452a1-11

It is implied again that wonder has an absolute value in itself.
Furthermore, the degree of surprise, the amount of the marvel-

lous, in the plot of a tragedy is the measure of the pity and fear it provokes, so that in the strict mathematical sense wonder is a function of pity and fear: $PF = W$.

Two further passages may be cited in this connection. In discussing the kinds of incidents which will produce the tragic pleasure of pity and fear, Aristotle remarks:

> A better situation [than the one previously discussed] is for the deed to be done in ignorance, and the relationship [of the parties involved] discovered afterwards, since there is nothing odious in it, and the Discovery will serve to astound us.
>
> 14. 1454a2-4

And later, in analyzing the kinds of Discovery, he remarks:

> The best of all Discoveries, however, is that arising from the incidents themselves, when the great surprise comes about through a probable incident, like that in the *Oedipus* of Sophocles.
>
> 16. 1455a16-18

In brief, let wonders happen, but make them—at least at the moment of their happening—plausible and convincing. This can best be accomplished by making the tragic incident unexpected, and yet, as soon as it has happened, obviously logical and supported by the situation and the preceding action. The incident is not what we expected, but what, as soon as we see it, we realize that we should have expected. Something of this sort is involved when we understand a person: he acts spontaneously at a crisis in a way we would never have predicted, yet the moment the thing has happened we know that we knew that was the sort of person he was. The point will be clear if we contrast this with our attitude toward the critical actions of those whom we do not understand: their actions simply puzzle us, and the measure of our bewilderment is the measure of our lack of understanding.

There is no need to think all this original with Aristotle: both rhetoric and poetic—the latter in Antiquity is only partially distinguishable from the former—had already a long history by this time. Much of the evidence, it is true, has been lost, and much must be reconstructed by divining earlier features in later texts.[4] But it is clear from the remarks of the rhapsode Ion in Plato's dialogue that fear, pity, and wonder were the commonly recognized effects of the recitation of epic, and particularly of the striking passages: for the whole point of the dialogue, which is simple-mindedly ironic, is that what Ion says should represent common opinion:

> ION: ... When I speak of anything piteous, my eyes are filled with tears; when I mention anything fearful or terrible, my hair stands on end with fear and my heart throbs ...
>
> SOC: And do you not know that you produce the same effects on many of the spectators?
>
> ION: I know it right well, for when I look down from the platform I see them weeping and showing signs of terror and astonishment at my words.
>
> *Ion*, 535B-C[5]

Nevertheless, most of the subsequent history of the concept of wonder can be derived from the Aristotelian texts. Wonder is, first of all, the natural effect of a marvellous story, and hence of those myths which furnished the plots of ancient tragedy and epic, as well as of those extraordinary events which in later Hellenistic times, as earlier in Herodotus, are narrated in certain types of history and in the marvellous tale. Apuleius, for instance, in the first sentence of the *Metamorphoses* claims that his purpose is to evoke wonder: "I have told these stories," he says, "in this style that you may wonder (*ut mireris*)."

Wonder is, in the second place, the result of a surprising and unexpected turn in events, and is thus intimately involved in the tragic catastrophe and in its proper effect. Furthermore, since in tragedy the turn is toward the worse, the effect of surprise will be inwoven with sorrow or pity as well as astonishment, and the astonishment will take that form which is akin to fear. From this line of thought, though not necessarily from Aristotle, is derived the following passage from a little scrapbook of short treatises by the famous rhetorician Hermogenes of

Tarsus, which goes under the title of *How to Speak Effectively*:

> Philippics, dialogue, comedy, tragedy, and the Socratic
> symposia weave the whole by a kind of double method.
> . . . The web and woof of tragedy are woe and wonder,
> as is to be seen both in the tragedies of tragic writers
> and in those of Homer whom Plato called the father of
> tragedy and the choregus.[6]

Thirdly, wonder is an end of poetry. This concept is generalized in the Neo-Platonist Plotinus, to whom wonder is an
effect of beauty:

> This is the effect that Beauty must ever induce, wonder-
> ment and a pleasant astonishment, longing and love
> and a dread that is pleasurable.
> *Enneades*, 1. 6. 4[7]

However, the more restricted view, which we found in Aristotle, that wonder is along with pleasure the end of poetry is a
commonplace in later Antiquity; it is chiefly associated with the
name of Eratosthenes, the poet-scholar, friend and disciple of
Callimachus. We gain our knowledge of his position principally
from the criticisms which Strabo levels against it in the *Geography*. "Eratosthenes," he says, "is wrong in his contention that
the aim of every poet is to entertain, not to instruct." (1. 1. 10)[8]
The argument is long and somewhat tedious. In brief, Strabo
holds that the poet either pleases or instructs—pleases when
what he says is false, instructs when what he says is true. (1. 2.
3, and 7-9) On this basis the ends of the various branches of
composition are distinguished:

> Now the aim of history is truth, . . . the aim of rhetorical
> composition is vividness, as when Homer introduces
> men fighting; the aim of myth is to please and excite
> amazement.
> 1. 2. 17

The purpose of myth—that is, of a story—is pleasure and wonder.

Eratosthenes' distinction, as preserved by Strabo, appears also in the historian Polybius. He is criticizing one of his predecessors, Phylarchus, of whom he says:

> Leaving aside the ignoble and womanish character of such a treatment of his subject, let us consider how far it is proper or serviceable to history. A historical author should not try to thrill his readers by such exaggerated pictures, nor should he, like a tragic poet, try to imagine the probable utterances of his characters or reckon up all the consequences probably incidental to the occurrences with which he deals, but simply record what really happened and what really was said, however commonplace. For the end of tragedy is not the same as that of history but quite the opposite. The tragic poet should amaze and charm his audience for the moment by the verisimilitude of the words he puts into his characters' mouths, but it is the task of the historian to instruct and convince for all time serious students by the truth of the facts and the speeches he narrates, since in the one case it is the probable that takes precedence, even if it be untrue, the purpose being to create illusion in spectators, in the other it is the truth, the purpose being to confer benefit on learners.
>
> 2.56[9]

The passage is intellectually more respectable, of course, than that from Strabo. For Polybius, though he does not exclude—as no one should since literature is a part of life—general ethical judgments ("Leaving aside the ignoble and womanish character of such a treatment of his subject"), is nevertheless capable of discussing literature on its own terms and with reference to its own proper ends ("let us consider how far it is proper and serviceable to history"). The end of tragedy is to astonish and please—but not without qualifications, for he points out in the passage that follows this quotation that unless we know the causes of a catastrophe and the course of events which led up to it, it is impossible to feel due indignation or pity. In brief, the effect must be adequately motivated.

Plutarch in his essay on *How the Young Man Should Study Poetry* repeats the commonplace:

> But when poetic art is divorced from the truth, then chiefly it employs variety and diversity. For it is the sudden changes that give to its stories the elements of the emotional, the surprising, and the unexpected, and these are attended by very great astonishment and enjoyment; but sameness is unemotional and prosaic.
>
> 7. 25[10]

In an earlier passage he applies Eratosthenes' formulation of the end of poetry to a play by Aeschylus:

> But it is patent to everybody that this is a mythical fabrication which has been created to please or astound the hearer.
>
> 7. 17

The following passage from the ancient *Life of Aeschylus* obviously springs from the same context of critical notions: Aeschylus has "few devices for drawing tears" and "uses the spectacle and plot more to strike by the marvellous than to effect (artistic) illusion."[11]

II

The marvellous is pleasurable. Thus wonder is an end of poetry, or it is with pleasure the end of poetry. Hence it would obviously be involved in the effect of any particular kind. It is, however, associated with the specific, rather than with the generic, effect of tragedy even in Aristotle, since the specific effects of pity and fear are most truly effective when they also involve wonder. Indeed, the marvellous is required in tragedy. Consequently, it becomes traditional to distinguish the purpose of fiction, especially of epic and tragedy, from that of history and of rhetoric on these grounds: fiction aims at wonder and pleasure; history at truth and instruction; rhetoric at vividness and persuasion. But, of course, these lines of distinction were not fixed and unalterable in Antiquity, since the subjects of the distinctions were not simple. Poetry and rhetoric had a great deal in common; fiction commonly involved history, and history fiction. Furthermore, from the time of Aristotle poetry was often identified with fiction, and the mythical was a characteristic property. Thus, the end of poetry was often said to be pleasure and instruction, as in Horace and Strabo, and its methods were usually rhetorical.

However, wonder is not only an effect of a story or of a subject matter, it is also an effect of language and of style. It is precisely the effect of characteristically poetic, or tragic, style, as opposed to the plain straightforward style proper to prose and to dialectic. For the fundamental distinction which prevails in Antiquity and informs the traditional theory of the three (or four) styles is the distinction in diction between the unornamented language native to prose and the unusual, figurative, ornamented language of poetry, and especially of tragedy. The distinction remained current even though poetry appropriated the language of prose, as in the later tragedians, and prose in the rhetorical tradition of Gorgias appropriated the language of poetry (Aristotle, *Rhet*. 3. 1. 1404a20-34; Strabo, 1. 2. 6). The point is made clear by Aristotle in the *Rhetoric*. The effect of poetic diction is wonder:

> People do not feel towards strangers as they do towards their own countrymen, and the same thing is true of their feeling for language. It is therefore well to give everyday speech an unfamiliar air: wonder is a characteristic of things off the beaten track, and the wonderful is pleasant. In verse such effects are common, and there they are fitting: the persons and things there spoken of are comparatively remote from ordinary life. In prose passages they are far less often fitting because the subject-matter is less exalted.
>
> 3. 2. 1404b8-15[12]

The later theory on the subject derives partly from such passages as this, probably by way of Theophrastus' work on style, and partly no doubt from Sophistic theory as developed by Gorgias among others. (Diodorus, 12. 53; Gorgias, *Helena*, 9.) It seems to have been based, at least originally, upon a distinction between style which employs plain language and to the point, whose aim is merely truth, and whose concern is simply with content (*rem tene, verba secuntur*), and a style cultivated as such. The former uses proper expressions only; the latter intermingles figurative. Its aim is to move, to convince, to please; its concern is with the effect on the audience. The former is the style of dialectic and, in general, of philosophy; and the latter is the style of poetry and of rhetoric. So Theophrastus in a passage preserved in one of the later commentaries on Aristotle's logic:

> Language is divided into two types, according to the philosopher Theophrastus, the one having reference to the hearers, the other to the matter concerning which the speaker aims to convince his audience. To the division with reference to the hearers belong poetry and rhetoric. Therefore its function is to choose the more stately words, and not those which are common or vulgar, and to interweave them with each other harmoniously, to the end that, by means of them and the effects which result from the employment of them, such as vividness, sweetness and other qualities of style, together with studied expansion and contraction, all employed at the suitable moment, the listener shall be charmed and astonished and, with respect to the intellectual persuasion, overmastered. The division looking to the matter will be the especial concern of the philosopher, refuting the false and setting forth the true.[13]

The effect of astonishment or wonder is the natural correlative of unusual diction, as it is of the unusual event. The proper word satisfies by its exactness; the unusual pleases or displeases by its startling effect. Upon this basis, which though obvious is not unimportant, together with the doctrine of the appropriateness of style to subject, rests the whole later theory of the kinds and characters of style in all its elaboration. Hence, the theorists will ascribe to any style which is noticeable as such the quality of wonder. That style which is elaborated for the purpose of charm or pleasure—the *genus floridum*—will evoke the kind of pleasant wonder that the marvellous story does, and will be appropriate to such subjects: for instance, the Milesian style of Apuleius, for the effect of wonder is ascribed in the passage cited above not only to the subject matter but also to the style. The high style, the forceful, the grand—the style of Demosthenes and of Aeschylus—will evoke that wonder which is akin to fear, and will be especially appropriate to tragedy. Yet wonder may be on a lesser scale than this: it corresponds to the displacement, large or small, that initiates internal movement: with respect to the intellect, inference, the processes of logic, and learning; with respect to the irrational part of the soul, feeling and emotion. Hence style can evoke emotion in the audience, and at the same time by the law of decorum the degree of unusual diction should be proportionate to the height and intensity of the feeling inherent in the subject matter. Again, to wonder at style is to regard it highly, to approve of it, to admire in the modern sense, but this attitude, though not unaccompanied by feeling, nevertheless implies no specific shade of emotional coloring.

This much may serve to introduce the following citations in which is exhibited the continuity in Antiquity of the Peripatetic and Sophistic tradition that wonder is an effect of style, and especially of the high style appropriate to tragedy. The treatise on style by Demetrius (probably first century A.D.) is clearly in this tradition. He cites a line of Homer in which a figurative shift in construction elevates the style, and contrasts this with the ordinary way of saying the same thing. "But everything ordinary is trivial," he says, "and so fails to attain wonder." (59-60) Again, to take a longer quotation:

> The sayings of Demades, too, possess power, although their expression sounds peculiar and unusual. Their power arises partly from their significance and partly from their allegorical form and lastly from their exaggerated character.
> This is an example: "Alexander is not dead, Athenians. If he were, the whole world would smell the

corpse." The use of the word "smell" for "perceive"
involves both allegory and exaggeration. The fact that
the world perceived it signifies Alexander's strength,
and at the same time the sentence has an effect of astonishment which is due to a combination of three
causes. Everything that astonishes is powerful, because
it creates fear.

282-83[14]

The rhetorical concept of wonder is the subject of the famous treatise on elevated style (*On the Sublime*), which has
been ascribed to Longinus. The subject is announced in the
opening chapter. The author premises that the eminence and
renown of great writers, both in prose and in verse, is derived
from distinction in language. (1. 3) The effect of such distinction he conceives of in the traditional way—the doctrine is precisely that of the passage cited above from Theophrastus—as
astonishment, which overpowers the hearer and puts him in a
state of transport. This effect is differentiated from that of persuasion, and incidentally of pleasure, on the grounds that this
is irresistible while persuasion for the most part involves voluntary assent, and secondly that this is a matter of detail and that
of the work as a whole. (1. 4)

In this way the differences which Eratosthenes, Polybius,
and Strabo, among others, had established between the various
kinds of literary works are here applied in the context of rhetorical theory to single out the special effect of certain details in a
work. The analysis gets sometimes a little complicated. Thus,
in discussing the kind of image in which out of an inspired passion the writer thinks he sees what he is describing and makes
his hearer see it—a well-known rhetorical device in Antiquity—
Longinus distinguishes between the purpose of such images
in oratory and in the poets. In poetry the end is astonishment;
in prose vividness; though both alike seek to stir up excitement.
(15. 36) But the poetic image tends to be fabulous, exaggerated,
and to go beyond what is believable, whereas the virtue of imagery in prose is always its reality and truth. (15. 40) Nevertheless, imagery in prose can exceed persuasion and attain astonishment, combining vigor and passion with argument and

fact so that the hearer is not merely persuaded but actually en-
slaved, for the stronger effect of wonder will absorb the weaker
of persuasion. (15. 41)[15]

The notion also appears, as we might expect, in the Latin
authors. Cicero, for example, in the teacher-pupil dialogue on
the *Classification of Oratory* associates wonder with ornate or
figurative diction, and hence with the charming style (*genus
suave*). He points out that style will be charming if something
unusual, original, or novel is said—he is thinking of phrasing—
"for anything wonderful pleases." (22) Again, a charming account is one that has causes of wonder, suspense, and emotional
outcomes, along with interpolated emotional passages, dialogues,
sorrow, anger, fear, joy, and desire. (32) Cicero is here speaking of those expositions of events which form part of a speech,
but the description could easily apply to a play, and particularly
to such as *The Winter's Tale* or to many of Beaumont and
Fletcher. In another passage he says that in developing a subject
in the decorative style we should take up those aspects that
produce suspense, wonder, and delight. (58) Finally, he points
out in an extended passage that in epideictic speeches, whose
chief purpose is to please and entertain an audience, the speaker
should make use of striking phrases, which have a great deal of
charm; that is, he should use coined words, archaisms, and metaphors; should construct phrases such that one echoes another
by similarity of rhythm and ending, thus giving doublets and
a verbal rhythm, not sounding like verse yet satisfying the ear
with an appropriate harmony. But the ornament should not be
merely verbal; there should also be in the matter a good deal
of what is wonderful and unexpected, things foreshadowed by
portents, prodigies, and oracles, and what seems to the man
to whom this happens to be the result of divine intervention
or of fate. For the feeling of suspense in the audience, and wonder, and the unexpected outcome always give a certain pleasure
in the hearing. (72-73)[16] What is described here is represented
in Elizabethan times by Lyly's *Euphues*, and all its progeny in
the Elizabethan drama. Wonder is an effect both of style and
of subject.

The doctrine of Antiquity on wonder is summed up and
transmitted to posterity by Quintilian:

. . . those words are the most to be commended which express our thoughts best, and produce the impression which we desire on the minds of the judges. Such words undoubtedly must make a speech both worthy of admiration and productive of pleasure; but not of that kind of *admiration* with which we wonder at monsters; or of that kind of *pleasure* which is attended with unnatural gratification, but such as is compatible with true merit and worth.

8. *Pr.* 32-33

It was the sublimity, magnificence, splendour, and dignity of his [Cicero's] eloquence, that drew forth that thunder of approbation. No such extraordinary commendation would have attended on the speaker, if his speech had been of an everyday character, and similar to ordinary speeches. I even believe that his audience were insensible of what they were doing, and that they gave their applause neither voluntarily nor with an exercise of judgment, but that, being carried away by enthusiasm, and unconscious of the place in which they stood, they burst forth instinctively into such transports of delight.

But this grace of style may contribute in no small degree to the success of a cause; for those who listen with pleasure are both more attentive and more ready to believe; they are very frequently captivated with pleasure, and sometimes hurried away in admiration. Thus the glitter of a sword strikes something of terror into the eyes, and thunder storms themselves would not alarm us so much as they do if it were their force only, and not also their flame, that was dreaded. Cicero, accordingly, in one of his letters to Brutus, makes with good reason the following remark: *That eloquence which excites no wonder, I account as nothing.* Aristotle, also, thinks that to excite wonder should be one of our greatest objects.

8. 3. 3-6[17]

III

So much for Antiquity. It will be sufficient now to establish the continuity of the tradition in the Middle Ages, and later in the Renaissance. The effect of wonder will be a familiar notion to any Christian since it is frequently noted in the New Testament as the effect of the words and works of Christ:

> And the disciples were astonished at his words.
> *Matt.* 13:54

> And straightway the damsel arose and walked, for she was of the age of twelve years. And they were astonished with a great astonishment.
> *Mark* 5:42

Wonder, of course, is the natural effect of miracles, real or apparent. St. Augustine makes the point in the text which furnishes the standard definition for medieval theology: "I call a miracle anything great and difficult or unusual that happens beyond the expectation or ability of the man who wonders at it" (*De Utilitate Credendi*, 16. 34).[18] And St. Thomas, in turn, integrates the Augustinian definition with the Aristotelian. In the *Summa* he takes up the question, "Whether everything that God does outside of the natural order is miraculous?" He cites an authoritative text from St. Augustine: "When God does anything contrary to the course and custom of nature as we know it, we call it a miracle." For the term is indeed derived from the word for wonder, and wonder arises whenever an effect is manifest and its cause hidden, as Aristotle says in the *Metaphysics*. Consequently, what is wonderful to one man may not be wonderful to another, but a miracle is fully wonderful since it has a cause—namely, God—absolutely hidden from all. (*ST*, 1. 105. 7)

The marvellous event, and so the marvellous story, provokes wonder. The explicit recognition of this effect is common throughout the literature of the Middle Ages, and has behind it a tradition derived from Christian dogma. Thus the German *Niebelungenlied* of the twelfth century begins by promising us

that now we will hear a wonder told, and so likewise in count-
less romances.

But with the recovery of the Aristotelian writings in the
twelfth and thirteenth centuries, the concept of wonder as the
end of poetry again enters firmly into the tradition under the
authority of Aristotle and in association with most of the other
elements in the tradition which were distinguished in the preceding sections of this essay. One of the most interesting texts
is to be found in the works of St. Albert the Great, the teacher
of Thomas Aquinas. It occurs in Albert's *Commentary on the
Metaphysics of Aristotle*; I cite it at length:

> Ch. 6: *In which it is shown that philosophy is a specu-
> lative, not a practical, science.*
> That philosophy is speculative, not practical, is clear
> from the motive that first moved men to philosophize.
> For everyone who has philosophized, now or in the
> past, has been motivated only by wonder. Now, wonder
> is defined as a constriction and suspension of the heart
> caused by amazement at the sensible appearance of
> something so portentous, great, and unusual, that the
> heart suffers a systole. Hence wonder is something like
> fear in its effect on the heart. This effect of wonder,
> then, this constriction and systole of the heart, springs
> from an unfulfilled but felt desire to know the cause
> of that which appears portentous and unusual: so it
> was in the beginning when men, up to that time un-
> skilled, began to philosophize—they marvelled at cer-
> tain difficulties, which were, as a matter of fact, fairly
> easy to solve. The Pythagoreans, for example, were
> concerned with the theory of number, with even and
> odd numbers, with complete, increasing, and dimin-
> ished number. Then men advanced bit by bit in learning
> and, becoming more proficient, raised graver questions
> whose causes were not easy to see: such as the changes
> of the moon with respect to mansions, accessions, and
> eclipses, or questions about the sun and the stars. . . .
> In like fashion they advanced in Physics, and began to
> wonder about generation in general, asking whether
> the universe was created or given.

Now the man who is puzzled and wonders apparently does not know. Hence wonder is the movement of the man who does not know on his way to finding out, to get at the bottom of that at which he wonders and to determine its cause. A token in proof is that the famous Philomithes according to this way of looking at the matter is a Philosopher, for he constructed his stories out of wonderful events. I hold that Philomithes was a poet who loved to fashion stories: for *mithes*, with the first syllable long, is the word for stories, and *Philomithes*, then, means a lover of stories, if you make the penultimate syllable long. Thus Aristotle shows in that branch of logic which is called poetic that the poet fashions his story for the purpose of exciting wonder, and that the further effect of wonder is to excite inquiry. Such is the origin of philosophy, as Plato shows with respect to the stories of Phaeton and Deucalion. The single purpose of these stories is to excite one to wonder at the causes of the two deluges of fire and of water (which issued from the circuit of wandering stars), so that through wonder the cause would be looked for, and the truth discovered.

Hence poetry offers a method of philosophizing, just as do the other sciences of logic. But the other sciences or branches of logic offer a method of proving a proposition by reasoning, that is, by conclusive or probable argument; poetry, however, offers no method of proof but rather a method of wonder by which we are incited to inquiry. Therefore, though poetry is a subdivision of grammar with respect to prosody, with respect to its purpose it is one of the branches of logic.

To get back to the point: we define the man who wonders as one who is in suspense as to the cause, the knowledge of which would make him know instead of wonder.

In I Met., Tr. 2, ch. 6[19]

The poet Philomithes, of course, is a character that grew from a misreading of the Greek text in the passage in which Aristotle states that "the lover of myth (*philomuthos*) is in a sense a lover of Wisdom, for the myth is composed of wonders" (*Meta-physics*, 1. 2. 982b18-19). But he is a charming character, and he makes the point. The end of poetry is wonder, and the end of wonder is to excite inquiry; thus poetry is a branch of logic with respect to its purpose, and distinguished from other branches in that they offer methods of proof but poetry offers a method of motivation. Its physiological effect is similar to that of fear.

St. Thomas holds substantially the same position, and cites Aristotle in the *Poetics* to the same effect. He is discussing the causes of pleasure, and comes finally to the question, Does wonder cause pleasure? He first takes up the objections:

> Apparently it doesn't 1) since wonder is a property of ignorance, and ignorance is not pleasurable, but rather knowledge. 2) Furthermore, wonder is the beginning of wisdom, being as it were a way of looking for the truth, as is said in the *Metaphysics*, 1, 2. But it is more pleasurable to contemplate what is already known than to inquire into the unknown, as Aristotle says in the *Ethics* X, 7. (1177a23*ff*.), since the latter offers difficulties and impediments, but the former does not, and pleasure arises from unimpeded operation. Therefore, wonder is not a cause of pleasure, but rather a hindrance. 3) Furthermore, everyone delights in what he is used to; hence, the operation of habits acquired through daily use is pleasurable. But what one is used to is not wonderful, as Augustine says (at the beginning of *In Joan.*, tr. 24). Therefore, wonder is precisely not a cause of pleasure.
>
> But to the contrary is the text of Aristotle (*Rhet.* 1. 11. 1371a31): *wonder is a cause of pleasure.*
>
> My position is that to attain anything one feels a want of is pleasurable; and the measure of anyone's desire for something he loves is the measure of his pleasure in attaining it. Indeed, in the very augmentation of desire there is an augmentation of pleasure, in that there arises a hope of what is loved, and desire itself is pleasurable in its aspect of hope. But wonder

is a kind of desire for knowledge. The situation arises when one sees an effect and does not know its cause, or when the cause of the particular effect is one that exceeds his power of understanding. Hence, wonder is a cause of pleasure insofar as there is annexed the hope of attaining understanding of that which one wants to know.

For this reason, everything wonderful is pleasurable: for example, anything that is infrequent, as well as any representation of things, even of those that are not in themselves pleasant. For the soul delights in comparing one thing with another, since this is a proper and connatural activity of reason, as Aristotle says in his *Poetics*. (4. 1448b13*ff*.) And for this reason even to be released from great danger is quite pleasurable, as is said in the *Rhetoric*. (1. 11. 1371b10*ff*.)

As to the first objection, wonder is not pleasurable insofar as it involves ignorance, but insofar as it involves learning the cause, and learning something new: namely, that such-and-such is such-and-such, though we had not thought it was.

As to the second objection, there are two kinds of pleasure: acquiescence in the Good, and awareness of such acquiescence. With respect to the former, since it is a more complete experience to contemplate known truth than to inquire into the unknown, the contemplation of things known is in itself more pleasurable than inquiry into things unknown; nevertheless, it sometimes happens that, with respect to our awareness of experience, inquiry is more pleasurable in that it has more drive and springs from a greater desire. For desire is especially aroused by the awareness of ignorance, and consequently a man takes the greatest pleasure in those things which he discovers for himself or learns from the ground up.

As to the third objection, doing what we are used to is pleasurable insofar as it is in a way natural to us. Still, on the other hand, what is unusual can be pleasurable, either with respect to the process of learning, since our desire for knowledge is proportional to the marvellousness of the subject, or with respect to the actual doing, since the mind is strongly impelled by desire to that which is felt intensely because of its novelty. But an activity, the more full it is, the greater the pleasure it causes.

ST, 1-2. 32. 8[20]

Wonder is also a species of fear, as the Damascene teaches. To the objection that wonder and amazement (*admiratio et stupor*) are not species of fear, since fear refers only to evil, and wonder and amazement refer to the unusual, whether good or evil; and again, to the further objection that philosophers are moved by wonder to inquire into the truth, whereas fear does not move one to investigate but rather to run from the scene of investigation; St. Thomas answers that the authority of the Damascene and of Gregory of Nyassa is sufficient to establish the point. He then solves the objections by dividing the six traditional species of fear into three whose source is internal and three whose source is external—wonder (*admiratio*), which arises when one contemplates some great evil whose issue he cannot see; amazement (*stupor*), which arises when one contemplates some unaccustomed evil, for it will seem to be great because it is unaccustomed; shocked surprise (*agonia*), which arises from the unforeseen. Hence, to the former objection Thomas answers that only that wonder and amazement which arises from the contemplation of evil is a species of fear; to the latter objection he answers that a man who wonders does fear at the moment to give a judgment, fearing that he will fail, but that he looks into the matter in the future; the amazed man, however, fears both now and in the future; hence wonder is the beginning of philosophizing, but amazement an impediment to it. (*ST*, 1-2. 41. 4)

IV

Whatever appears in the scholastic philosophers and at the same time in Aristotle, as well as in Cicero and Quintilian, is likely to appear anywhere in Renaissance literature. It will be commonplace. Thus the rhetorical tradition is gathered up, assimilated, and integrated into a consistent structure in Pontanus' dialogue on poetry (*Actius*, about 1500). There the end of poetry is said to be "to speak well and appropriately so as to attain wonder," and this is later corrected by one of the speakers into the form, "to speak exceptionally well," so as to distinguish the poet from the orator who also must speak well and appropriately. The wonder referred to is conceived under two aspects: it is admiration, in the modern sense, for the eloquence of the poet himself, who from this source derives his fame and glory; at the same time, it is the emotion of wonder in the audience. The poet moves wonder not only by sublime words, but also by his subject matter, and since truth alone cannot guarantee this he shades truth with fiction and myth. Nor is wonder only the effect of the grave and serious; it is also the effect of the pleasant and delightful. And in speaking so sweetly, sublimely, and marvellously, the poet teaches others to speak well, so that every literary form derives from poetry.[21]

The same line of thought is developed in Fracastoro's dialogue *Navagero* (published 1555), in which the emphasis, however, is laid on the final remark, and poetry is distinguished from all other forms in that it is the master-art of eloquence. For, though poetry excites wonder, this is not its exclusive characteristic since wonder is also the effect of oratory and history: "Who can read Cicero himself without wonder?"[22]

The idea is common throughout the Renaissance. Minturno, who is in the same line of tradition as Pontanus and Fracastoro, begins his dialogue on the poet, *De Poeta* (1559), with the statement that "no one can be called a poet who does not excel in the power of arousing wonder." Minturno, however, goes beyond the rhetorical tradition, making a good deal of Aristotle's *Poetics* which had lately been translated, paraphrased, and expounded by a good many of his fellow countrymen. Thus he introduces the notions of wonder and pleasure in connection with tragedy:

> The poet does not deal with what does not please, nor does he move the emotions without delight. Rather, excited by the force of language and the weight of his

ideas he rouses, attracts, and moves the audience intensely to the point of wonder—either through fear or pity, or both.[23]

In fact, the idea of wonder is so commonplace in the Renaissance it would be surprising not to find it in Sidney or in Shakespeare. Hence, to establish the availability of the idea, I will only add to these citations and that from Sidney's *Defense* the following passages from Spenser:

A.   Wonder is the effect of theological discourse, being, of course, the highest subject matter and hence affording by its very nature the highest eloquence; as such, however, it is an effect of subject, not style:

> And that her sacred Booke, with blood ywritt,
> That none could reade, except she did them teach,
> She unto him disclosed every whitt,
> And heavenly documents thereout did preach,
> That weaker witt of man could never reach,
> Of God, of grace, of justice, of free will,
> That wonder was to heare her goodly speach:
> For she was hable with her wordes to kill
> And rayse againe to life the hart that she did thrill.
> *Faerie Queene*, 1. 10. 19

Compare Milton's *Paradise Lost*: At Raphael's speech Adam,

> with his consorted Eve,
> The story heard attentive, and was filled
> With admiration and deep muse, to hear
> Of things so high and strange.
> 7. 50-53

B.   The palmer finds good Guyon, "slumbering fast, in senseles dreame":

> Whom when the palmer saw, abasht he was
> Through fear and wonder, that he nought could say.
> *FQ*, 2. 8. 7. 1-2

Fear and wonder is the effect of apparent unexpected death.

C. Ruth (that is, pity or woe) and wonder is the effect
on the bystanders at a mortal combat:

> With that they both together fiercely met,
> As if that each ment other to devoure;
> And with their axes both so sorely bet,
> That neither plate nor mayle, whereas their power
> They felt, could once sustaine the hideous stowre,
> But rived were like rotton wood a sunder,
> Whilest through their rifts the ruddie bloud did showre,
> And fire did flash, like lightning after thunder,
> That fild the lookers on attonce with ruth and wonder.
> *FQ*, 4. 3. 15

"Attonce" means "both."

D. The following marvellous events quite properly provoke great wonder of a kind akin to fear, as do the prodigies
of Nature:

> Then forth he brought his snowy Florimele,
> Whom Trompart had in keeping there beside,
> Covered from peoples gazement with a vele.
> Whom when discovered they had throughly eide,
> With great amazement they were stupefide;
> And said, that surely Florimell it was,
> Or if it were not Florimell so tride,
> That Florimell her selfe she then did pas.
> So feeble skill of perfect things the vulgar has.

> Which when as Marinell beheld likewise,
> He was therewith exceedingly dismayd;
> Ne wist he what to thinke, or to devise,
> But, like as one whom feends had made affrayd,
> He long astonisht stood, ne ought he sayd,
> Ne ought he did, but with fast fixed eies
> He gazed still upon that snowy mayd;
> Whom ever as he did the more avize,
> The more to be true Florimell he did surmize.

As when two sunnes appeare in the azure skye,
Mounted in Phoebus charet fierie bright,
Both darting forth faire beames to each mans eye,
And both adorn'd with lampes of flaming light,
All that behold so strange prodigious sight,
Not knowing Natures worke, nor what to weene,
Are rapt with wonder and with rare affright:
So stood Sir Marinell, when he had seene
The semblant of this false by his faire beauties queene.
                    FQ, 5. 3. 17-19

Then Artegall steps forth and says this " 'is not (I wager) Florimell at all' . . . For proofe whereof he bad them Florimell forth
call."

Then did he set her by that snowy one,
Like the true saint beside the image set,
Of both their beauties to make paragone,
And triall, whether should the honor get.
Streight way so soone as both together met,
Th' enchanted damzell vanisht into nought:
Her snowy substance melted as with heat,
Ne of that goodly hew remayned ought,
But th' emptie girdle, which about her waste was
    wrought.

As when the daughter of Thaumantes faire
Hath in a watry cloud displayed wide
Her goodly bow, which paints the liquid ayre;
That all men wonder at her colours pride;
All suddenly, ere one can looke aside,
The glorious picture vanisheth away,
Ne any token doth thereof abide:
So did this ladies goodly forme decay,
And into nothing goe, ere one could it bewray.

Which when as all that present were beheld,
They stricken were with great astonishment,
And their faint harts with senseless horrour queld,

To see the thing, that seem'd so excellent,
So stolen from their fancies wonderment:
That what of it became none understood.
And Braggadochio selfe with dreriment
So daunted was, in his despeyring mood,
That like a lifeless corse immoveable he stood.

FQ, 5. 3. 24-26

E.   "Calidore sees young Tristram slay / A proud discourteous knight":

Which when he saw, his hart was inly child
With great amazement, and his thought with wonder fild.

FQ, 6. 2. *Argum*. and 4. 8-9

F.   In *The Ruines of Time*:

Before mine eyes strange sights presented were,
Like tragicke pageants seeming to appeare.

489-90

Then follows a series of visions in which a gold image, a stately tower, a pleasant paradise, a giant, a gold bridge over the sea, and two white bears successively fall to ruin:

Much was I troubled in my heavie spright,
At sight of these sad spectacles forepast,
That all my senses were bereaved quight,
And I in minde remained sore agast,
Distraught twixt feare and pitie; when at last
I heard a voyce, which loudly to me called,
That with the sudden shrill I was appalled.

"Behold," said it, "and by ensample see,
That all is vanitie and griefe of minde,
No other comfort in this world can be,
But hope of heaven, and heart to God inclinde;
For all the rest must needs be left behinde."

575-86

The effect of these tragic pageants is wonder ("That all my senses were bereaved quight") which suspends and mediates between fear and pity. The ultimate effect is to teach the rejection of this life.

V

Certainly the aesthetic effect of wonder was a notion easily available to Shakespeare. But if Horatio's *aught of woe or wonder* is to be taken as aesthetically significant, it must be shown not only that Shakespeare could have been but also that he was aware of the tradition. Does Shakespeare use the notion of wonder, and the synonymous *amazement, astonishment,* and *to be struck senseless,* in any other contexts that this one in *Hamlet*? He does. In fact, he uses almost the full range of meanings which are to be found in the tradition.

Wonder is the effect of such an incident, conventional to tragedy, as the appearance of the Ghost in *Hamlet* and the recognition of his likeness to the dead King:

> BERNARDO: Looks it not like the King? Mark it, Horatio.
> HORATIO: Most like. It harrows me with fear and
>   wonder.
> 1. 1. 43-44

The appearance is regarded by Horatio (1. 1. 113-25) as of the same nature as those signs and portents, those foreshadowings of tragic consequences, which preceded the death of Caesar. Indeed, such "precurse of fierce events," such "harbingers preceding still the fates / And prologue to the omen coming on" have precisely the same effect upon Casca in the play of *Julius Caesar*:

> CASCA: It is the part of men to fear and tremble
>   When the most mighty gods by tokens send
>   Such dreadful heralds to astonish us.

To which Cassius replies:

> CASSIUS: ... You look pale, and gaze
> And put on fear, and cast yourself in wonder,
> To see the strange impatience of the heavens.
>   1. 3. 54-56, 59-61

Wonder, then, is an emotion which is a kind of fear and is produced by striking and supernatural events. But, truly, one doesn't have to see the ghost in order to experience the effect: the Ghost in the closet scene is invisible to Hamlet's mother, yet the effect on her of Hamlet's apparently wild actions, his holding discourse with the incorporeal air, and the communicated effect of his manifest fear and wonder:

> Forth at your eyes your spirits wildly peep;
> And, as the sleeping soldiers in th' alarm,
> Your bedded hairs, like life in excrements,
> Start up and stand an end.

are characterized by the Ghost himself as an effect of amazement:

> But look, amazement on thy mother sits.
>   3. 4. 119-22, 112

Wonder is also an effect of the plot as a whole, and not merely of incident. Theseus and Hippolyta in *Midsummer Night's Dream* discuss the events of the same play, the plot of the crisscrossing lovers, from the point of view of literary criticism (the passage contains the famous remarks on "the poet's eye in a fine frenzy rolling"):

> HIPPOLYTA: 'Tis strange, my Theseus, that these lovers
>   speak of.
> THESEUS: More strange than true. ...
> HIPPOLYTA: But all the story of the night told over,

> And all their minds transfigur'd so together,
> More witnesseth than fancy's images
> And grows to something of great constancy;
> But howsoever, strange and admirable.
>   5. 1. 1-2, 23-27

The plot, whether true or not, is certainly strange and wonderful ("admirable").

Wonder, however, is especially the effect of the denouement of those plays which the literary historian calls romances, especially if they conclude with a marvellous and surprising turn of events. Thus, in *The Winter's Tale* the "discovery" that Perdita is the King's daughter is described by the First Gentleman as "a little amazedness." He goes on:

> But the changes I perceived in the King and Camillo
> were very notes of admiration. They seem'd almost,
> with staring on one another, to tear the cases of their
> eyes. There was speech in their dumbness, language in
> their very gesture. They look'd as they had heard of a
> world ransom'd, or one destroyed. A notable passion
> of wonder appeared in them; but the wisest beholder
> that knew no more but seeing, could not say if th' im-
> portance were joy or sorrow; but in the extremity of
> the one it must needs be.
>   5. 2. 5-6, 11-21

He, however, had been commanded out of the chamber, and did not have the full story; hence, so far as he was concerned, it was "a little amazedness," provoked mainly by the wonder of the King and Camillo. The Second Gentleman, who now enters, is better informed and tells us:

> Such a deal of wonder is broken out within this hour
> that balladmakers cannot be able to express it.
>   5. 2. 25-27

Wonder, then, is the effect of the surprising and the marvellous; it is an extremity of feeling, and hence may be either joy or sorrow, fear or rapture. It is, if not the actual effect of such plots as *The Winter's Tale*, at least the effect aimed at. Thus Paulina, the mistress of ceremonies in the following scene, remarks as she discloses Hermione standing like a statue:

> I like your silence; it the more shows off
> Your wonder.
>
> 5. 3. 21-22

And the disclosure certainly has such an effect on Perdita; witness the King's speech:

> O royal piece,
> There's magic in thy majesty, which has ...
> From thy admiring daughter took the spirits,
> Standing like stone with thee!
>
> 5. 3. 38-39, 41-42

But there is more wonder still! Paulina warns her audience that they remain at their own risk:

> Quit presently the chapel, or resolve you
> For more amazement.
>
> 5. 3. 86-87

And when the King commands, "No foot shall stir," she speaks to the statue:

> 'Tis time; descend; be stone no more; approach;
> Strike all that look upon with marvel.
>
> 5. 3. 98-100

So, if the reader finds the events of the play improbable, that is the point. They are intended to be improbable. The effect aimed at is pleasurable wonder.

In comparable circumstances, at the denouement of the serious plot of *Much Ado About Nothing*, when Hero appears alive, the Friar says:

>   All this amazement can I qualify . . .
>   Meantime let wonder seem familiar.
>   5. 4. 67, 70

Wonder, then, is associated not only with extreme fear but also with extreme joy, and is marked by silence and immobility. It is the shocked limit of feeling. Hence, Descartes a few years later chose wonder as the first, and indeed the principal, passion of the soul (*Les Passions du Ame*, 2. 53; 69-78).

It is easy to understand that the marvellous is intended to be wonderful, whether in fact the reader finds it so or not. But tragedy should not so fly from all probability. In what way, then, does Shakespearean tragedy in general, and the tragic catastrophe in particular, admit of the effect of wonder? I have already shown how certain conventional tragic incidents and certain conventional appurtenances of tragic atmosphere involve fear and wonder. But a tragedy is not merely a spectacle and a plot, it is also something written and spoken; it is in large measure a series of declamations. This is obviously true of Elizabethan tragedy and of Shakespearean.

In fact, the revolution in the English theater of the 1580s out of which came the great plays of the succeeding decades consisted largely in the introduction of an adequate rhetoric. Nashe, for example, characterizes the pre-Shakespearean *Hamlet* and related plays as "handfuls of tragical speeches." Again, it is Greene's dying complaint against the companies of actors that he has been "of them forsaked," "those puppets . . . that spake from our mouths, those antics garnished in our colors"—that is, in our colors of rhetoric. It is his complaint against Shakespeare himself that he "supposes he is as well able to bombast out a blank verse as the best of" Greene's companions.[24] Marlowe's *Tamburlaine, Parts I* and *II* are, according to his printer, "tragical discourses"; and Marlowe himself enunciated in the prologue to *Tamburlaine I*, in those lines which constitute the charter of the greater Elizabethan tragedies, the rhetorical principle of high style in tragedy and its concomitant effect of wonder or astonishment:

>   From jigging veins of rhyming mother wits

And such conceits as clownage keeps in pay,
We'll lead you to the stately tent of war
Where you shall hear the Scythian Tamburlaine
Threatening the world with high astounding terms
And scourging kingdoms with his conquering sword.
View but his picture in this tragic glass,
And then applaud his fortunes as you please.

Though these lines have often been quoted, they are worth noticing again, for they are packed with critical doctrine. They are a manifesto. The first two lines constitute an explicit rejection of the old theatrical tradition of the fourteener with its rhyme and its marked regularity of meter ("jigging veins"); of the uneducated, unartful writer ("mother wits"); and of the tradition of the irresponsible clown. In its stead is proposed the modulated and rhymeless line, and the wholly serious play. This play involves a high subject, *war*, and by implication and the enjoinment of decorum a *stately* style, a high and royal style. The effect will be largely one of language and of rhetoric, for there "you shall hear," and you shall hear what is grand, or even grandiose, a "threatening the world," expressed in "high astounding terms."

Let us dwell on this phrase. A *term* is not any word, but a word belonging to a special vocabulary; so we speak of logical terms, and philosophical terms, and in the field of rhetoric there is, for example, that specialized literary diction which the Scots called "aureate terms." And Chaucer says in the *Canterbury Tales*:

Youre termes, youre colours, and youre figures—
Keep hem in stoor til so be that ye endite
Heigh style, as whan that men to kinges write.
Clerk's Prologue, 16-18

Tamburlaine will speak, then, in a choice and sifted language, the diction of *high* style, whose effect is here defined as that of wonder or astonishment, the "astounding." This effect is supported by the kind of action involved, "scourging kingdoms with his conquering sword."

The manifesto concludes with the proposition that the work of literature should merely present the object and leave the question of judgment to the spectator. This last, it seems to me, is Marlowe's one distinctive contribution to literary theory (I do not say that it is correct), and *Tamburlaine* is perhaps the only play of the period—perhaps the only play of Marlowe's —that clearly adheres to the doctrine. Yet it is only an extreme statement of a general trend in Elizabethan drama, the trend toward emancipating the story from the exemplum. However, it is the other ideas which are of concern here, and these ideas are the common critical property of the time. They enunciate the principle of high style, high characters, and high matters, to which Shakespeare gave allegiance, though a less thorough-going allegiance. The significance of this passage is that they are here expressed for the first time in Elizabethan drama, that they are expressed memorably, that the play to which these ideas are prologue is, if we leave aside Kyd and *The Spanish Tragedy*, the first notable application of the ideas, and, finally, that the play itself was a great success and had great influence on the course of Elizabethan drama.

The reader today is fairly unmoved by grand speeches, but the testimony of our fathers as to the overwhelming effect of the grand style is explicit and fairly unanimous. It should cause no surprise, then, to find that Shakespeare ascribes the quality of wonder to eloquence. He echoes *Tamburlaine* at the beginning of *1 Henry VI* (if the passage be indeed his); there the Dauphin, deeply impressed by Joan of Arc's long speech, exclaims seriously:

Thou hast astonish'd me with thy high terms.
1. 2. 93

Again, in *Henry V* the Archbishop of Canterbury in delineating the ideal character of the King ascribes the same quality to the eloquence of theology and to the sweet style:

Hear him but reason in divinity,
And, all-admiring, with an inward wish
You would desire the King were made a prelate . . .

> Turn him to any cause of policy,
> The Gordian knot of it he will unloose,
> Familiar as his garter; that, when he speaks,
> The air a charter'd libertine, is still,
> And the mute wonder lurketh in men's ears
> To steal his sweet and honey'd sentences.
>   1. 1. 38-40, 45-50

But the point is clear enough in *Hamlet* itself, and in connection with "tragical speeches." In the graveyard scene, after Laertes' outburst of rhetoric, Hamlet discloses himself and answers rant with rant:

> Nay, an thou'lt mouth,
> I'll rant as well as thou. . . .

> What is he whose grief
> Bears such an emphasis? whose phrase of sorrow
> Conjures the wand'ring stars, and makes them stand
> Like wonder-wounded hearers?
>   5. 1. 306-07, 277-80

The terms "emphasis" and "phrase" make quite clear that Hamlet refers to Laertes' style, which is at least intended to wound (that is, "to strike") the hearers with wonder.

Wonder in Shakespeare is the effect of tragic incident and tragic style, as well as of the marvellous turn in events. But this does not exhaust the complexity of the notion of wonder: one more strand at least remains to be unraveled. For the notion derives not only from the tradition of literary criticism, as the proper effect of marvellous events, and the tradition of rhetoric, as the proper effect of marvellous eloquence, but it derives also from the tradition of philosophy, in which wonder is the primary cause of learning.

Wonder, in this sense, is that which strikes our attention and provokes intensity of interest and intensity of curiosity. Hence it is obviously relevant to drama and fiction, for a story that does not interest us may as well not exist, as Mine Host will instruct us, who commented on the Monk's famous, but deadly, tragedies:

> Sire Monk, namoore of this, so God you blesse! ...
> Nor certeinly, as that thise clerkes seyn,
> Where as a man may have noon audience,
> Noght helpeth it to tellen his sentence.
> VII. 3978, 3990-92

It is especially relevant to the conclusions of Shakespearean plays, which are as persistently occupied with the explanation of "How these things came about" (*Hamlet*, 5. 2. 391) as are the conclusions of the modern detective story. For wonder, as the motive for acquiring knowledge, demands explanation and is satisfied by it. Now, to satisfy by explanation, though it may seem a misguided impulse to the modern reader who lives by the current maxim of "Never explain," was not unimportant to the Elizabethan: it is the chief concern of the dying Hamlet. He charges Horatio:

>   report me and my cause aright
> To the unsatisfied. ...
> O good Horatio, what a wounded name
> (Things standing thus unknown) shall live behind me!
> If thou didst ever hold me in thy heart,
> Absent thee from felicity awhile,
> And in this harsh world draw thy breath in pain,
> To tell my story.
> 5. 2. 350-51, 355-60

For this reason, to satisfy the unsatisfied as to Hamlet's motives and actions, Horatio soon summarizes the events of the play, but not for this reason only. The unexplained gives scope to the irrational; hence:

> let this same be presently perform'd
> Even while men's minds are wild, lest more mischance
> On plots and errors happen.
> 5. 2. 404-06

There is, then, in the resolution of wonder a kind of *catharsis*, a further effect of the effect of the catastrophe, and one appropriate to Shakespearean drama. To understand is to acquiesce. The movement of the drama is from this point of view an increasing intensity of interest which culminates in the striking events of the climax. These astonish the spectator so that he stands for the moment stone still, but at the same time they demand explanation, and with the explanation his emotion subsides and order prevails, as on the stage at the close of the play order prevails in the state.

Certainly the philosophical notion of wonder enters into the explanation of the catastrophe. In the passage already cited from *Much Ado About Nothing*, the Friar hastens to remark on the marvel of the catastrophe:

> All this amazement can I qualify,
> When, after that the holy rites are ended,
> I'll tell you largely of fair Hero's death.
> 5. 4. 67-69

First wonder, then explanation. So also in *As You Like It*, Hymen, who enters to conclude the comedy, speaks thus:

> Peace ho! I bar confusion.
> 'Tis I must make conclusion
>   Of these most strange events . . .
> Whiles a wedlock hymn we sing,
> Feed yourselves with questioning,
> That reason wonder may diminish
> How thus we met, and these things finish.
> 5. 4. 131-33, 143-46

And the general scheme is very well explained by Quince, as prologue to the "tragical mirth" that concludes *A Midsummer Night's Dream*:

> Gentles, perchance you wonder at this show;
> But wonder on, till truth make all things plain.
> 5. 1. 128-29

VI

To sum up: the primary effect of tragedy is sorrow or woe, of which pity is a species. The tragic atmosphere and the incidents leading to the catastrophe are fearful. This is the Donatan tradition in which the tragic fact is violent, unexpected death, and corresponds to the medieval tradition of psychology in which the anticipation of death is fearful and its accomplishment woeful. But since the catastrophe is unexpected, it will startle the audience, and so the emotion of fear which has accompanied the course of tragic incident will become attached in special measure to the catastrophe. But this will be that fear which results from external events: wonder, astonishment, or shocked surprise. Hence woe or wonder are the effects of the tragic spectacle. Horatio's phrase, then, as is Sidney's, is only a distillation of the tradition, and *woe* is even a more proper term than "pity," *wonder* than "fear."

In the preceding section, I have cited texts in which Shakespeare explicitly names wonder as an effect of tragic incident, of tragic style, and as the principal effect of the catastrophe of those nontragical plays which involve marvellous events, being the natural correlative of marvels and the motive for understanding them. But is wonder named in any other work of Shakespeare as an effect of the tragic catastrophe, or does it appear only in the one passage from *Hamlet*? Again, is it customary to name explicitly the intended effect at the end of other Elizabethan plays?

It will be expected that woe or pity will be the most commonly named, and in fact there are more texts than anyone wishes to look through. To cite one example, the anonymous *Tragedy of Locrine* is drenched with mournful complaints. These occur after each of the successive tragic catastrophes which constitute the play (1. 1. 227*ff*.; 3. 1. 1*ff*.; and especially 43*ff*.; 3. 6. 1*ff*.; 5. 1. 1*ff*. and especially 16*ff*.), but most notably at the end. Here in Estrild's lament over the death of Locrine, the concept of lamentation and pity is explicitly associated with the concept of tragedy as involving both the fall and death of the great, and the lesson of the instability of this world—for here as in glass we plainly see that all our life is but as a tragedy, a confused chaos of mishaps:

> Break, heart, with sobs and generous suspires!
> Stream forth, you tears, from forth my watery eyes!
> Help me to mourn for warlike Locrine's death!
> Pour down your tears, you watery regions,
> For mighty Locrine is bereft of life!
> O fickle Fortune! O unstable world!
> What else are all things that this globe contains
> But a confused chaos of mishaps?
> Wherein as in a glass we plainly see
> That all our life is but as a tragedy,
> Since mighty kings are subject to mishap.
>   5. 4. 111-21[25]

But the effect of wonder is common enough. In Greene's *Orlando Furioso* the Emperor of Africa, who is the representative of the state, replies after hearing an account of the action from Orlando:

> I stand amazed, deep overdrenched with joy,
> To hear and see this unexpected end:
> So will I rest content.
>   5. 2. 1425-27[26]

This is the kind of wonder we have already met at the end of *The Winter's Tale*. Of like kind is the effect of the discovery in Marston's *Malcontent* that Malevole is Altofont, the former and legitimate Duke of Genoa:

> MALEVOLE: Banish amazement; come, we four must stand
>   Full shock of fortune. Be not so wonder stricken....
> PIETRO: ... Give leave to recollect
>   My thoughts dispersed in wild astonishment.
>   4. 5

This is the principal catastrophe of the play, though there follows in the fifth act, amid masquing and comedy, a second re-versal—the fall of Mendoza. Of a similar nature is the discovery of Andrugio at the end of Marston's *Antonio and Mellida*:

> We are amazed, our royal spirits numbed
> In stiff astonished wonder at thy prowess.

And, a little later, when Antonio rises from the coffin:

> Stand not amazed, great states! ...
> Most wished spectators of my tragedy.[27]

There is a different, but not too dissimilar, kind in the 1610 *Mucedorus*, the version played before King James. Here Comedy and Envy in the Epilogue suddenly kneel before the majesty of James:

> ENVY: My power has lost her might; Envy's date's
>   expired.
>   Yon splendent majesty hath felled my sting,
>   And I amazed am. *Fall down and quake.*
>   65-67[28]

    But for wonder as the immediate effect of the catastrophe of a tragic, rather than of a comic or heroic, catastrophe, Shakespeare himself gives precedent. The catastrophe of Shakespeare's poem *The Rape of Lucrece* is Lucrece's suicide—at which:

> Stone-still, astonish'd with this deadly deed,
> Stood Collatine and all his lordly crew.
>   1730-31

This is the wonder that is a species of fear; but, as the shock subsides, woe and pity rise:

> About the mourning and congealed face
> Of that black blood a wat'ry rigoll goes,
> Which seems to weep upon the tainted place;
> And ever since, as pitying Lucrece's woes,

Corrupted blood some watery token shows.
>   1744-48

The poem ends finally with Brutus' speech, which again provokes wonder:

> This said, he struck his hand upon his breast
> And kiss'd the fatal knife to end his vow;
> And to his protestation urg'd the rest,
> Who, wond'ring at him, did his words allow.
>   1842-45

Quite parallel to this is the conclusion of Jonson's *Sejanus*.
Here signs and prodigies precede the fall of Sejanus:

> But now a fiery meteor in the form
> Of a great ball was seen to roll along
> The troubled air, where yet it hangs unperfect,
> The amazing wonder of the multitude!
>   5. 4. 48-51

The fall itself provokes wonder:

> MACRO: Wherefore, fathers,
>   Sit you amazed and silent.
>   5. 10. 246-47

But the final effect is a curious kind of terror, emotionally rather
subtle, for, though terror is not directly named, no one can miss
it: the more our pity is solicited in the subsequent speeches for
the attendant circumstances of Sejanus' fall, the more our terror rises. The pity which these accounts summon is really a kind
of aghast terror at the mob and at the political corruption which
still persists and is not resolved with Sejanus' fall. The pity we
feel is certainly not pity for Sejanus himself, who had disclaimed
any such softness:

> When I do fear again, let me be struck
> With forked fire, and unpitied die.
>   5. 6. 75-76

to whom it had been denied by Macro:

> And no man take compassion of thy state.
> 5. 10. 242

and whose fall is described thus by Lepidus:

> And this man fall! Fall? Ay, without a look
> That durst appear his friend, or lend so much
> Of vain relief to his changed state as pity!
> 5. 10. 283-85

Finally Arruntius at the very end of the play sums it all up:

> Forbear, you things
> That stand upon the pinnacles of state
> To boast your slippery height: when you do fall
> You pash yourselves to pieces, ne'er to rise;
> And he who lends you pity is not wise.
> 5. 10. 458-62[29]

The immediate effect of the fall is wonder, but its final effect is a terror begotten by the detailing of the occasions for pity. But the pity is simply for the human state and the innocent bystanders; there can be no real pity for the fall of a thorough villain. And here is disclosed how fear or terror enters properly into the catastrophe of an Elizabethan play. We feel pity for the death of the good and for death itself, but the violent end of the wicked begets fear. Thus Shakespeare's Queen Margaret anticipates the fall of Richard III:

> But at hand, at hand
> Ensues his piteous and unpitied end.
> 4. 4. 73-74

and Richmond later comes from the field of battle:

> God and your arms be prais'd, victorious friends!

> The day is ours; the bloody dog is dead.
>
> 5. 5. 1-2

Contrast this with Bolingbroke's comment on Richard II, who was weak but not villainous:

> Lords, I protest my soul is full of woe
> That blood should sprinkle me to make me grow.
> Come, mourn with me for what I do lament.
>
> 5. 6. 45-47

In like fashion the death of Macbeth is not mourned—he is spoken of as "this dead butcher and his fiendlike queen" (5. 8. 69)—though that of Siward's son is:

> Your cause of sorrow
> Must not be measur'd by his worth, for then
> It hath no end.
>
> 5. 8. 44-46

Sorrow and pity are reserved for the deaths of the good, or for the human fact itself—even Richard III's end will be piteous, though unpitied. Hence, at the end of *Lear*, Albany, the representative of the state, says after the deaths of Lear and Cordelia:

> Bear them from hence. Our present business
> Is general woe.
>
> 5. 3. 318-19

But on the earlier reported deaths of Goneril and Regan, one of whom was his wife, he only says:

> This judgement of the heavens, that makes us tremble,
> Touches us not with pity.
>
> 5. 3. 231-32

Fear, then, is the effect of the violent death of the wicked as distinguished from that of the good, whose fall evokes sorrow and pity.

The striking effect of pity and sorrow is explicitly named at the end of two later Shakespearean tragedies. Octavian, the representative of the state, sums up *Antony and Cleopatra*:

> High events as these
> Strike those that make them; and their story is
> No less in pity than his glory which
> Brought them to be lamented.
>
> 5. 2. 363-66

The verb "strike" here denotes the effect of wonder—at least, this is its ordinary meaning. Aufidius utters similar sentiments at the end of *Coriolanus*:

> My rage is gone,
> And I am struck with sorrow. Take him up.
>
> 5. 6. 148-49

Again, to be struck is the effect of wonder. Consequently, these three plays at least—*Hamlet, Antony and Cleopatra, Coriolanus* —together with *The Rape of Lucrece*, are intended explicitly to evoke the emotional effect of woe and wonder.

From the later tradition I will quote only the following close parallel: The Cardinal in Middleton's *Women Beware Women* characterizes the catastrophe thus:

> The greatest sorrow and astonishment
> That ever struck the general peace of Florence
> Dwells in this hour.
>
> 5. 1. 240-42[30]

Reason Panders Will

~~~~~~

The emotional effect of the catastrophe, of course, is not equivalent to the experience of the work. It is a final element in that experience, enters into it, and in part determines it. But there is more to the experience of art than the emotional effect even of the whole, and certainly more than the effect of the conclusion. There is, among other things, the experience of the language of the work. There is, especially in the Renaissance, the intellectual experience of persistent sententious thought. And there is in the typical play the central intellectual experience of plotting, counter-plotting, and mistakes: the events of *Hamlet* are characterized by Horatio at the end of the play as "mischance" that "on plots and errors happen" (5. 2. 405-06). This is an experience of the same sort as that of a game of chess, and is like chess intense in its kind, for though it is intellectual it is not without emotion: otherwise it would not be experience. Nevertheless, the other aspects of a work are related to the effect of the conclusion, and not only as elements in the larger experience of the whole. They are related in this way: though the effect itself is largely a result of the bare fact, of what happens, it is not sufficient merely to attain an effect; the effect must be justified. We must acquiesce in the conclusion.

We acquiesce out of a feeling of inevitability: what will be will be. But what is the source of this feeling? A conclusion is inevitable *within the closed system of a work of art* when it satisfies a pattern or principle of order acceptable to the audience. Such patterns are of different kinds, some larger, some smaller. They may be external, as, for example, the full circuit of Fortune's wheel, the fulfillment of the retributive justice of God, or the progression from order to disorder, concluding sadly in deaths. The pattern may exhibit the causal sequence of realistic fiction, which consists in an exemplification of a syllogistic conclusion (more precisely, an enthymeme) made persuasive. For a causal sequence shows a probable course of action, and by probability we mean a conformity to some accepted commonplace about how men of a certain type will behave under certain conditions. This is persuasive when sharply and compellingly presented so that we do not explicitly recognize the syllogistic nature of the conclusion. We merely believe it, speak of it as if it were really determined, and hence inevitable. We say the conclusion was logical.

The pattern may, however, be internal and involve artistic foreshadowing and completion, suggestion and fulfillment. Artistic devices of this nature are usually referred to and grounded on the personality of the characters, and so exhibit that adjustment of feeling which comprises the ethics of sensibility. Or, and this is quite different, the pattern may be internal and involve the structure of character. In this case it will exhibit responsibility and moral choice, and will exemplify the ethics of character. Of this sort is the pattern or principle of order which is the subject of this essay. It is only one among many, but it will serve to illustrate the kinds of principles I have in mind and the relationship of these to the emotional effect of the conclusion.

The basic text for this principle of order in Renaissance tragedy is the definition of tragedy in Averroës' paraphrase of Aristotle's *Poetics*, which was current throughout the later Middle Ages and was probably more widely reprinted in the Renaissance than the work of any other commentator. The definition reads:

> Tragedy is the imitative representation of a notable action, brought to completion by a voluntary decision, and having in it a certain force of generalization with

respect to matters of some import, as distinguished
from a particular proposition about some individual
fact. By means of this imitative representation there
is induced in the minds of the audience a rightness of
feeling which springs from the pity and terror which
the representation begets in them.[1]

The final effect of tragedy according to this definition is ethical:
it results in an ordering of the irrational by means of a presentation which evokes specific emotional effects. The internal
spring of the plot is a willed act, or moral choice. The final cause
is right feeling, which is obviously the correlative of the ethical
principle of right reason. This rightness of feeling comes through
the tragic emotions, but apparently the effective cause of ordered
feeling is the force of generalization in the plot. The universal
here is an immanent power, not explicit or allegorical, and not
singular or particular.[2]

Some of the greater tragedies of Shakespeare correspond
well enough to this definition, which supplements the Donatan
tradition with, among other principles, the principle of action
involving moral choice. But choice in tragedy is usually a choice
of evil, and hence the question in Renaissance terms is one of
sin. How does a man sin? There are two main views in the Renaissance, the intellectualist view of the Aristotelian and Thom-
istic tradition, and the voluntarist view whose tradition is more
complex. In the former the act of sin is primarily intellectual
so that the process involves erroneous reasoning: action follows
on reasoned deliberation as the conclusion of a syllogism follows on its premises. The will is considered to be subservient
to reason and to embrace almost necessarily what reason proposes. Erroneous choice, then, from this position will be ascribed primarily to sophistry. Practical reason in the possession
of the immutable principles of right action fails in the particular
application, and so sins. In Duns Scotus' phrase, "We sin by
paralogism." For the will never moves except "under the show
of goodness," as St. Thomas says,[3] or, as Iago puts it in *Othello*:

> Divinity of hell!
> When devils will the blackest sins put on,

> They do suggest at first with heavenly shows,
> As I do now.
>
> 2. 3. 356-59

We may account for sin, then, by saying that it is the result of a logical confusion, a failure to discriminate between *a* good and *the* good. Thus in the case of Macbeth it will be granted that the kingship is *a* good, but it was not for Macbeth *the* good. The irrational part of the soul, the passions and perturbations, will affect man, so long as he remains man and is in the possession of his faculties, only to the extent that his reason may be sophisticated so that he accepts invalid for valid argument. For, "if the passions of the mind be strong," Hooker relates, "they easily sophisticate the understanding; they make it apt to believe upon very slender warrant, and to imagine infallible truth where scarcely any probable show appeareth." (*EP*, 5. Dedication) In brief, reason is not dethroned or suspended, but is perverted, commits an error in logic, and is actively enlisted on the side of false desire. The process is one of reasonable choice though the reasonableness be unreasonable. It is briefly summed up in a phrase in *Hamlet*: "reason panders will."

The phrase occurs in the closet scene. It is in its context the last and most violent in a series of illustrations of the perversion of the natural order of things. Hamlet says to his mother:

> Rebellious hell,
> If thou canst mutine in a matron's bones,
> To flaming youth let virtue be as wax
> And melt in her own fire. Proclaim no shame
> When the compulsive ardour gives the charge,
> Since frost itself as actively does burn,
> And reason panders will.
>
> 3. 4. 82-88

Rhetorically, this is a very curious passage. It is a series of adynata, of impossibilities. As such, it employs the tritest device of classical and Renaissance rhetoric. We are accustomed to sigh when we meet it. But these are adynata in an ethical context; they are impossibilities only to right reason and uncorrupted nature. To be sure, frost from the point of view of Renaissance science cannot burn as if it were active. But every observer of Renaissance and fallen man knew that lust not only could but regularly did break out, even in those in whom by age and station it was especially indecorous. And every Christian knew that man was inherently sinful, and that the state of sin was that in which reason pandered will. Yet he knew that these perversions of the due order were not right, and he would feel the moral horror that Hamlet, and Shakespeare, expresses by this rhetorical device: the horror that these impossibilities, repugnant to Reason and true Nature, should be not merely possible but actual and in our sense almost natural.

The phrase, then, expresses nothing new in the history of thought. The idea is at least as old as Aristotle; it is, in fact, a compendious statement of the Aristotelian analysis of the act of erroneous moral choice which had been taken up, developed, and rendered almost conventional by a long line of medieval and Renaissance philosophers. In this tradition when reason panders will the due and proper subordination of the irrational to the rational is overturned, and overturned the more grievously in that reason is not merely suspended or dethroned but is actively enlisted in the service of desire. The man who is swept away by emotion acts unreasonably and wrongly but not perversely; the man whose reason is bent to further his unreasonable desires is in that measure diabolical.

As idea, then, it was available and in a sense trite. It had already been employed by Shakespeare, most clearly in one passage which may be regarded as the direct ancestor of this. The passage is in the reply of Adonis to the arguments of Venus in *Venus and Adonis*, for it was the quaint device of the Elizabethans to believe in discourse of reason, and they would seem, if we may accept the testimony of their literature, even to have attempted seduction by the method of disputation, and by the same method to have repelled it. Such is the case with Comus and the Lady in Milton's poem. And as the Lady in *Comus* extricates herself from the designs of the villain by opposing true reason to false reasoning, true love to earthly lust:

I had not thought to have unlockt my lips

> In this unhallowed air but that this juggler
> Would think to charm my judgement as mine eyes,
> Obtruding false rules pranked in reason's garb.
>
> 756-59

so Adonis answers Venus' arguments and defines in context the nature of sin:

> What have you urg'd that I cannot reprove?
> The path is smooth that leadeth on to danger.
> I hate not love, but your device in love,
> That lends embracements unto every stranger.
> You do it for increase. O strange excuse,
> When reason is the bawd to lust's abuse!
>
> 787-92

Here the idea is more fully and more analytically presented than in the phrase in *Hamlet*, though less fully and less analytically than in St. Thomas or Aristotle. To achieve the later phrase there remained only to subject this passage to the Shakespearean transmutation: to turn idea into intuition, to condense it to three words, and by the metaphorical *panders*, a violent and sensuous word, to exhibit reason and will as sinful and shabby figures in a disreputable world.

But though this was the orthodox view, resting on the long Aristotelian tradition, it was not the only view at that time. Erroneous action was often presented in Elizabethan drama as the result of the dethroning of reason. This latter possibility is allowed for in the Scholastic scheme, for it is an obvious fact of experience, but it is minimized. St. Thomas says, for example, that in cases of sudden and violent emotion, when reason cannot come to the opposition, mortal sin is not involved. But this is only a limiting case. For if the passion, say of love or anger, were in its origin voluntary the consequences would involve sin even though the passion took away the use of reason entirely. The critical point of decision is simply moved further back. Only if the cause were not voluntary but natural, as for example some bodily sickness, would the consequences be excused of sin. (*ST*, 1-2. 77. 7)

Nevertheless, interest in the limiting case grew in the Renaissance. The full history of this development is somewhat obscure but the principal lines are clear. In the first place, there was the development of a mechanistic psychology, the Galenic psychology of humors, with its emphasis on the involuntariness of strong passion; the most famous text in English is Burton's *Anatomy of Melancholy*. In the second place, there was the development of a voluntaristic metaphysics in the Franciscan school associated with the name of Duns Scotus, and the subsequent extension of this point of view to ethics. The issue of this movement was the predestinarianism of the Reformation with its emphasis on the helplessness of man, and particularly of his reason, and the corollary interest in Stoic Fate, which was supported by the prestige of Seneca's tragedies. Here, especially in the *Phaedra*, as also in Ovid's *Medea*, were classic exemplars of tragic characters swept away by an overmastering passion: "I see the better course, and approve of it; I follow the worse."[4] It is curious that this view of human action which ascribes to the will, the faculty of inner motion in man, the ultimate control of his destiny should in practice have issued often in an extreme determinism. Perhaps this is a sign of the thoroughgoing rationalism of the period; the more the will was considered to be irresponsible to the dictates of reason and free to act arbitrarily, the more some principle of compulsion must be invoked to account for the irresponsible arbitrariness of the will.

But whatever the reasons, there are at least four sorts of compulsion to be found in Elizabethan drama. There is, first, the compulsion which is accounted for by a mechanistic physiology and psychology, a type that has been studied a good deal in recent years, notably by Hardin Craig. He points out, for example, that the sudden and apparently unmotivated jealousy of Leontes in *The Winter's Tale* is explainable in such terms.[5]

> Too hot, too hot!
> To mingle friendship far, is mingling bloods.
> I have tremor cordis on me; my heart dances,
> But not for joy; not joy.
>
> 1. 2. 108-11

I have tremor cordis on me. But Leontes' jealousy is conceived also as voluntaristic, as involving the primacy of feeling. This is explicit in the key line of the speech in which Leontes embraces his unjustified jealousy:

> Can thy dam—may't be?
> Affection! thy intention stabs the centre.
> 1. 2. 137-38

Affection denotes the passions, emotions, and feelings which are associated with the will in the moving faculty of the soul, as distinguished from the rational faculty to which the will is attached as the rational appetite. *Intention* denotes the directed movement of a faculty of the soul toward realizing a possibility. It is that which is required to raise the potentiality of knowledge to act, and it is also the movement by which the rational will tends toward and embraces the end of action proposed by reason.[6] The passage means, then, that affection directing its own movement penetrates to the knowledge of the fact which gives the grounds for being jealous, and at the same time embraces the decision to be jealous. Hence we may translate Leontes' speech into modern terms: "Feeling rather than reason hits the mark and furnishes the decision." This is explicit voluntarism.

The third type of compulsion is that exercised by the Stoic Fate, and operating often through the influence of the stars. The fourth is the theological compulsion of grace and predestination. The two are conjoined and offered as alternative explanations of the tragic action in Heywood's *A Woman Killed with Kindness.* The tragic villain speaks:

> I am a villain if I apprehend
> But such a thought! Then, to attempt the deed,
> Slave, thou art damn'd without redemption.—
> I'll drive away this passion with a song.
> A song! Ha, ha! A song! As if, fond man,
> Thy eyes could swim in laughter, when thy soul
> Lies drench'd and drowned in red tears of blood!
> I'll pray, and see if God within my heart
> Plant better thoughts. Why, prayers are meditations,
> And when I meditate (oh, God forgive me!)

It is on her divine perfections.
I will forget her; I will arm myself
Not t'entertain a thought of love to her;
And, when I come by chance into her presence,
I'll hale these balls until my eye-strings crack,
From being pull'd and drawn to look that way.
>   *Enter, over the Stage, Frankford, his Wife,*
>   *and Nick*

O God, O God! With what a violence
I'm hurried to mine own destruction!
>   2. 3. 1-18

And again:

I will not; zounds! I will not. I may choose,
And I will choose. Shall I be so misled,
Or shall I purchase to my father's crest
The motto of a villain? If I say
I will not do it, what thing can enforce me?
What can compel me? What sad destiny
Hath such command upon my yielding thoughts?
I will not;—ha! Some fury pricks me on;
The swift fates drag me at their chariot wheel,
And hurry me to mischief.
>   2. 3. 96-105

The tragic action follows. And since the first citation above is
a soliloquy and the second an aside, they may be taken as representing the view of tragic motivation which the author himself
proffers. This is one of sheer fatalism. The character attempts
to distract his thoughts, as St. Thomas for example suggests he
should (*ST*, 1-2. 77. 2: "Whether reason can be overcome by passion against its knowledge"), but the divine sensuality of love
overpowers him. He attempts to exercise rational choice, but
fury and Fate hurry him to mischief, and with him the other
characters. He sees the better course and approves it, but follows
the worse. Yet an alternative explanation, which could be regarded as the same explanation under another aspect, is given
at the end of the play. Here the leading character, a good man,
sums up the whole:

> God, that hath laid this cross upon our heads,
> Might (had He pleas'd) have made our cause of meeting
> On a more fair and more contented ground;
> But He that made us made us to this woe.[7]

For what seems to man to be a result of Fate or fury is but the concealed operation of the Providence of God.

The contrast between the intellectual and voluntarist positions can be made clear by comparing Sextus Tarquin's soliloquy before committing the rape in Heywood's play *The Rape of Lucrece* with the similar soliloquy in Shakespeare's poem of the same title. In the former, Tarquin enters Lucrece's bedchamber carrying a drawn sword and a lighted taper. He speaks:

> I am bound
> Upon a black adventure, on a deed
> That must wound virtue and make beauty bleed.
> Pause, Sextus, and, before thou runnst thyself
> Into this violent danger, weigh thy sin ...
> Back! yet thy fame
> Is free from hazard and thy style from shame.
> O Fate! thou hast usurped such power o'er man
> That where thou pleadst thy will no mortal can ...
> Forward still!
> To make thy lust live, all thy virtues kill.
> 4. 3[8]

Certainly reasonable deliberation in the sense of rational awareness is involved here as it was in the previous citation from *A Woman Killed with Kindness*. But it does not enter into the decision. The character in the grip of strong emotion must act contrary to the dictates of reason: Fate sweeps him on. He makes no attempt to justify his sin; the end is not presented under the show of goodness.

But in Shakespeare's poem, the poet himself explains the course of Tarquin's soliloquy:

> Thus, graceless, holds he disputation
> 'Tween frozen conscience and hot burning will,

And with good thoughts makes dispensation,
Urging the worser sense for vantage still;
Which in a moment doth confound and kill
   All pure effects, and doth so far proceed
   That what is vile shows like a virtuous deed.
      246-52

God for his own inscrutable reasons does not assist Tarquin on this occasion with his grace (*Thus, graceless*). Hence Tarquin must reach this moral decision on a human and ethical plane. And how is the process described? It is described in medieval terms as the holding of a disputation. In this disputation Tarquin urges the worser sense for vantage still; reason is actively enlisted in the service of desire. When the process reaches the point of decision it doth in a moment confound all pure effects, for Tarquin by the decision has sinned mortally. Consequently, the undoing—not of his character, really, in the modern sense, but of his moral principle—doth so far proceed that what is vile shows like a virtuous deed. He sins by paralogism under the show of goodness.

II

The act of decision in the intellectualist tradition has as a further characteristic mark that it is divided into two steps: the choice of the end (*intentio*) and the choice of means (*electio*). The steps are distinct, though the second is dependent on the first. (*ST*, 1-2. 8. 3) I shall now analyze two scenes in Shakespearean tragedy, one in *Othello* and one in *Macbeth*, each of which portrays an act of moral choice that leads to the catastrophe; and I shall conclude with a discussion of the whole scope of *Hamlet*.

The scene in *Othello* concerns the choice of the end, for there is here no serious question of means. Othello has it in his power to kill Desdemona at any time, and presuming his grounds are correct the killing is justified. "Cassio did top her," he says to Emilia:

> Oh, I were damn'd beneath all depth in hell
> But that I did proceed upon just grounds
> To this extremity.
>
> 5. 2. 136-39

As for the death of Cassio, Iago promises to take care of that. The only question, then, is the question of fact; for it is assumed in the play, and made more plausible by locating the action in Venice and Cyprus, that if Desdemona has been unfaithful she must die.

The action of the play, so far as it concerns the moral act, is roughly this: Iago plants in Othello's mind the idea that his wife may be unfaithful, and he does it so skillfully that he is not himself open to attack. The mere idea is sufficient to upset most men:

> Dangerous conceits are in their nature poisons
> Which at the first are scarce found to distaste,
> But with a little act upon the blood
> Burn like the mines of sulphur.
>
> 3. 3. 326-29

But Iago does more than plant the idea; he insinuates a number of fairly vivid and violent images; he raises an efficient head of passion. More than this, he brings to bear on the question a number of commonplaces which make the fact more credible: women are weak; most husbands are cuckolds. He shows that in this special situation infidelity is even more likely, for as Desdemona has deceived her father so she may deceive him. Besides, there is the fact of their disproportion in race, in age, and in social position. Any man would be almost convinced of his wife's infidelity after such insinuation.

But its effect on Othello is only to get him into a passion in which he may do anything. He may even, as he threatens, kill Iago. At this point Iago intervenes with an appeal to reason:

> Are you a man? have you a soul? or sense?[9]
>
> 3. 3. 374

That is, "Are you a man or beast? Have you a rational soul, since reason is the distinguishing characteristic of man? or merely sense, the sensitive soul, the distinguishing characteristic of animals?" He appeals to reason because he does not want to put Othello merely in a passion: there can be no directed action without a reasoned conclusion. And Othello answers this appeal by stating the disjunctive syllogism upon which the play turns:

> I think my wife be honest, and think she is not;
> I think that thou art just, and think thou art not.
> I'll have some proof.

3. 3. 384-86

But he has prefaced this with the statement, "Nay, Stay. Thou shouldst be honest." And it has been reiterated throughout the play, not without purpose, that Iago is honest. So when the disjunction is presented almost in technical form: Either Iago is honest or Desdemona is honest, the conclusion that: Iago is honest, therefore Desdemona is not, is almost guaranteed by the assumption that Iago is. Hence Othello goes on:

> Her name, that was as fresh
> As Dian's visage, is now begrim'd and black
> As mine own face.

Nevertheless, Othello's feeling is so strong he does not yet assent; he demands some proof. If he cannot see his wife strumpeted before his eyes, let him at least have some circumstantial sign. However, as Iago has confided to the audience (3. 3. 321-24), Othello, in the distraught state of mind in which he is prepared to assent to the syllogism proposed, will accept as proof the flimsiest trifle of a sign, a mere handkerchief which he saw really but a moment ago. When to this is added Iago's account of Cassio's remarks in his sleep, which is accepted substantially as testimony to a confession on Cassio's part, the cause is finished. Othello consents. "Patience, I say," Iago interposes, "your mind perhaps may change." "Never, Iago." (3. 3. 452-53) The choice is made and solemnly ratified by oath. The following scene (3. 4

together with 4. 1 and 2) supports the decision but is subsequent to it. The play moves on to the catastrophe.

No one cares to see such things happen. Nevertheless, we can acquiesce since we can see "How these things came about." A man "not easily jealous" is operated on by a skillful insinuator and becomes so "perplex'd in the extreme" that his passions easily sophisticate his understanding: "they make it apt to believe upon very slender warrant, and to imagine infallible truth where scarcely any probable show appeareth." Othello is perplexed both intellectually and emotionally, but primarily intellectually. For, as Francis Bacon relates in the *Advancement of Learning*, there is a seducement that works by the subtlety of the illaqueation and another by the strength of the impression. The latter overmasters the reason by power of sense and imagination; the former works by perplexing the reason.[10] The process is described more fully in a sermon by Bishop Andrewes with reference to the fall of Eve:

> For this is not the least policy of the Devil, not to set upon her bluntly, but like a serpent slily and slowly to creep in her little by little, until he has espied some vantage. Therefore his order is: to bring her from questioning in talk to a doubt in opinion, and from that to an error in judgement, and so at last to a corrupt action in practice. And to corrupt her mind within, first he useth this order, to tickle her ears with curiosity, and by that to cause her to have a giddiness and swimming in the brain by fantastical imaginations and surmises; and then to make her secure and careless of the truth, and so at last maketh her somewhat inclinable to error and falsehood.[11]

But Othello's transition to jealousy and sin has not seemed plausible to every reader. It is not true to life, we are told, and the theatrical convention of the calumniator credited has been invented to solve the difficulty.[12] But the crediting of calumny is no mere convention of the theater; it is a fact of daily life. The truth is, the modern critic is concerned to defend the niceness of life, to maintain that successful hypocrisy is unlikely, that no one omits speaking up when he should, that no decent husband suspects his precious wife, and that if he does they just talk it over like civilized people. Anyway, no woman of character will sleep with a man's best friend.

Such critics make the optimistic assumption that men are not likely to go wrong unless there is sufficient cause. But this is modern, and not too well founded in fact. The general assumption of the Renaissance was that men were not likely to go right unless there was a supernatural cause. "Such is the propensity of all creatures unto evil," Bishop Jewel says, "and the readiness of all men to suspect, that the things which neither have been done, nor once meant to be done, yet may be easily both heard and credited for true."[13] The modern critic feels that women do not tend to be unfaithful; the Renaissance man, who was still smarting under Eve's transgression, felt that women were pretty likely to be unfaithful if they only had a chance. He would take Othello's remarks on cuckoldry as hardly exaggerated:

> 'Tis destiny unshunnable, like death.
> Even then this forked plague is fated to us
> When we do quicken.
>
> 3. 3. 275-77

Furthermore, the appeal of Desdemona's innocency is much greater for the reader than it was for Othello; the reader knows she is innocent, which is precisely what Othello does not know.

Anyone who is willing to believe in evil, and personally I do not find this difficult to do, will not find Othello's jealousy implausible. He may be worried, however, that it all seems to happen in so short a time, and he may wonder just how it is that Othello seems to be convinced that his wife is unfaithful —not how Iago persuades him, for that is clear enough, but by what process he comes to accept the proposition himself. I have held that the process is the traditional one of moral choice and intellectualist in character. For all his passion Othello is not swept away; he is presented with a disjunctive syllogism, draws what seems to him a proper conclusion, confirms the conclusion with a sign, and proceeds upon what he thinks are just grounds to this extremity. The process of choice itself takes place in a point of time and is properly represented as occurring within a single scene.

The restriction of the process of choice to a point of time and a single scene contributes to the feeling of implausibility. Our natural tendency, as can be seen in the novel, is to consider the process of choice as distributed through a number of scenes and as in large measure unconscious. We tend to find the condensed incredible and the diffused plausible. We regard decision as so implicated in the circumstances that condition it that neither can profitably be distinguished from the other. We can believe anything if only it be an indistinct compound of environment and heredity, and if we can be persuaded that it has evolved. For what is perhaps the greatest single difference between our habits of thought and those of the Middle Ages and Renaissance is located in the problem of continuity. We believe in the continuous. We believe that contraries shade off into each other. We believe a character is real when he is neither good nor bad but a middling gray. We disbelieve in, though we have not yet disproved, the law of the excluded middle. But the Renaissance believed firmly in Aristotelian logic: for them, B was either A or Not-A.

They also believed firmly in sin and repentance, each of which takes place in a point of time. Sin and grace were precise contraries that could not shade off into each other. Hence their view of the moral life was radically different from ours; it was essentially theological. Man's destiny hung on each decisive act, a life of grace could be cancelled by one mortal sin, and conversely the departing soul of an old and confirmed sinner could, though it was not likely, at the furthest margin of life repent of his sins and so pass joyously into the company of the elect. Such a view was held by both the great parties in the theological wars of the sixteenth century; it was proclaimed openly by those who emphasized man's free choice, but it was also maintained, if paradoxically maintained, by many of the fieriest proponents of predestination. For though a man be predestined to Hell, still he must willfully embrace that act by which he is eternally condemned, for the responsibility must be his and not the predestinating God's. So likewise, if he be predestined to Heaven,

though he make an ungodly life his profession, still at the predestined moment he shall have grace to repent and his will
must embrace that repentance. It is clear, then, that the restriction of the process of choice in Elizabethan drama to a single
scene is not the result merely of foreshortening and condensa-
tion for dramatic purposes, but is a result of the Elizabethan
view of the moral life. At the same time, of course, it is more
dramatic.

The process of the decisive choice of evil can be seen more
clearly, and this time with respect to the choice of means, in
one scene in *Macbeth*.[14] It is the seventh of the first act. Macbeth
enters and announces in a soliloquy that he has already fallen
from the state of grace, that he has preferred the show of goodness in things temporal to the solid goodness of things eternal:

> If it were done when 'tis done, then 'twere well
> It were done quickly. If th' assassination
> Could trammel up the consequence, and catch,
> With his surcease, success; that but this blow
> Might be the be-all and the end-all here,
> But here, upon this bank and shoal of time,
> We'ld jump the life to come.
>   1. 7. 1-7

His will has already moved to embrace the end, the kingship,
but he is disturbed. He does not see how to accomplish it; he
does not see how he can get away with the murder of Duncan:

> But in these cases
> We still have judgement here, that we but teach
> Bloody instructions, which, being taught, return
> To plague th' inventor.
>   1. 7. 7-10

Thus there is a consequent weakening of the will:

> I have no spur
> To prick the sides of my intent, but only

> Vaulting ambition, which o'erleaps itself
> And falls on th' other side.
>
> 1. 7. 25-28

Enter Lady Macbeth.

To understand what follows it will be well to recapitulate the requirements for a moral act. Reason must propose an end as good, and when the end is proposed the will moves naturally to embrace it. This has already happened in Macbeth, but it is not sufficient to constitute moral choice. The practical reason must discover means by which to accomplish the end (*consilium*), and not until the means are available is the choice finally made. There must follow sufficient emotion (*consensus*) so that the choice is actually put into operation (*usus*). This emotion precedes, accompanies, and follows the act of choice. It is the steam pressure that makes the engine move; there must be a certain excitement in the will to account for the step to choice and from choice to action. It is the office of rhetoric to supply this excitement; its function is to persuade. So Bacon defines it in a passage that has often been quoted but usually not properly understood: "The duty and office of rhetoric is to apply reason to imagination for the better moving of the will."[15] By *apply* here is meant "to put into practical contact with," so that if one were to use these words in a modern context he would rather say that imaginaion is applied to reason.

The traditional analysis, popularized and lacking the complication of multiplied distinctions, is expounded by the character of Tragedy himself in a play presented by Shakespeare's company (ca. 1598) a few years before *Hamlet. A Warning for Fair Women* begins with an argument between Tragedy, Comedy, and History. Later in the play, at the moment of moral choice, Tragedy steps forward and explains the process:

> Prevailing sin having by three degrees
> Made his ascension to forbidden deeds,
> At first, alluring their unwary minds
> To like what she proposed, then practising
> To draw them to consent; and, last of all,
> Ministering fit means and opportunity
> To execute what she approved good;

> Now she unveils their sight, and lets them see
> The horror of their foul immanity.
>
> 2. 865-74[16]

But to return to *Macbeth*. He has embraced the end, and now falters in resolution because he does not see how the end can be accomplished. There is required now fit means and opportunity to execute what he approved good, together with a concurrent sustaining and heightening of resolution, the maintaining of an efficient head of passion. To fulfill this last requirement, the Ghost had appeared to Hamlet in the closet scene, and for the same reason Hamlet was made to observe Fortinbras and his army marching across "a plain in Denmark." For the same reason in this scene Lady Macbeth speaks in such shockingly violent terms:

> I have given suck, and know
> How tender 'tis to love the babe that milks me.
> I would, while it was smiling in my face,
> Have pluck'd my nipple from his boneless gums
> And dash'd the brains out, had I so sworn as you
> Have done to this.
>
> 1. 7. 54-59

So also, to Macbeth's assertion:

> I dare do all that may become a man.
> Who dares do more is none.

which is sound doctrine, implying the notion of decorum and the mean. Lady Macbeth answers with the old commonplace that Iago had used, of soul and sense, distinguishing man from beast through the characteristic of willed action:

> What beast was't then
> That made you break this enterprise to me?
> When you durst do it, then you were a man;
> And to be more than what you were, you would
> Be so much more the man.
>
> 1. 7. 46-51

This is obvious sophistry. It makes the will and not reason the distinguishing characteristic of man; it opposes rashness to timidity, excluding from consideration the reasonable mean of right courage. But it takes Macbeth in. His only question now is as to the means: "If we should fail?" Lady Macbeth outlines the way in which the murder can be accomplished and suspicion diverted. As soon as the means are proposed Macbeth assents and the moral choice is complete:

> I am settled and bend up
> Each corporal agent to this terrible feat.
> 1. 7. 79-80

This final decision of the soul, accompanied of course by disordered emotion, persists unaltered through the catastrophe.

But in *Hamlet* the process of moral choice extends throughout the play. The first half is concerned with the choice of end, which rests here as in *Othello* on a question of fact: did Claudius really kill the old King, Hamlet's father? or, what is the same question, is the Ghost a true ghost or a diabolical apparition? To resolve this question of fact Hamlet devises the play scene as an *experimentum crucis*: "If he but blench," Hamlet says in a soliloquy, "I know my course." (2. 2. 625-26) At the close of the play scene, when the King does blench, Hamlet turns to Horatio and says, "I'll take the ghost's word for a thousand pound! Didst perceive?" (3. 2. 297-98) The question of fact is now resolved and Hamlet embraces the end which the Ghost had proposed in an early scene of the play: "Revenge his foul and most unnatural murther." (1. 5. 25) The rest of the play concerns the choice of means, but the means in this case is not easy to find. The King cannot be killed at his prayers and so dispatched to Heaven: "Why, this is hire and salary, not revenge!" (3. 3. 79) He does kill him in the Queen's closet, or so he thinks, but it turns out to be only Polonius, that "wretched, rash, intruding fool." And so on to the close of the play. The proper means to accomplish the end is never discovered until it is too late, until Hamlet when he knows that he is dying stabs the King with the envenomed sword. It is too late, now, for a successful plot.

Hamlet, of course, is a touchy subject. I do not wish to imply that his character is equivalent to this analysis; he is something more and something other. He is an imitation of a person, and thus has an imputed reality. He has a name, which is a chief instrument of individualization. He is implicated in circumstances of some particularity. He does and says much that is not reducible to the central choice. He is presented in a specific body of writing. Nevertheless, a fictional character is not a given, a brute fact of existence. He is a construction, a fiction, and hence he must be constructed according to a scheme and must have a scheme to be intelligible. I am maintaining only that both the play and the character of Hamlet are in part constructed according to the scheme of moral choice as it was analyzed in the scholastic tradition.

It would follow that those who interpret Hamlet's character in terms of irresolution are in a way right, for here the process of choice is extended over the whole play. But they are wrong when they see in this a trait of character. Hamlet delays, not because he is irresolute, but because he is reasonable. His reason must be satisfied as to the end before his will moves to embrace it; his reason must discover the appropriate means before the moral choice can be ratified and action move on to the conclusion. He is irresolute because, as Hooker says, "the Will notwithstanding does not incline to have or do that which Reason teacheth to be good, unless the same do also teach it to be possible." (*EP*, 1. 7. 5) Hamlet could quote in his defense against his detractors, who perhaps like Coleridge are mightier with the pen than with the sword, the apology of the old counsellor in *The Winter's Tale*:

> if ever fearful
> To do a thing where I the issue doubted,
> Whereof the execution did cry out
> Against the non-performance, 'twas a fear
> That oft infects the wisest.
> 1. 2. 258-62

Yet in a sense the resolution of the plot is apprehended partly in terms of moral action. Everyone knows the famous line in Hamlet's soliloquy, "Thus conscience," that is, knowledge and awareness, "does make cowards of us all":

> And enterprises of great pith and moment
> With this regard their current turn awry
> And lose the name of action.
> 3. 1. 83, 86-88

and the later speech prompted by the sight of Fortinbras' exploits:

> What is a man,
> If his chief good and market of his time
> Be but to sleep and feed? A beast, no more.

Here again is the commonplace of soul or sense.

> Sure he that made us with such large discourse,
> Looking before and after, gave us not
> That capability and godlike reason
> To fust in us unus'd. Now, whether it be
> Bestial oblivion, or some craven scruple
> Of thinking too precisely on th' event,—

in which *event*, of course, means "outcome" or "upshot." The problem here involves a choice between no action, rational action with a view to consequences, and action at any cost. The contrast between the latter two resembles that between the chivalric rashness of Hotspur and the staid courage of Prince Hal. In this case it is solved in favor of Hotspur. Hamlet decides:

> Rightly to be great
> Is not to stir without great argument
> But greatly to find quarrel in a straw
> When honour's at the stake.

and concludes:

> O, from this time forth,
> My thoughts be bloody, or be nothing worth!
> 4. 4. 33-41, 53-56, 65-66

From this time forth his actions as well as his thoughts are as bloody as anyone could wish. To the earlier death of Polonius he adds the deaths of Rosencrantz and Guildenstern, of Laertes by accident, and the King by design. He acts now partly from "perfect conscience," in the ethical sense of that which incites or binds us either to do or not to do something, and partly in the rashness of honor. Reasonable action has proved inadequate in the circumstances, and is abandoned:

> Being thus benetted round with villanies,
> Or I could make a prologue to my brains,
> They had begun the play.
>   5. 2. 29-31

Deliberation is fatal; only rashness has a chance of success:

> Rashly—
> And prais'd be rashness for it; let us know,
> Our indiscretion sometime serves us well
> When our deep plots do pall; and that should learn us
> There's a divinity that shapes our ends,
> Rough-hew them how we will—
>   5. 2. 6-11

Man proposes, and God disposes. Indeed, Heaven is ordinant even in the accidental details. And so Hamlet gives up the human attempt to achieve justice by rational action, by the calculation of means, abandons himself to the tide of circumstance which is the Special Providence of God, and proceeds to the catastrophe despite his misgivings. He is resigned to destiny, which is God's will; "the readiness is all." The play whose plot had displayed the scheme of moral action ends with the renunciation of it.

Appendix I

The Ancient Quarrel Between History and Poetry

~~~~~~

A work of art is the embodiment of an intention. To realize an intention in language is the function of the writer. To realize from language the intention of the author is the function of the reader or the critic, and his method is historical or philological interpretation. For Philology, in the older sense of the term, is concerned with the relationship of expression and intention; it revivifies the letter by ascertaining its spirit. And when Philology has accomplished this task, there remains not even the appreciation of the spirit, since the task cannot be accomplished without this.

This premise resolves the quarrel between the historical and the aesthetic approach to literature and to other branches of art. Everyone is familiar with the distinction, and apparently everyone agrees that there is a distinction. Even those who have defended the historical attitude against the onslaughts of the aesthetes have maintained the dualism of the two approaches. For they have held either that the historical is an independent discipline with its own rights to existence, or, more commonly, that though the historical is subordinate, it is a necessary hand-maid to the aesthetic: we need historical knowledge to remove the hindrances to appreciation.

The two positions are, of course, compatible: one can hold that the discipline of literary history has independent validity and at the same time hold that it furnishes useful aids to literary appreciation. Furthermore, it is true enough that there is a body of knowledge associated with literature that is in itself worth knowing: not only literary history proper, but also history in the ordinary sense of the term, and indeed many other fields of learning. What is more, all these are useful; in fact, it is doubtful if there be any kind of knowledge that will not at some point or other prove useful in the study of literature. Furthermore, the ways of understanding and the habits of attention which are developed by some of these disciplines are of the greatest value, both in themselves and for the study of literature, and there is much to be said for the old argument that a thorough grounding in Anglo-Saxon and textual criticism form a good preparation for the study of the English essay or the poetry of T. S. Eliot. But the general habits formed in this way can be acquired without these disciplines; the information needed to understand a given work can be picked up from those who have it; and as to the associated learnings, the aesthetic critic can grant them validity and prop-erly ignore them on the grounds that a man can only do so much and that his business is appreciation. Let the historian write history, let the aesthetic critic appreciate—or let the one man alternately do both.

Such is the common resolution of the problem, and the only argument is over the spoils: which shall have the greater pres-tige or make the more money. But the dualism is not only un-necessary, it is pernicious.

It rests apparently upon an empirical basis. We are told that works of art take on new color with each succeeding generation if not with each succeeding reader, that they are complexes of symbols that seem to offer an almost inexhaustible variety of interpretations. They are all things to all men and all ages. And the living greatness of a work of art is often thought to reside in this chameleon character. It is this, we are told, which dis-tinguishes the major from the minor work, which marks the difference between *Hamlet* and *The Spanish Tragedy*, or the work of living interest from the work of mere historical interest.

But is this really the case? The difference is obviously in part one of merit, or of imputed merit. The case is not that the one is better because it is more living, but simply that it is more living because it is better. The argument, then, mistakes an effect for the cause, or is naïvely circular. There is, moreover, a second consideration which is usually unnoticed in these discussions. The work that is thought to be more alive and more universal usually turns out to be simply more familiar, for the familiar is that with which we feel we can take liberties. Donne, for instance, achieved universality by becoming fashionable, and so with Gerard Hopkins. Thus the contemplative spirit becomes fashion or custom.

But the position rests in truth, as a distinguished scholar tells us, not so much upon an empirical basis as upon an assumed distinction between the work of art "as artistic phenomenon and historical fact," a distinction which leads logically to the disappearance of the work of art itself. The distinction is made clear by Walter Curry in the following passage:

> But as historical fact it [the work of literature] must inevitably bear upon it, in both form and content, the stamp of historical associations which influenced its production and from which it emerged. Criticism, we may say, attempts to report faithfully upon the efficacy of an artistic construction as a stimulus of aesthetic experience; historical interpretation, on the other hand, is concerned with orienting the historical fact in relation to the historical events—traditional or otherwise—which urged the dramatist to create it. But wherever these scattered events originally focussed upon the drama have been forgotten, it is evident that criticism cannot exercise its function properly and completely without relying upon the findings of historical interpretation.[1]

Although in the last sentence the scholar suggests that historical interpretation is the handmaid of criticism or appreciation, the dualism he erects does not leave room even for this.

For the distinguishing mark of literature, insofar as it is true art, he asserts, is its universality, and by this is meant that "as art-work it may be immediately possessed by the contemplative spirit of men in any age and under any circumstances; as a stimulus to aesthetic experience it is timeless, self-sufficient, and free."

From this account it is not at all evident how criticism and historical interpretation can have anything to do with each other. On the one hand, the historian is concerned with the origin of the stimulus, with what urged the writer to create it. On the other hand, criticism reports on the "timeless" response to the stimulus—any response, and the only question is: Does it get a response? So the multiplicity of wild and inconsistent interpretations of *Macbeth*, as Curry hastens to explain, testify to the virility of the Macbeth-stimulus, and not at all to the stupidity, confusion, and selfishness of the interpreters. But who is going to look at the stimulus itself? Here are ancestors and descendants, but where is the man? Who is going to look at *Macbeth*? And if the scholar himself looks very closely and very accurately at *Macbeth*, this only refutes his theory by his practice, for his practice exhibits that fusion of accuracy and feeling which we have defined as genuine historical interpretation.

But, according to the theory, appreciation is the actual response to the work of art, though usually it is the response of certain selected persons. For it is not held to be, except by some cultural anarchists, any response of any person, but rather that of what is generally called the man of sensibility who appreciates in the light of universal aesthetic values. Now, few will deny that there are men of sensibility and men of insensibility, that there are those who are capable of responding to works of art and those who should not be allowed to try, though there may be some disagreement as to who belongs in what category. But when we have settled on the elect, what have we? We have contemplative spirits who immediately possess the aesthetic experience, which is timeless, self-sufficient, and free. There is apparently a kind of Oversoul of Culture in which are absorbed all the aesthetic monuments of the past, which have put off the body of this death and the material clothing of their particular expressions, and in which the elect participate by a parody of the Beatific Vision.

The more cautious will bring this heaven down to earth, and will allow the work of art its material embodiment. But they will regard the historical nature of the work only as a hindrance to the universality of the artist's vision, or as an accident to be disengaged from the substance. They will maintain that historical interpretation is necessary, but that its purpose is to remove the ignorance or misapprehensions which hinder our direct appreciation of the text.

On the contrary, the accidents are integral to the substance. Hindrances are not merely hindrances; they are in themselves important. They are the points at which we become conscious that the text cannot be understood on our own terms. We are reading another, not ourselves. This fact should provoke us to look with some skepticism on what is meant by the universal in the context of aesthetic appreciation. By the universal is usually meant that which concerns you; hence as a principle of aesthetic importance, it is the principle of selfishness and ignorance. For what you immediately understand you regard as essential; what you do not, as accidental.

However, we need not deny that the appreciation of a work of art on one's own terms and even in defiance of the known historical intention of the work is more valuable than a dry and desiccated antiquarianism. For the one has life and the other has not. And such appreciation is especially valuable to the man who would integrate in his own experience the monuments of the past. But the man who does this should remember that he is not integrating in his experience the experience of the past. By being unhistorical he has abjured that experience; he is abusing the monuments of history to inform them with his own life. At the best, if he is himself a competent artist and if the material is tractable, he may produce a new and different work, and this may in itself have value.

This is sometimes accomplished, for example, in the transcription and arrangement of old music, as in Bach's transcription of Vivaldi or Chavez' of Buxtehude. In literature the best and most obvious examples are to be found in the seventeenth and eighteenth century adaptations of the classics. Today, it is usually done in critical essays for the reviews. But in such cases we are dealing with a new, though derived, work. The new work may throw some light upon its source, and an understanding of the source may be an important element in the understanding of the work. But the point is: an adaptation is an independent work and not primarily an interpretation.

On the other hand, translation and intepretation are essentially alike. For, although a translation is manifestly other than its original, nevertheless we can designate a translation as correct or incorrect, as more or less adequate to the original. Now, it is that understanding of the original which enables us to say that a given translation is more or less adequate, which is the aim of historical interpretation. Furthermore, this understanding of the original is the work of art. Hence, the work of interpretation consists precisely in the recovery, so far as is possible, of the original; that is, of the author's intentions as realized in the particular text under consideration.

For this is the way in which the genuinely sensitive man approaches a work of literature. It is a method that, as a matter of fact, does have close analogies with the method of religious surrender. It consists in yielding as completely as possible to the experience of the work, with the intention of formulating afterwards the alterations which this surrender has wrought. As such, it is not only unobjectionable but necessary, both in art and in life. It is the initial act of abandonment, of faith and sympathy, without which we will never penetrate any human experience.

But, unless it is protected by the constant awareness that the experience we are penetrating is that of another, such aesthetic surrender can only be an elaborate game by which we discover with surprise that the attitudes and preconceptions with which we view the object are really there, although in fact we put them there in a somnambulistic trance. Thus the aesthetic experience proves often enough to be only an affirmation of solipsism, and the aesthetic soul a parody of the Neo-Platonic God whose spirit infuses all things, which are but degradations of Itself. However, if the act of faith and sympathy with which we surrender ourselves to an object be one which involves a scrupulous responsibility toward the object in all its specificality, this is nothing other than historical interpretation.

It is in fact nothing other than morality, if it is not too out of fashion to connect morality with such pursuits as poetry and scholarship. For the understanding of an author in the scholarly sense involves the exercise under defined conditions of the two fundamental principles of morality in the Western tradition: 1) the principle of dignity, or of responsibility to the external fact, in the special form of respect for another person as revealed in his works; and 2) the principle of love, the exercise of sympathetic insight, or of imaginative transformation.

For (to sum up) the premise of historical interpretation is that a piece of writing is a historical document, and by this is meant that it is to be interpreted, understood, and experienced as nearly as possible in the way in which it was originally intended to be interpreted, understood, and experienced. Hence, in historical interpretation our allegiance is to the external, to the historical experience implicated in the system of signs which is the work under consideration.

For whatever be the case with the other arts, the arts of language consist of statements, and a statement means what it says. We look at what a work says to find out what it means, and the apprehension of its meaning is the work of art. Insofar as the meaning is not expressed in or not recoverable from the statements, the work is deficient. Furthermore, it is a simple principle of ethics, provable in daily conversation, that the meaning of a statement is not what anyone chances to attribute to it—how hurt we are when we are misconstrued—but what it was intended to convey. The intention is the intention of the author as expressed in the language which he used and qualified by the circumstances under which he expressed it. Hence every statement is a historical statement, and it is properly understood only by historical interpretation.

Thus, since a work of literature is precisely the apprehension of its proper meaning, the appreciation of literature resides in historical interpretation. There are not two approaches to the study of literature, but only one: historical interpretation is aesthetic appreciation. If the two are distinguishable, they are distinguishable only as aspects of one another. The historical is that act of respect by which we recognize otherness: to this the various historical disciplines are subsidiary. The aesthetic is that act of sympathy by which we realize the other and make it our own.

I add: There is a distinction to be made in the use of the term *historical*. In the wider sense, it denotes that interpretation which takes into account the time, place, and conditions of an utterance. But there is a fundamental difference in methodology between the literary approach to a text and the approach of the historian in the narrower sense of the term. The literary interpreter is interested solely in understanding what the text was intended to say, neither more nor less. The historian, in the narrower sense, is interested primarily in the reality supposed to lie behind the text. He is as interested in what the text does not say as in what it does. His method consists in breaking down the text, in destroying its literary finish in order to penetrate to the reality that the words conceal. In brief, the historian treats a text as evidence, the literary interpreter treats it as a composition whose surface is inviolate. The historian's allegiance is to the facts which the text enables him to conjecture, to infer, or to establish. The allegiance of the literary interpreter is to the text itself.

Perhaps a trivial example will make the distinction clear. The notorious seacoasts of Bohemia in *The Winter's Tale* are evidence to the historian of a certain casualness and vagueness about geographical matters on Shakespeare's part. To the literary interpreter this is irrelevant. Bohemia to him is precisely what it was to Shakespeare, a remote kingdom which may as well have a seacoast as not.

Appendix II

Tragedy as Essence

~~~~~~

The humanist in areas that are of special concern to him, as in the case of tragedy, tends to be an uncritical Realist, a simple-minded believer in a realm of essences. Let us take the case of tragedy and see what this belief entails. The assumption that there is a stable and external reality corresponding to the idea of tragedy, the assumption, indeed, that there is an Idea of tragedy, and the subsequent inquiry into its definition always presupposes at least that there is a given and prior body of material associated with a common name in common use. Otherwise, one could never begin. Furthermore, the name itself, being a term in common use, has associated with it a group of notions whose content and relationship is only partly fixed and defined. A certain vagueness and slipperiness is part of their meaning. The process of investigation, then, consists in introducing a more explicit structure into the notions associated with the term and a more limited reference into the term itself. In this way the element of slipperiness and vagueness, if not eliminated, is considerably reduced. The term in its more closely defined sense is then reintroduced into the body of the material so that some items are excluded from consideration, while others are arrayed in degrees of importance on the basis of their approximation to

128

the definition. *The Spanish Tragedy* is not really a tragedy but a melodrama, and *King Lear* is more tragic than *Richard III*.

The result of such investigation is a definition which cannot be regarded as merely arbitrary, as simply stipulated. It refers to reality and proposes to get to the heart of it. And the heart of it is an essence. But if what one arrives at by this process be an essence, in any of the normal senses of this term, we must suppose that the terms of ordinary language, or at least some of them, derive their content and reference from some source other than the historical process of usage, and that this source is to a sufficient extent controlled by a realm of essences. We must further suppose that the methods by which we clarify the definition of the word and thing is the reverse of that by which the word in the historical process of actual usage became corrupted by vagueness of content and slipperiness of reference, and we must assume that the process is reversible. These assumptions seem to me to entail a Platonism that is denied by my experience and by what historical knowledge I have of, for example, the notions of tragedy in various literatures and various times.

I should prefer to define such a notion as tragedy in terms of those principles of order that enter into the intention of a given work or given body of works insofar as the explicit recognition by the author of those principles as the principles of what he calls tragedy and their intended recognition by the reader is guaranteed by historical evidence. There may thus be a relationship between tragedies of various authors, groups, and periods so far as similar principles of order can be defined in different traditions. There is in this sense a continuity in the tradition of tragedy between Classical Antiquity and the English Renaissance. In this the chief mediating source was not Aristotle's *Poetics* but the definition of tragedy gathered by the grammarians of later Antiquity out of Classical theory and practice and transmitted to the writers of the Renaissance as a scheme to be realized. Consequently, it is possible to construct a history of tragedy from Aeschylus to John Ford that would be a genuine history without presupposing that any such entity as tragedy really exists except in the notions of tragedy that writers and readers have entertained.

II

**Tradition and
Poetic Structure**

Poetry,
Structure, and Tradition

~~~~~~

I

These chapters are about poetry, and particularly about the structure of individual poems and their relationship to a tradition. Consequently, I shall begin with some more general remarks on the nature of poetry, of structure, and of tradition.

To begin with the definition of poetry. It is said that poetry is difficult to define, and the difficulty would seem to be of two sorts. In the first place, there is in different definitions a difference in what is being defined. Poetry is regarded as a kind of literature, a quality of experience, a way of knowing. It is contrasted with verse, with prose, and with science. It is defined in such a way as to favor a special view of experience or to promote the writing or approval of a special kind of poem. The difficulty, then, lies in the fact that the object of definition is not constant. The hesitations, the scruples, the blurring in the act of definition result from this. There remains, however, a constant point, if not of reference at least of departure, in all these formulations, and this is poetry as it is ordinarily understood: the body of linguistic constructions that men usually refer to as poems.

The second difficulty springs from the need to defend and

to praise poetry. Very nice things are said of it. In fact, it is felt
that one has not only to define poetry but also in so doing to put
it in a place of honor, to recover some of the prestige that once
accrued to the Muses. A particularly happy definition, one is led
to believe, might elicit a donation from some elderly recluse or
from a foundation. But these claims for poetry, which invade
the description and definition of it, this concern with a higher
something, knowledge or feeling, while they might seem designed
to improve its estate, have in fact weakened it. They have on the
one hand erected pretensions that no linguistic construction, no
poem, could ever hope to satisfy. The statements, in brief, are
not true. Poets, for example, are not "the unacknowledged legis-
lators of the world," and a good thing it is that they aren't. And
the claims have, on the other hand, by qualifying the conception
of poetry both limited the kinds of poetry that can be written
and the audience that is prepared to receive it. They have exiled
most of human experience from the poet's page, and he is left
with an image and a mood:

> For all the history of grief
> An empty doorway and a maple leaf[1]

If one glances through the history of criticism it would
appear that there are in general three definitions of poetry that
have persisted throughout the tradition. The commonest is that
which regards it as a quality of experience associated with a
special selection and use of language, and the quality of experience is normally one that is thought to command prestige. A
representative formulation is offered by one of the standard
dictionaries, where poetry is characterized as: "The expression
of beautiful or elevated thought, imagination, or feeling, in appropriate language, such language containing a rhythmical element and having usually a metrical form."[2] Of such a definition
we may say that it appears to isolate and explore the activity
and subject matter of poetry, but that in fact it introduces a
principle of value which is prescriptive as to what kinds of
poetry should be written or cherished. Furthermore, the principle which arrogates to poetry a higher kind of experience is
pretentious. Finally, we may observe that such definitions are

fairly reticent about meter, but firmer with respect to rhythm, which is usually regarded as primitive and emotional, and hence, no doubt, higher. Nevertheless, it is true that at different times certain attitudes toward the kinds of experience and certain associated selections of language have been comprised in the idea of poetry. Hence, as a method of defining, not poetry, but the poetry of a given tradition, this is an appropriate and useful method.

The second of the definitions that are commonly offered is usually ascribed to Aristotle in the *Poetics*. In that work Aristotle attempts to distinguish a kind of what he calls imitation which had been, he says, up to that time without a name. It is the kind of imitation in which an action is represented by means of language, and he cites as examples the Platonic dialogue and the mimes of Sophron. Of the same kind, with the exception that music as well as language is used as a means of imitation, are epic, comedy, and tragedy. For this more general kind he appropriates the name of poetry, a name which had been more customarily applied, as he points out, to compositions in meter.[3] Aristotle, of course, is simply developing and systematizing a notion already available in the tradition, the notion Socrates accepts in the *Phaedo* (61B) that a poet to be really a poet must employ fiction. It follows, then, that for poetry in this sense meter is not essential; it can be at most a contributory means appropriate to the end. For what is being defined is what we call fiction, and this may be, as it is in Plato's dialogues, in prose, or as in Homer and Sophocles, in verse. However, the use of a common term implies a common object of reference and so the question has arisen again and again since Aristotle's day whether a poem need be written in meter, and whether a poem that is not in some sense an imitation of an action, that is, fiction, is really a poem or rather something else—perhaps rhetoric. But fiction and metrical composition are simply two different things: a work may be both, or either, or neither.

However, though every composition in meter need not have a narrative structure, need not be fiction, it is pretty likely to have some sort of structure analogous to the narrative structure of fiction. If we use *fiction*, then, in a wider sense, if we generalize the notion to extend to the device, whatever it is, that orders the material of the poem in outline, we may regard a metrical composition as having a principle of fiction, and we may discuss what is the fiction of this particular poem, what kinds of fictions various poems exhibit, and perhaps what kinds of fictions are possible or practical in poetry. A fiction in this broader sense is a major principle of order in a work, and I shall discuss a number of such principles in the following chapters.

I prefer with respect to poetry the third, the common or garden variety of definition. I mean by poetry what everyone means by it when he is not in an exalted mood, when he is not being a critic, a visionary, or a philosopher. I mean by poetry what a man means when he goes to a bookstore to buy a book of poems as a graduation gift, or when he is commissioned by a publisher to do an anthology of sixteenth century poems. Poetry is what looks like poetry, what sounds like poetry. It is metrical composition.

To define a poem in this way will seem trivial to some and offensive to others. It will seem to depreciate the importance of poetry. It will seem to signal out what is thought to be an accidental and to ignore the essential quality of poetry. It will be objected to, in addition, as affording no principle of value by which one could distinguish a good poem from a bad, for certainly that distinction will not lie solely or even largely in the meter. But all of these objections, where they are not motivated by a concern to advance the prestige and practice of a special kind of poetry or by the inveteracy of old habit now appalled, spring from a tacit and perhaps unconscious assumption about the nature and function of a definition. It is assumed that the definition is offered in the form and spirit of the Aristotelian tradition. It is assumed that a definition, in marking off an object from all other objects of the more general kind to which it belongs, purports to distinguish the peculiar virtue of the object, and in terms of the point of difference to offer a principle of judgment, a scale of values. And it is assumed that the point of difference is more important than, is important to the detriment of, the general class to which the object is assigned. But there is no need to assume this. The purpose of the definition is simply to mark off the territory and to describe the thing unmistakably.

How these assumptions tacitly operate can be seen in the traditional definition of man as a rational animal. This formulation was preferred to the alternatives, that man is a two-legged or a laughing animal, largely because it was felt that in his rationality lay his peculiar glory and claim to prestige, and that this was a worthy principle of evaluation that could be applied to the rating of particular men. There is not much glory in two-leggedness or laughter, and neither would offer an acceptable scale of values. Again, in the traditional definition, and in the views that grew out of it, the rationality of man was attended to to the depreciation of his animality; the specific took precedence over the generic. But the tacit demands here made on a definition are demands of a different order than the requirements for clarity and accuracy of definition, and the alternative formulations might have served the latter purpose as well or better.

II

To begin, then, with the general class to which poems belong: a poem is a composition; that is, it is a system of propositions. I take *proposition* in a more general sense than is usual; a proposition is a determinate relationship of signs forming an element in a composition consisting of successive elements of this nature. Thus an algebraic equation is a proposition, and that equation subjected to a successive series of transformations would constitute a system of propositions. The syllogism in logic is of the same order, as is a piece of music insofar as the musical signs are grouped into elements, for example, into what are called phrases. Of the same order is a recorded game of chess, in which the elements, of course, are the distinct moves: P-K4, P-K4. But each of these differs from such things as an incident, a statue or picture, a football game or a horse race. We can formulate propositions about these; we can describe the incident, the picture, or the game, and the formulation refers to the object, but it is not the object. The poem, however, is the text; the equation is the equation; and the game of chess is the recorded series of moves. Whatever the source of the propositions and however the man who wrote them down may have arrived at them, once the formulation has been recorded the experience it refers to and the experience it directs are properly confined to the meanings of the terms and the meanings of their relationship and succession.

Consequently, there is an exact analogy between poetry and chess, since they are things of the same kind. The poet in writing a poem has a good many experiences that do not appear in the propositions he puts on paper, the completed poem. The player at chess has a good many experiences that do not appear in the moves he makes on the board, the moves that recorded in the standard notation constitute for him and for anyone who knows chess the game he played. This game is repeatable as the poem is repeatable, and the experiences that properly belong to it are the repeatable experiences. In fact, the game as played and the poem as written constitute a principle of order, a method, for discriminating the relevant from the irrelevant among one's immediate experiences as he plays or reads or writes, and among one's retrospective experiences as he sums up after the game or after the completion of the poem. To be repeatable and to be a method for discriminating relevant from irrelevant experiences are characteristics of all composition.

There is a further characteristic. The player at chess in making each move envisages a variety of alternative moves, and we in replaying the same game must do alike if we are to achieve the recorded experience. Similarly the text of a poem consists of what little is left, out of the wide-strewn wreckage of alternative phrases, lines, and possibilities of development. No one has read a poem who has not constructed and rejected as he read some of the alternative poems whose nonexistence gives timbre and resonance to the text.

There is also an inexact analogy between poetry and chess. It is slightly fanciful, but not untrue and not without its applications. The player at chess has an opponent. He makes his moves not only within the rules of the game and the limitation of the board and his pieces, but also within the possibilities afforded by his opponent's moves and by the potentiality of his future moves. The player is not free to erect what structure he pleases within the rules of the game. If he chooses to be whimsical, there are consequences that must be dealt with. If he moves his pieces merely to accomplish a pretty design, an apparent pattern, he moves to disaster. The poet, too, has an opponent. His opponent is experience. The nature and quality of the game the two of them play will depend not only on his own skill but also on the adroitness and resourcefulness of his opposing experience. If experience is simple, unseasoned, without depth, the poet may have an easy time of it but the game suffers; it lacks depth and interest. And if the opponent is dishonest, if he throws away a queen to extricate the poet from a difficult spot, the game will be shoddy and not worth the playing. There are poems that are praised for their order, simplicity, and charm that so far as I can see represent a victory over nothing at all. We must distinguish between the simplicity of a Capablanca against a Nimzowitsch,[4] of a master of chess against a master of chess, and the simplicity with which one defeats a friend when he negligently forgets to castle. But this is a digression.

To return: it is characteristic of a composition that it is repeatable, that it is a method for discriminating the repeatable from the unique in experience, and that it is the specification of a range of possible compositions. There is a further characteristic which all compositions have. They all conform to the rules of the game, by which is stipulated beforehand what kinds of terms, of propositions and successions of propositions are admissible. For example, the rules of the traditional syllogism of the type *All men are mortal* are fairly simple and fairly easily stated. In brief, there will be three propositions and in this order: all items belonging to a certain general class have a certain property; this item belongs to that general class; therefore, this item has that property. The rules are a method for inventing further syllogisms with the same structure. The rules of chess are more complex, but of the same order. The rules of poetry, or rather the rules of the various traditions of poetry, are of the same order, but even more complex. Nevertheless, they are describable, and to describe the rules of the game is to define a tradition. A tradition is all the ways a particular poem could have been written; it is the potentiality of realized structures, as the rules of chess contain all the games that may be played.

III

But a poem is not only a composition; it is a composition of a special sort. What distinguishes a poem from all other items in its general class is that the propositions are in meter, and hence if poetry has any peculiar province this issues from the fact that it is metrical. There are three possibilities. Since meter is an aspect of language it is possible that certain special meanings can be conveyed by meter that cannot be conveyed by unmetrical language, either different kinds of meaning or more or less refined versions of similar meanings. It is said, for example, that metrical language can deal more subtly and more accurately with feeling. Again, meter may have some special effect on those who use it. Poetry, for example, tends to be more memorable than prose and tends to support a greater extraordinariness of language. The third possibility is this: wherever one finds alternative forms in a language, the existence of a distinction in form tends to beget a distinction in function or purpose, and usually by an unnoticed historical process. In time, then, certain areas of experience will be assigned to metrical and others to unmetrical composition, and this is what has happened in the history of literature. Furthermore, the areas assigned to each medium shift and vary from time to time and place to place. It follows, then, that poetry of a given time and place will tend to deal with those areas of experience which convention and history have assigned to writing in meter. In brief, a poem is the sort of thing that poets write, and what they write is the sort of thing their society has come to regard as poetry. By their society here I mean the larger or smaller group at a given time and place who are concerned with the production and appreciation of poetry. What that society regards as poetry is what I mean by tradition. What it regards as poetry will furnish the rules of the game.

Consequently, though a tradition is historical in that it issues from a historical process, it is not in itself its history. It exists at each moment in completed form. For a tradition is rather, both in the terms in which it must be described and reconstituted by the literary historian and in the actual way in which it is attained and apprehended by a given writer at a given time, a context of notions, often jumbled and sometimes not too consistent with one another, together with the methods and attitudes by which these notions are grasped and applied. A tradition can be located in the body of texts and interpretations current among a given group of writers and readers. Such a description applies equally to the traditions in which Chaucer or Shakespeare wrote and to those which are now current: one must be learned as well as the other, and in the same way.

A tradition, however, is not simply a body of learning. It is a body of learning capable of being applied to the production of what are called original works. It is the method by which the sentences of a poem are discovered: it demarks the field of discovery and orders the succession of sentences. It is the potentiality of any work in the tradition.

Hence, the notions which constitute a tradition are not ideas merely, but principles of order. They are schemes which direct the production of works. For a principle of order is that which directs and determines the selection of the materials that enter into a work, and their succession and importance. Such principles may relate to language as such. Meter and rhyme are of this sort, and so is what we ordinarily call language. A poem in Latin is not a poem in English. But even within a given language there are many sublanguages, and there have been in all periods of the history of poetry special selections of language appropriated to poems, or to certain kinds of poems, or to certain groups of poets.

By selection of language I mean not merely a limited and special vocabulary (the aureate diction of the Scottish Chaucerians, for example) but also certain possibilities of phrasing allowed and others disallowed, certain syntactical patterns predominant and others seldom or never used. The language of Lyly's *Euphues* is an obvious and easily characterized sublanguage of this sort.

The principles of order may relate to literature as such, regarded as a separate activity and not as an imitation of life, and of this sort are the numerous literary conventions which both writers and historians have recognized. The conventions of the Petrarchan sonneteer are only partly to be found in the unliterary life of his times; to a considerable extent they exist rather in the experience of literature. The idea of tragedy in a given tradition, though not unrelated to life, is a literary idea. I shall discuss at length in a later essay a principle of order of this sort, the medieval literary convention of the dream vision.

Lastly, principles may be derived from sources external to literature, and may be of the sort that order the material of nonliterary experience. Of this nature are the methods of logic, and I shall subsequently discuss such principles at length, or notions proper to theology which I shall take up in connection with *The Phoenix and Turtle*. Principles of a similar nature are common in fiction, those principles, namely, which deal with how men generally act and feel, which have been appropriated by the science of psychology from the ancient art of rhetoric, together with those abstractions as to life and the universe, which belong as abstractions to the province of philosophy and in exemplification to the province of fiction. But all these, though they may be regarded as material or conclusions in other branches of endeavor, are for the man who writes primarily the methods by which he both finds what he has to say, and says it in succession and with appropriate emphasis and development.

Consequently, there is a sense in which a work of literature is nothing but an adjustment of a congeries of principles of order. In another sense, it is only a specification of the potentialities of a tradition. The specification is the structure of the poem. For the poem itself is a structure and it has a structure. By the structure of a poem, then, I mean the principles of order that determine it and their interrelationships with each other. It should be remarked that no poem could have only a single principle: meter, for example, is always an independent principle. However, to give a full description in every case of the principles that enter into a work would be difficult, certainly clumsy, and largely unnecessary. And so in the following essays I shall in practice discuss only one or two of the leading principles of order in a work and the tradition to which these are related.

IV

If a poem is a system of propositions, and if the propositions are discovered and ordered by a system of principles, then these principles are not extrinsic to the work; they are not merely possible ways of viewing the object, but are intrinsic to it. They are formative elements in the work itself and hence in the experience of the work.

Consequently, it will be relevant to ask at this point, How do we experience a poem? By what process do we apprehend it? And we will find that the question we are raising is really the question, Where and in what way does the poem or work of art exist? What is its mode and locus of existence?[5] It is obvious that the poem is not simply in the text, in the closed book. *Hamlet* as an experience, in fact, is neither in the text, nor, for that matter, on the stage. It can exist as an experience only in the experience of some person, some reader or member of the audience. But there are difficulties in this statement, and not merely the difficulty that the experience of each reader is different, and different at each separate reading, and that some of these experiences, no doubt, are quite far removed from others. There is another difficulty, and one whose resolution will perhaps resolve the difficulty which has just been stated. *Hamlet* is not in the immediate experience of a member of the audience as he is seeing or reading the play. If it were we could never think or speak of the play as a whole. We could only deal with this moment in my experience of the play, and we would have to treat our aesthetic experiences as Rochester treated his erotic, regarding each moment as absolute: "All my past life is mine no more. . . . The present moment's all my lot."

The play is rather the experience of having experienced the play. It is the result of a reconstruction in memory and a summing up in judgment after the play is over. The process is described by St. Augustine in one of those passages in the *Confessions* in which his extraordinary genius for introspection is given full scope. He is describing the act of reciting a Psalm:

> I am about to repeat a Psalm that I know. Before I begin, my expectation is extended over the whole; but when I have begun, how much soever of it I shall separate off into the past, is extended along my memory; thus the life of this action of mine is divided between my memory as to what I have repeated, and expectation as to what I am going to repeat; but "consideration" is present with me, that through it what was future may be conveyed over so as to become past. Which the more it is done again and again, so much the more the ex-

pectation being shortened, is the memory enlarged; till the whole expectation be at length exhausted, when that whole action being ended shall have passed into memory.

11. 38[6]

So I know a poem or play thoroughly when the beginning, middle, and end are comprehended in one synthetic act of recollection, and that synthetic act of recollection is the play.

That is, one leaves the theater or lays down his book, lights a cigarette, and held within the spell of the experience the experience grows steady; it seems to come together. This is the unity of the work. The process is not wholly intellectual, nor wholly describable in intellectual terms since it is an experience, yet experience never comes together except when ordered by some principles, implicit or explicit, and the principles are describable. Nor is it a matter of indifference what the principles are, for in consolidating the experience they alter it. The difference between the ordinary view of *Hamlet* and the one I shall later urge does not lie primarily in a difference in antecedent experiences, nor in a difference in experiences simultaneous with the experience of the text, since the text is a method of discriminating between the relevant and the irrelevant in those experiences. It does not lie primarily in the varying meaning that various readers impute to the words and constructions of the poem. It lies in the principles allowed and employed in constructing the final experience of the work.

The process is not peculiar to poetry. St. Augustine draws this moral himself in the passage which follows the one just quoted. He says:

> And this which takes place in the whole Psalm, the same takes place in each several portion of it, and each several syllable; the same holds in that larger action, whereof this Psalm may be a part; the same holds in the whole life of man, whereof all the actions of man are parts; the same holds through the whole age of the sons of men, whereof all the lives of men are parts.

It is the process by which each one of us sums up and unifies his life, so far as it can be unified. It is the process by which each constructs his personality. In this precise analogy may be located the moral, or as we now say the emotional or educational, importance of literature: it is an exercise in the recollection, the gathering up, of the elements of personality and in their ordering. And it is moreover true that the kinds of material which we notice, select, and emphasize in this process, together with the principles of order which we elicit from or impose on this material, are—in our society at least—largely derived from the art we favor.

But, though the process here described is not in general peculiar to poetry, there is a feature in the experience of poetry and of similar systems of propositions that is peculiar to it. It is that the object of experience in that case remains steady. In the case of our autobiography, for example, the experience does not remain steady unless we have formulated it and reduced it to a system of propositions. If we sit musing on our past the events shift with the transition of feeling. What was important a moment ago recedes and what was excluded as irrelevant grows large. Images and judgments waver and transform themselves into others, structures dissolve, as in our memory of a dream.

But it is different with a poem. Our experience there derives from and refers to an object that stays steady and persists. The text remains. Our experience is subject to verification and correction, and hence it has an element of externality in it. Furthermore, since it is the peculiar nature of a composition that the experiencing of the work may be repeated, and that we may be assured that this experience refers to the same work as did our previous experience, there is an element not only of externality in each experience, but also of stability, or of what may be called eternality. So in the cumulative re-experience of a given composition, except insofar as habituation ("That monster, custom, who all sense doth eat") deadens the impact, we may hope to come nearer and nearer to the norm of that experience which is ideally implicit in the work. It is the ideal implicit norm of, for example, *Hamlet* that enables us to say that we have seen *Hamlet* five times, though one of the performances was "hardly *Hamlet!*" The ideal implicit norm is the structure of the work; it is the congeries of principles of order that determines the work; it is the work itself. It is a thing external and eternal, a potentiality of experience waiting to be realized. It is the poem.

Classical and Medieval
Statius on Sleep

~~~~~~

There are different kinds of poems. There is, for example, a poem by Statius, the lovely invocation to sleep, which has captured the fancy of many critics, especially the English. They like it so well they call it almost a sonnet, and they would excise three lines in the middle of the poem to make it more sonnet-like. But the poem is not a sonnet and the lines should not be excised, for to do so is to convert a poem of one kind into a poem of another. The poem reads:

> Crimine quo merui, iuuenis placidissime diuum,
> quoue errore miser, donis ut solus egerem,
> Somne, tuis? Tacet omne pecus uolucresque feraeque
> et simulant fessos curuata cacumina somnos,
> nec trucibus fluuiis idem sonus, occidit horror
> aequoris et terris maria adclinata quiescunt.
> Septima iam rediens Phoebe mihi respicit aegras
> stare genas; totidem Oetaeae Paphiaeque reuisunt
> lampades et totiens nostros Tithonia questus
> praeterit et gelido spargit miserata flagello.
> Unde ego sufficiam? non si mihi lumina mille,
> quae sacer alterna tantum statione tenebat

Argus et haud umquam uigilabat corpore toto.
At nunc heu! si aliquis longa sub nocte puellae
brachia nexa tenens ultro te, Somne, repellit,
inde veni, nec te totas infundere pennas
luminibus compello meis—hoc turba precatur
laetior—: extremo me tange cacumine virgae,
sufficit, aut leuiter suspenso poplite transi.[1]

I have translated this as literally as possible, taking care
at the same time to represent those formal aspects of the poem
which will come under discussion so that the reader whose English is better than his Latin may be at ease in the argument:

What was my crime, youthful most gentle god,
What folly was it that I alone should lack,
Sweet Sleep, thy gifts? All herds, birds, beasts are still,
The curved mountains seem wearily asleep,
Streams rage with muted noise, the sea-wave falls,
And the still-nodding deep rests on the shore.
Seven times now returning Phoebe sees
My sick eyes stare, and so the morning star
And evening, so Tithonia glides by
My tears, sprinkling sad dew from her cool whip.
How, then, may I endure? Not though were mine
The thousand eyes wherewith good Argus kept
But shifting watch, nor all his flesh awake.
But now, alas! If this long night some lover
In his girl's arms should willingly repel thee,
Thence come, sweet Sleep! Nor with all thy power
Pour through my eyes—so may they ask, the many,
More happy—: touch me with thy wand's last tip,
Enough, or lightly pass with hovering step.

The conventional opinion of this poem is based on Mackail's
comments. "Perhaps the finest, certainly the most remarkable,"
he says of Statius' occasional verses, "is the short poem (one
might almost call it a sonnet) addressed to Sleep." He then
quotes the text and remarks:

Were the three lines beginning *Unde ego sufficiam* struck

out—and one might almost fancy them to have been inserted later by an unhappy second thought—the remainder of this poem would be as perfect as it is unique. The famous sonnet of Wordsworth on the same subject must at once occur to an English reader; but the poem in its manner, especially in the dying cadence of the last two lines, recalls even more strongly some of the finest sonnets of Keats.[2]

This judgment has been accepted, extended, and hardened by English critics and literary historians. Tyrrell says: "This beautiful and pathetic little poem seems to have (more than any other ancient poem except, perhaps, the *Sirmio* of Catullus) the effect of a sonnet." Slater speaks of Statius' "short poem on sleep, which is admitted to be a masterpiece," paraphrases Mackail's comments, and quotes Fyfe's translation of the poem in the form of a sonnet (published 1903), remarking that the translator "has excised what Mackail considers a blemish in the original, the allusion to Argus of the thousand eyes." Garrod in *The Oxford Book of Latin Verse* quotes Fyfe's translation in the appendix, "Translations and Imitations," and follows it with six sonnets to sleep by Sidney, Daniel, Drummond, Wordsworth, Keats, and Hartley Coleridge. E. E. Sikes preserves the comparison with the English sonnet—the poem "is deservedly famous and may well take rank with the sonnets to Sleep by Wordsworth and Keats"—but translates the poem himself in three six-line stanzas and defends the Argus passage. In this he is a lone dissenter. Mozley in the introduction to the Loeb translation comments: "Best known of all the *Silvae*, probably, is the little sonnet-like poem addressed to the god Sleep." Duff quotes Mackail's "one might almost call it a sonnet," and adds that "if certain mythological lines are dropped, it can be reduced to the requisite proportions." He then prints his own early translation (published 1906) of the poem in the form of a sonnet. Finally, Philip Schuyler Allen says in introducing an English rendering by Howard Mumford Jones: "the translation has been designedly cast into a form suited to display to English readers the virtues of its original: a verse scheme after Sir Philip Sidney's hexameter sonnet."[3]

It is time now to examine Mackail's judgment. One must

admit there is a nice sensitiveness in the comparison between the "dying cadence" in Statius' last lines and a similar effect in the last lines of some of Keats' sonnets, though not particularly, as the later critics have assumed, of the sonnet *To Sleep*. But the close of the sonnet *On the Sea*:

> Sit ye near some old cavern's mouth, and brood
> Until ye start, as if the sea-nymphs quired!

and especially of the sonnet *On a Leander Gem:*

> see how his body dips
> Dead-heavy; arms and shoulders gleam awhile:
> He's gone: up bubbles all his amorous breath![4]

have a close similarity of effect to the close of Statius' poem. The similarity, however, is not mysterious; it is not the result of some affinity of spirit that can only be intuited by the literary tact of the critic. It resides in, and wholly in, the use of precisely the same technical devices by both poets, with such differences only as are required by the difference in language and in poetic tradition. In both the Leander sonnet and Statius' poem there is a kind of semidramatic colloquialness ("He's gone" and "sufficit") and the use of a more specialized statement for the direct statement it implies ("up bubbles all his amorous breath," which implies "He is drowned," and "leviter suspenso poplite transi," which implies "May I be even the least bit asleep.").

But these similarities only support and limit the kind of similarity Mackail points to. This is the similarity in the movement of the verse. One may ask, What determines the movement of a verse line? It is determined by the metrical principles of the line itself, and by the relation of syntactical units to the ends of lines. In these terms there is a distinction between two traditions of verse movement, and this will ultimately turn out to be a distinction between two kinds of poetry. To one of these traditions both the passage from Statius and those from Keats belong.

It will be well to make this distinction clear by citing two other passages, both in English. The first is the invocation at the beginning of Gascoigne's *The Steele Glas*, the earliest non-dramatic poem of any length in blank verse; the second is Milton's invocation at the beginning of *Paradise Lost*. That the one is universally conceded to be better than the other is for the present beside the point—we are interested in making a distinction:

> The Nightingale, whose happy noble hart,
> No dole can daunt, nor fearful force affright,
> Whose chereful voice, doth comfort saddest wights,
> When she hir self, hath little cause to sing. . . .
>
> Of Mans First Disobedience, and the Fruit
> Of that Forbidden Tree, whose mortal tast
> Brought Death into the World, and all our woe.[5]

The differences are obvious. The meter of the one, though not without certain discreet variations, displays and enforces in every line the simple metrical pattern. Every line conforms strictly to type: a regular alternation of unaccented and accented syllables with a pause after the fourth syllable.[6] The lines in the second passage also conform to a metrical type, but they conform in a different sense. They conform in the sense that the type can be inferred from a collection of lines; it is implicit in them. In the first passage the type is apparent and, as it were, explicit in any single line. Milton, as he himself says, observes "apt Numbers" and "fit quantity of Syllables";[7] that is, his metrical practice is based on the concept of decorum, or the reasonable adherence to an implicit norm. Gascoigne's practice is based on the concept of law, or the rational adherence to an explicit norm.

The passages differ also with respect to the relation of syntax to the metrical structure. In Gascoigne each line is end-stopped, and the internal pause occurs at precisely the same point in each line. The thought is apprehended in units of alternately four and six syllables. But it is a principle of Milton's prosody that the sense should be "variously drawn out from one Verse into another," that the thought should be apprehended in units that cut across the metrical structure. The difference is not simply one of merit or skill, a question of monotony and variety; it is a difference in kind. For the first passage, though not distinguished, is not without merit. What it needs is rhyme, and for two reasons. Rhyme would sustain the verse line, which tends as it is to disappoint the ear, and would impart, if not a singing quality, at least a kind of conviction to the rhetoric—for example:

> The nightingale whose happy noble heart
> No dole can daunt, no fearful force can start

Secondly, since conformity to an external pattern is the guiding principle in this tradition of poetry, the articulation of rhyme in a fixed stanza would impose on the poem that order and articulation of thought, the lack of which is here more offensive than is the apparent monotony of the verse line. For the poem is conceived in couplets, but not written in couplets.

Clearly the method of Milton is that of Keats and of Statius. The metrical line in each, though it conforms to the patterns of their respective traditions, yet exhibits considerable variety in the permissible substitution of feet, in the placing of the pause, and in the playing of accent against quantity in the quantitative meter[8] and of quantity against accent in the accentual meter. In each the syntactical structure of thought deviates from and plays against the verse line. These formal elements carry with them a disposition of feeling which is inherent in the method and which is of the same general nature in each poem. But the agreement between the close of the Leander sonnet and the close of Statius' poem is much more particular; it is almost coincidental:

> see how his body dips
> Dead-heavy; arms and shoulders gleam awhile:
> He's gone: up bubbles all his amorous breath!

> hoc turba precatur
> laetior—: extremo me tange cacumine virgae,
> sufficit, aut leviter suspenso poplite transi.

　　so may they ask, the many,
More happy—: touch me with thy wand's last tip,
Enough, or lightly pass with hovering step.

The types of syntactical structure and their placing relative to the metrical line are almost identical in the two passages. There could hardly be found for one ignorant of Latin a better illustration of the formal effect of Statius' lines than this passage from Keats.

Thus far I have approved of Mackail's remarks, and have even extended them. There remain now the two propositions, that the poem is sonnet-like and that the Argus passage should be excised. It is clear what Mackail and his successors have in mind. If you excise the three lines on Argus the poem falls into two parts of ten and six lines, which is close enough to the proportions of a sonnet. Furthermore, you may consider that the four lines (7-10) which precede the Argus passage (11-13) and which relate with four mythological references how the poet has been sleepless for a full week could be reduced to two lines at the most and could at the same time be improved by being disencumbered of mythological adornment.[9] What the modern reader fails to see, it may be remarked in passing, is that myth for the Latin poet is a field of poetic details parallel to and comparable with the field of natural landscape, as is illustrated in this poem. However, in this way a poem is begotten that corresponds precisely to the eight and six lines of the sonnet. Moreover, the octave can be conceived to present the situation, and the sestet the reflection upon the situation, and thus the poem could be said to exhibit perhaps the commonest type of internal form to to be found in the sonnet. But this is not Statius' poem; it is one the critic has written himself in a form familiar to him.

The form of the original can be studied by comparing it with the famous sonnet by Wordsworth on the same subject to which Mackail and his successors allude:

A flock of sheep that leisurely pass by,
One after one; the sound of rain, and bees
Murmuring; the fall of rivers, winds and seas,

> Smooth fields, white sheets of water, and pure sky;
> I have thought of all by turns, and yet do lie
> Sleepless! and soon the small birds' melodies
> Must hear, first uttered from my orchard trees;
> And the first cuckoo's melancholy cry.
> Even thus last night, and two nights more, I lay,
> And could not win thee, Sleep, by any stealth:
> So do not let me wear to-night away:
> Without Thee what is all the morning's wealth?
> Come, blessed barrier between day and day,
> Dear mother of fresh thoughts and joyous health![10]

The resemblance of the two poems is quite close—the parallels in the third and fifth lines are particularly striking. This similarity in subject will consequently afford a surer basis than might otherwise have been for the comparison of formal qualities.

The sonnet has in common with Statius those elements that have already been discussed, a complex meter and the run-over line. In fact, if the run-over lines are scrutinized more closely they will be seen to be in both of a special type: in both the phrase halts early in the subsequent line:

> the sound of rain, and bees
> Murmuring. . .

> I have thought of all by turns, and yet do lie
> Sleepless. . .

> donis ut solus egerem,
> Somne, tuis?

In the first and third instances, at least, and less obviously in the second, the grammatical construction could be considered completed at the end of the line: "the sound of rain, and bees" and "donis ut solus egerem" are phrases sufficient in themselves. Yet the additional word or phrase at the beginning of the next line is by no means otiose: what it does is to extend the construction from one recognized syntactical pattern to another so that the addition, though it is not required, nevertheless affords when it has been made that effect of inevitability which arises from a completed pattern. Hence the resolution of the latter carries with it the special effect that it is the resolution of a pattern which emerged out of a former one.

In these respects, then, the poems are similar. But the respects in which they differ are more numerous, more obvious, and more important. The most obvious is that Wordsworth's poem is a sonnet, a fixed form, whereas Statius' could have been of any length. There was nothing in the ancient poet's tradition that prescribed the exact number of lines. In fact, it is a characteristic of Latin antiquity that even poems with a fixed refrain have an irregular number of verses between the refrains: for example, Vergil's Eighth Eclogue and Catullus lxii. Consequently, the particular length of this poem could only have been determined by chance, as Coleridge tells us the length of *Kubla Khan* was determined, or, as seems rather to be the case here, by what may be called an internal necessity: that is, the length was determined by the law of decorum or tact, by the fitness and aptness of the external form to the internal form of what was to be said. But the law of the sonnet is law in the strict sense: it is fixed, eternal, and given. It has the characteristics of Jehovah's pronouncements.

Thus the form of a sonnet does not emerge like the more modern God and take shape in the process of writing; it is an Idea and prior to the specific poem. The case is not that the poet has an inspiration in the sense of having a subject that moves him to write and that the poem turns out when he is finished to be a sonnet of exactly fourteen lines. If this were so, there would be few sonnets. The case is quite otherwise: he who would write a sonnet must begin with the idea of the form, and one can almost say, for paradox is sometimes an instrument of truth, that he hopes it will turn out to have a subject.

Of course, it is possible, and I have done it myself, for a poet relatively late in the process of writing to expand or reduce to the compass of a sonnet what was originally conceived as a poem, say, in quatrains, though scarcely one in blank verse. He may even begin scribbling lines, poetically exploring some subject, with no defined notion of its ultimate form apart from the meter, and even that may be changed at an early stage in the process of composition. Finally, when a certain number of lines and approximate formulations are scattered on the page, pages, or backs of envelopes, he may suddenly realize that the whole can best be redacted in the form of a sonnet. But at what point was the poem as it finally exists in the text first conceived? It was conceived when its potential realization was envisioned, when the poet saw that it would make a sonnet. But the kind of form which is envisioned alters essentially both the experience of writing and the final text so that a distinction in kinds of form is a distinction in kinds of experience and in kinds of poetry; in the one the external form is fixed and given in the tradition; in the other the external form presents at least the illusion of being a free determination.

But a sonnet is not only a poem of a given length; it is also a poem that conforms to one of a very few patterns, and patterns that are for the most part established in the tradition. The pattern of Wordsworth's sonnet is the familiar one in which two units of expression of four lines each comprise the first major division, and three units of two lines each comprise the second. Furthermore, the divisions are marked by an obvious device of external form, the arrangement of rhymes, and the divisions of thought correspond point for point with the external divisions. An outline of the rhyme-scheme and an outline of the thought of the poem would coincide. Even the relation of the two major divisions is an accepted one; the first is an exposition of the situation, the second a reflection on it.

But Statius' poem falls into two, or three, divisions, and the uncertainty on this point is characteristic of his kind of poetry. The first division comprises the first ten lines, in which are presented, as in Wordsworth's poem, the fact of the poet's sleeplessness and the contrast with the peace and quiet of external nature. But the passage is not subdivided into equal parts. The opening question, "Why do I alone lack sleep?" occupies two and one-third lines. The illustration of the uniqueness of the poet's experience by contrast with the due and proper rest after exertion which external nature enjoys is expressed in three and two-thirds lines. And the return to his own situation, the complaint that he has been sleepless for a full week so that the gods pitied him, is expressed in four lines. Here is no point for point correspondence of the internal to the external form, no units of expression that bear a simple mathematical ratio, one to the other.

So it is with the rest of the poem, whether the Argus passage is taken as a separate major division or as a part of the concluding section of nine lines. The passage itself occupies three lines: "I could not endure to lie thus open-eyed"—an aspect of sleeplessness—"even though I had the thousand eyes of Argus and could open and close ones by turn." Then in two lines: "But, taking the situation as it is, if there are those who can sleep, being happy in love, and will not since they would enjoy their love"—and now in one-third of a line: "transfer their rights in sleep to me." The paraphrase may be halted at this point since the second point of difference between the two poems is now sufficiently clear; the one conforms to an established pattern, the other establishes its own.

There is a third point of difference. If the above paraphrase is compared with the actual text, it will be found that little of what is made, and must be made, explicit in the paraphrase is explicit in the poem. It is true that the opening proposition is relatively explicit, yet it is given a rhetorical treatment that removes it from the bluntness of plain statement. The poet does not say directly that he alone has been sleepless; rather he asks why he alone has lacked thy gifts, Sleep. And the whole is framed in a rhetorical question as to the causes why sleep has been denied him, which by the gravity of the causes suggested (*crimen, error*) implies the gravity of the effect. Thus something else is said by indirection than could have been said in the same compass by direct statement, and this something else requires the active participation of the reader in finding it out. The reader must actively assist in constructing the poem.

For example, Statius does not say as one translator has him say:

But my sad eyes their nightly vigil keep.

He does not say that he has been sleepless a full week, though this is clearly what he means. He says:

Septima iam rediens Phoebe mihi respicit aegras
stare genas; totidem Oetaeae Paphiaeque reuisunt
lampades et totiens nostros Tithonia questus
praeterit et gelido spargit miserata flagello.

Seven times now returning Phoebe sees
My sick eyes stare, and so the morning star
And evening, so Tithonia glides by
My tears, sprinkling sad dew from her cool whip.

Is this nothing but rhetorical amplification? It is that, of course,
but with a purpose. The sad plight of the poet is essential to the
poem, and there is required a certain bulk of language to give it
due importance. Such is the primary function of amplification.
But the passage in its precise wording has further purposes. The
succession of the moon, the morning star, and then the evening
star, and finally dawn again indicates by its very succession the
continuity and duration of time. It is the implying of a process
by a kind of poetic imitation of the process.

There are other types of implication in the poem. In the
last line of this passage the poet says that Tithonia sprinkles
from her cool whip. There seemed no way of excluding the word
dew from the translation; English style will hardly permit the
omission. In the original, however, the reader is not told what
the dawn goddess sprinkles but must himself complete the inference from the material furnished by the poet, and the completion of the inference is an integral part of the experience of
the poem. Furthermore, in the same line there is involved another process of completing the inference, the process that has
come to be called fusion in modern criticism. For Tithonia who
sprinkles dew also takes pity on the poet. But to take pity on
someone is to shed a tear for him, and that tears are the dew
of the eyes has been established by generations of poets.[11] Consequently, the reader must not only elicit both dew and tears
from a passage that makes no mention of either; he must also
through a feeling for literary tradition fuse or identify the image
of dew and of tears.

Of the four kinds of poetic implication which have been
analyzed so far—implication by rhetorical figure, by a kind of

imitation of a process, implication in the proper logical sense, and implication by fusion—the two latter may be discussed a little more fully. Why is it that the poet cannot sleep? Is it, as Vollmer conjectures, because the poem was written during a spell of illness? Certainly insomnia accompanies some illnesses, and from another poem we learn that the poet was once quite ill.[12] But when we ask why the poet asserts that he cannot sleep, we must answer in terms of the particular poem. He cannot sleep in this poem because he is that conventional figure, the unhappy lover. For this reason Tithonia, rising from the bed of her senile husband, pities his condition; and for the same reason he begs of Sleep that if some happy lover willingly gives up his sleep, since being happy in love he could sleep if he would, some portion of that rejected sleep should be transferred to him. But the request is strictly qualified. He disclaims any petition for full or contented sleep, for it would be impious of the unhappy lover to pray for what is not his due. In the ancient erotic tradition sleeplessness is an inseparable accident of the unrequited lover; hence he asks only for the least bit of sleep. Thus the reader construes what is said in the poem in the light of the literary tradition, and infers what the situation of the poet is. The process is similar to, though not quite the same as, the construction of a hypothesis that saves the phenomena. It is different in that a poem is a closed system, and that tradition furnishes the lines of construction.

Implication by fusion will account for the Argus passage. The poet asks only for a little sleep, in fact, only for so much as Argus had who could close some of his thousand eyes while the others kept vigil. In this lies the function of the passage which Mackail would excise; it is the turning point in the poem, the hinge upon which the whole swings. It announces for the first time the conceptual basis of the poem, for this is not the contrast between no sleep and full sleep, but between a lack of sleep and the least degree of it. The Argus passage, then, foreshadows the final prayer, and being held in memory fuses with the last lines. The reader sees at that moment that the poet wishes to be Argus with respect to sleep.

To sum up, the paraphrasable meaning of Statius' poem is implicit in the text rather than explicit. But in Wordsworth's sonnet, on the contrary, the paraphrasable meaning is quite explicit. "I have thought of all by turns," he says, and by *all* he means the images of external nature which constitute the opening lines, "and yet do lie Sleepless." The poet himself gives in explicit statement the paraphrasable content of the octave; the wording of a paraphrase would be the wording of the text. This is clear also in the sestet:

> Even thus last night, and two nights more, I lay,
> And could not win thee, Sleep! . . .
> So do not let me wear to-night away.

The fourth and final point of difference between the two poems emerges from what has already been said. The conceptual basis of Statius' poem is not the contrast between sleeplessness and its logical contrary, but between degrees of sleeplessness. But Wordsworth's sonnet takes no note of such humanistic quibbling. The contrast there is plainly between one state and its logical opposite: the poet is either A or Not-A with respect to sleep, and there is in the text no middle ground.

In the course of this chapter six characteristics of one kind of poetry have been discriminated and opposed to six characteristics of another kind. The one employs a complex and modulated meter; the other an obvious meter conforming to a simple mathematical scheme. The one plays the syntactical structure against the metrical line; the other shows a marked coincidence of the two. In the one tradition the length of the poem tends to be a free determination; in the other it tends to be fixed and given. The outline of thought in the one tends not to correspond to the units of the external form; in the other it tends to correspond. The paraphrasable meaning of the one is largely implicit and to be inferred from the text; with the other it is explicit. Finally, the conceptual basis of the first kind of poetry will tend to be one of continuity and degree; in the second kind it will tend to be one of discontinuity, identity, and contradiction. The first kind is exemplified by the poetry of Horace, Vergil, and Statius, by Milton's *Lycidas* and most of his sonnets, and by a great deal of more modern poetry. The second kind is exemplified in most medieval and Tudor lyric. The first may be called

the classical method, the second the medieval, and the history
of the English lyric may be construed in terms of the transition
from the second to the first.

Logic and Lyric
Marvell, Dunbar, and Nashe

~~~~~~

The discussion in the previous chapter raises the question, May the principal structure of a poem be of a logical rather than an alogical sort? For example, to confine ourselves to the Old Logic, May a lyric be solely or predominantly the exposition of a syllogism? and may the propositions of the lyric, one by one, be of the sort to be found in a logical syllogism?

The incautious romantic will deny the possibility, and with a repugnance of feeling that would preclude any further discussion. For logic and lyric are generally regarded as opposites, if not as contradictory terms. "It is a commonplace," says a recent writer on logic, "that poetry and logic have nothing to do with each other, that they are even opposed to one another."[1] You will find this explicitly stated, sometimes with the substitution of "science" for "logic," in most of the school handbooks on the study of literature, in most of the introductions to poetry. "The peculiar quality of poetry," we read in one of these,

> can be distinguished from that of prose if one thinks of the creative mind as normally expressing itself in a variety of literary forms ranged along a graduated scale between the two contrasted extremes of scientific exposition and lyrical verse.

162

And, a little later:

> [Poetry] strives for a conviction begotten of the emotions rather than of reason.

Consequently, we are told:

> The approach of poetry is indirect. It proceeds by means of suggestion, implication, reflection. Its method is largely symbolical. It is more interested in connotations than in denotations.[2]

This is common doctrine. Poetry is in some way concerned with emotion rather than reason, and its method is imaginative, indirect, implicit rather than explicit, symbolic rather than discursive, concerned with what its terms suggest rather than with what they state. The kind of poetry which most fully possesses and exhibits these concerns, methods, and qualities is generally thought to be the lyric, and hence it, of all poetry, is regarded as the most antithetical to reason, logic, and science.

This was not always the case. In the eighth century, for example, a scholiast of the school of Alcuin regarded not only grammar and rhetoric but dialectic or logic also as the disciplines that nourish and form a poet. In the medieval and renaissance traditions of commentary on Aristotle's logic, poetic is sometimes regarded as a part, a subdivision, of logic—as, indeed, I consider it myself. As late as the eighteenth century David Hume writes in an essay, *Of the Standard of Taste*:

> Besides, every kind of composition, even the most poetical, is nothing but a chain of propositions and reasonings; not always indeed the justest and most exact, but still plausible and specious, however disguised by the coloring of the imagination.

And even today the writer on logic whom I quoted earlier asserts, in denial of the commonplace: "Every poem, except in rare extreme cases, contains judgments and implicit propositions, and thus becomes subject to logical analysis."[3]

But may the chain of propositions and reasonings be not merely plausible and specious but even sufficiently just and exact? May the poem be not merely subject to logical analysis but logical in form? May, to return to our point, the subject and structure of a poem be conceived and expressed syllogistically? Anyone at all acquainted with modern criticism and the poems that are currently in fashion will think in this connection of Marvell's *To His Coy Mistress*. The apparent structure of that poem is an argumentative syllogism, explicitly stated. "Had we but world enough, and time," the poet says,

> This coyness, lady, were no crime; . . .

> But at my back I always hear
> Time's winged chariot hurrying near; . . .

> Now, therefore . . .
>   let us sport us while we may.

If we had all the time and space in the world we could delay consummation. But we do not. Therefore. The structure is formal. The poet offers to the lady a practical syllogism, and if she assents to it the appropriate consequence, he hopes, will follow:

> Had we but world enough, and time,
> This coyness, Lady, were no crime;
> We would sit down and think which way
> To walk and pass our long love's day.
> Thou by the Indian Ganges side
> Shouldst rubies find: I by the tide
> Of Humber would complain. I would
> Love you ten years before the Flood,
> And you should, if you please, refuse
> Till the conversion of the Jews.
> My vegetable love should grow
> Vaster than empires, and more slow;
> An hundred years should go to praise
> Thine eyes and on thy forehead gaze;
> Two hundred to adore each breast;

But thirty thousand to the rest;
An age at least to every part,
And the last age should show your heart;
For, Lady, you deserve this state,
Nor would I love at lower rate.

But at my back I always hear
Time's winged chariot hurrying near;
And yonder all before us lie
Deserts of vast eternity.
Thy beauty shall no more be found,
Nor in thy marble vault shall sound
My echoing song: then worms shall try
That long preserved virginity,
And your quaint honor turn to dust,
And into ashes all my lust:
The grave's a fine and private place,
But none, I think, do there embrace.

Now, therefore, while the youthful hue
Sits on thy skin like morning dew,
And while thy willing soul transpires
At every pore with instant fires,
Now let us sport us while we may,
And now, like amorous birds of prey,
Rather at once our time devour
Than languish in his slow-chapt power.
Let us roll all our strength and all
Our sweetness up into one ball,
And tear our pleasures with rough strife
Thorough the iron gates of life:
Thus, though we cannot make our sun
Stand still, yet we will make him run.[4]

The logical nature of the argument here has been generally recognized, though often with a certain timidity. Mr. Eliot hazards: "The three strophes of Marvell's poem have something like a syllogistic relation to each other." And in a recent scholarly work we read: "The dialectic of the poem lies not only or chiefly in the formal demonstration explicit in its three stanzas, but in all the contrasts evoked by its images and in the play between the immediately sensed and the intellectually apprehended."[5] That is, the logic is recognized, but minimized, and our attention is quickly distracted to something more reputable in a poem, the images or the characteristic tension of metaphysical poetry. For Mr. Eliot the more important element in this case is a principle of order common in modern poetry and often employed in his own poems. He points out that the theme of Marvell's poem is "one of the great traditional commonplaces of European literature . . . the theme of . . . *Gather ye rosebuds*, of *Go, lovely rose*." He continues: "Where the wit of Marvell renews the theme is in the variety and order of the images." The dominant principle of order in the poem, then, is an implicit one rather than the explicit principle of the syllogism, and implicit in the succession of images.

Mr. Eliot explains the implicit principle of order in this fashion:

> In the first of the three paragraphs Marvell plays with a fancy that begins by pleasing and leads to astonishment. . . . We notice the high speed, the succession of concentrated images, each magnifying the original fancy. When this process has been carried to the end and summed up, the poem turns suddenly with that surprise which has been one of the most important means of poetic effect since Homer:
>
> > But at my back I always hear
> > Time's winged chariot hurrying near,
> > And yonder all before us lie
> > Deserts of vast eternity.
>
> A whole civilization resides in these lines:
>
> > Pallida Mors aequo pulsat pede pauperum tabernas
> > Regumque turres . . .
>
> A modern poet, had he reached the height, would very likely have closed on this moral reflection.

What is meant by this last observation becomes clear a little later where it is said that the wit of the poem "forms the crescendo and diminuendo of a scale of great imaginative power."[6] The structure of the poem, then, is this: it consists of a succession of images increasing in imaginative power to the sudden turn and surprise of the image of time, and then decreasing to the conclusion.

But is there any sudden turn and surprise in the image of time? and does the poem consist of a succession of images? This talk of images is a little odd since there seem to be relatively few in the poem if one means by image what people usually do— a descriptive phrase that invites the reader to project a sensory construction. The looming imminence of Time's winged chariot is, no doubt, an image, though not a full-blown one since there is nothing in the phrasing that properly invites any elaboration of sensory detail. But when Mr. Eliot refers to "successive images" and cites "my *vegetable* love," with *vegetable* italicized, and "Till the conversion of the Jews," one suspects that he is provoking images where they do not textually exist. There is about as much of an image in "Till the conversion of the Jews" as there would be in "till the cows come home," and it would be a psychiatrically sensitive reader who would immediately visualize the lowing herd winding slowly o'er the lea. But "my *vegetable* love" will make the point. I have no doubt that Mr. Eliot and subsequent readers do find an image here. They envisage some monstrous and expanding cabbage, but they do so in mere ignorance. *Vegetable* is no vegetable but an abstract and philosophical term, known as such to every educated man of Marvell's day. Its context is the doctrine of the three souls: the rational, which in man subsumes the other two; the sensitive, which men and animals have in common and which is the principle of motion and perception; and, finally, the lowest of the three, the vegetable soul, which is the only one that plants possess, and which is the principle of generation and corruption, of augmentation and decay. Marvell says, then, my love, denied the exercise of sense, but possessing the power of augmentation, will increase "Vaster than empires." It is an intellectual image, and hence no image at all but a conceit. For if one calls any sort of particularity or detail in a poem an image, the use of the wrong word will invite the reader to misconstrue his experience in terms of images, to invent sensory constructions and to project them on the poem.

A conceit is not an image. It is a piece of wit. It is in the tradition in which Marvell was writing, among other possibilities, the discovery of a proposition referring to one field of experience in terms of an intellectual structure derived from another field, and often enough a field of learning, as is the case in "my vegetable love." This tradition, though it goes back to the poetry of John Donne, and years before that, was current in Marvell's day. The fashionable poetry at the time he was writing this poem, the poetry comparable to that of Eliot or of Auden in the forties and fifties, was the poetry of John Cleveland, and the fashionable manner was generally known as Clevelandizing. It consisted in the invention of a series of witty hyperbolical conceits, sometimes interspersed with images, and containing a certain amount of roughage in the form of conventional erotic statements:

> Thy beauty shall no more be found,
> Nor in thy marble vault shall sound
> My echoing song.

It was commonly expressed in the octosyllabic couplet. Cleveland, for example, writes *Upon Phillis Walking in a Morning before Sun-rising*:

> The trees, like yeomen of the guard,
> Serving her more for pomp than ward.

The comparison here does not invite visualization. It would be inappropriate to summon up the colors and serried ranks of the guard. The comparison is made solely with respect to the idea: the trees like the guard serve more for pomp than ward. Again:

> The flowers, called out of their beds,
> Start and raise up their drowsy heads,
> And he that for their color seeks
> May see it vaulting to her cheeks,
> Where roses mix—no civil war
> Divides her York and Lancaster.[7]

One does not here picture in panorama the Wars of the Roses. One sees rather the aptness and the wit of York and Lancaster, the white rose and the red, reconciled in her cheeks, or one rejects it as forced and farfetched. This is a matter of taste.

But if the poem is not a succession of images, does it exhibit that other principle which Mr. Eliot ascribes to it, the turn and surprise which he finds in the abrupt introduction of time's chariot and which forms a sort of fulcrum on which the poem turns. Subsequent critics have certainly felt that it has. In a current textbook we read:

> The poem begins as a conventional love poem in which the lover tries to persuade his mistress to give in to his entreaties. But with the introduction of the image of the chariot in l. 21, the poet becomes obsessed by the terrible onrush of time, and the love theme becomes scarcely more than an illustration of the effect which time has upon human life.

And the leading scholar in the field, a man who is generally quite unhappy with Mr. Eliot's criticism, nevertheless says:

> the poet sees the whole world of space and time as the setting for two lovers. But wit cannot sustain the pretense that youth and beauty and love are immortal, and with a quick change of tone—like Catullus' *nobis cum semel occidit brevis lux* or Horace's *sed Timor et Minae* —the theme of time and death is developed with serious and soaring directness.[8]

These, I believe, are not so much accounts of the poem as accounts of Mr. Eliot's reading of the poem. Let us question the fact. Does the idea of time and death come as any surprise in this context? The poem began, "Had we but world enough, and time." That is, it began with an explicit condition contrary to fact, which by all grammatical rules amounts to the assertion that we do not have world enough and time. There is no surprise whatever when the proposition is explicitly made in line 21. It would rather have been surprising if it had not been made. Indeed, the only question we have in this respect, after we have read the first line, is, How many couplets will the poet expend on the ornamental reiteration of the initial proposition before he comes to the expected *but*. The only turn in the poem is the turn which the structure of the syllogism had led us to await.

Mr. Eliot compares the turn and surprise which he finds in this poem to a similar turn in an ode of Horace's, and the scholars seem to corroborate the comparison. This is the fourth ode of the first book:

> Solvitur acris hiems grata vice veris et Favoni,
>   trahuntque siccas machinae carinas

The poem begins with a picture of spring and proceeds by a succession of images, images of the external world and mythological images:

> Sharp winter relaxes with the welcome change to Spring and the west wind, and the cables haul the dry keels of ships. The herd no longer takes pleasure in its stalls or the farmer in his fire, and the pastures no longer whiten with hoar frost. Cytherean Venus leads her dancers beneath the overhanging moon, and the beautiful graces and nymphs strike the ground with alternate foot, while blazing Vulcan visits the grim forges of the Cyclops. Now is the time to wind your bright hair with green myrtle or with the flowers that the thawed earth yields. Now is the time to sacrifice to Faunus in the shadowed woods, whether it be a lamb he asks or a kid:

> > Pallida mors aequo pulsat pede pauperum tabernas
> >   regumque turres.

> Pallid death with indifferent foot strikes the poor man's hut and the palaces of kings. Now, fortunate Sestius, the brief sum of life forbids our opening a long account with hope. Night will soon hem you in, and the fabled ghosts, and Pluto's meagre house.[9]

Death occurs in this poem with that suddenness and lack of preparation with which it sometimes occurs in life. The structure of the poem is an imitation of the structure of such experiences in life. And as we draw from such experiences often a generalization, so Horace from the sudden realization of the abruptness and impartiality of death, reflects:

> vitae summa brevis spem nos vetat incohare longam.

> The brief sum of life forbids our opening a long account with hope.

But the proposition is subsequent to the experience; it does not rule and direct the poem from the outset. And the experience in Horace *is* surprising and furnishes the fulcrum on which the poem turns. It has, in fact, the characteristics which are ascribed to Marvell's poem but which Marvell's poem does not have. The two are two distinct kinds of poetry, located in distinct and almost antithetical traditions; both are valuable and valid methods, but one is not to be construed in terms of the other.

In brief, the general structure of Marvell's poem is syllogistic, and it is located in the renaissance tradition of formal logic and of rhetoric. The structure exists in its own right and as a kind of expandable filing system. It is a way of disposing of, of making a place for, elements of a different order: in this case, Clevelandizing conceits and erotic propositions in the tradition of Jonson and Herrick. These reiterate the propositions of the syllogism. They do not develop the syllogism, and they are not required by the syllogism; they are free and extra. There could be more or less of them since there is nothing in the structure that determines the number of interpolated couplets. It is a matter of tact, and a matter of the appetite of the writer and the reader.

The notion of a structure as a kind of expandable filing system may deserve a few sentences. The narrative structure of a Shakespearean play can be regarded as a structure of this order. It exists in its own right, of course, but it is also a method for disposing various kinds of material of other orders, a set speech or passion here, an interpolated comic routine in another place. The structure offers a series of hooks upon which different things can be hung. Whether the totality will then form a whole, a unity, is a question of interpretation and a question of value. It is a question, for example, of what sort of unity is demanded, and whether there are various sorts.

In Marvell's poem, only the general structure is syllogistic; the detail and development are of another order, and critics have been diligent in assigning the poetic quality of the whole to the nonsyllogistic elements. Is it possible, then, to write a lyric that will be wholly or almost wholly syllogistic? It is. There is such a lyric in *The Oxford Book of English Verse*, a lyric of somewhat lesser repute than Marvell's, but still universally praised and universally conceded to possess the true lyrical power. It is Dunbar's *Lament for the Makaris*.

The structure of Dunbar's poem is the structure of the traditional syllogism with which everyone is acquainted: "All men are mortal, I am a man"; together with a concluding practical syllogism, "What must be, must be accepted, but I must die." The syllogism is developed in two ways, both characteristic methods in the logical tradition of the later Middle Ages. It begins with the immediate induction from experience of the leading principle, the major premise:

> I that in heill wes and gladnes,
> Am trublit now with gret seiknes,
> And feblit with infermite;
> *Timor mortis conturbat me.*

The experience, then, is the sudden alteration from health to illness, and this yields the generalization:

> Our plesance heir is all vane glory,
> This fals warld is bot transitory,
> The flesche is brukle, the Fend is sle:
> *Timor mortis conturbat me.*

The premise, then, is: this false world is but transitory; and it is presently expressed in more restricted terms:

> The stait of man dois change and vary,
> Now sound, now seik, now blith, now sary,
> Now dansand mery, now like to dee:
> *Timor mortis conturbat me.*

The syllogism is now developed by another form of induction, and this development accounts for the remainder of the poem, except for the last stanza. It is developed through induction by simple enumeration in support and explication of the major premise, but with this special feature, that the induction proceeds by a hierarchical method. Nothing could be more characteristic of medieval logic. The argument is: if everything sublunary changes and varies, is mortal, then every estate of man is mortal, and the poet enumerates the estates:

> On to the ded gois all Estatis,
> Princis, Prelotis, and Potestatis,
> Baith riche and pur of al degre:
> > *Timor mortis conturbat me.*

> He takis the campion in the stour,
> The capitane closit in the tour,
> The lady in bour full of bewte:
> > *Timor mortis conturbat me.*

> He sparis no lord for his piscence,
> Na clerk for his intelligence;
> His awfull strak may no man fle:
> > *Timor mortis conturbat me.*

> Art, magicianis, and astrologgis,
> Rhetoris, logicianis, and theologgis,
> Thame helpis no conclusionis sle:
> > *Timor mortis conturbat me.*

> In medicyne the most practicianis,
> Lechis, surrigianis, and phisicianis,
> Thame self fra ded may not supple:
> > *Timor mortis conturbat me.*

If all estates must die, then poets too must die. And now Dunbar proceeds by a simple enumeration, a roll call, of poets:

> He has done petuously devour
> The noble Chaucer, of makaris flour,

> The Monk of Bery, and Gower, all thre:
> *Timor mortis conturbat me.*
>
> The gude Syr Hew of Eglintoun,
> And eik Heryot, and Wyntoun,
> He has tane out of this cuntre:
> *Timor mortis conturbat me.*

He continues to enumerate poet after poet whom death has taken, until he comes finally to his friendly enemy, the poet, Kennedy, and to himself:

> Gud Maister Walter Kennedy
> In point of dede lyis veraly,
> Gret reuth it wer that so suld be:
> *Timor mortis conturbat me.*
>
> Sen he has all my brether tane,
> He wil nocht lat me lif alane,
> Of forse I man his nyxt pray be:
> *Timor mortis conturbat me.*

Therefore, I must die, concludes the syllogism. And now follows the practical syllogism, the act of resignation:

> Sen for the deid remeid is none,
> Best is that we for dede dispone,
> Eftir our deid that lif may we.
> *Timor mortis conturbat me.*[10]

Almost every proposition in the poem is strictly controlled by the syllogistic structure. The exceptions are the refrain and a certain number of affective phrases and affective sentences: "He has done petuously devour / The noble Chaucer" and "Gret reuth it wer that so suld be." These direct the feeling of the poem. Yet though the poem is so completely determined by logical method and logical structure it has seemed, and justly, to generations of readers to be a moving poem and properly poetical.

I shall conclude with another poem of the same sort, a lyric of even greater renown in modern criticism. This is the song from *Summer's Last Will and Testament* by Thomas Nashe, "Adieu, farewell, earth's bliss!" It too has a refrain, though in English, a response from the Litany of Saints, which was cus· tomarily recited through the streets of London in time of plague. The poem, like Dunbar's, consists of a series of discrete, self-enclosed stanzas, in which each line is end-stopped. The structure of the poem is, like Dunbar's and Marvell's, a practical syllogism explicitly propounded, though not quite so formally as in the preceding poem. It opens with the rejection of earthly happiness. The argument is, to begin with the suppressed premise: true happiness is certain, but the world is uncertain; therefore wordly happiness is not true happiness. The world is uncertain since it is subject to the certainty of death and change. Nor can the goods of this world buy continued life, nor the art of medicine procure it: the plague increases. What is best in this life—and here we have the structure of the next three stanzas—beauty, prowess, and wit, all fade:

> Haste therefore each degree
> To welcome destiny.

For the world after death is certain, and its happiness true happiness:

> Adieu, farewell, earth's bliss!
> This world uncertain is:
> Fond are life's lustful joys,
> Death proves them all but toys.
> None from his darts can fly;
> I am sick, I must die—
>   Lord, have mercy on us.

> Rich men, trust not in wealth,
> Gold cannot buy you health:
> Physic himself must fade;
> All things to end are made;
> The plague full swift goes by;
> I am sick, I must die—
>   Lord, have mercy on us.

Beauty is but a flower
Which wrinkles will devour;
Brightness falls from the air;
Queens have died young and fair;
Dust hath closed Helen's eye;
I am sick, I must die—
 Lord, have mercy on us.

Strength stoops unto the grave,
Worms feed on Hector brave;
Swords may not fight with fate;
Earth still holds ope her gate;
Come, come! the bells do cry—
I am sick, I must die—
 Lord, have mercy on us.

Wit with his wantoness
Tasteth death's bitterness;
Hell's executioner
Hath no ears for to hear
What vain art can reply;
I am sick, I must die—
 Lord, have mercy on us.

Haste therefore each degree
To welcome destiny;
Heaven is our heritage;
Earth but a player's stage;
Mount we unto the sky;
I am sick, I must die—
 Lord, have mercy on us.[11]

The poem is a series of fairly literal propositions, some exactly in logical form: "This world uncertain is, All things to end are made, Queens have died young and fair, Haste therefore each degree." They are such propositions as might have been translated from the *Summa Contra Gentiles* of Thomas Aquinas, and they are located in that general tradition. St. Thomas, for instance, discusses the following questions: That human happiness does not consist in carnal pleasures; that man's happiness does not consist in glory; that man's happiness does not consist in wealth; that happiness does not consist in worldly power; that happiness does not consist in the practice of art; that man's ultimate happiness is not in this life, "for if there is ultimate happiness in this life, it will certainly be lost, at least by death."[12] But these are the propositions of Nashe's lyric, some literally, some more figuratively put.

Of the propositions in the poem, perhaps the most figurative is "Strength stoops unto the grave," which yet is fairly literal, as we see the suggestion of an aged figure bent over more and more until he is almost prone. And there are, of course, affective elements in the poem, as in "death's bitterness" and "Hell's executioner." But the special distinction of the poem and the source of an unusual quality of feeling perhaps lies in the meter as much as in anything else. The six-syllable line glides from a regular iambic pattern into a triple movement—accented, unaccented, accented—and back again as if both were its mode of being and neither had precedence over the other.

> Beauty is but a flower
> Which wrinkles will devour;
> Brightness falls from the air;
> Queens have died young and fair.

The poem in this respect belongs to a curious episode in the history of English meter; for this phenomenon appears only to my knowledge in the songs written within a fairly short period, of perhaps ten or twenty years, in the 1590s and early 1600s. Of a similar sort is Shakespeare's:

> Come away, come away, death,
>   And in sad cypress let me be laid;
> Fly away, fly away, breath;
>   I am slain by a fair cruel maid.

But the special distinction of the poem has usually been found in the line, "Brightness falls from the air." This is certainly a proposition of a different order from those we have discussed, and one that has excited the sensibilities of innumerable modern readers. It is a line in the symbolist tradition. One remembers how Stephen Dedalus in *A Portrait of the Artist as a Young Man* recalls the line, though at first in an altered form:

> She had passed through the dusk. And therefore the air was silent save for one soft hiss that fell. And therefore the tongues about him had ceased their babble. Darkness was falling.
>
> *Darkness falls from the air.*
>
> A trembling joy, lambent as a faint light, played like a fairy host around him. But why? Her passage through the darkening air or the verse with its black vowels and its opening sound, rich and lutelike?
> He walked away slowly towards the deeper shadows at the end of the colonnade, beating the stone softly with his stick to hide his revery from the students whom he had left: and allowed his mind to summon back to itself the age of Dowland and Byrd and Nashe.
> Eyes, opening from the darkness of desire, eyes that dimmed the breaking east. What was their languid grace but the softness of chambering? And what was their shimmer but the shimmer of the scum that mantled the cesspool of the court of a slobbering Stuart. And he tasted in the language of memory ambered wines, dying fallings of sweet airs, the proud pavan. . . .
> The images he had summoned gave him no pleasure. They were secret and enflaming but her image was not entangled by them. . . .
> Yes; and it was not darkness that fell from the air. It was brightness.
>
> *Brightness falls from the air.*
>
> He had not even remembered rightly Nashe's line. All the images it had awakened were false.[13]

But all the images it had awakened were false for still another reason. The line as Joyce quotes it is certainly an evocative line, a line in the symbolist tradition, and hence apt and fitted to entangle itself in revery. But it seems out of place in the poem. It is so much a line in the symbolist tradition that the historical scholar grows wary and suspicious. He turns to the text. He looks in the great modern edition of Nashe, the edition of Mc-Kerrow, and he finds that the editor records with a sigh: "It is to be hoped that Nashe meant 'ayre,' but I cannot help strongly suspecting that the true reading is 'hayre,' which gives a more obvious, but far inferior, sense."[14] So we have the alternatives: "Brightness falls from the air" or " Brightness falls from the hair." But the latter is a literal account of the effect of age and death. The proposition so read is of the same order as all the other propositions in the poem, of the same order as "Queens have died young and fair." There is no doubt, then, as to the correct reading. In fact, the symbolist line, however good, is a bad line in context since it is out of keeping. And so the poem loses its last claim to modernity. It becomes a Renaissance poem. It returns to the park of logic from the forest of revery. The experience of the poem is the experience of syllogistic thinking with its consequences for feeling, attitude, and action. It is a mode of experience that the Renaissance practiced and cherished, and expressed with power, dignity, and precision. It is a poetical experience and a logical one, and it is both at once.[15]

Convention as Structure
The Prologue to the *Canterbury Tales*

~~~~~~

A literary convention is obviously a principle of order in poetry.
I shall maintain in this chapter, against the consensus of scholarly opinion, that Chaucer derives the structure of the Prologue
to the *Canterbury Tales* from one of the most common of the
literary conventions of his time.

The Prologue is the only one of Chaucer's major works for
which there is said to be no model, no genuine antecedents in
the tradition. The *Book of the Duchess*, the *House of Fame*, the
Parliament of Fowls, and the Prologue to the *Legend of Good
Women*, for example, all belong to the well-recognized tradition
of the dream vision, whose history and peculiar features have
been described at length in a number of standard monographs.
The antecedents of the *Troilus* are well known, and Chaucer himself assigns it to the medieval category of tragedy. The shorter
complaints belong to a common literary type. But the most
familiar of Chaucer's works and the one generally thought to be
the best seems, as a whole, to be without literary predecessors,
though there are, of course, sources for particular aspects and
details. This circumstance has been construed by the literary
historians in Chaucer's favor. They have seen in it the triumph
of originality over convention and of realism over artifice. They
have pictured Chaucer going directly to reality and reporting

what he found. And so the defect of literary history becomes the glory of literary criticism.

The state of the question is summarized by one scholar: "For the *Prologue*, as for the general device of the Canterbury pilgrimage, no real model has been found." Another remarks: "There had never before . . . been the like of that singularly *modern* thing—to use our most complacent term of approbation —the Prologue." And a third: "no source for" the Prologue, "the most distinctive of Chaucer's works, has ever been discovered,"[1] The features which scholarship has particularly distinguished as unprecedented are the series of portraits in the Prologue and the device of a journey, and especially of a pilgrimage, as the frame for a series of stories. For example, the scholar continues in the passage just alluded to, "No such series of descriptions [of characters] is to be found in any work of ancient or medieval literature which could have come to Chaucer's attention."[2] It is recognized, of course, that "individual sketches of knights or priests or peasants are common enough," that the "allegorical writings of the age, both sacred and secular, abound in personified types . . . some of which Chaucer clearly imitates." But the general conclusion is that "in none of his predecessors has there been found a gallery of portraits like that in the *Prologue*, and there is very little that is comparable in later English poetry except in Chaucer's avowed imitators."[3]

For the second feature—the general idea of a frame story— it is agreed that no particular model need be sought. Chaucer had already used it in the *Legend of Good Women*, and the idea was common in the tradition. For the device of a journey, and especially of a pilgrimage, there is a distant analogue in Boccaccio's *Decameron* and a closer one in a contemporary Italian work in which the tales are actually told by a single figure in the course of a journey. But the difficulty here has been that, though Chaucer could have been acquainted with these works, we have no evidence that he was. Furthermore, what has seemed to modern scholarship the special merit of Chaucer's device—the interplay of personalities on the journey—is only rudimentary in these possible models. The conclusion has been, as a recent writer on the subject puts it: "There is really no necessity to search for the 'source' of Chaucer's pilgrimage. It would, indeed, have been strange had there been no reflections in imaginative literature of the common medieval custom of going on a journey with a party of travellers."[4] This is the general opinion. "For his particular device of a group of persons on a pilgrimage to Canterbury on horseback," we are told in the standard work, "he needed only to draw on life about him. . . . Thus the device of a pilgrimage as a narrative framework was repeatedly presented to him in actual life, and he was at liberty to adopt it for his literary purpose with whatever degree of realism he found convenient."[5]

It is noteworthy that this flight to reality on the part of eminent scholars is always subsequent to a search for an antecedent of the motif and a failure to find it. This is almost too obviously making a virtue of necessity and suggests that perhaps the search for antecedents has been misconducted. It has been a search for the prior appearance of the particular motif. And when this search fails, it has been felt that the only alternative is the recourse to reality. But the alternative is as unsatisfactory as the original undertaking, for it does not explain what it pretends to explain.

The pilgrimage was undoubtedly a common occurrence in Chaucer's day, and he had in all likelihood seen a good many groups of pilgrims among whom were to be found close analogues to the characters in the Prologue. Scholars have been concerned to establish that he lived in Greenwich on the Canterbury road, where he could have seen groups of pilgrims passing before his window, perhaps while he was writing the *Canterbury Tales*. Kittredge is willing to wager he had undertaken a Canterbury pilgrimage himself.[6] The argument is that what he found day after day in real life he needed no literary precedent to invent. But this is not so. It is not the direct observation of murders and of the process of detection that leads to the construction of a detective story. Nor was it the perception of violent death in high places that prompted the Elizabethan dramatist to compose a tragedy. What a writer finds in real life is to a large extent what his literary tradition enables him to see and to handle.

It may be conceded that experience is sometimes obtrusively at odds with tradition. We can see that it is, for we can see how

tradition has been modified to render it more supple to experience. But the one term is always tradition, not unalterable but
never abandoned, as, of course, the other term is always experience. The one is form, method, a way of apprehending; the other
is matter, realization, and what is apprehended. What we should
be concerned with, then, is to discover, if possible, a literary form
extant in Chaucer's tradition of which the Prologue to the *Canterbury Tales* is a realization. It must be a form that will account
not only for particular motifs, for the device of the journey or
the series of portraits, but also for the other elements of the
work and for their order and succession.

A literary form exists only in what I call a tradition. I use
that word in the sense in which we speak of the tradition of the
hard-boiled detective story or say that Shakespeare's sonnets
are in the tradition of the *Astrophel and Stella* sequence or, more
generally, in the Petrarchan tradition. A tradition is the body of
texts and interpretations current among a group of writers at
a given time and place. The description of literary traditions is
a principal subject of literary history, and the nature of a tradition can be reconstructed only by the methods of literary history. If one were to construct, for example, the tradition of a
number of contemporary poets in America, it could be described
in terms of the poetry of Eliot, of Pound, Hopkins, Auden, and
some fragments of Donne and Marvell, together with the associated body of commentary, the "new criticism." When a poet in
this tradition undertakes what he has learned to distinguish as
a metaphysical poem, the principles that determine the realization of what he regards as a particular literary form—the appropriate subject, devices, and structure—are principles located
in that tradition.

It follows from this that a literary form is not simply an external principle of classification of literary works, as is the Dewey
Decimal System in the public library, nor is it an Idea. It is rather a principle operative in the production of works. It is a
scheme of experience recognized in the tradition and derived
from prior works and from the decriptions of those works extant in the tradition. It is, moreover, a scheme that directs the
discovery of material and detail and that orders the disposition
of the whole. If a literary form is an Idea, it is an idea only in

the sense that it is the idea that the writer and reader have of the form. Thus a literary form may vary somewhat from work to work, since it is only a summary description of those elements of the tradition that entered into the conception and realization as into the appreciation by a qualified reader of the particular work.

I come now to my thesis, which may as well be stated clearly and simply at the start. The literary form to which the Prologue to the *Canterbury Tales* belongs and of which it is a special realization is the form of the dream-vision prologue in the tradition of the *Romance of the Rose* and of the associated French and English poems of the subsequent century and a half. This is certainly to find the answer in the most obvious place, to find it, like the purloined letter, in plain sight. For if one were to look for the source of anything in Chaucer, the first place an experienced scholar would look is in the *Romance of the Rose* and its tradition. The *Romance*, it has been said, "probably exerted on Chaucer a more lasting and more important influence than any other work in the vernacular literature of either France or England."[7] There are throughout Chaucer innumerable borrowings in detail from that work, and four of Chaucer's most extended poems are clearly in the form of the dream vision: one of them, indeed, is explicitly a prologue framing a series of tales, as is the masterwork of Chaucer's contemporary and friend, John Gower. If one asks why the similarity of the *Canterbury* Prologue to this well-known type has not been seen before, the answer lies in the method by which the form has been described in the scholarship on the subject. It has been described in terms of particular motifs, but the motifs have not been generalized and regarded as functional in a structure. One scholar, for example, enumerates "the regular features of the love-vision": "the introductory device of reading a book, the discussion of sleeplessness and dreams, the setting on May-day or in the spring-time, the vision itself, the guide (who in many poems takes the form of a helpful animal), the personified abstractions, Love, Fortune, Nature, and the like."[8] There is only one element in this description that is also to be found in the *Canterbury* Prologue, and that is the setting in spring, an element which is common to many other literary forms in the Middle Ages.

But if we describe the *Canterbury* Prologue in terms of the scheme of experience which orders it, in terms of its elements and their succession, we will find a striking similarity to—in fact, an identity with—the scheme of the dream vision. The Prologue can be described accurately enough in this fashion: at a certain time of the year—and the season is then described—the author comes to a place, to the Tabard Inn in Southwark. He there meets a company, who are then depicted, one after the other in panel fashion. After a brief digression, one of the company, not described so far (our host, Harry Bailly), is singled out as a master of ceremonies and proposes the device that orders the remainder of the poem, the telling of tales on the journey.

I shall now describe in the same fashion the opening of the *Romance of the Rose* and of a number of English poems in the same tradition. The *Romance* begins with some expository remarks on the truth of dreams, illustrated by the dream related in this book whose name is the *Romance of the Rose* and whose subject is an autobiographical account—for everything fell out just as this dream relates—containing the art of love. After a brief prayer and praise of the lady, the dream begins. It is May, and there is an extended description of the season. The author walks out into the fields, crosses a stream, and comes to a garden inclosed by a wall. He then describes, one after the other, a series of allegorical portraits painted on the wall, ten in number. He wants to enter the garden but can find no way in. Walking around the wall, he comes finally to a wicket gate and pounds on it. The porter Idleness, "whose hair was as yellow of hue as any basin newly scoured," opens the door and leads him into the garden, which is described at length. He finds Sir Mirth dancing and singing there in company and depicts the company in a series of set portraits, fifteen in number. He then walks in the garden, followed by the God of Love with his arrows ready. The garden is leisurely described, including the well where Narcissus died, which leads to the interpolated tale of Narcissus. In the well he sees a rose bush full of roses; there is one bud in especial which he has a great longing to pluck. At this point the God of Love, who has been stalking him, looses an arrow, and the author is committed to the sentimental enterprise which directs the remainder of the poem.

These are the elements and their order: after the preliminary matter and the dream, at a given time of the year—and there is a description of the season—the author comes to a place where he sees a number of allegorical characters painted on a wall and describes them; a guide then appears and leads him to another place, where he sees a company in action, though the characters are personifications, and describes them in the same manner. There follows a framed tale, and then one of the characters initiates the action which leads to the remainder of the poem. This character is not strictly a master of ceremonies, but he might in another poem and in other hands develop into one. The form is clearly not too unlike the form of the *Canterbury* Prologue, particularly if we collapse into one movement the two instances of an author's coming to a place and substitute for allegorical characters and personifications realistic portraits of representative members of society.

In other poems of this tradition the dream-vision prologue appears now as a separable and independent form, now as an element and sometimes a repeatable element in a work of larger scope, and most commonly as an introduction to a poem that continues now in one way, now in another. It is so used in the *Confessio Amantis*. In this poem, after a discursive and sententious preface, similar to, but more extensive than, the one in the *Romance of the Rose*, the author comes to his *matere*. He walks out in May and comes to a wood, where he begins to complain of his woe and falls into a swoon. On recovering, he utters a prayer to Cupid and Venus, whereupon he sees both of them come by. The King of Love, as he passes, throws an arrow through his heart, but the Queen pauses and speaks to him. On hearing what he has to say, she proposes the device: he shall confess to her priest, Genius. The essential structure of the Romance is here preserved, though in summary fashion. The nature description is quite brief, as are the descriptions of the characters. A swoon supplants the dream, and the interpolated prayer, an element in the opening of the *Romance*, occasions the appearance of the figures. Nevertheless, the author goes out at a certain time of the year and comes to a place where he sees figures riding by, one of whom proposes the device that directs the remainder of the poem.

The scheme of the vision is repeated, this time without the dream, in the course of one of the tales that form the bulk of Gower's work. This is the tale of Rosiphelee.[9] Before dawn on a May morning she walks out in a park through which runs a great river. She bids her women withdraw. She sees the flowers blooming, hears the birds singing, and sees all the animals, male paired with the female. As she looks around, she sees a company of ladies riding by, whose dress is then described. She wonders who they are and then sees a woman on a horse, who is described at length. She questions her about the company of ladies and receives the answer which changes the course of her life. Here is the typical nature description, the character who comes to a place where he sees a company, and, finally, the master of ceremonies, who disposes the particular device of this poem. And in this case it is no dream.

So much for Gower. Chaucer himself had written, if we allow the accepted chronology of his work, four dream visions by the time he undertook the Prologue to the *Canterbury Tales*; indeed, while he was engaged in the composition of the *Tales*, he rewrote with considerable thoroughness the last of these, the Prologue to the *Legend*. The earliest, the *Book of the Duchess*, begins with preliminary matter on the melancholy and sleeplessness of the author, who reads a book to pass the time, the tale of Ceyx and Alcyone. At one point in the tale Alcyone prays Juno for sleep and a dream, and the author decides to try the same method, whereupon he falls asleep and dreams. It is a May morning, with birds singing. He finds himself in a room with glass windows and full of pictures depicting the whole story of Troy and the whole *Romance of the Rose*, both text and gloss. He hears the sound of hunters, rises, takes his horse, and comes to a field, where he overtakes a great company of hunters. He inquires of one of them, "Who is hunting here?" and is told the Emperor Octavian. He follows the chase. When the hunt ends, he walks from a tree and follows a whelp into a field full of flowers, where he becomes aware of a man in black. This is the figure that introduces the device of the poem.

The *House of Fame* is a poem in the same tradition. It begins with preliminary matter similar to that in the *Romance* and the *Book of the Duchess*, a proem on dreams and an invocation. It continues with the dream. Exactly on the tenth of December—there is in this case no description of the season—the author falls asleep and in a dream finds himself in a temple made of glass. There are many images there, finely wrought portraits, among them one of Venus, "naked fleeting in a sea," of Cupid, and of Vulcan, "that in his face was full brown." As the dreamer walks about, he sees on the wall the story of the *Aeneid*, portrayed in a series of panels. These are described at length, one after the other—"There saw I," "There saw I"—in a manner and in a position in the scheme of the poem analogous to the portraits on the wall in the *Romance* or the portraits of the pilgrims at the Tabard. The author then leaves the temple, finds himself in a barren desert, looks up to heaven in prayer, and becomes aware of an eagle larger than any he has ever seen. The eagle is the figure who disposes the device which accounts for the remainder of the poem.

I come now to the Prologue to the *Legend of Good Women*. The later of the two versions is more relevant to our purpose, since it is closer in form to the scheme of the *Canterbury* Prologue, though the differences between the versions are not sufficient to call for separate treatment. The poem begins with preliminary matter, in this case of exceptional distinction, and then the poet late in the month of May falls asleep and dreams. He finds himself in a field—"With floures sote embrouded was it al" —where "The smale foules, of the seson fayn" sing a hymn to St. Valentine. There appear the God of Love and his Queen, Alceste, whose dress in particular is described at some length. Behind the god the author sees nineteen ladies in royal dress, and after them an extraordinary number of women. There follows the action which leads to the device: the King and especially the Queen as masters of ceremonies impose on the author the task of writing a series of tales of true lovers as penance for his heresy in love.

The underlying scheme of the dream-vision prologue should now be clear. If we set aside the preliminary matter as not relevant to the form of the *Canterbury* Prologue and begin, as it does, after the dream, we will find the following elements in this order. The poem is set at a given time of the year, generally in May, but perhaps exactly on the tenth of December, or sometime in the latter part of April, as the astrology of the *Canterbury* Prologue indicates. The time of the year leads in many cases to a description of the season, which may be brief or leisurely, simple or, as in the case of the *Canterbury* Prologue, ornate, with elements drawn from the introductory nature descriptions of other literary forms. The author, usually as the dreamer, is a character in his own poem, though when the scheme is used in a narrative, as in the tale of Rosiphelee, the principal character takes the place of the author. He comes to a place, usually a field, but sometimes a chamber or temple of glass, and in one case the Tabard in Southwark. He sees there a company, or occasionally one or two persons, and sometimes some birds who are treated as characters. Or he sees a number of portraits depicted on a wall, or incidents in a famous story, and then, after another journey, comes to a company. These may be described at length, one after another, in panel fashion, or they may, especially if the material is common in the tradition, be briefly and summarily denominated. At this point, or after another journey, or, as in the case of the *Canterbury* Prologue, after a brief digression, one of the company or another character who is now met—the man in black or Harry Bailly— initiates the action of the poem. This may consist, as in the Prologue to the *Legend* and the Prologue to the *Canterbury Tales*, in proposing the relation of a series of tales.

But the *Canterbury Tales* extend beyond the Prologue. Is there any precedent in the tradition for the particular way in which Chaucer proceeds to develop the poem? Of course, there is precedent in the *Legend* and in Gower for the framed tales, but I have in mind something more definite and limited than this. I have in mind the problem of the principles of order in the work as a whole, of which the idea of the frame story is only one. I have in mind a very restricted question: Is there in the tradition or in those realizations of the tradition that Chaucer had already accomplished any scheme of development from the dream-vision prologue that is similar to the development in the *Canterbury Tales*?

The whole problem of the construction of the *Canterbury Tales* is a vexed and difficult one. The work as it has come down to us consists of a number of fragments, each disjoined from

the others and each consisting of several tales and of the pro-
logues to and links between the tales. The general Prologue, for
instance, is followed by three tales with the links between them
and breaks off abruptly, shortly after the beginning of a fourth
tale. This section is usually called the "A Fragment." I will concern myself only with this.

It is clear from the state of the manuscripts, then, that the
project was never one that was complete in design though incomplete in execution. The design itself was in a fluid state.
The general outlines of the framework were perhaps clear: it
would involve a pilgrimage, and the completion of the journey
would coincide with the completion of the design. The characters of most of the pilgrims, at least, were determined. There
was to be a leader of the party, the Host, whose word was law.
Each pilgrim was to tell a given number of tales, and the tales
he told were to accord with his rank and nature according to
the ancient principles of decorum. But within what was already
determined there was much that was indeterminate, especially
the principle or congeries of principles that would determine
the succession of speakers and tales.

What principles had Chaucer? He begins with the principle
of lots which could have served to order the whole, but he uses
it only to determine the first speaker. Again, the principle of
lots, whether by chance, by Providence guiding chance, or by
the manipulation of the Host, serves to pick out the man of highest rank in the company as the first to speak. This again would
have served as a sufficient principle; the order of precedence in
society could have determined the order of precedence in the
telling of tales, and the Host, who was a proper man to be a
marshal in a hall, could easily have settled the questions of eti-
quette. But this principle breaks down immediately after the
Knight's tale. The Host calls on the Monk, who would probably
be considered next in social rank, to relate something that will
fit in with the Knight's tale. But the Miller, who is a churl and
will abide no man for courtesy, cries out in Pilate's voice, "I
know a noble tale with which I will repay the Knight's." His
tale, of course, is just the opposite: it is an ignoble tale of churls
and obsenity rather than a noble tale of princes and high love.

Is there any precedent for this in the tradition? There is,

in the scheme of experience of a dream vision which Chaucer wrote some years before this, the *Parliament of Fowls*.[10] In that poem, after the customary preliminary matter, the author falls asleep and dreams. A guide leads him to a spring scene, a garden full of birds and trees, where he sees Cupid and Will, his daughter, and many other allegorical figures and a temple of brass with more figures inside it and the story of many famous lovers painted on the wall. He walks forth again from this place and comes on the figure who disposes the device that orders the rest of the poem. This is Nature, who is holding a parliament of birds on St. Valentine's Day. The birds are then summarily described. Nature opens the parliament and stipulates that the birds shall speak in order of rank; and so they do until suddenly the lower orders break out, crying. "Have don, and lat us wende! . . . Whan shal youre cursede pletying have an ende?" The subject has been high courtly love, and now the vulgar point of view is urged by a vigorous churlish personality amid a certain amount of general uproar.

Obviously, the scheme of progression at the beginning of the *Canterbury Tales* is similar in these general respects to the scheme of the *Parliament of Fowls*. It is not only the form of the Prologue that derives from the dream vision, but from the particular scheme of a particular dream vision that Chaucer had written some time before derives the underlying principle of order of the A Fragment as a whole. In both, the master of ceremonies, by stipulation and by lot, appoints the highest in rank to speak first. The discourse is on high courtly love. It is interrupted by the lower orders of society who urge a vulgar point of view, and there follows strife among the churls. This is developed in the A Fragment by a new principle, the principle of retaliation. The Miller tells a tale about a carpenter, and the Reeve, who had been a carpenter, answers with a tale about a miller. The Cook offers to go on in this vein, begins, and the fragment breaks off. It is open to question whether or not in this instance the form of the dream vision itself broke down, whether or not it was inadequate to handle the material which Chaucer wished to explore by its means. But it does not seem to me open to question that the form of the Prologue and indeed of the A Fragment is, if we understand by a "literary form" the method by which material is discovered and ordered, the form of the dream vision in whose terms Chaucer himself had learned to feel and think through many years of love and apprenticeship.

The identity of the literary form of the Prologue to the *Canterbury Tales* with the conventional form of the dream-vision prologue can be regarded as established. It may be felt, however, that the distinctive feature of the *Canterbury* Prologue—the series of portraits—has not adequately been accounted for. No one, I trust, will ask one to account for the greatness of Chaucer's portraits, for his peculiar skill in writing. If such matters can be explained, certainly they lie outside the scope and method of this chapter. The question is rather, I should say, Is the technique of portraiture in the dream-vision convention of the same kind as Chaucer's technique in the Prologue? It is. The model in the tradition—and the model to which Chaucer recurred here—is the double series of portraits at the opening of the *Romance of the Rose*, the portraits that occupy the same place in the scheme of that poem as Chaucer's do in the scheme of his.[11]

I would distinguish several points of similarity of technique in the portraits themselves and two further points in their connection with the remainder of the poem. The portraits are given in succession in both poems, without transition or with the most summary form of transition: "And next was peynted Covetise," "Elde was paynted after this," "And alderlast of everychon / Was peynted Povert al aloon," "And next hir wente, on hir other side," "Love hadde with hym a bacheler." Chaucer's technique is similar: "With hym there was his sone, a yong squier, / A lovyere and a lusty bacheler," "A Monk ther was." There are a number of such portraits, a group of ten and of fifteen in the *Romance* and twenty-one in the Prologue, plus the five guildmen who are treated as a unit and several others who are just named. The portraits are of varying length, but they vary roughly within the same range: in the *Romance* they run from four to ninety-six lines, averaging around thirty-two; in the Prologue they run from nine to sixty-two lines, averaging around thirty-one. The peculiar coincidence in the averages, of course, is of no significance. The portraits in each are introduced by brief critical remarks in which the terms derive from the medieval arts of poetry. The second series in the *Romance* begins (I quote the medieval translation of the poem which is often ascribed to Chaucer):

> Then gan I loken ofte sithe
> The shap, the bodies, and the cheres,
> The countenaunce and the maneres
> Of alle the folk that daunced there,
> And I shal telle you what they were.[12]

Chaucer begins with an explicit remark, "Me thynketh it accordaunt to resoun," that is, *secundum rationem*, in accordance with the law of the kind. He begins the *Complaint of Mars* with a similar remark, indicating an awareness of the requirements of a literary kind:

> The ordre of compleynt requireth shylfully.

He proceeds:

> Me thynketh it accordaunt to resoun
> To telle you al the condicioun
> Of ech of hem, so as it semed me,
> And which they weren, and of what degree,
> And eek in what array that they were inne.

These are the principle technical correspondences. But one might observe further that the method in both poems is one that allows not only objective presentation and analysis but also author's comment and that the portraits in both contain a good deal of sharp realistic detail of the same type. For example, of Hate:

> Hir heed ywrithen was, iwis,
> Full grimly with a greet towayle.

Avarice is clad

> Al in an old torn courtepy
> As she were all with doggis torn.[13]

There are two further points that concern the relation of the portraits to the remainder of the poem. The first is that at least some of the characters described act and interact as the poem goes on—this is obvious in the *Canterbury Tales* but is also true in some measure of the *Romance*. The second is that the author who describes these characters as an external observer becomes involved in action with them.

In brief, the technical features of the portraits in the *Canterbury* Prologue have exact analogues in the portraits of the *Romance*. There are in each a number of portraits of moderate length, containing realistic detail, introduced by critical remarks, described by the author in his own person, and presented one after another with the minimum of transition, as in the description of a panel of portraits on a wall. If a composition instructor were to assign the portraits in the *Romance* as a model for imitation and stipulate that the method there exhibited be applied to a range of figures from contemporary society, his better students would produce a series of characters not too unlike the series in the Prologue. And if he should extend his assignment to the whole scheme of the opening portion of the *Romance* and of the associated poems in the tradition, the result could well be the Prologue to the *Canterbury Tales*.

In these terms the development of Chaucer's career becomes intelligible. We must give up the naïve conclusion of literary criticism and literary scholarship that in his earlier work Chaucer had yielded "with docility to medieval schematism" and then suddenly broke "with all such rigid notions of order." We can no longer say, as a recent writer on the subject does, that "one of the most astonishing things about the *Canterbury Tales* is that Chaucer, a courtly artist, steeped in French, Latin, and Italian models, chose as a framework a direct departure from them. He did not have to go to sleep and dream in order to get started..."[14] For Chaucer did not simply go to reality; he apprehended reality by the means he had learned and cultivated. He was original and traditional at the same time, and his originality lay in the application to fresh material of the old method—new wine in the old bottle. He brought to life a tradition that had grown, perhaps, too contrived, though the Prologue to the *Legend* is an exquisite thing of its kind. But he brought it to life within the framework of the tradition. He was an artist, and he worked by artifice, for he knew that realism is artifice.

Idea as Structure

The Phoenix and Turtle

~~~~~~

I am concerned in this chapter with another of the principles of order that determine the structure and detail of a poem. This is the use of some field or system of ideas in the writer's tradition which serves as a scheme or paradigm by which material of another order is apprehended and expounded. I have already appropriated in an earlier essay the term "conceit" for this procedure. Here I shall show how the material of courtly love in Shakespeare's *The Phoenix and Turtle* is treated in terms of scholastic theology.

I

The characteristic feature of scholasticism for our purpose is its terminology. The whole system, in fact, may be said to be implicit in the definition of its terms, as in our own times the systems of clinical psychology are implicit in such terms as "regression," "libido," "flight from reality," and "inferiority complex." Consequently, if we find that Shakespeare uses such a scholastic term as "essence" in its technical sense and in a technical context, we may presume not only that he was acquainted with scholastic notions but also that he was capable of thinking and feeling in those terms.

196

"Essence" occurs three times in Shakespeare. It appears in a well-known passage in *Measure for Measure*:

> Merciful heaven,
> Thou rather with thy sharp and sulphurous bolt
> Split'st the unwedgeable and gnarled oak
> Than the soft myrtle. But man, proud man,
> Drest in a little brief authority,
> Most ignorant of what he's most assur'd
> (His glassy essence), like an angry ape,
> Plays such fantastic tricks before high heaven
> As make the angels weep.
>
> 2. 2. 114-22

This is the scholastic notion in a scholastic context: man's essence is his intellectual soul, which is an image of God, and hence is "glassy" for it mirrors God. "Glassy" is used in this sense in *Hamlet*:

> There is a willow grows aslant a brook,
> That shows his hoar leaves in the glassy stream.
>
> 4. 7. 168-69

and in *1 Henry VI*:

> As plays the sun upon the glassy streams,
> Twinkling another counterfeited beam.
>
> 5. 3. 62-63

The full context of the notion here involved is given in the following passage from Ralegh's *History of the World*:

> But man, to cover his own ignorance in the least things
> . . . that is ignorant of the essence of his own soul, and
> which the wisest of the naturalists, (if Aristotle be he)
> could never so much as define, but by the action and
> effect, telling us what it works, (which all men know as
> well as he,) but not what it is, which neither he, nor any-
> one else, doth know, but God that created it; (*for though
> I were perfect, yet I know not my soul*, saith Job;)—

man, I say, that is but an idiot in the next cause of his own life, and in the cause of all the actions of his life, will, notwithstanding, examine the art of God in creating the world.[1]

"Glassy essence" is, of course, a sharp poetic phrase. But there is no need to fuse the denotation of the adjective "glassy" with connotations which are not exacted by the noun it qualifies in order to render it poetic. "Brittleness," "clarity," and "pellucidness" may be charming notions but they are inaccurate in context and beside the point. It is not irrelevance that makes a phrase poetic. Shakespeare's is poetic in that it initiates a moment's reflection and invites the energy of a linguistic inference by which one sees that the phrase means "image of God" through the ascending aspect of imaging rather than through the more customary descending aspect of being imaged.

"Essence" is also used technically in Valentine's speech about Silvia in the *Two Gentlemen of Verona*:

> And why not death rather than living torment?
> To die is to be banish'd from myself;
> And Silvia is myself. Banish'd from her
> Is self from self—a deadly banishment!
> What light is light, if Silvia be not seen?
> What joy is joy, if Silvia be not by?
> Unless it be to think that she is by
> And feed upon the shadow of perfection.
> Except I be by Silvia in the night,
> There is no music in the nightingale.
> Unless I look on Silvia in the day,
> There is no day for me to look upon.
> She is my essence, and I leave to be
> If I be not by her fair influence
> Foster'd, illumin'd, cherish'd, kept alive.
> 3. 1. 170-84

The speech begins on a relatively human level, for the assertion that Silvia is myself and the question, "What light is light, if Silvia be not seen?" may both be taken sufficiently metaphorically. Nevertheless, Silvia is designated as perfection, for to imagine her present when she is absent is to feed upon the shadow, the image, of perfection. If she were here one would be in the presence of perfection. However, when a Christian of Elizabeth's time comes right down to it, there is only one true perfection, God, and only one set of terms in which to discuss it, the theological language of the Schools. And it is precisely in these terms that Valentine speaks. His language and thought are those, for example, of Hooker, except that Silvia is substituted for God:

> God hath his influence into the very essence of all things, without which influence of Deity supporting them their utter annihilation could not choose but follow. Of him all things have both received their first being and their continuance to be that which they are. All things are therefore partakers of God, they are his offspring, his influence is in them. . . . Otherwise, how should the same wisdom be that which supporteth, beareth up, and sustaineth all. . . .
>
> So that all things which God hath made are in that respect the offspring of God, they are *in him* as effects in their highest cause, he likewise actually is *in them*, the assistance and influence of his Deity is *their life*.
>
> 5. 56. 5[2]

Silvia, consequently, is regarded as perfection, as Love in the absolute sense, as the ultimate principle of the lover's being, as that by which he is fostered, illumined, cherished, sustained. She is God. She is immanent and transcendent, and the lover's relation to her is that of scholastic creature to scholastic Creator. Apart from the blasphemy involved, there is only one difficulty in the passage: this resides in the proposition, "She is my essence." The proposition is technically incorrect with regard to the relation of creature and Creator in the scholastic system, for it is manifestly false to say that the soul is of the substance of God. Although the soul is a simple form in its essence, it is not its own being but is a being by participation.

Therefore, it is not pure act like God (*ST*, 1.90.1.c. and ad 2).[3] For man is made to the image and likeness of God, but "the preposition *to* signifies only a certain approach, as of something at a distance." (*ST*, 1.93.1)[4]

Valentine's relation to Silvia, it is true, conforms in general to the centuries-old scheme of courtly love; the lover is to the beloved as vassal to lord, of if the scheme be construed in Neo-Platonic terms, as it often was, as shadow to substance or as image to archetype. But the commonest and most available source of Neo-Platonic ideas in the sixteenth century was the scholastic doctrine of the Christian God, who is only protected from utter Neo-Platonism by an unceasing vigilance in qualification. If one abandons the qualification, locates the infinite Idea in the finite beloved, maintains the theological language of the Schools regarding God's immanence and ceaseless providence and yet ascribes all reality to the Idea to the extent that the lover's essence is the Idea, he arrives at this passage. It is worldly Neo-Platonism, precipitated out of the latent Neo-Platonism of Christian dogma. However, there remain two difficulties for anyone familiar with these schemes of thought: 1) the analogical relationship of the derived and Underived is contradicted by the predication of identity of essence, and 2) the identity of essence takes the special form that the essence of the derived *is* the Underived.

II

The difficulties can be understood and their source located in the light of the third passage in Shakespeare in which "essence" occurs. The passage is found in his "poetical essay" on "the former subject, viz., the Turtle and Phoenix," one of a group of poems on this theme "by the best and chiefest of our modern writers"[5] which was appended to Robert Chester's *Loves Martyr* (1601). The poem represents a memorial service for the Phoenix and Turtle, the beloved and lover, and is divided into three parts. In the first part the poet appoints "the bird of loudest lay" as Herald, the swan as Celebrant, and the "treble-dated crow" as one of the mourners, and interposes an interdict against the presence of certain others. There follows the anthem, with which we will be concerned, in which is stated the relationship of the lovers:

> So they lov'd as love in twain
> Had the essence but in one.

Reason concludes the poem by pronouncing a threne over the urn where their cinders lie, to the effect that Beauty and Truth, Love and Constancy, in their ideal forms are now dead:

> Leaving no posterity:
> 'Twas not their infirmity,
> It was married chastity.

There are a number of problems here, some integral to the text and some only associated with it, but nevertheless troublesome. The characters in the poem, for example, are birds, and the ordinary Elizabethan expectation would be that they represent persons in the situation the poem derives from and refers to, but who they are is unknown, and the situation can only be inferred from the text. It is apparently a poem with a key, and the key has been lost. Read with a certain literal-mindedness, and this is generally a good way to read poetry, it would appear to commemorate the more or less simultaneous deaths of a married couple who had taken and kept vows of marital chastity, and hence in all likelihood were Recusants.[6] But Time and Chance have destroyed or mislaid the evidence, with the consequence that the uncertainty of reference imputes, illegitimately perhaps, a kind of uncertainty to the poem as a whole.

And a similar uncertainty arises from the literary context of the poem. It is one of a series of poems, signed by Vatum Chorus, Ignoto, Shakespeare, Marston, Chapman, and Jonson, and dedicated to the recently knighted Sir John Salusbury of Lleweni. What is clear from the text is that the poems were severally written on a theme propounded to the poets and do not refer to a common situation. Both Marston and Jonson make this clear. In Shakespeare's, the first of the poems on the theme, the birds die without issue. Marston in the poem that follows

Shakespeare's begins with a direct comment: "O 'twas a moving epicedium!" and then proceeds by inquiring, "can blackest Fate consume / So rare creation? No . . . Then look. For see what glorious issue . . . now springs from yonder flame." In brief, his poem is on a different situation, has another reference: in this case there is posterity. Jonson in his turn begins: "We must sing too? What subject shall we choose?" That is, clearly it is a command performance. And characteristically he asserts that there could not be

> A beauty of that merit that should take
>
> Our Muse up by commission. No, we bring
> Our own true fire. Now our thought takes wing,
> And now an Epode to deep ears we sing.[7]

And he copies out a poem he had had around the house for some time.[8] But beyond this it is difficult to go, though there is enough partial evidence available on the literary situation in 1601 so that a patient and divining spirit may some day make it all clear, particularly if he finds more evidence.

We are concerned, however, only with the central part of the poem, which states clearly, technically, and reiteratively the relationship of the lovers, and here there is no uncertainty:

> Here the anthem doth commence:
> Love and constancy is dead,
> Phoenix and the turtle fled
> In a mutual flame from hence.
>
> So they lov'd as love in twain
> Had the essence but in one;
> Two distincts, division none:
> Number there in love was slain.
>
> Hearts remote, yet not asunder;
> Distance, and no space was seen
> 'Twixt this turtle and his queen;
> But in them it were a wonder.

So between them love did shine
That the turtle saw his right
Flaming in the phoenix's sight:
Either was the other's mine.

Property was thus appalled,
That the self was not the same;
Single nature's double name
Neither two nor one was called.

Reason, in itself confounded,
Saw division grow together,
To themselves yet either neither,
Simple were so well compounded;

That it cried, How true a twain
Seemeth this concordant one!
Love hath reason, reason none,
If what parts can so remain.

Here is stated in exact, technical, scholastic language the relationship of the lovers. They are Love and Constancy, Beauty and Truth, Phoenix and Turtle. The nature of their love was such that love in each had the essence (the defining principle by which anything that is, is what it is) only in one. Obviously, then, the effect of their love was unitive. But in what way? in terms of what scheme of ideas is this union conceived? Let us examine the possibilities. It is not unlike, of course, the Neo-Platonic union, in which the soul, being reduced to the trace of the One which constitutes its resemblance to it, is absorbed, submerged, and lost in the presence of the One. There is no more distance, no doubleness; the two fuse in one.[9]

But the language here is Latin and has passed, as had the doctrine of Plotinus, through the disputations of the Schoolmen: *essence, distincts, division, property, single nature's double name, simple, compounded.* Furthermore, the chief point of Shakespeare's poem is lost in the Plotinan formulation: for the central part of the poem consists wholly in the reiteration—line after line as if the poet would have you understand even to exhaustion

—of the paradox that though identical the two are distinct; they are both truly one and truly two. Thus, for example, in the Plotinan union there is no interval between the two—"And no space was seen"—but the contrary element of the paradox— "distance"—is lacking.

The language and the ideas of the poem, then, are technical and scholastic. But is this the scholastic doctrine of love? Is the scheme of thought here of the same order as the material of the poem? The doctrine of Thomas Aquinas on this point is sufficiently representative of the scholastic position. Love, he tells us (he is quoting the Neo-Platonist, the Pseudo-Dionysius), is a unitive force. The manner of this union, the way in which the beloved can be said to be in the lover, can be comprehended by an analogy. For just as when someone understands something there is a certain notion of the thing in the man who understands, so when someone loves something there is a certain impress, so to speak, of what is loved in the feeling of the lover, and with reference to this one can say that what is loved is in the lover as what is understood is in him who understands. (*ST*, 1. 37. 1) But union in this sense by no means amounts to absolute identification; it is not possible to say according to this account that she is my essence.

St. Thomas in another place distinguishes a three-fold sense in which union is related to love. There is the union which is the cause of love, and this is a genuine and substantial union with respect to one's love of himself; it is a union based on similitude with respect to one's love of others. Secondly, there is that union which is essentially love itself, and which involves a certain conformation of feeling toward the object. (see *ST*, 1-2, 28. 5) If this is the love of friendship, the nature of the relationship is similar to the substantial union spoken of above, for the lover loves the other as himself; if it is the love of desire, he loves the other as something that belongs to him. There is, finally, a third kind of union which is an effect of love, and that is that union of the parties involved which the lover seeks of the loved. This union is in accordance with the demands of love, for, as Aristotle says in the *Politics* (2. 4. 1262b11), "Aristophanes said that lovers desire from being two to become one," but since "the result of this would be to destroy either one of them or both," they seek a suitable and proper union, namely to live and speak together and to be joined in other ways of this nature. (*ST*, 1-2. 28. 1 ad 2)

From this much it is clear how carefully St. Thomas distinguishes and how painstakingly he points out that the effect of union in love, together with those other related effects which he goes on to discuss—a mutual inherence of one in the other, an ecstatic going out of oneself, and a zealousness in appropriating the good which one loves (1-2. 28. 2-4)—only take pláce in a certain sense. The love of desire, it is true, does not rest with attaining any external or surface enjoyment of what it loves, but seeks to possess it absolutely, penetrating as if to the very heart of the beloved. (1-2. 28. 2) But it is only *as if*. For human love admits of no real identification. Though we desire it, if it were attained, one or both would be destroyed.

In Shakespeare's poem, however, the lover is identified with the beloved; the beloved is his essence; they become one and yet neither is annihilated. The lovers are of course destroyed in that they have passed in a mutual flame from this life, but clearly they have only passed into the real life of Ideas from the unreal life of materiality.

It might be suspected, looking back on the passage in the *Two Gentlemen of Verona*, that the relation implied here is that of the Beatific Vision, in which our love of God and God's love for us finds its ultimate fulfillment. If this were so it would certainly offer us what we are looking for. It would offer us a model or paradigm by means of which the relationship of the lovers in this poem is constructed and construed. But though the doctrine of the Beatific Vision be thorny and difficult to understand, nevertheless one thing is clear: even in that last eternal embrace, in which, no longer through a glass darkly, we see the essence of God face to face (*ST*, 1. 12. 1: "We shall see Him as He is." 1 John 3: 2), there is no absolute identification of essence. St. Thomas makes this clear in the following passage, which I translate paraphrastically in order to render it as easy as possible to the uninitiated (italics mine):

> Since some form is required in any cognition by which the object can be cognized or seen, there is required

for the cognition of separated substances nothing less than the separated substance itself which is conjoined to our intellect as the form, being both the object and the means of understanding. In fact, whether this apply or not to other separated substances, it behooves us to accept that mode of understanding as applying to the vision of God through His essence, because in no other way could we be conducted to the divine essence. *But this explanation is not to be taken in the sense that the divine essence is really the form of our intellect, or that there results an absolute unity from the fusion of the divine essence and our intellect,* as is the case with form and matter in natural, as distinguished from supernatural, things. Rather, there is a proportion of the divine essence to our intellect on the analogy of form to matter. For, whenever there are two things in the same receptacle, of which one is more perfect than the other, they maintain a proportionate relationship of the more perfect to the less perfect, like that of form to matter.

3. 92. 1. c. sub fin.

III

But anything is forgiven a lover, the reader may exclaim at this point, even the grossest hyperbole. Perhaps this is so; our present business, however, is simply with interpreting a text. Now, if anything be clear in the history of the lyric, it is that *The Phoenix and Turtle*, whatever its merits, is not a gracious and charming trifle, and could not have been intended as such. One half of the poem consists of a grimly reiterated paradox, stated with the minimum of decoration and the maximum of technical exactitude. The inference is that the poet was trying to say something precisely, and this lays on us the obligation, if we wish to read the poem at all, of trying to find out precisely what he was saying.

The doctrine of the poem is not sanctioned by the scholastic doctrine of human love, nor indeed, so far as I know, by the facts of nature. It is not sanctioned by the doctrine of the Beatific Vision. Is there a source in the tradition from which is derived the structure of thought and the technical terms by which it is displayed? There is, in fact, only one model in the tradition for the notion that distinct persons may have only one essence, and that is the doctrine of the Trinity. Not, of course, the Incarnation, for the two Natures (or Essences) of Christ are distinct. (*ST*, 3. 2) The relation of lover and beloved in Shakespeare's poem is that of the Persons of the Trinity, and the technical language employed is that of scholastic discussion on the subject. With this clue, all the difficulties of the expository part of the poem are resolved, and if it still remains difficult to understand, it is no more difficult than the Trinity.

The principal point of the doctrine of the Trinity in this connection is summed up in Hooker's *Laws of Ecclesiastical Polity*:

> The Persons of the Godhead, by reason of the unity of their substance, do as necessarily remain one within another, as they are of necessity to be distinguished one from another. . . . And sith they all are but one God in number, one indivisible essence or substance, their distinction cannot possibly admit separation. . . . Again, sith all things accordingly love their offspring as themselves are more or less contained in it, he which is thus the only-begotten, must needs be in this degree the only-beloved of the Father. He therefore which is in the Father by eternal derivation of being and life from him, must needs be in him through an eternal affection of love.
>
> 5. 56. 2-3

The Father and Son are distinct persons, yet one essence. Furthermore, as the learned Doctors tells us, the Son proceeds from the Father by way of the intellect in that he is the Father's understanding of Himself; and the Holy Ghost proceeds from both by way of the will in that He is the mutual love of both. But when anyone understands and loves himself, he is in himself not only through the identity of the subject, but also in the way in which what is understood is in the one who understands, and what is loved is in the lover. Thus the Holy Ghost, who proceeds from the reciprocal relation of the Father and Son, is a distinct person, but is at the same time the bond between Them, inasmuch as He is Love (*ST*, 1. 37. 1. c and ad 3):

> So they lov'd as love in twain
> Had the essence but in one.

In the next line—"Two distincts, division none"—the terminology is obviously scholastic, and its context is the doctrine of the Trinity. "To avoid the Arian heresy," St. Thomas says, "we must avoid the terms *diversity* and *difference* so as not to take away the unity of essence; we can, however, use the term *distinction* . . . So also to avoid taking away the simplicity of the divine essence we must avoid the terms *separation* and *division*, which apply to parts of a whole. . . . " (*ST*, 1. 31. 2.)

"Number there in love was slain," for plurality is always the consequence of a division, as St. Thomas points out; but the division of a continuum from which springs number, which is a species of quantity, is found only in material things. But number in this sense cannot be applied to God. When numerical terms are used they signify only the things of which they are said, and so we may say one essence, signifying only the essence undivided, and many persons, signifying only those persons and the undividedness of each. (*ST*, 1. 30. 3) "Hearts remote, yet not asunder" repeats the central paradox. "Distance, and no space was seen"; the Son is co-eternal with the Father in order of time (1. 42. 2) and hence in order of space. (1. 42. 1., and see 1. 81. ad 3.) "But in them [and in God!] it were a wonder."

The next stanzas are based on the scholastic distinction of *proprium* and *alienum*: what is proper is what belongs to the one, but not to the other; what is alien is what belongs to the other, but not to the one. The terms are contraries, and exclude each other. But in the Trinity the relations which constitute the three Persons are their several Properties. Though property is the same as person, yet in the Father and the Son, as there is one essence in the two persons, so also there is one property in the two persons. (*ST*, 1. 40. 1.) So also in *The Phoenix and*

Turtle: love so shone between them (and Love is the relationship of the Father and the Son in the Holy Ghost—1. 37. 2) that the one saw what belonged to him ("his right": *suum proprium*) in the sight of the other; but the other's sight was the instrument by which the second saw reciprocally what belonged to him in the sight of the first. Each was the other's "mine": *meum*. No wonder "Property was thus appalled": for "property" is the personification of *proprium*.

"Single nature's double name": Each of the Persons of the Trinity has His proper name, yet they are all of one nature, one essence (1. 13; 1. 33. 2; 1. 34. 1-2; 1. 36. 1; and especially 1. 39. 2-7), and the name *God* stands of itself for the common nature—hence, "Neither two nor one was called."

"Reason, in itself confounded,"—for reason is the principle of distinction and its method is division—"Saw division grow together"; each of the two was distinct ("To themselves"), yet neither one of them was one or the other ("yet either neither"). And the last line of this stanza repeats again the same paradox, and again by one of the common scholastic dichotomies: "Simple were so well compounded." Any separated substance is simple; thus the Phoenix and the Turtle are simples, but are so compounded as to form a simple. Hence, at the final recapitulation of the paradox, Reason confesses its inadequacy to deal with the mystery of love: "Love has reason, reason none / If what parts" can remain unparted ("can so remain").

The relation of the Phoenix to the Turtle is now clear. It is conceived and expressed in terms of the scholastic doctrine of the Trinity, which forms in this sense the principle of order of the poem. The Phoenix and Turtle are distinct persons, yet one in love, on the analogy of the Father and the Son in the Holy Ghost. If the reader does not immediately understand this mystery, the point of the poem is that it is a mystery at which Reason is confounded and confesses that true Reason is above it and is Love.[10]

Plots and Errors

Hamlet and *King Lear*

∿∿∿∿∿∿∿∿∿∿∿∿∿∿∿∿∿∿∿∿∿∿∿∿∿∿∿∿∿∿∿∿∿∿∿∿∿∿

We read some works, even literary ones, coldly for what they are, as we read a menu or a casual novel. But not works of prestige. These we approach differently, under one of two kinds of context. Some we read possessively; they are the favorites of a group, whether socially broad or narrow. They are Works of Fashion. We come to them, either initially or in time, with a prepared attitude and verify that attitude in rehearsing the text. There is, for example, within the academic community that consistent and repetitive attitude toward the more popular works of Chaucer which may be called the Chuckle School of Criticism, or "Good old Chaucer." There is, more narrowly, the attitude toward Statius' *To Sleep* illustrated in an earlier essay, or the dominance of the Eliot gloss in our experience of Marvell's *To His Coy Mistress*. In each case there is a possessiveness of the group toward the text and a limitation of the experience of the text to the form of the prevailing gloss. It is a fixed point from which raids are made on the detail of the work.

But with such texts as *Hamlet* and *King Lear*, though antecedent glosses do in part direct our experience, as it is only human they should, there is something else involved. These are texts of a special sort in our society. They are not simply works of prestige: they are Scripture. They are much more than works;

210

they are iron magnets for innumerable filings. And they must, in our society at least, be serious, if not solemn; they must engage our humanity. When we come to interpretations we do not simply interpret a text but rather attempt to order a massed experience of discussion, quotation, and concern that has a ghostly yet substantial existence distinct from the page. This constitutes a field, comparable to, or almost of the same kind as, the field out of which in one of the current modes of composition a poem is precipitated. There is involved a process of divination and emotional accommodation. The result must come together; it must satisfy. In the case of Scripture it must satisfy by attaining a unity ordered by the modes of our own emotional life and by alluding to those deeper concerns set loose by the autonomy of religion: human destiny, the human heart, tragedy and the plight of modern man. We write our own poems in the form of literary criticism, and what we divine are our own forms.

Consequently, for many years we have tended to regard the greater Shakespearean tragedies as primarily concerned with the psychological or spiritual nature and development of the main character, to regard character, routinely said to be indistinguishable from action, as the guiding principle of order that directs the construction of the plays. In this way we get rid of the action. Bradley, for example, says of *Hamlet*: "the whole story turns upon the peculiar nature of the hero." And Allardyce Nicoll, to choose one more example among many, speaks of "that which forms the very core of the tragedy, the mental and spiritual Hamlet."[1] Again, almost everyone assumes that the spiritual development of Lear is the principle of that play, and that all that is not directly concerned with Lear is nevertheless related. The story of Gloucester, it is said, repeats the design of the main plot; it forms a second, a sub- or echo-plot, and in the repetition emphasizes, intensifies, and even universalizes the significance of the main plot, the development of Lear's character. Hence we regard the political and local circumstances of the story as of little consequence; it is a universal and a domestic tragedy. Finally we view the internal method of construction according to the familiar analysis of high school lore: it consists of the initial exposition, followed by the rising action which culminates in the emotional climax or crisis, and then falls away to the resolution.

It is a curve of feeling which rises and falls, and the only problem is to locate the point of highest tension, whether in the storm scenes on the heath or later in the reconciliation with Cordelia.

Such ways of viewing experience and its reflections in fiction are familiar to us: they are common in the modern novel. But they are not necessarily the principles of all fiction. Indeed, for our present purposes we may distinguish broadly two kinds of fiction, corresponding roughly to the two kinds of lyric previously distinguished.[2] The one exhibits—to use our commonplace —artificial or mechanical form; the other aims at organic form. The former is found in Roman comedy, in Jonson, in many of the comedies and some of the greater tragedies of Shakespeare. It is differentiated by having as a major principle of order a plot in the old sense, a contrivance, a sequence of actions moved by scheming and mistakes. The latter would appear uncontrived. In it character is indeed indistinguishable from action, action from character, and in fact the parts subsist only in the impression of the whole. In the former things are brought about. In the latter they happen. Toward the end of Henry James' *Ambassadors*, for example, the principal character remarks: "I don't think there is anything I have done in such a calculated way as you describe. Everything has come as a sort of indistinguishable part of everything else."[3] This is not the sort of thing that Davos or Mosca, Iago or Edmund, or indeed Claudius or Laertes could with any accuracy say.

For what is missing in the modern accounts of Shakespearean tragedy is precisely the plot of the play, the series of intrigues and mistakes by which the situation as initially expounded comes to the catastrophe. For this reason the modern critic has always had special difficulties with *King Lear*. He wonders at the disappearance of the Fool, as if the Fool had some bearing on the issue of the action. And he finds that the play falls off after the storm scenes. It falls off after the storm scenes because the poet has action to deal with, a story to tell, a plot to unfold, and the modern critic is not interested in this. He would like to leave out the plot.

He would like to leave it out because in the modern view it is a good thing to be rid of. Mark Twain threatened to shoot anyone attempting to find a plot in his narrative of Huckleberry

Finn. André Gide resolved in his *Journal of "The Counterfeiters"* "to avoid the artificiality of a 'plot'." And E. M. Forster commenting on that novel, apparently with approval, described Gide's attitude in these terms: "As for plot—to pot with plot, break it up, boil it down. Let there be those 'formidable erosions of contour' of which Nietzsche speaks. All that is prearranged is false." Sherwood Anderson: "The plot notion did seem to me to poison all story-telling. What was wanted, I thought, was form, not plot." Elizabeth Bowen asked: "What about the idea that plot should be ingenious, complicated—a display of ingenuity remarkable enough to command attention?" gives no answer, and passes on. The distinguished poet and critic, Edwin Muir, said: "It was Thackeray who first made a clear break with the plot both as a literary and a popular convention" so that in *Vanity Fair* "All the plot that remains is the series of incidents which widen and diversify the picture, and set the characters in different relations . . . What we ask [of the incidents] is that they should arise as naturally as possible, that the plot should not appear to be a plot." And again: "There is no external framework, no merely mechanical plot; all is character, and all is at the same time action." "This spontaneous and progressive logic is the real distinguishing feature of the dramatic novel."[4]

But "spontaneous and progressive logic" is not a characteristic of Shakespearean tragedy, and indeed was not a notion available at that time. I suggest a return from the concerns of modern fiction and modern life to the commonplaces of Shakespeare's own tradition, commonplaces that fit his work with a remarkably unsubtle obviousness. If this method of interpretation seems not to enrich our experience of the works but rather to limit and simplify that experience, I can only confess that this is my intention. Interpretation, I feel, should sharpen and define, subtract, not add. One does not make progress in this field; the trick is to go back, to recover.

If in the process of recovery we ask what traditions were available to Shakespeare, from what sources could he draw those structures and schemes of language, person, scene, and action which he used, and in what context would his audience perceive and feel them, we shall find that with respect to the theater there were, among others, three important traditions. The first, which will not concern us here, is the tradition of pageantry and court entertainment, of hermits, allegorical and supernatural characters, of special scenery, dance, song, and "the study of magnificence."⁵ It is a tradition relevant to many of Shakespeare's comedies, and one that receives its final realization in the masques of Jonson.

The second is the tradition of show business, of the professional actor and the popular stage. It is a tradition of juggling, tumbling, comic beatings, of Tom o' Bedlam and "Exit, pursued by a bear," of fencing matches and vaudeville skits. In this tradition a narrative is only partly useful for its own sake; it is at the same time a device for disposing and arranging a series of theatrical routines, just as the story of the modern musical play is largely an occasion for songs, dances, comedy acts, and what not. It forms, as was earlier maintained, a sort of expandable filing system. Hence the story or plot of an Elizabethan play has in this sense a double function. It is presented for its own sake, and at the same time it forms a sort of framework or outline allowing a number of independent acts or routines. It is a way of plotting out, of arranging, a wide variety of theatrical material—comic scenes, songs, and exhibitions of odd characters, such as Osric in *Hamlet* or Clove and Orange in Jonson's *Every Man Out of His Humour*:

> MITIS: What be these two, signior?
> CORDATUS: Marry, a couple, sir, that are mere strangers
>   to the whole scope of our play; only come to walk
>   a turn or two in this scene of Paul's, by chance.
>   3. 1. 16-19

It allows for soliloquies or passions, and scenes of the same sort, such as the scenes on the heath, expressing the feeling attached to the story. It leaves room, as Jonson says in discussing unity of action, "for digression and art."⁶ The critical rule that pertains to these is not that they should blend together and be integrated into a single and organic effect, that they should exhibit some kind of qualitative progression. It is rather the rule of decorum, the negative rule that they should be not inappropriate.

Plot in this sense, then, is a method for disposing and arranging the heterogeneous material of the play. And the difference in aesthetic effect between two plays with approximately the same quantity of plot but with greater and less digression and episode will be, as Coleridge noted of *Hamlet* and *Macbeth*: "the one proceeds with the utmost slowness, the other with a crowded and breathless rapidity."[7] Or, to put it less perceptively: the one in a school text I have at hand runs to fifty pages, the other to thirty.

The third tradition is academic, the tradition of literary criticism and analysis employed in the reading and discussion of Roman comedy in the schools. We shall find that Shakespeare constructs the plots of *Hamlet* and *King Lear* consciously and deliberately according to the rubrics of this tradition. The basic texts are the classics of ancient rhetoric and Donatus on Terence, and the general context is elementary school learning, rehearsed and repeated with the single-mindedness of a Freudian interpreter. We could assume that Shakespeare knew this tradition, knew it by heart, even without the work of the many scholars who in recent years have firmly established the fact,[8] for it was the tradition of prestige in his time. But how well he understood and how easily he handled the basic terms and distinctions of that tradition can be illustrated by the exegesis of a phrase in Polonius' speech about the players in which the councilor displays his familiarity with current literary and dramatic terms:

> The best actors in the world, either for tragedy, comedy, history, pastoral, pastoral-comical, historical-pastoral, tragical-historical, tragical-comical-historical-pastoral; scene individable, or poem unlimited.
> 2. 2. 415-18

The enumeration of dramatic genres begins like the enumeration in a patent for a company of players, and then introduces that contamination of genres which was being currently discussed and explicitly practiced, as in Guarini's *Il Pastor Fido* (1590), a pastoral tragicomedy, or in the comical satires of Jonson. The last two phrases in the enumeration, culminating in the quadrate contamination of "tragical-comical-historical-pastoral," are not in the text of 1604 (the second quarto) but appear for the first time in the folio text of 1623. They may represent an addition, gagging up the passage. However, the phrases we are specially concerned with are "scene individable" and "poem unlimited." The commentators do not know what is meant, and have settled on the guess that it is a reference "to dramas that observe the unities of time and place and also those that give no heed to such limitation."[9] It is a distant guess. A better guess and a more obvious one would be that "scene individable" refers to the question, which was receiving some attention at the time, of whether the acts of a play should be divided into scenes. Muretus in his notes to Terence (1550), which were incorporated in the later editions of that author, comments, "As to dividing the acts of a play into scenes, designating scene one, scene two, and so on, how skillfully and intelligently it is done is, I think, questionable. For my own part I take it that this distinction comes from the teachers of literature and not from the poets"; and he advises a friend whose tragedy he had read "to remove entirely the useless and superfluous and dreamed up by teachers division of acts into scenes."[10] Jonson may well have had such comment in mind in the following passage from *Every Man Out of His Humour* (1599, published 1600), in which Shakespeare was a principal actor:

> MITIS: Does he observe all the laws of comedy in it?
> CORDATUS: What laws mean you?
> MITIS: Why, the equal division of it into acts and
>   scenes, according to the Terentian manner. . . .
> CORDATUS: O no, these are too nice observations.
> Induction, 235-42

But there is no need to guess what "poem unlimited" means. All that is needed is an elementary Elizabethan education, a familiarity with the basic distinctions of Cicero and Quintilian, and a willingness to countenance the persistent Renaissance habit of using rhetorical concepts in the discussion of poetry. Let us translate the phrase, as an Elizabethan would naturally do, into Latin: *poema infinitum*. Of course. He had learned from rhetoric that there are two kinds of topics one could write or speak on: *quaestiones esse aut infinitas aut finitas.*[11] They are unlimited or limited; either general, without reference to persons, time, or place, or they are implicated in circumstance. "Should men marry?" is unlimited; "Should Antony marry Octavia?" is limited. An unlimited poem, then, is an expository poem on a general topic, such as *De Rerum Natura* or John Davies' *Nosce Teipsum* (1599).

The concepts of this tradition enter into the structure of Shakespeare's drama in various ways. The principle of social rank, for example, that tragedy involves heads of state and comedy the affairs of the citizen class, is retained and modified. It serves, to use our own terms, to distinguish domestic from true tragedy, and romantic from realistic comedy. One of the most interesting consequences of this principle in Shakespearean comedy is the implicit stipulation that romantic love is only possible to the wellborn, so that to introduce this element into the citizen comedy of the *Merry Wives of Windsor* the author must introduce a wellborn lover, a Mr. Fenton who is a courtier and so of necessity a Throckmorton, a Knyvett, or a Blount.

There is another principle relating to comedy that Shakespeare sometimes scrupulously observes and sometimes deliberately violates. It seems to have had a fascination for him. This is the stipulation that comedy should be *sine periculo vitae,* "without the threat of death." The action in one of his earliest comedies, the *Comedy of Errors,* is deliberately set in the frame of a violation of this law. Indeed, the observance of the law in the *Merry Wives of Windsor* is sufficient to distinguish that play absolutely in kind from *Much Ado About Nothing* and *Measure for Measure.* The knot of error in *Much Ado* is tied by a supposed death, and *Measure for Measure* exploits to the full the tragic attitudes of fear and resignation to death: "Be absolute for death." The former is simply comedy; the latter are tragicomedy in the form in which it was being developed at this time in practice and theory. For "he who composes tragicomedy," says Guarini, "takes from tragedy its great persons but not its great action . . . its danger but not its death."[12]

In brief, Cicero and Donatus, Quintilian and Diomedes furnish Shakespeare and his interpreter with the relevant notions. Consequently, when Viola exclaims in *Twelfth Night*:

O Time, thou must untangle this, not I;
It is too hard a knot for me t'untie!
                    2. 2. 41-42

we recognize the allusion to the Donatan tradition of analysis,
and we perceive that the plot of *Twelfth Night* is constructed
precisely according to that tradition. In general Donatus describes the structure of Terence's comedies in terms of the error
that furnishes the problem of the play, and the plots and errors
that complicate and lead to the tying of the knot whose resolution yields the catastrophe. He comments, for example, on *Andria*
2. 4: "This scene ties the knot of error of the play, and the difficulty proper to comedy; it also sets in motion the schemes."
On 2. 6: "This scene contains the plots of both characters, by
which each marvellously takes, and is taken, in." On 5. 4: "And
here the error of the play is wholly revealed." Again, on *Hecyra*,
4. 4: "In this scene is the final error before the catastrophe."[13]
So in *Twelfth Night*, after the situation is expounded in a series
of scenes, the plot begins with the initial error, an error like
that in the *Silent Woman*, "error personae"[14]: Olivia falls in love
with the disguised Viola, thinking her a man, and there follow
later the subsequent errors springing from the twinness of
Sebastian. Immediately after the initial error the first plot begins, Maria against Malvolio. This is a separate plot that has
its own issue and has no bearing on the catastrophe. The next
plot, however, does. Sir Toby and Fabian's practice on Sir An-
drew, leading to the duels, precipitates the catastrophe. In brief,
the action of the play develops simply and solely through plots
and errors; they constitute the engine that runs the show.

Likewise in *Hamlet*, when Horatio after the catastrophe of
that play proposes to "speak to th' yet unknowing world / How
these things came about" and goes on after Fortinbras' assent
to say:

But let this same be presently perform'd,
Even while men's minds are wild, lest more mischance
On plots and errors happen.
                    5. 2. 404-06

one who knows that tradition understands the terms and perceives that it is being authoritatively stated that the catastrophe resulted from a series of plots and errors. As it does. It would not particularly bother him that the mechanisms of comedy are employed in tragedy, for he would know with Jonson and many others who wrote on the subject that "the parts of a comedy are the same with a tragedy."[15]

The action of *Hamlet*, the busy part of the play, begins with Hamlet's assumption of madness, an alteration that amounts to a disguise. The subsequent scenes are produced by the plots of the King and Polonius through Rosencrantz and Guildenstern, Ophelia, and the Queen to find out "The very cause of Hamlet's lunacy," and of Hamlet against the King to discover his guilt. This movement culminates in the killing by error of Polonius as an accidental consequence of his plot to use the Queen in discovering Hamlet's secret. Hamlet is immediately packed off to England—this is the King's plot; and Rosencrantz and Guildenstern "go to 't" by a plotted error:

> O 'tis most sweet
> When in one line two crafts directly meet.
>   3. 4. 209-10

In the final scene of the play the carefully contrived scheme to murder Hamlet, as it were accidentally, goes awry:

> purposes mistook
> Fall'n on th' inventors' heads.

In error the foils are exchanged; in error the Queen drinks the poisoned cup.

This is a plot of intrigue, a tale of "mischance that on plots and errors happen," enriched by scenes and speeches of comedy, passion, satire, hung on the framework of the plot and not inappropriate to the whole. To our modern question, What is Hamlet's tragic flaw? or, In what way are we to construe his final death as issuing out of the depths of his personality? we answer: His tragic flaw is Claudius and Laertes. He was cold-bloodedly murdered by means of a contrived diabolical plot. One need not assume, therefore, that he was in our current jargon "murder-prone."

Lear, too, is a play of mischance that on plots and errors happen. There is in it also the spiritual story of Lear and the spiritual story of Gloucester, of course, but neither of these nor both together furnish the structure of the whole. It is not these that bring about the catastrophe.

The action begins with the first plot at the end of the scene of state that opens the play. Goneril and Regan, fearful of the threat to their new eminence from the King's character and his very kingness, as also from his hundred knights who with their retainers constitute a sizable army, begin to scheme:

> If our father carry authority with such dispositions as
> he bears, this last surrender of his will but offend us.
> 1. 1. 308-10

Regan says, "We shall further think on't," but Goneril fiercely replies, "We must do something, and in the heat." What she proposes to do becomes clear in a later scene. The second strand of the play is now introduced with the soliloquy of Edmund, who expounds his plot:

> Legitimate Edgar, I must have your land . . .
> Well, my legitimate, if this letter speed
> And my invention thrive, Edmund the base
> Shall top the legitimate.
> 1. 2. 16, 19-21

And with the entrance, first of Gloucester, then of Edgar, he immediately puts it into execution. The next scene shows Goneril's plot in operation: Lear is to be treated with such disrespect, offensive to the name of King as well as father, that, given his character which she knows, he will leave in a huff. "And let his knights have colder looks among you," she tells little Oswald:

> What grows of it, no matter; advise your fellows so:
> I would breed from hence occasions, and I shall,
> That I may speak; I'll write straight to my sister
> To hold my very course.
> 1. 3. 23-26

The difficulty between Lear and Goneril is not the spontaneous consequence of differing temperaments, nor is it the result of the offensive and riotous senility of an old man. These are merely Goneril's allegations, and have no standing against the claim of duty to a King and father. Rather, the difficulty between Lear and Goneril is coldly and explicitly provoked. It is the consequence of a plot.

The next scene shows Kent in disguise taking service with Lear, and Oswald furthering Goneril's plot, though he is tripped up for his pains in a comic routine. Up to this point, from the conclusion of the exposition, all has been plots on the part of Goneril and Edmund, and in the case of Kent's disguise an error. There follows an interlude, the Fool's routine with Lear, which, however important it may be to our feeling about the play, is irrelevant to the plot. Its primary purpose is to drive home the wrongness of Lear's initial mistake, and to display some wit. The plot resumes with the entrance of Goneril who has, as she planned, bred occasions to insult Lear. He hurries off in a rage to the other daughter, and she sends Oswald with a message urging Regan to a similar course of action. This plot comes to a head when Lear, rejected by Regan, goes out into the storm. Meanwhile, Edmund's plot against Edgar has been successful; Edgar flees, is proclaimed, and assumes the disguise of Tom o' Bedlam. Kent in the storm discloses his political plot against the Dukes, the alliance with France which culminates in the battle. But this leads to the furtherance of Edmund's second plot, the plot against Gloucester, who has been approached by Kent's party and confides this to Edmund. By revealing the intrigue to Cornwall he destroys his father and attains his title and lands. This is the culmination of his original plot.

Gloucester is blinded, Cornwall slain, the French Army landed at Dover, Goneril and Regan vie for Edmund's favor, and Albany comes to the side of the good. Oswald, carrying a letter from Goneril to Edmund, runs across Gloucester, is slain by the disguised Edgar, and the crucial error of the plot occurs—Edgar finds on Oswald's body Goneril's letter. This leads to the unloosing of the knot of the play. For, with the defeat of Cordelia, Edmund is at the height of his power. He plots by way of the Captain the death of Cordelia and Lear. Meanwhile, Albany has been shown Goneril's letter and has consented to Edgar's scheme of a trial by combat. In the quarrel for pre-eminence between Albany and Edmund, Regan openly espouses Edmund; it is a marriage ceremony:

> Witness the world, that I create thee here
> My lord and master.
>
> 5. 3. 77-78

And Albany, on the evidence of the letter that went astray, forbids the banns:

> For your claim, fair sister,
> I bar it in the interest of my wife;
> 'Tis she is sub-contracted to this lord,
> And I, her husband, contradict your banns.
>
> 5. 3. 84-87

Regan has been poisoned by Goneril, and is led off. The trial by combat ensues, with Edgar triumphant and Edmund mortally wounded. Goneril is exposed, exits, and commits suicide. The death of Gloucester is announced, and then on the repentance of Edmund, who discloses his plot against Lear and Cordelia, his orders are recalled. But it is too late. Cordelia is dead and Lear soon dies. This is hardly the story of the psychological development of Lear and Gloucester.

We have left out much, and much that conduces to the richness and deep feeling of the play—the scenes on the heath, the mighty passions of Lear corresponding to the soliloquies of Hamlet, the regeneration of Lear and Gloucester—but we have left out none of the action, nothing that is necessary to the plot. In *Lear*, this is the plot of Goneril and Regan against Lear, of Edmund against Edgar and Gloucester, of Kent against the Dukes, of Goneril against Regan, of Edmund against Lear and Cordelia, and the counteraction stemming from the errors of Edgar's disguise and the letter gone astray.

Nor is there in the modern sense a double plot in the play, though there is in a Renaissance sense. A prominent Italian critic, for example, writing in the 1540s says:

I call that plot double which has in its action diverse

kinds of persons of the same station in life, as two
lovers of different character, two old men of varied
nature . . . and other such things, as they may be seen
in the *Andria* and in the other plots of the same poet,
where it is clear that these like persons of unlike habits
make the knot and solution of the plot very pleasing.
And I believe that if this should be well imitated in tragedy by a good poet, and the knot so arranged that its
solution will not bring confusion, double structure in
tragedy will be no less pleasing (always remembering
the reverence due to Aristotle) than it is in comedy. . . .[16]

Obviously, in these terms *King Lear* has a double plot, for Lear
and Gloucester are two old men, though in this case of similar
rather than of varied nature; Edgar and Edmund, and Cordelia
on the one hand and Goneril and Regan on the other yield further
doublings. But this is not what the modern critic has in mind
when he speaks of the main and sub- or echo-plot of that play.
Rather, a plot in this tradition consists of several lines of action,
separately developed at the beginning, but impinging on each
other to form the complication, and each necessary to the final
solution or catastrophe. It follows in this tradition that a line
of action necessary to the complication and solution does not
constitute a separate or sub-plot but is an integral part of the
plot itself. There is, consequently, on this view no double, no
main and sub-plot, in *King Lear*, for Edmund and Edgar are the
principal agents in the catastrophe.

The method and intention of such doubling in Renaissance
drama is illuminated by a later critic, Guarini. "It now remains
to defend this grafting in of subordinate stories," he says, and
we recall that Shakespeare grafted the Gloucester story from
Sidney's *Arcadia* onto the old story of Lear:

In order to do this I shall consider four agents indispensable to the plot of the *Andria* . . . : Pamphilus the
first, Glycerium the second, Philumena the third, and
Charinus the fourth . . . the principal subject is nothing
else than the love of Pamphilus and Glycerium, not interrupted by that of Charinus, but greatly aided. And
if that love alone had been represented, with the preg-

nancy of Glycerium and the displeasure of Simo, the
father of Pamphilus, how insipid the story would have
been! A young man fallen under the displeasure of the
father because he had married a woman of no standing,
who at last, when she is discovered to be a free woman,
is given to him as his wife—what is there in that to
make a plot? The plot might indeed have been pathetic
and have displayed character, but there would have
been no activity, which is the strength of the dramatic
art. How would the plot have come to a crisis? From
the indignation of the father and the love of the son
strong feelings could have resulted, but not intrigues.[17]

The author's exclamation, "What is there in that to make a
plot?" is clearly applicable to the plot of *Lear* as it is ordinarily
summarized for us. An old man acts foolishly, estranges the
child who loves him, is brutally rejected by his other children,
goes into a feverish delirium, is finally reconciled to the good
child, and then by a trick of fate she is killed and he dies broken-
hearted. The story is repeated about another old man. One could
say with our Renaissance author: "The plot might indeed have
been pathetic and displayed character, but there would have
been no activity, which is the strength of the dramatic art. How
would the plot have come to a crisis? . . . strong feelings could
have resulted, but not intrigues."

Tradition and Modernity
Wallace Stevens

~~~~~~

I have defined tradition in such a way that every poem necessarily has a tradition, but this is not the common meaning of
the term. For we distinguish between what is traditional and
what is not, and in the latter case the principle is a negative
one. This is a concern for tradition that is a modern concern,
and provoked by something so simple as a sense of alienation
from the past, a feeling for history as distinct. It is motivated
by the persuasion that tradition has been lost and is only recoverable in novelty. From this arises a corollary concern with
modernity in poetry, for which the poetry of Wallace Stevens
will serve as an illustration. He himself writes in the poem entitled *Of Modern Poetry*:

> The poem of the mind in the act of finding
> What will suffice. It has not always had
> To find: the scene was set; it repeated what
> Was in the script.
>   Then the theatre was changed
> To something else. Its past was a souvenir. (239)[1]

To be modern in this sense is not the same thing as to be
contemporary, to be living and writing in our time, or to have

lived and written within our normal life span. There are many contemporary poets who are not modern. The modern poet writes the new poetry, as it was called some years ago. His poetry is modern in that it is different from the old, the traditional, the expected; it is new. This is the sense in which *modern* has always been used in these contexts: the modern poets in Roman antiquity were Calvus and Catullus who wrote in new and untraditional poetic forms, in forms borrowed from another language and regarded by the traditionalists of the times as effete and decadent; whose subjects were novel and daring; and whose attitudes were in conscious distinction from those of the old morality. Again, the *moderni*, the modern thinkers in the late Middle Ages, were those who advocated and embraced the new logic of that time and whose attitudes were thought to be dangerous to the established order; it was later said that they caused the Reformation.

The modern poet, then, is modern only in the light of tradition, only as distinguished from the old. His forms, his models, his subjects, and his attitudes are different from and in opposition to the customary and expected forms, models, subjects, and attitudes of his own youth and of his readers. Consequently to be modern depends on a tradition to be different from, upon the firm existence of customary expectations to be disappointed. The new is parasitic upon the old. But when the new has itself become the old, it has lost its quality of newness and modernity and must shift for itself.

This is the situation with respect to what is still called modern poetry; it is rapidly becoming the old and the traditional. There appeared some years ago a number of articles in the leading conventional journals of this country in defense of modern poetry. Had the poetry still needed defense, the articles would never have been accepted by the editors of those journals. But modern poetry is, in fact, in secure possession of the field, and its heroes are aged men with a long public career behind them. Wallace Stevens, in fact, died in 1955 at the age of seventy-six after a public career of forty years. Yet the attitude of modernity still persists. These poets still represent to the young writer of today the new, the adventurous, the advance guard, the untried. Their names are still sacred to the initiate.

For it is the condition of modernity in art that it appeal to the initiate, that it provoke the opposition of the ordinary reader who has the customary and old expectations which it is the purpose of modern art to foil. Hence it lives in an attitude of defense; is close and secret, not open and hearty; has its private ritual and its air of priesthood—*odi profanum vulgus et arceo*, "I despise the uninitiated crowd, and I keep them at a distance." It is obscure, and its obscurities are largely calculated; it is intended to be impenetrable to the vulgar. More than this, it is intended to exasperate them.

There is something of this in all art that is genuine. For the genuine in art is that which attains distinction, and the distinguished is uncommon and not accessible to the many. It is different, it must be different, and as such provokes the hostility of the many, and provokes it the more in that its difference is a claim to distinction, to prestige, and to exclusion. This claim is diminished by time. Wordsworth is now regarded as quite traditional, quite stuffy and conventional. For the particular qualities of difference in an older body of poetry that has been absorbed into the tradition become part of that tradition, and so something that the reader actually need not see since he does not know it is different. He may then in his early years and through his school days develop a set of social responses to the received body of poetry; he may enjoy that poetry without effort, be pleased by his conditioned responses, and think of himself as a lover and judge of poetry. When the audience for poetry becomes satisfied with a customary response to a customary poem, when they demand of the poet that he write to their expectations, when distinction is lost in commonness, there is need for the modern in art, for a poetry that is consciously different, even if it often mistakes difference for distinction. The poet must exasperate his reader, or succumb to him.

Such was the situation out of which Stevens wrote, at least as it seemed to him and to those of his contemporaries who have become the aged fathers of modern poetry. They sought to appear different, and hence distinguished, and they succeeded perhaps too well. The first thing that strikes the reader of Wallace Stevens, and the quality for which he was for a long time best known, is the piquant, brilliant, and odd surface of his poems.

They are full of nonsense cries, full of virtuoso lines, such as:

> Chieftan Iffucan of Azcan in caftan
> Of tan with henna hackles, halt![2] (75)

which unexpectedly make grammar and sense if you read them slowly with closed ears. They are thronged with exotic place-names, but not the customary ones of late romantic poetry; instead of "Quinquereme of Nineveh from distant Ophir" there is "a woman of Lhassa," there is Yucatan. Rare birds fly, "the green toucan," and tropical fruits abound, especially the pineapple. Odd characters appear—Crispin, Redwood Roamer, Babroulbadour, black Sly, Nanzia Nunzio—and are addressed in various languages—my semblables, Nino, ephebi, o iuventes, o filii. And they wear strange hats.

A good deal of this, of course, is simply the unexpected in place of the expected; a new and different collection of proper names, for example, instead of the old collection, but used largely for the same purpose while seeming to deny this by being designedly different:

> Canaries in the morning, orchestras
> In the afternoon, balloons at night. That is
> A difference, at least, from nightingales,
> Jehovah, and the great sea-worm.(142)

The process is common in Stevens, and can be seen neatly in one of his most engaging stanzas. The theme of the stanza is the traditional one of Tom Nashe's:

> Brightness falls from the hair,
> Queens have died young and fair.

But instead of Helen and Iseult there are references to the beauties in Utamaro's drawings and to the eighteenth-century belles of Bath:

> Is it for nothing, then, that old Chinese
> Sat tittivating by their mountain pools

> Or in the Yangtse studied out their beards?
> I shall not play the flat historic scale.
> You know how Utamaro's beauties sought
> The end of love in their all-speaking braids.
> You know the mountainous coiffures of Bath.
> Alas! Have all the barbers lived in vain
> That not one curl in nature has survived? (14)

A woman's hair is here used as a synecdoche for her beauty. Have all those who have cared for and cherished her hair, have all the barbers, lived in vain, that though much has survived in art, none has survived in nature? The poet concludes then, expressing the sense of the couplet of a Shakespearean sonnet:

> This thought is as a death, which cannot choose
> But weep to have that which it fears to lose.

in the more specialized terms of his synecdoche, but almost as movingly:

> Why, without pity on these studious ghosts,
> Do you come dripping in your hair from sleep? (14)

Much of this is rather amusing, and even, as we say now, intriguing. Sometimes, indeed, it is much more than that, as in the stanza just quoted which is poetry of a rare though too precious kind. But Wallace Stevens had a public career in poetry for forty years, and forty years is a little too long for this sort of pepper to retain its sharpness and piquancy. We have to ask, then, What is the motive and purpose in this?

It is usually said that these aspects of Stevens' work derive from a study of the French poets of the latter nineteenth century, the Symbolists and Parnassians, and this explanation no doubt is true enough. But it is not a sufficient explanation. The prestige of that poetry was not so high in Stevens' youth as to serve as a motive, though it might be sufficient now. The motive is rather a more human one. It is disdain—disdain of the society and of the literary tradition in which he grew up, of himself as a part of that society, and of his readers so far as they belonged to it. He sought, he tells us:

> when all is said, to drive away
> The shadow of his fellows from the skies,
> And, from their stale intelligence released,
> To make a new intelligence prevail. (37)

How did he go about it? He celebrated the rankest trivia in the choicest diction. He was a master of the traditional splendors of poetry and refused to exercise his mastery in the traditional way; he displayed it in the perverse, the odd:

> he humbly served
> Grotesque apprenticeship to chance event.(39)

He became "a clown" though "an aspiring clown." In his own summary, in the passage that immediately follows the lines quoted above, he explains:

> Hence the reverberations in the words
> Of his first central hymns, the celebrants
> Of rankest trivia, tests of the strength
> Of his aesthetic, his philosophy,
> The more invidious, the more desired:
> The florist asking aid from cabbages,
> The rich man going bare, the paladin
> Afraid, the blind man as astronomer,
> The appointed power unwielded from disdain.(37)

He possessed "the appointed power"—the Miltonic and Scriptural phrasing is blasphemous in this context, and deliberately so—but would not wield it from disdain. The question then is, Why should he have felt such disdain? The answer can be collected from various of his poems but is given full and detailed exposition in the one from which I have just quoted. This is *The Comedian as the Letter C*, the showpiece and longest poem in his first book. The poem is sufficiently complex to have several centers of concern. I shall interpret it, however, in terms of our question, and we shall find that this will turn out to be a primary concern of the poem.

The poem consists of six sections, each of a little under a hundred lines of blank verse. It is in form and subject a poem that depicts the growth of a poet's mind, and though the main character is given the fictitious name of Crispin, he may be taken as an aspect of the author, a mask for Wallace Stevens the poet, so that the poem in effect is autobiographical. It belongs, then, to that literary form of which the model and prototype is Wordsworth's *Prelude*. It is not a wholly easy poem to read, partly because much of it is written in Stevens' fastidious and disdainful manner, partly because its structure is not adequately adjusted to its theme. The hero of the poem makes a sea voyage to a strange and exotic country, in this case Yucatan, and back to his own land. The motive for the voyage is explicitly given late in the poem in the passage already quoted:

> What was the purpose of his pilgrimage,
> Whatever shape it took in Crispin's mind,
> If not, when all is said, to drive away
> The shadow of his fellows from the skies,
> And, from their stale intelligence released,.
> To make a new intelligence prevail? (37)

His voyage is a rejection of his society as banal and trite, of its intelligence as stale, and his quest is the quest of a new intelligence. His problem was the problem that every teacher of freshman composition sets his better students, the problem of striking through routine phrasing and syntax to the genuine, the honest, the possibly distinguished.

The hero is portrayed as having been before this trip a man who was master of his environment, but he was a little man, "the Socrates of snails," "this nincompated pedagogue," and the environment itself was trivial; it was a land "of simple salad-beds, of honest quilts." It was, in fact, to quote Stevens' own summary of his early environment in an essay of later date, "the comfortable American state of life of the 'eighties, the 'nineties, and the first ten years of the present century."[2] It was the time and place when the sun

> shone
> With bland complaisance on pale parasols,
> Beetled, in chapels, on the chaste bouquets. (29)

It was that middle class culture of business, public chastity, **and** official Christianity which we often call, with some **historical** injustice, Victorianism. In this world Crispin wrote the conventional poetry of the times. He was one

>   that saw
> The stride of vanishing autumn in a park
> By way of decorous melancholy . . .
> That wrote his couplet yearly to the spring,
> As dissertation of profound delight.

However, he found that

> He could not be content with counterfeit. (31, 39)

It was this dissatisfaction with the conventional—in society and in poetry—"That first drove Crispin to his wandering." He alludes to it as "The drenching of stale lives," a life of "ruses" **that** was shattered by the experience of his voyage.

He found the sea overwhelming; he "was washed away by magnitude." "Here was no help before reality." It was **not so** much that he was cut off from the snug land; he was cut off **from** his old self:

> What counted was mythology of self,
> Blotched out beyond unblotching.

and hence from his environment. He was destitute **and bare:**

> The salt hung on his spirit like a frost,
> The dead brine melted in him like a dew
> Of winter, until nothing of himself
> Remained, except some starker, barer self
> In a starker, barer world. (28, 29)

From this experience he came to Yucatan. The poetasters **of that** land, like the poetasters at home, in spite of the vividness of experience around them

> In spite of hawk and falcon, green toucan
> And jay. (30)

still wrote conventional verses about the nightingale, as if their environment were uncivilized. But Crispin's conversion at sea— for it was obviously a conversion—had enlarged him, made him complicated

> and difficult and strange
> In all desires. (31)

until he could reduce his tension only by writing an original and personal poetry, different and unconventional.

The experience at sea is now reinforced by another experience in Yucatan, of the same elemental, overwhelming sort:

> one
> Of many proclamations of the kind,
> Proclaiming something harsher than he learned

from the commonplace realism of home:

> From hearing signboards whimper in cold nights.

It was rather "the span / Of force, the quintessential fact,"

> The thing that makes him envious in a phrase.

It was the experience that altered and reinvigorated his poetry, the source from which he drew that distinction of style that marks off his published work from the sentimental verses he had printed in the college magazine some twenty years before. The experience was of the type of a religious experience:

> His mind was free
> And more than free, elate, intent, profound
> And studious of a self possessing him,
> That was not in him in the crusty town
> From which he sailed. (32-33)

The poetry he now wrote issued from this context. It was conditioned by the kind of dissatisfaction that drove Crispin to his wandering, by such an experience as Crispin's on the voyage and in Yucatan, and by its results. This dissatisfaction lies behind a good many of Steven's poems, which deal, if one looks beneath the distracting surface, simply with the opposition between the aridities of middle class convention and the vivid alertness of the unconventional, as in *Disillusionment of Ten O'Clock*. Some repeat in smaller compass and with other properties the subject of *The Comedian*: as *The Doctor of Geneva*. In others he attempts to deal directly with the experience of the sea, but this was a religious experience without the content of traditional religion. In fact, it had no content at all beyond the intuition of a bare reality behind conventional appearance, and hence was an unfertile subject for poetry since it was unproductive of detail. He treated it in one of his best short poems, *The Snow Man*, but when he had stated it, there was nothing more to be done with it, except to say it over again in another place. This he has repeatedly done, though with a prodigality of invention in phrasing that is astounding.

Most of what is interesting in Stevens issues from this problem. It can be put in various terms. It is the problem of traditional religion and modern life, of imagination and reality, but it can be best put for Stevens in the terms in which it is explicitly put in *The Comedian*. The problem is the relationship of a man and his environment, and the reconciliation of these two in poetry and thus in life. The two terms of this relationship are really Wordsworth's two terms: the one, what the eye and ear half create; the other, what they perceive. The reconciliation in Wordsworth is in a religious type of experience:

> With what strange utterance did the loud dry wind
> Blow through my ear! the sky seemed not a sky
> Of earth—and with what motion moved the clouds!
>
> Dust as we are, the immortal spirit grows
> Like harmony in music; there is a dark
> Inscrutable workmanship that reconciles
> Discordant elements, makes them cling together
> In one society.[3]

The reconciliation in Stevens is sought in poetry, in

> those
> True reconcilings, dark, pacific words,
> And the adroiter harmonies of their fall. (144)

For poetry is the supreme fiction of which religion is a manifestation:

> Poetry
>
> Exceeding music must take the place
> Of empty heaven and its hymns,
>
> Ourselves in poetry must take their place. (167)

What Crispin is seeking is such a reconciliation, a oneness between himself and his environment. He began in the illusion that he was the intelligence of his soil, but the experience of reality overwhelmed him, and he came to believe that his soil was his intelligence. At this extreme he wrote poems in which a person is described by his surroundings. But he perceived that this too was sentimental, and so he settled for the ordinary reality of daily life, married, had four daughters, and prospered. However, he did not give up poetry entirely; he recorded his adventures in the poem, and hoped that the reader would take it as he willed: as a summary

> strident in itself
> But muted, mused, and perfectly revolved
> In those portentous accents, syllables,
> And sounds of music coming to accord
> Upon his lap, like their inherent sphere,
> Seraphic proclamations of the pure
> Delivered with a deluging onwardness. (45)

Such is Stevens' account of the source of his distinctive style and distinctive subjects. But he owed more than he acknowledged to the old and the traditional. He owed "the appointed power" which was "unwielded from disdain."

That he once had the appointed power is clear in his greatest poem, and one of his earliest, *Sunday Morning*. The poem is traditional in meter—it is in eight equal stanzas of blank verse—and has as its subject a deep emotional attachment to traditional Christianity and a rejection of Christianity in favor of the clear and felt apprehension of sensory detail in this life, together with an attempt to preserve in the new setting the emotional aspects of the old values.

The poem depicts a woman having late breakfast on a Sunday morning, when of course she should have been at church. She is for the moment at one with her surroundings, which are vivid, sensory, familiar, and peaceful. All this serves to dissipate the traditional awe of Christian feeling, but the old feeling breaks through:

> She dreams a little, and she feels the dark
> Encroachment of that old catastrophe,
> As a calm darkens among water-lights. (67)

Her mood "is like wide water, without sound," and in that mood she passes over the seas to the contemplation of the Resurrection. The remainder of the poem consists of the poet's comment and argument on her situation, on two short utterances she delivers out of her musing, and finally on the revelation that comes to her in a voice.

The poet asserts that Christianity is a religion of the dead and the unreal. In this living world of the sun, in these vivid and sensory surroundings, there is that which can assume the values of heaven:

> Divinity must live within herself:
> Passions of rain, or moods in falling snow;
> Grievings in loneliness, or unsubdued
> Elations when the forest blooms; gusty
> Emotions on wet roads on autumn nights;
> All pleasures and all pains, remembering
> The bough of summer and the winter branch.
> These are the measures destined for her soul. (67)

The truly divine is the human and personal in this world: it consists in the association of feeling with the perception of natural landscape, in human pleasure and pain, in change, as in the change of seasons.

He then argues that the absolute God of religion was originally inhuman, but that the Incarnation by mingling our blood with His, by mingling the relative and human with the Absolute, satisfied man's innate desires for a human and unabsolute Absolute. Certainly, if "the earth" should "Seem all of paradise that we shall know," we would be much more at home in our environment:

> The sky will be much friendlier then than now . . .
> Not this dividing and indifferent blue. (68)

At this point the woman speaks in her musing, and says that she could acquiesce in this world, that she could find an earthly paradise, a contentment, in the perception of Nature, in the feel of reality, except that the objects of her perception change and disappear. Nature is an impermanent paradise. The poet, however, answers that no myth of a religious afterworld has been or ever will be as permanent as the stable recurrences of Nature:

> There is not any haunt of prophecy,
> Nor any old chimera of the grave,
> Neither the golden underground, nor isle
> Melodious, where spirits gat them home,
> Nor visionary south, nor cloudy palm
> Remote on heaven's hill, that has endured
> As April's green endures; or will endure
> Like her remembrance of awakened birds,
> Or her desire for June and evening, tipped
> By the consummation of the swallow's wings.

The woman speaks again, and says:

> "But in contentment I still feel
> The need of some imperishable bliss." (68)

There remains the desire for the eternal happiness of tradition.

The lines that comment on this present some difficulties to interpretation until it is seen that the poet in his answer proceeds by developing the woman's position. Yes, he says, we feel that only in death is there fulfillment of our illusions and our desires. Even though death be in fact the obliteration of all human experience, yet it is attractive to us; it has the fatal attractiveness of the willow in old poetry for the lovelorn maiden. Though she has lovers who bring her gifts—that is, the earth and its beauty—she disregards the lovers and, tasting of the gifts, strays impassioned toward death.

Yet the paradise she would achieve in death is nothing but an eternal duplicate of this world, and lacking even the principle of change, leads only to ennui. Therefore, the poet creates a secular myth, a religion of his irreligion. The central ceremony is a chant, a poem to the sun,

> Not as a god, but as a god might be. (70)

It is an undivine fiction that preserves the emotions of the old religion but attaches them to a poetry in which the sensory objects of a natural landscape enter into a union in celebration of the mortality of men:

> And whence they came and whither they shall go
> The dew upon their feet shall manifest. (70)

The biblical phrasing creates a blasphemous religion of mortality.

The poem now concludes with a revelation. Out of the woman's mood a voice cries to her, saying that the place of the Resurrection is merely the place where a man died and not a persisting way of entry into a spiritual world. The poet continues:

> We live in an old chaos of the sun,
> Or old dependency of day and night,
> Or island solitude, unsponsored, free,
> Of that wide water, inescapable.
> Deer walk upon our mountains, and the quail
> Whistle about us their spontaneous cries;

Sweet berries ripen in the wilderness;
And, in the isolation of the sky,
At evening, casual flocks of pigeons make
Ambiguous undulations as they sink,
Downward to darkness, on extended wings. (70)

We live, in fact, in a universe suggested by natural science, whose principle is change, an island without religious sponsor, free of the specific Christian experience. It is a sensory world, it has its delights, its disorder, and it is mortal.

The poem is an argument against the traditional Christianity of Stevens' youth, and especially against the doctrine and expectation of immortality, in favor of an earthly and mortal existence that in the felt apprehension of sensory detail can attain a vivid oneness with its surroundings and a religious sense of union comparable to the traditional feeling. The former is undeniably traditional, and much of the deep feeling of the poem is derived from the exposition in sustained and traditional rhetoric of the position which is being denied. In this sense it is parasitic on what it rejects. But the positive argument is almost as traditional in the history of English poetry and in the literary situation of Stevens' youth: it is, with the important difference of a hundred years and of the denial of immortality, Wordsworthian in idea, in detail, in feeling, and in rhetoric. Passages comparable to the appositive enumeration of details of natural landscape associated with human feeling, as in:

Passions of rain, or moods in falling snow;
Grievings in loneliness, or unsubdued
Elations when the forest blooms. (67)

are scattered throughout Wordsworth's poetry, especially through the blank verse. I have already quoted a short passage, let me quote another:

What want we? have we not perpetual streams,
Warm woods, and sunny hills, and fresh green fields,
And mountains not less green, and flocks and herds,
And thickets full of songsters, and the voice

> Of lordly birds, an unexpected sound
> Heard now and then from morn to latest eve,
> Admonishing the man who walks below
> Of solitude and silence in the sky?

The movement of the verse is Stevens', the syntax, and the relation of syntax to the line-ends. The kind of detail is the same. And the idea, if one reads it out of the specific context of Wordsworth's system, is Stevens' idea; for the passage in isolation says, What does man need, what need he desire, more than a live appreciation of the detail of natural landscape, for the world beyond, the birds admonish us—or, Nature tells us—is a world of solitude and silence. This is not precisely what Wordsworth would have endorsed, but certainly what a young man who was drenched in Wordsworth could make of it. And as he read on in the poem—it is *The Recluse*—he would come to the rhetoric of one of his greatest stanzas and the theme of his greatest poem: he would read in Wordsworth:

> Paradise, and groves
> Elysian, Fortunate fields,—like those of old
> Sought on the Atlantic Main—why should they be
> A history only of departed things,
> Or a mere fiction of what never was?
> For the discerning intellect of Man,
> When wedded to this goodly universe
> In love and holy passion, shall find these
> The simple produce of the common day. [4]

and he would write:

> There is not any haunt of prophecy,
> Nor any old chimera of the grave. (68)

The central concern of Stevens' poetry, the concern that underlay Crispin's voyage and the poet's meditative argument with the woman in *Sunday Morning*, as well as most of the more or less curious divergencies of his career, is a concern to be at peace with his surroundings, with this world, and with himself.

He requires for this an experience of the togetherness of himself and Nature, an interpenetration of himself and his environment, along with some intuition of permanence in the experience of absoluteness, though this be illusory and transitory, something to satisfy the deeply engrained longings of his religious feeling. Now, there is an experience depicted from time to time in the romantic tradition—it is common in Wordsworth—and one that has perhaps occurred to each of us in his day, a human experience of absoluteness, when we and our surroundings are not merely related but one, when "joy is its own security." It is a fortuitous experience; it cannot be willed into being, or contrived at need. It is a transitory experience; it cannot be stayed in its going or found when it is gone. Yet though fortuitous and transitory, it has in its moment of being all the persuasion of permanence; it seems—and perhaps in its way it is— a fulfillment of the Absolute:

> It is and it
> Is not and, therefore, is. In the instant of speech,
> The breadth of an accelerando moves,
> Captives the being, widens—and was there.(440)

Stevens attempted to will it into being. He constructed a series of secular myths, like the one in *Sunday Morning*, that affirm the traditional religious feeling of the nobility and unity of experience, but the myths remain unconvincing and arbitrary, and conclude in grotesqueries that betray the poet's own lack of belief in his invention, as in *A Primitive Like an Orb*, in which he evokes:

> A giant, on the horizon, glistening,
>
> And in bright excellence adorned, crested
> With every prodigal, familiar fire,
> And unfamiliar escapades; whirroos
> And scintillant sizzlings such as children like,
> Vested in the serious folds of majesty. (442)

For, as he asks in an earlier poem:

But if
It is the absolute why must it be
This immemorial grandiose, why not
A cockle-shell, a trivial emblem great
With its final force, a thing invincible
In more than phrase? [5]

He has attempted to contrive it by a doctrine of metaphor and resemblances, which is precisely Wordsworth's doctrine of affinities. He has sought to present in a poem any set of objects and to affirm a resemblance and togetherness between them, but all the reader can see is the objects and the affirmation, as in *Three Academic Pieces*, where a pineapple on a table becomes:

1. The hut stands by itself beneath the palms.
2. Out of their bottle the green genii come.
3. A vine has climbed the other side of the wall. . . .

These casual exfoliations are
Of the tropic of resemblance. [6]

But there is a poem in *Transport to Summer*, one of the perfect poems, as far as my judgment goes, in his later work, that achieves and communicates this experience. It is a short poem in couplets entitled *The House Was Quiet and the World Was Calm*. There is no fiddle-dee-dee here. The setting is ordinary, not exotic. It is about a man reading alone, late at night. The phrasing is exact and almost unnoticeable. The style is bare, less rich than *Sunday Morning*, but with this advantage over that poem, that none of its effect is drawn from forbidden sources, from what is rejected. The meter is a loosened iambic pentameter, but loosened firmly and as a matter of course, almost as if it were speech becoming meter rather than meter violated. It has in fact the stability of a new metrical form attained out of the inveterate violation of the old. If is both modern and traditional:

The house was quiet and the world was calm.
The reader became the book; and summer night

Was like the conscious being of the book.
The house was quiet and the world was calm.

The words were spoken as if there was no book,
Except that the reader leaned above the page,

Wanted to lean, wanted much most to be
The scholar to whom his book is true, to whom

The summer night is like the perfection of thought.
The house was quiet because it had to be.

The quiet was part of the meaning, part of the mind:
The access of perfection to the page.

And the world was calm. The truth in a calm world,
In which there is no other meaning, itself

Is calm, itself is summer and night, itself
Is the reader leaning late and reading there. (358-59)

III

The Problem of Form

~~~~~~

I shall stipulate that there is a problem of form in the poetry of our day, but I shall treat *form*, for the moment, as an undefined term, and I shall not until later specify the nature of some of the problems. I am, at the outset, interested in pointing to certain generalities, and to certain broad, simpleminded, pervasive attitudes and dualisms, of which the problem in poetry is to a large extent only a localization. These will give in outline the larger context of the problem.

To begin with, it is apparent that in our society we have too many choices. When we ask the young what they are going to do when they grow up, we should not be surprised or amused that the answers are whimsical and bewildered. The young poet today has a large and not too discriminated anthology of forms to realize: only illiterate ignorance or having made the pilgrimage to Gambier or to Los Altos will reduce the scope of options to manageable size—and even then there will be a hankering for further options. On the other hand, the young poet 250 years ago had it easy in this respect. He wrote octosyllabic or decasyllabic couplets, and the rhetoric and areas of experience of each were fairly delimited. For recreation he wrote a song in quatrains, and once or twice in a lifetime a Pindaric ode.

We come now to those attitudes and dualisms that make the problem of particular forms peculiarly our problem. We are a democratic society and give a positive value to informality,

247

though some of the ladies still like to dress up. We will have nothing to do with the formal language and figured rhetoric of the *Arcadia*, for that is the language and rhetoric of a hierarchical and authoritarian society in which ceremony and formality were demanded by and accorded to the governing class. Instead, we praise, especially in poetry, what we call the accents of real speech—that is, of uncalculated and casual utterance, and sometimes even of vulgar impropriety. Now, if this attitude is a concomitant of the Democratic Revolution, the value we give to antiformality, to the deliberate violation of form and decorum, is a concomitant of its sibling, the Romantic Revolution. The measured, or formal, the contrived, the artificial are, we feel, insincere; they are perversions of the central value of our life, genuineness of feeling. "At least I was honest," we say with moral benediction as we leave wife and child for the sentimental empyrean.

If informality and antiformality are positive values, then the problem of form is how to get rid of it. But to get rid of it we must keep it; we must have something to get rid of. To do this we need a method, and we have found it in our dualisms of science and art, of intellectual and emotional, of regularity and irregularity, of norm and variation. We have been convinced, without inquiry or indeed adequate knowledge, that the regularities of ancient scientific law, of Newton's laws of motion, are regularities of matter, not of spirit, and hence are inimical to human significance. And so we embrace the broad, pervasive, simpleminded, and scarcely scrutinized proposition that regularity is meaningless and irregularity is meaningful—to the subversion of Form. For one needs only so much regularity as will validate irregularity. But Form is regularity.

So we come to definition. The customary distinctions of form and matter, or form and content, are in the discussion of writing at least only usable on the most rudimentary level. For it is apparent to any poet who sets out to write a sonnet that the form of the sonnet is the content, and its content the form. This is not a profundity, but the end of the discussion. I shall define form, then, without a contrasting term. It is that which remains the same when everything else is changed. This is not at all, I may say, a Platonic position. It is rather a mathematical and, as it should be, linguistic notion: $a^2 - b^2 = (a+b)(a-b)$ through all the potentialities of a and b. The form of the simple declarative sentence in English is in each of its realizations.

It follows, then, that form is discoverable by the act of substitution. It is what has alternative realizations. And the generality or particularity of a form lies in the range or restriction of alternatives. It follows, also, that the form precedes its realization, even in the first instance, and that unique form, or organic form in the sense of unique form, is a contradiction in terms. For it is the essence of form to be repetitive, and the repetitive is form. It follows, further, that there may be in a given utterance simultaneously a number of forms, so that the common literary question, What is the form of this work? can only be answered by a tacit disregard of all the forms other than the one we are momently concerned with.

It is time for illustration. Donne has a little epigram on Hero and Leander:

> Both robbed of air, we both lie in one ground,
> Both whom one fire had burnt, one water drowned.

What are the forms of this poem? First, both lines are decasyllabic in normal iambic pattern. Second, they rhyme. Third, it is phrased in units of four and six syllables in chiasmic order. Fourth, there are three "both's" and three "one's" in overlapping order. Fifth, the whole story of the lovers is apprehended, summarized, and enclosed in the simple scheme or form of the four elements. Finally, it is recognizably an epigram. Now Sir Philip Sidney, a few years earlier, in one of the *Arcadia* poems has the following lines:

> Man oft is plagued with air, is burnt with fire,
> In water drowned, in earth his burial is.[1]

The lines are decasyllabic in normal iambic pattern. The adjacent lines do not rhyme, for the form of the poem is terza rima, an alternative form. It is phrased in units of six and four in chiasmic order. The first line repeats "with," the second "in." Man, not Hero and Leander, is apprehended in the scheme of the four elements, and in both cases the order of the elements is not formally predetermined. Finally, it is not an epigram, but part of an eclogue.

I have illustrated in these examples and in this analysis something of the variety of what may be distinguished as form: literary kind, conceptual distinctions, and all the rhetorical figures of like ending, equal members, chiasmus, and the various modes of verbal repetition. That some of the forms of Sidney's lines are repeated in Donne's, with the substitution of Hero and Leander for man, shows they have alternate realizations, and that so many operate simultaneously shows, not that a literary work has form, but that it is a convergence of forms, and forms of disparate orders. It is the coincidence of forms that locks in the poem.

Indeed, it is the inherent coincidence of forms in poetry, in metrical writing, that gives it its place and its power—a claim for poetry perhaps more accurate and certainly more modest than is customary. For this is the poet's *Poetics*: prose is written in sentences; poetry in sentences and lines. It is encoded not only in grammar, but also simultaneously in meter, for meter is the principle or set of principles, whatever they may be, that determines the line. And as we perceive of each sentence that it is grammatical or not, so the repetitive perception that this line is metrical or that it is not, that it exemplifies the rules or that it does not, is the metrical experience. It is the ground bass of all poetry.

And here in naked reduction is the problem of form in the poetry of our day. It is before all a problem of meter. We have lost the repetitive harmony of the old tradition, and we have not established a new. We have written to vary or violate the old line, for regularity we feel is meaningless and irregularity meaningful. But a generation of poets, acting on the principles and practice of significant variation, have at last nothing to vary from. The last variation is regularity.

The Problem of Style

~~~~~~

This is a book intended to ask questions, though most of the authors represented have given answers. But the answers are sometimes different, and often enough to different questions. For different answers: Aristotle, as Cicero points out, does not distinguish between the two figures of thought, metaphor and metonymy (by which a word associated with the expected word is used instead of it); to Roman Jakobson they are polar opposites. And for different questions: anyone who has taken a course in English composition knows about clichés, how awful they are and how he should avoid them. He will be amused at Frank Sullivan's "Cliché Expert." Yet the late Milman Parry, as Denys Page explains, showed that the *Iliad* and the *Odyssey* are composed very largely of formulaic phrases, that is, of clichés, yet for twenty-five centuries they have been justly regarded as summits of the Western tradition. And Walter Raleigh quietly points out that clichés are part of our public civilization, not to be lightly set aside. And so an answer becomes a question.

The initial question is, Is there such a thing as style? To the believer in organic form there cannot be. He will hold, with Benedetto Croce, that how a thing is expressed is indistinguishable from the expression, that a difference in manner is a differ-

---

This essay was originally the Introduction for an anthology edited by J. V. Cunningham, *The Problem of Style*, a collection from thirty-four authors.

251

ence in meaning. And so anyone who wishes to consider style must premise that something may be said in different ways and that the ways may be compared. He may even hold, what is something else again, that manner is a potentiality looking for and limiting a meaning, that style precedes any realized expression. For him, then, style is an absolute.

But if there is such a thing as style, what sort of a thing is it? Is it a Platonic Idea, as Cicero holds, an "unsurpassable ideal which seldom appears throughout a whole work but does shine forth at some times and in some places, more frequently in some speakers, more rarely perhaps in others," and so, like the Sublime of Longinus, that striking distinction in speech that bowls one over? Or is it a neutral concept, so that everything has style, though one may contrast various styles and find this good and that bad? Or good and bad for this purpose or that, and so invoke the criterion of decorum, of appropriateness. It is curious that Aristotle, the interminable definer, does not define style, but proceeds at once to characterize the qualities of good style, and then of bad.

And if there is such a thing as style, what sorts of things have it? The notion was first applied to speech, and particularly to written composition. In recent centuries it has been applied to art and artifacts, and defined, as Meyer Schapiro defines it, as "the constant form . . . in the art of an individual or group." Other historians seek to divine in these constant forms the inner forms of a personality or civilization as represented in their art, artifacts, and sometimes literature. But is a linguistic composition an artifact in the sense that a Pueblo Indian pot is? Or only by metaphor? And if style is a form of form, is not the inner form of the cultural historian a contradiction, since form is external? But if it is a contradiction, is it a purposeful and useful one enabling the historian to intuit or posit some pervasive principle, some formal cause, that will account for and supplant in value the observable external forms? Some spirit of the age, perhaps, or some oscillating or developing principle of the human spirit or of human history.

Again, is style rather a process, as Robert Louis Stevenson and Raleigh suggest, so that the realization of the design transforms the design? And, if it is a process, can language be regarded as material the speaker shapes as the potter shapes clay? If so, then the result is form, of which style may be taken as a species; it is then both process and shape. But the material itself may have its own inherent style, as Stanley S. Newman shows of a language. Then the style of a particular work, if linguistic, will be only a sublanguage, a dialect so to speak, of the larger language, and describable by the methods of linguistics. And does it then have itself a history, as languages have?

Finally, does it have an opposite? And is that opposite thought or matter, or bad style, or lack of style? Such are the questions that definition raises.

After definition comes division: Are there kinds of style? Certainly actual speech and speech in writing differ, for writing abstracts part of a speech situation and records it in repeatable form. It is possible to abstract more than conventional writing does, as James Sledd shows in his phonetic transcriptions, and, indeed, some linguists are now attempting to record intonation and gesture by a system of signs. Nevertheless, an actual utterance is not repeatable except by disc or tape. But is not this, too, an abstraction? And if it is, is it an abstraction of the same order as writing?

Another distinction is between styles that are unnoticeable and those that are noticeable. The first, according to Aristotle, gives clarity, the second weight. And from this comes the Ciceronian distinction between low, middle, and high style, and all the ancient and traditional lore of the figures of speech. For language, at least as abstracted in writing, is noticeable in detail either in its components or in its arrangement. The diction may be unusual, let us say that sort characterized as poetic, or, though not in itself unusual, unusually used. The various describable ways in which words may be unusually used comprise the tropes or figures of thought of traditional rhetoric, of which metaphor and metonymy are most commonly discussed. Yet these discussions are not always conducted with proper tact. If you are thinking of bridge cables as "swinging places where birds alight," you may translate this by metonymy into "The agile precincts of the lark's return."[1] This is figurative since the retranslation requires inference. But if there is a certain slant of light, winter afternoons, that

> When it goes 'tis like the distance
> On the look of death.[2]

"look" is not figurative for "face" since it is precisely the look that is being referred to. So, too, the Ancient Mariner's "At one stride comes the dark" is not metaphorical, for we all are making great strides these days. But the famous Gorgianic figure, that vultures are "living graves," is metaphorical, whether a good or, as Aristotle and Longinus think, a bad metaphor.

What is noticeable in arrangement is either unusual syntax, such as inversion or asyndeton (omission of connectives), or obtrusive repetition. The lack of conjunctions in "I came, I saw, I conquered" is not usual in speech and hence is noticeable. The figures of repetition, though they occasionally occur by chance in casual utterance, have generally the appearance of design and attract attention: "We have nothing to fear but fear itself." Since repetition is form, it gives to an utterance a form other than and concurrent with grammatical form, and hence tends, as verse does, to make a saying memorable. Since opposites imply each other, antithesis is a form of repetition: "Good is what we can do with evil." Finally, repetition is rhythm,[3] for "it is number that limits all things," and to number is to count, to note repetition, either exact or approximate. And since numerical recurrence can be anticipated, its completion gives finality, as in metrical lines which consist of speech-segments of equal length.

The transfer from verse to prose of the figures of arrangement marks the beginning of the history of style in the Western tradition as a conscious subject of discussion, as something to be taught and to be learned. The event can be plausibly dated 427 B.C., if truth may be tied to particular occasions. "This year the Leontines," writes an ancient annalist, "dispatched ambassadors to Athens":

> The leader of the embassy was Gorgias the rhetorician, who in eloquence far surpassed all his contemporaries. He was the first man to devise rules of rhetoric and so far excelled all other men in the instruction offered by the sophists that he received from his pupils a fee

of one hundred minas. Now when Gorgias had arrived in Athens and been introduced to the people in assembly, he discoursed to them upon the subject of the alliance, and by the novelty of his speech he filled the Athenians, who are by nature clever and fond of dialectic, with wonder. For he was the first to use the rather unusual and carefully devised structures of speech, such as antithesis, sentences with equal members or balanced clauses or similar endings, and the like, all of which at that time was enthusiastically received because the device was exotic, but is now looked upon as laboured and to be ridiculed when employed too frequently and tediously.[4]

The effect of such speech, by all the testimony of Antiquity, and indeed of the Middle Ages and Renaissance, is astonishment, open-mouthed wonder at the gift of gab. But if it fails it seems frigid, bombastic, artificial. It is both offensive and impersuasive. And so the problem arises of hedging against failure, employing the art that conceals art, or alternatively, of developing an unrhetorical plain style whose "careful negligence" may yet permit distinction.

Such are some of the themes of *The Problem of Style* and their attendant questions. You may write the answers in the margin.

How Shall the Poem be Written?

How shall the poem be written? I answer, In metrical language. In most periods of English literature this was a sufficient answer. One could explain meter but need not. It was learned as one learns his language, and indeed it was a language; it was, in a sense I shall later define, a dialect. But it is not now a sufficient answer. For metrical theory, description, and practice are a shambles.

The principal causes of this in metrical practice are the wide diversity of metrical forms and systems, and, in particular, the prevalence of what I shall call parasitic meter, the characteristic meter of our time. In theory and description it is partly a consequence of phonetic ignorance, even in high places—assonance is illustrated by "In Xanadu did Kubla Khan / A stately . . . "—conjoined with that mystique of sensitivity that was encouraged by the New Criticism. We read: "The richness and variety of sounds and rhythms heard in reading a poem of the highest order . . . is and always will remain indescribable." The sounds and rhythms of poems good and bad, as well as of lectures and conversation, are no more and no less than the sounds and rhythms of English, or of one of the varieties of English, and these are describable.

256

But it is also a consequence of that same mystique achieving insights in commentary by the application of the doctrine of norm and variation. One posits a metrical norm, and then searches for the significance of this and that deviation. For example:

> Rhythm . . . can . . . express the most delicate feelings and moods. No words can adequately paraphrase the effect of hopeless, absolute despair conveyed by the final line of the stanzas of Keats' *La Belle Dame Sans Merci:*
>
>> O what can ail thee, Knight-at-arms,
>>   Alone and palely loitering?
>> The sedge has withered from the lake,
>>   And no birds sing!
>
> The final line is half the length of the preceding three. We have been prepared to find the final line rhythmically symmetrical with the others. Compelled by the rhythmic vacancy, our defeated expectation produces a desolation of spirit no other poetic device could produce.

Now, in the first place, if you are reading that in print, you can see the line is shorter; but even heard without text the rhyme tells you it is over. There is no vacancy, no defeated expectation to express what the poem literally says: "And no birds sing!" And what of the desolation of:

> A man is swimming in the lake
>   With no clothes on.

which has an identical stress contour.

Another remarks about Chaucer's "Wondring upon this word, quaking for drede": "the double inversion, at the start of the line and again after the caesura, gives the two participial verbs a special quiver." The quiver, of course, is begotten by the literal sense, "quaking for dread." Again, on Yeats' "Speech after long silence, it is right," we are instructed: "the fact that the reader must hurry over the two unaccented syllables of *after* before he can rest on the accent of *long* makes the emphasis on *long* greater than it would otherwise be; and this heavy emphasis on *long* fortifies the meaning of the word." It is a long *long*. But you don't hurry over anything or rest on anything; you speak English:

> Beer after sweet sherry, it is wrong.

Finally, "The heavy pause after *silence* . . . is dramatically right." A pause is silence.

Meter on this view has no inherent rights, but in its betrayals and its phonetic allegories is significant.

Nevertheless, it is clear from what is being published as poetry, approved of and commented on, that there is not only uncertainty with respect to the old tradition but also a widely felt need for some system of meter other than the traditional, and that none has been agreed on and established. There seem to be two conditions: the new meter will avoid both structural rhyme and the characteristic stress patterns of the old. The motive is rebellion, now become a habit, which is sufficient to destroy but not to establish.

This is the inconclusive issue of that revolution in the arts, poetry among the rest, which began in the first decade of this century, culminated in the twenties, and achieved almost universal cultural acceptance in the forties. I myself came into it in the late twenties, the latest possible moment to be touched by the original impulse. Soon afterward—let us date it by Eliot's tenure of the Charles Eliot Norton professorship at Harvard in 1933-34—what had been the advance guard had become practically the whole army. Everyone felt special in belonging to a club to which everyone belonged.

There is, as you know, a natural progression in time in such matters, from personal impulse to communication to and within a group, conversion of outsiders, institutionalization of the coterie spirit, and finally the establishment of sacred texts, *The Waste Land* and *Ulysses*, and orthodox commentary, Brooks and Warren, and the fixed formulas of The Creed whose repetition aids identification with the institution, but identification no longer with a cohesive group in ferment. Such is the natural history of revolution. In the beginning the slogans, the aims, do not especially matter; what is important is the revolutionary spirit, the destruction of the past. The revolutionaries are united in destruction, however different their explicit goals. In the end only the slogans matter, and the revolutionary stance. But the life has gone out of it. And so we ask, In the debris of revolution how shall the poem be written?

What are our metrical languages? Of the untraditional there is that heterogeneity of procedures, often on no discernible principles, that we call free verse, from the scriptural line of Whitman to the letters falling down the page in organic form as they spell "rain." Much of this is based on writing, on print. The lineation is determined by stipulation and whimsy, by the placing on the page, with no phonetic principle unless in reading and reciting it one gives a phonetic signal at the arbitrary line-ends. But such signals, unless they coincide with idiomatic ones, are affected pronunciation.

Early free verse, however, and much still written, has a discernible principle. I call it grammatical meter: a line may end at any terminal juncture, any completed grammatical unit. If the line is short, as in much Imagistic verse, the sentence is, in effect, diagrammed; one might call it parsing meter. Some charming things were done in it; for example, Stevens' *Disillusionment of Ten O'Clock:*

> The houses are haunted
> By white night-gowns.
> None are green,
> Or purple with green rings,
> Or green with yellow rings,
> Or yellow with blue rings.
> None of them are strange,
> With socks of lace
> And beaded ceintures.
> People are not going
> To dream of baboons and periwinkles.
> Only, here and there, an old sailor,
> Drunk and asleep in his boots,
> Catches tigers
> In red weather.

There was a moment in history for this sort of thing, and some nice things are still done in it, notations that might have been journal entries, but it is not properly a meter, which requires, as I shall later maintain, an independent and concurrent metrical principle. It is rather a form of punctuation that may display or distort by emphases the grammatical principle.

Some early free verse was intended to be an accentual meter, determined only by count of stress. But the problem with accentual meters in modern English is to determine which syllables are prosodically accented. As you know, there is one, and only one, primary stress in each phrase, and the others have varying degrees of stress determined partly by the grammatical function and partly by the internal stress contour of the word. In the old Germanic tradition prosodic stresses were pointed by structural alliteration:

In a somer seson   when softe was the sunne

supported by the repetitiveness of formulas, and limited by the two and two phrasing of the lines. But we have no viable formulas, would be appalled by consistent structural alliteration, and would feel hemmed in by two and two phrasing. Yet without such support the meter remains wavering and ambiguous. It will not do.

There is more to be said for a syllabic meter, determined by count of syllables only. It is, like the accentual, an old tradition in English; it accounts for the decasyllabic line of Wyatt and Donne:

So, if I dream I have you, I have you.[1]

and sometimes of Sidney:

If you hear that they seem my heart to move[2]

"observing only number (with some regard to the accent)," as Sidney himself describes it. In the modern tradition it has these rules: the syllabification is that of ordinary educated speech, not of careful enunciation, and elision is optional. Final unaccented syllables count. And there is a negative principle, testifying to the power of traditional meter, that no succession of lines should establish the expectation of a repetitive stress pattern. Consequently, verses of seven or of nine syllables are best. It is an interesting, though probably limited, meter. It can handle the ordinariness of experience, as in *Monday Morning*:

> The flattery has been infrequent
> And somewhat grudging. There is junk mail
> And no letter. The weather cloudy
> With more snow. Fortuitous meeting,
> The rustle of flirtation, the look—
> Self-esteem sustained by any excuse,
> By any misconstruction? No. No.
> It is now a January world,
> An after-Christmas waiting. For what?
> Not for this snow, this silence. There is
> No resonance in the universe.
> I must buy something extra today
> And clutter up my house and my life.[3]

I should like now to seem to digress. Literary judgments, in general, are hand-me-downs. Or they are acts of belonging. In a time in which metrical experiment is thought to be in itself a good, the Renaissance experiment in classical prosody is universally condemned, even by those ignorant of classical prosody. Yet it was more rationally conducted, and was, perhaps, no greater a failure, than the metrical experiments of this century. The poetry of prestige at that time was Classical Latin, and only Latin prosody had been adequately described. Latin poetry had been written, was still being written, both in rhymed accentual-syllabic and in classical quantitative meters. Why not English? Furthermore, Latin was then pronounced with the sounds of English. The classical tunes were learned in childhood, and in one's native phonemic system. The problem would seem to be simple: to substitute English words and syntax for Latin. It had to be tried; it didn't work. It did not work primarily, I should think, because one does not hear in English length by position, which is essential to the classical system; it is not a perception relevant to our language habits. And because at the same time, in the 1580s and 1590s, there appeared a poetry in the native tradition to challenge "the comparison / Of all that insolent Greece or haughty Rome / Sent forth, or since did from their ashes come." And because the native tradition developed a rhymeless measure, blank verse, and an internal structuring of the line with alternative varieties of modulation, analogous to the potentialities of a quantitive prosody. So it wasn't needed.

In like fashion the current experimental procedures may not really be needed. For why have generations of poets set out to destroy the iambic pentameter and its predecessor, the iambic octosyllable? Partly because it was the fashion, but also because traditional meter carried with it the rhetoric, subjects, attitudes, and values the revolution was directed against, the linguistic and social notions of correctness. But that rhetoric, those subjects, and those values have been lost.

I turn now to traditional and its bastard issue, parasitic meter. On the traditional I shall make only a few points; they are the points on which I have something to say.

First, it is a meter by law. One rejects the textbook distinction between the metrical norm and the rhythm of a line, defined as the actual stress-contour, as a fiction, and a harmful fiction. Meter is perceived in the actual stress-contour, or the line is perceived as unmetrical, or the perceiver doesn't perceive meter at all. Donne's decasyllabic line:

So, if I dream I have you, I have you.

is by the laws of traditional meter unmetrical; that is what Jonson was referring to when he said "Donne should be hanged for not keeping of the accent."

Second. Traditional meter consists in the repetition of one or more of the figures of diction, the *schemata verborum* of ancient rhetoric: homoioteleuton, or rhyme, like ending; isocolon, or equality, usually syllabic equality, of units; cursus, the repetition of one of a group of syllabic patterns, long and short, or stressed and unstressed. Nor is this surprising, for rhetoric, as Aristotle says, borrowed the figures from poetry. Since it is repetitive it may be thought monotonous; since it is rhetorical it may be thought artificial. To these charges we shall return in a moment.

Third. Of these the dominant principle in English poetry since the Norman Conquest has been rhyme. In the first edition of *The Oxford Book of English Verse* (1900), there are 883 selections; 16 are unrhymed, or minimally rhymed. Furthermore, rhyme is a sufficient principle, with the ancillary principle that the rhyming syllables be not so hidden or remote that the rhyme is unperceived:

> I might as well give you my opinion of these two
>   sorts of sin as long as, in a way, against
>   each other we are pitting them,
> And that is, don't bother your head about sins
>   of commission because, however sinful, they
>   must at least be fun or else you wouldn't be
>   committing them.

It determines the line. It tells you where the line ends. It does not determine the length and internal modulation of the line.

Off-rhyme, if used systematically as in some of Wilfred Owen, is a form of rhyme, and could be exploited much more than it has been, as in the following quatrain where *demand* answers *mend*, and *face fuss*:

> Prue loved her man: to clean, to mend,
> To have a child for his sake, fuss
> Over him, and on demand
> Sleep with him with averted face.[4]

But in current practice off-rhyme is usually parasitic on the tradition of rhymed verse; it is an act of naughtiness, answering the plea of the girl in the old song, "Oh, violate me in the vilest way you know."

Fourth. The basic English measure is the iambic octosyllable. Instead of "The curfew tolls the knell of parting day," read:

The curfew tolls the knell of day,

The herd wind slowly o'er the lea,
The ploughman homeward plods his way,
And leaves the world to night and me.

And so on through the poem.

It follows that if you wish to say something in verse that when read aloud to an audience will be immediately apprehended and responded to as an utterance, write it in octosyllabic couplets:

An Oedipean Mom and Dad
Made Junior Freud feel pretty bad,
And when they died he was so vexed
He never after hetrosexed.[5]

And if you are looking for novelty within the scope of standard meter, there are possibilities in octosyllabic blank verse, of which there are almost no instances in English:

The night is still. The unfailing surf
In passion and subsidence moves
As at a distance. The glass walls,
And redwood, are my utmost being.
And is there there in the last shadow,
There in the final privacies
Of unaccosted grace,—is there,
Gracing the tedium to death,
An intimation? Something much
Like love, like loneliness adrowse
In states more primitive than peace,.
In the warm wonder of winter sun.[6]

Fifth. Modes of recitation sometimes affect meter, for a mode of recitation is a dialect. I mean by a dialect a sublanguage, a system of enunciation, of grammar, and, in metrical speech, of lineation, as also of idiom and vocabulary, used by a particular group in specified social situations. Of the common modes associated with the recitation of poetry two are distinctly dialects.

The first is the scanning in unison which we learned in grade school:

> *This* is the *for*est prim*ev*al, the *mur*muring *pines*
> and the *hem*locks.

Or:

> Of *man's* first *disob*ed*ience and* the *fruit*

This is the experiential basis for what I shall call the fiction of a metrical norm. And notice, the whole phonetic structure of scanning aloud is unEnglish. If you spoke that way in any other situation you would probably not be understood, and certainly would be regarded as very odd. The second is the children's chant:

> Jóhnny ís a stínkér.

The chant has a definite tune, and the form imposes accents on syllables that would be unaccented in ordinary speech, on "is" and "ker." The tune demands its four heavy beats, its Germanic heritage. Contrast the mnemonic rhyme:

> Thirty days hath September,
> April, June, and November

with its accents on "hath" and "and," with "The payments will be due in September, April, June, and November."

The other modes I shall enumerate are distinct from one another but all clearly forms of ordinary English. There is the elocutionary and expressive, and its cousin the rhetorical and declamatory; there is the voice of the public lecture, and the slowed-down enunciation of reading aloud. There is also semi-chant, favored by some poets, which blurs the distinction between grades of more than minimal accent, and in this respect is like the scanning mode. There is, finally, on the one hand, considered conversation, and, on the other, humdrum casual utterance. This latter is often taken to be the exemplar of real speech, though most of it is ritual, the noises of sociability. Furthermore, casual utterance in some places reduces the number of syllables, and at times gives minimal instead of tertiary, secondary instead of primary accent, and so this mode of recitation has metrical consequences.

The descriptive problems raised by different modes of recitation can be avoided by regarding a meter, not as a schematic diagram of scansions, but as a collection of syllabic-syntactic types; any one fulfills the law. Any line of the type, "A rosy garland and a weary head," is an iambic pentameter; for example, "The raving beauty or the common scold." And, indeed, this is the way we perceive meter when we read without hesitation or analysis, that is, poetically. We do not hear diagrams.

I turn now to the two charges against traditional meter: that it is monotonous and artificial. Monotonous, of course, is a value judgment. But is monotony necessarily monotonous? Is it monotonous to have coffee every morning, or is it necessary? Should other activities be substituted for the essential elements in the sexual act to relieve the boredom of how often a week?

However, there is a legitimate objection to standard meter that is somewhat akin to this, and one that is not usually explicitly stated. It is that the line is overdetermined, particularly when rhymed. For syllable count, stress pattern, rhyme, each would sufficiently determine the line. And if the line consists, as very often it does, of complete grammatical units, that would reinforce the determination. But it may be urged on the contrary that rigor in poetry as in science is an instrument of discovery.

Again, traditional meter is felt to be artificial, which, of course, is why it is used, and to exclude the natural rhythms of real speech. It is said again and again, as if it were true, that people do not talk in iambic pentameters. But they do; not always, but often enough. Some months ago I sat in the sun and wrote down these lines at random. They are segments of real speech:

> I'll have the special and a glass of milk.
> The order will be ready when you come.
> We ought to be in Cleveland in an hour.

I haven't anything to say to you.
Goddamn it, what in hell is going on?
I'll think it over and I'll let you know.
Oh, go to hell! Who do you think you are?
She does her exercises every day.
How often shall I see you in a lifetime?

But perhaps more often people talk in the octosyllabic line, in iambic tetrameters:

I love her and I always will.
Young poets are a dime a dozen.
I'll be there anytime you say.
He doesn't love me anymore.
For Christ's sake, will you stop that noise?
I didn't ask you what you thought.
I've had a headache for two days.
Darling, I'd rather not tonight.
What's playing at the Paramount?
I put five dollars on the nose.
Some people do, some people don't.
Is there a doctor in the house?
We live in Massachusetts now.
Who do you think you are? The Pope?

If the ear for iambic pentameter and tetrameter has not been completely destroyed in our society, you will have heard each of these lines as simultaneously a completed grammatical segment and one of the various types of recognizable iambic lines. For as prose is written in sentences, without significant lineation, so poetry is written in sentences and lines. It is encoded not only in grammar, but also at the same time in meter, for meter is the principle or set of principles, whatever they may be, that determines the line. Consequently, grammar and prosody are separate and concurrent principles of the same order. And as we perceive of each sentence, without stopping to analyse it, that it is grammatical or not, so the repetitive perception that this line is metrical or that it is not, that it exemplifies the rules of its meter or that it does not, is the metrical experience.

It follows that metrical analysis is irrelevant to poetry; metrical perception is of the essence. You do not have to explain the iambic pentameter; you do have to recognize it.

It follows, also, that the notion of norm and variation is not relevant to traditional meter. There are alternative patterns, each of which satisfies the metrical requirements, some more common, some less. You may begin "To be or not" or "Whether 'tis nobler"; the choice is metrically indifferent. An absolutely consistent preference of one to the other would constitute another meter. Furthermore, the theoretical iambic norm of modern prosodists, described as an alternation of minimal and maximal stresses, is a very uncommon pattern. Since there is only one maximal stress to a phrase, the line must be phrased in two-syllable units, "The man, the maid, the bed, the child," or "I came, I saw, I won." The monotony of the theoretical norm is grammatical.

But norm and variation is relevant to, is, in fact, the generating principle of parasitic meter. The term is descriptive and pejorative. Such meter presupposes a meter by law which it uses, alludes to, traduces, returns to. To perceive it one must have firmly in mind the prior tradition from which it departs and to which it returns. The *locus classicus* is Eliot's "the most interesting verse which has yet been written in our language has been done by taking a very simple form, like the iambic pentameter, and constantly withdrawing from it, or taking no form at all, and constantly approximating to a very simple one. It is this contrast between fixity and flux, this unperceived evasion of monotony, which is the very life of verse."

Meter may be parasitic in various ways. One finds a fairly simple form of it, supported by rhyme, in *Lycidas* and *Dover Beach*: the lines are either iambic pentameter or fragments, and usually conventional half-lines, of iambic pentameter. In general, the lines of a poem in parasitic meter will be partly in standard meter, at times parts of what would be a standard line, or they are felt to be equivalent in some aspect of sound or feeling to a standard line, or they exhibit some marked variation of a standard line, or some other principle of meter is used intermittently and supported and given authority by the presence and recurrence of standard lines. If it seems from this account that meter can be parasitic in many and devious ways, this is true, for the only consistent principle is that it depart from and return to a norm. It is the nature of parasitism that it may feed in different ways, that it may be irresponsible since it always has the responsible thing it feeds on to sustain it and keep it alive.

I shall conclude with some illustrations. Yeats in an eight-line poem produces three deviants of the iambic pentameter line by the transformation of a legitimate syllabic-syntactic pattern:

> Speech after long silence; it is right,
> All other lovers being estranged or dead,
> Unfriendly lamplight hid under its shade,
> The curtains drawn upon unfriendly night,
> That we descant and yet again descant
> Upon the supreme theme of Art and Song;
> Bodily decrepitude is wisdom; young
> We loved each other and were ignorant.

"Speech after lengthy silence" is transformed to "long silence" by substituting a monosyllabic for a disyllabic adjective; similarly "hidden by its shade" is transformed to "hid under its shade," and "the highest theme" to "the supreme theme."

Again, in many of Tate's poems most of the lines are fugitives from the iambic pentameter. It is, as he says, "a little like the man who either avoids or steps upon all the cracks in the sidewalk." In *The Wolves* he stepped upon five cracks out of twenty-seven.

In Stevens' *Hibiscus on the Sleeping Shores* nine of the fifteen lines are iambic pentameter, and the presence and recurrence of these supports the whole:

> I say now, Fernando, that on that day
> The mind roamed as a moth roams,
> Among the blooms beyond the open sand;
>
> And that whatever noise the motion of the waves
> Made on the sea-weeds and the covered stones
> Disturbed not even the most idle ear.

Then it was that that monstered moth
Which had lain folded against the blue
And the colored purple of the lazy sea,

And which had drowsed along the bony shores,
Shut to the blather that the water made,
Rose up besprent and sought the flaming red

Dabbled with yellow pollen—red as red
As the flag above the old cafe—
And roamed there all the stupid afternoon.

But it was Eliot, perhaps, who most exploited parasitic meter. In *The Love Song of J. Alfred Prufrock* and *Portrait of a Lady* rhyme is the dominant principle: about five-sixths of the lines in each. A secondary principle is iambic pentameter, its observance and avoidance: about two-fifths of the lines observe, the rest avoid in different ways. And *Prufrock*, especially, is supported by a good deal of rhetorical repetition, 27 out of 131 lines: "In the room the women come and go," "And would it have been worth it, after all?" Now *Prufrock* may be parasitic partly by accident of composition. The poem would seem to be in inception an anthology of relevant passages from the poet's notebook—fragments written now in this meter, now in that, but often enough in pentameter—rather than a planned departure from and return to a norm. But within particular passages there is sometimes a planned departure. The *Portrait*, on the other hand, seems planned.

But the nature of parasitic meter can be more clearly seen in what is perhaps the best passage in Eliot's *Gerontion*:

After such knowledge, what forgiveness? Think now
History has many cunning passages, contrived corridors
And issues, deceives with whispering ambitions,
Guides us by vanities. Think now
She gives when our attention is distracted
And what she gives, gives with such supple confusions
That the giving famishes the craving. Gives too late
What's not believed in, or if still believed,

In memory only, reconsidered passion. Gives too soon
Into weak hands, what's thought can be dispensed with
Till the refusal propagates a fear. Think
Neither fear nor courage saves us.

Let us go through some of this, line by line. "After such knowledge, what forgiveness? Think now" is a normal iambic pentameter with feminine ending. It has a slightly odd movement, but
that has nothing to do with the metrical principle. The next line
consists of a complete clause forming a normal iambic pentameter, but with the appositive phrase "contrived corridors" tacked
on extra. "And issues, deceives with whispering ambitions" has
an unusual variation in the second foot. "Guides us by vanities.
Think now" contains an easily recognized part of a normal line,
with the repetition of "Think now" added. We return in the next
line and the line following to blank verse, with an unusual variation in the last foot of the latter. "That the giving famishes the
craving. Gives too late"; this will not fit a standard pattern. The
complete clause, however, could be taken as a headless pentameter, and the added phrase is supported by the repetition of
"gives." The next line returns to normal. Finally, "In memory
only, reconsidered passion. Gives too soon" is a standard line
with the repetitive "Gives too soon" added. And so on.

An inductive examination of these poems, with no antecedent knowledge of English metrical tradition, would yield no
metrical principle. This would not be true of Chaucer, Shakespeare, Milton, Wordsworth, or, in Antiquity, of Homer or Vergil.

We have lost the repetitive harmony of the old tradition,
and we have not established a new. We have written to vary or
violate the old line, for regularity we feel is meaningless and irregularity meaningful. But several generations of poets, acting
on the principles and practice of significant variation, have at
last nothing to vary from. The last variation is regularity.[7]

Graduate Training in English

A university is an institution of learning. The undergraduate acquires learning; the faculty contribute to learning. The graduate student is in transition from acquiring to contributing.

To contribute to learning one must know something, and to know something means there is much one does not know. One specializes because one must, and because it is human: curiosity aggrandizes its object. One becomes a professional.

If the university is regarded as a way of life, the life of an institutionalized leisure class pursuing the semispiritual exercises of culture, then matters are different. For this is the life of the amateur.

Such, in brief, is the conflict between the creative soul in the university and the pedant. I am a pedant. Some of the contributors to this symposium are, no doubt, creative souls: for them, their servants will do their scholarship for them.

If I read books I should know how books are made and where to find them. If I read Shakespeare I should know it may not be Shakespeare. We call the one bibliography, the other textual criticism. If I read a language I should know the language, whether it be of Tudor London or contemporary Western American. We call this philology. If what I read has any real

This piece was originally part of "A Symposium: Graduate Training in the Humanities," a special section, by nine contributors, of a *Carleton Miscellany* issue.

reference I should know something of the referent. We call this history. If the referent is, in part, as it is in *Lycidas*, prior literature, I should know that. We call this literary history. These are the disciplines of graduate study, together with the literary disciplines of undergraduate study.

It is true, many graduate instructors are dull and pedantic. And many graduate students in the humanities are dull and not even pedantic. They are fugitives from the worlds of business and the exact sciences, who come to graduate school to raskolnikov.

IV

Ideal Fiction

The Clerk's Tale

~~~~~~

My subject is Ideal Fiction, my instance *The Clerk's Tale*. The problems of *The Clerk's Tale* are in part problems of the subject matter, the relationship of the sexes in marriage, and these were problems to Chaucer and his audience as they are to us. But they are also in part problems of literary kind, for those exemplified in *The Clerk's Tale* are now in disfavor. In rejecting the kind we impute the fault to the instance.

I shall begin with Horace. It is difficult to make material in the public domain one's own. And yet it is better to rehandle the Trojan War in five acts than to produce something novel and so far unsaid. Hence, when Chaucer undertook to render Petrarch's prose tale in English rhyme royal, he did not, on the one hand, do it routinely or prepare a word-for-word crib, nor, on the other, in rivalry with Petrarch leap into difficulties by ignoring his own limitations and the limitations of the particular literary kind, the *lex operis*.[1] And there is our difficulty. For we do not recognize, and would not admit as valid if we did, that literary kind. What is it? and what is its law?

I shall, to begin with, premise that any work is a simultaneity of literary kinds, and shall in this instance deal with three. First, *The Clerk's Tale* is one of those fictions, common until fiction changed its nature in the nineteenth century, con-

ducted by a Manipulator, in this case an authoritarian monarch, like the Duke in *Measure for Measure*, who has the power
to manipulate. Another common form, of course, is the Practical
Joker, like Claudio and his associates in *Much Ado About Nothing*
who engineer the extreme case: a couple who hate each other
fall in love with each other. Officially, at least aesthetically, we
are repelled by this, or explain it away as with Beatrice and
Benedick, partly out of democratic and romantic feeling, and
partly out of the conviction that contrivance is inimical to art.
Yet art is contrivance, and the manipulator, God knows, is a
common figure in what we call real life. We need not like him,
but need not dislike the story because of him.

     This brings us to the second, the principal form. Current
theory permits us only two major ones, the fiction of ordinariness
and probability, or fairy tale, fantasy, allegory, the terms by
which we apologize for deviation from real life, as if real life
itself were not a fiction. We read in Forster: "The other novel-
ists say 'Here is something that could occur in your lives,' the
fantasist says 'Here is something that could not occur.' " But
The Clerk's Tale is in between; it is possible; it could occur, but
not in your lives. And so we watch and do not identify. The story
is distanced. It is Ideal Fiction.

     The essence of Ideal Fiction is that it presents the extreme
case, but yet a case. It is something that once happened to people
with such names as we have, living in a nameable place. As extreme, however, it is in the literary sense improbable, improbable by definition: "Yet sometimes it shall fall on a day / That
falls not afterward within a thousand years."[2] And this provokes two observations. First, the improbable is interesting.
Your wife says, "God, another day," and you turn off your hearing aid. She says, "The damnedest thing happened today, I never
would have believed it," and you are eager attention. Secondly,
the improbable is also probable.[3] Several years ago I hailed a
cab at 58th and Park Avenue, said "Grand Central Station,"
and the cabbie said, "How do you get there, buddy?"

     But the Fiction of the Extreme Case, though consonant with
medieval habits of thought and feeling, is not peculiarly medieval. It is also modern, though repugnant to our official ideas.
It is true we are not so partial to notable images of virtues and

vices, partly because we are routinely in revolt against what we take to be Sunday School morality, against the idea of extreme good and extreme evil. We will not accept More's or Shakespeare's Richard III, though we constructed such a character ourselves in Hitler and in Stalin. But the extreme case in our society deals rather with the little things and little people, with comedians, professors, cowboys, and not with the big things, death and supposed death, chiefs of state, their spouses and heirs. It flourishes particularly in oral literature; it is the point of many a joke.

There is the extreme case of W. C. Fields' "Who put water in my water?" as also the current story of the professor who taped his lectures, which were heard by fifty lonely tape recorders on fifty chairs. Or there is that classic of the two homosexuals on a street corner. A blonde walks by, wind blowing against her dress, and one says to the other, "Sometimes makes you wish you were a lesbian, doesn't it?" Or even more classic, the poker player hand to end the poker game in Eugene Manlove Rhodes' *The Trusty Knaves*. The slickers are setting the tenderfoot up for the kill, so our cowboy heroes sit in. In the climactic hand one cowboy calls the other, who lays down Ace, King, Queen, Jack, and ten of spades. He then lays down Ace, King, Queen, Jack, and ten of spades. "Well, well! It's a tie. We'll have to divide the pot."

What is notable in each case is the invention. There is nothing so simple as exaggeration: that yields a different sort of story, The Tall Tale or The Boast. Rather, the invention involves opposites, or what are taken to be opposites, whisky and water, man and machine. Or it finds that statement or that choice to which nothing but the point involved is relevant. So in Sidney's episode of Argalus and Parthenia, the hopeless and constant lover, offered an exact replica of his love—indeed it is Parthenia herself, unidentified—courteously declines. "It is only happiness I refuse, since of the only happiness I could and can desire I am refused." He is in love with her identity. Invention has found the extreme case, and found it with a special flourish; the thing clicks, and one thinks, What else? There is an apt ingenuity, a striking propriety. This, too, is a quality now officially in disfavor; it falls under suspicion of contrivance. Yet, here again, in nonaesthetic matters we still sometimes appreciate the apt invention. There is a useful allowance horse running at Aqueduct named Brooklyn Bridge. He is by Swaps out of Conniver. What else?

The ideality of invention in *The Clerk's Tale* is a matter of detail, of the premise, and of the conduct of the story. Of detail: "She was not idle until she slept," for Nature requires that idleness. Of premise: Walter is solicited by his subjects to marry, to provide for the succession. To this the wealth and rank of the mother-to-be is irrelevant, and so excluded in the choice, excluded by their opposites: "the poorest of the poor, the lowliest of the low." The invention is controlled by the form, by the *lex operis*. In the larger conduct of the story there is appropriateness in the sequence. The first trial is the supposed death of the daughter, the second of the heir apparent, the third the rejection of the marriage itself, and in the joyful catastrophe the supposed bride is the restored daughter. Who else? In one scene of discovery all is reversed. And the trials themselves are not the incidentals but the essentials of marriage, children and the marriage itself. A modern Walter would leave faucets dripping.

In one scene of discovery. Here we have the third of our literary kinds, for *The Clerk's Tale* is both the *historia*, the story, of rhetorical tradition, "an account of exploits actually performed, but removed in time from the recollection of our age," and a narrative based on persons, displaying "particular traits of character, such as austerity and gentleness," or patience in marriage, and showing "the vicissitudes of life, reversal of fortune, unexpected disaster, sudden joy, and a happy outcome."[4] In such narrative character is narrowed to relevance, and the elements of action are extremes, high and low, joy and disaster, and they are not gradual but sudden. They invite the extreme case.

It follows, then, that in Ideal Fiction the characters are flat. But it is a fiction of our fiction that people are really round. The truth is we are not usually real life characters in real life. We are flat, and so are those we know. We are only round occasionally to others in a sympathetic moment, to ourselves in introspection, and now and again as a demand on others in the grim game of interpersonal relations: "I want to be treated as a person." We usually see others as truck drivers or neighbors, bore or blonde. And we are flat to ourselves when working efficiently, when we are most ourselves. When I write a poem I am a poet; I am narrowed to relevance.

Nor was the extreme case in Chaucer's world as extreme as one might think. In that Christianity which has been almost liquidated in my lifetime, each of us is an extreme case, destined for Heaven or for Hell. There is no individualistic Limbo in which we as real characters can hide. We are flat, flatly saved, or flatly damned. The ultimate world is ideal, and the ultimate our ultimate concern.

The Renaissance in England

In dealing with the past, as in dealing with our own autobiography, we parcel it out in periods. And these need not be merely arbitrary. What is arbitrary is that we mark off a period in light of some aspect of the times that interests us; in light of other aspects we would mark it off differently. For some, at least, of the authors in this book there was such a thing as the Renaissance in England. It was an event in the history of literature and of learning.

The time is the hundred and some years after Columbus' discovery of America, from the youth of Thomas More to the publication of Shakespeare's collected plays in 1623. It is the time of the diffusion of printing, the exploitation of gunpowder, the exploration of the New World. It is the time of the Reformation and of an increasing nationalism in Western Europe: Christianity became regional, and theology an instrument of international affairs.

The place is England, a small northern country on the edge of the great world of that time, and with about the same secondary importance in the international scene of its day as Great Britain has in the larger scene of today. But it was not, at the start, Great Britain. Scotland until 1603 was an independent king-

---

This essay was originally the Introduction for an anthology edited by J. V. Cunningham, *The Renaissance in England,* a collection of ninety-four selections from forty-some authors or sources.

dom and after 1603 still had an independent government under a common monarch. Moreover, in the preceding century it was often hostile and for the most part allied with France: Mary, Queen of Scots, for example, was for a time Queen of France. Nor was England itself a country unified and homogeneous. The North was remote, unruly border country, poor, feudal, and feuding. It was the world of the border ballads, of the Percys and the Dacres. Wales, to the west, was at the beginning of this period still thoroughly Celtic, a region where Owen Glendowers still called "spirits from the vasty deep," though toward the end it had been sufficiently assimilated to the central culture of England. Ireland was an outpost in uneasy subjection, and the relationship of English and Irish was precisely that of the English and the American Indian. We are concerned, in brief, with London and with central, southern, and eastern England.

And with very few people. There were fewer, indeed, in the 1490s than there had been a century and a half earlier, as a consequence of the Black Death and the subsequent recurrent plagues. However, from this time on the population was on the increase. We do not have, of course, any precise figures since there was nothing like the modern census, but we can make informed guesses. The population in 1490 was about equal to the present population of Connecticut; in 1623, to that of Florida. The striking increase was in the population of London: from the size of Portland, Maine, to almost the size of Portland, Oregon, in a hundred and some years.

At the beginning of this period the literary models in English were Chaucer, Gower, and Lydgate in verse; there were none in prose. The only prose work of general reputation in the world of letters, Thomas More's *Utopia* (1516), was written in Latin. At the end of this period there were for models the achievements of Shakespeare and Jonson, Beaumont and Fletcher, Sidney and Spenser, Bacon and Donne. There was a literature that, as Jonson said of Shakespeare in the commendatory poem to the first collected edition, could challenge comparison with "all that insolent Greece or haughty Rome sent forth." At the beginning is Leonard Cox's simple assumption that "logic"—the old Aristotelian logic—"is a plain and sure way to instruct a man of the truth of anything," and the lore of the four elements; at

the end, William Gilbert's conception of the earth as a giant lode-
stone, and William Harvey's demonstration of the circulation
of the blood.

This, then, was the Renaissance in England. For the Renaissance is a notion properly applicable to the world of letters and
of learning. It denotes, of course, a rebirth and referred originally to a revival of interest in the literature of Antiquity and
its associated learning after, so it was thought, the monkish
barbarism of the intervening centuries. The idea was then extended to the Early Modern rebirth of a special kind of intellectual excitement. So, at least, some of the authors in this book
themselves thought. Thomas Campian writes in 1602:

> Learning first flourished in Greece, from thence it was
> derived unto the Romans. . . . Learning, after the de-
> clining of the Roman Empire and the pollution of their
> language through the conquest of the barbarians, lay
> most pitifully deformed till the time of Erasmus, Reuch-
> lin, Sir Thomas More, and other learned men of that
> age, who brought the Latin tongue again to light, re-
> deeming it with much labor out of the hands of the il-
> literate monks and friars.[1]

Francis Bacon a few years later saw the literary and intellectual history of the immediate past in much the same terms,
only more explicitly developed, and with dispraise for both parties, as befitted the rhetorician of the New Learning of modern
science:

> Martin Luther, conducted no doubt by a higher provi-
> dence, but in discourse of reason finding what a prov-
> ince he had undertaken against the bishop of Rome
> and the degenerate traditions of the church and finding
> his own solitude being no ways aided by the opinions
> of his own time, was enforced to awake all antiquity,
> and to call former times to his succours to make a
> party against the present time. So that the ancient
> authors, both in divinity and in humanity, which had
> long time slept in libraries, began generally to be read

and revolved. This by consequence did draw on a necessity of a more exquisite travail in the languages original, wherein those authors did write, for the better
understanding of those authors, and the better advantage of pressing and applying their words. And thereof
grew again a delight in their manner of style and phrase,
and an admiration of that kind of writing; which was
much furthered and precipitated by the enmity and
opposition that the propounders of those primitive but
seeming new opinions had against the schoolmen; who
were generally of the contrary part, and whose writings
were altogether in a different style and form; taking
liberty to coin and frame new terms of art to express
their own sense, and to avoid circuit of speech, without
regard to the pureness, pleasantness, and, as I may call
it, lawfulness of the phrase or word. And again, because
the great labour that then was with the people (of whom
the Pharisees were wont to say, *Execrabilis ista turba,
quae non novit legen*), for the winning and persuading
of them, there grew of necessity in chief price and request eloquence and variety of discourse, as the fittest
and forciblest access into the capacity of the vulgar sort:
so that these four causes concurring, the admiration
of ancient authors, the hate of the schoolmen, the exact
study of languages, and the efficacy of preaching, did
bring in an affectionate study of eloquence and copy of
speech, which then began to flourish. This grew speedily
to an excess; for men began to hunt more after words
than matter; more after the choiceness of the phrase,
and the round and clean composition of the sentence,
and the sweet falling of the clauses, and the varying and
illustration of their words with tropes and figures, than
after the weight of matter, worth of subject, soundness
of argument, life of invention, or depth of judgment.
Then grew the flowing and watery vein of Osorius, the
Portugal bishop, to be in price. Then did Sturmius
spend such infinite and curious pains upon Cicero the
Orator, and Hermogenes the Rhetorician, besides his
own books of Periods and Imitation, and the like. Then

did Car of Cambridge, and Ascham with their lectures and writings almost deify Cicero and Demosthenes, and allure all young men that were studious unto that delicate and polished kind of learning. Then did Erasmus take occasion to make the scoffing Echo: *Decem annos consumpsi in legendo Cicerone*; and the Echo answered in Greek, *"Ove, Asine."* Then grew the learning of the schoolmen to be utterly despised as barbarous. In sum, the whole inclination and bent of those times was rather towards copy than weight.[2]

For Campian and Bacon, then, there is a clearly distinguished period in the history of literature and of learning beginning around 1500—Erasmus (1465-1536), Reuchlin (1455-1522), More (1478-1535), Luther (1483-1546)—and extending to their own day. The initiators were Northern: German, Dutch, English. Nothing is said of Italy. The culture opposed and displaced is that of the Old Church, the scholasticism of monks and friars. The New Learning is associated with the Reformation.

What did it involve? It involved, first of all, a revolution in style, a rebirth, as they saw it, of the Latin language itself. Not that Latin had ceased to be used in the Middle Ages: there is more medieval Latin in print in a large university library than a man could, or would, read in a lifetime. It was, in fact, the only language of learning and remained the principal language of learning until the nineteenth century. But medieval Latin had shed the idiomatic quirks of the language of Plautus and the stately period of the language of Cicero. It had become a kind of Basic Latin, a clear, dry, precise medium that welcomed and harbored all the technical words, "terms of art," of the medieval sciences. And so the revolution in style was inevitably a revolution in learning, and, since learning was in large part divinity, it was associated with the revolution in religion.

It was first a revolution in Latin and then a revolution in the vernacular. And though the re-realization of classical models and classical experience was only part of the story in the vernacular literatures, it was part of the story. Something of Vergil's descent into Hell had long before been assimilated in the medieval tradition, and is realized again in Thomas Sackville's

Induction (1563). But the worlds of ancient dialogue and Horatian satire are first naturalized in English in the early sixteenth century by More and by Thomas Wyatt. And the subjective erotic world of Propertius and Ovid is recaptured first by Donne in the Valedictions and Elegies of the 1590s. Indeed, the great stylistic achievement of the period, apart from the inimitable style of the later Shakespeare, the plain style of Jonson, and of Donne at his best, is consciously modeled on the classical plain style. It is a consequence of the Renaissance.

THE STRUCTURE OF SOCIETY

There were, to be simple about it, but no more simple than the views of the time warrant, two kinds of people in Renaissance England: those that mattered and those that did not. The latter were "the multitude, wherein be contained the base and vulgar inhabitants not advanced to any honor or dignity," as Sir Thomas Elyot puts it in *The Governor*. They were, for instance, the vulgar countrywomen at Dame Elinor's alehouse, figures of fun; the artisan, William Waring, doing ecclesiastical penance; the London rioters on Evil May Day; the gossipy servingmen in *A Yorkshire Tragedy*; or Annis Herd, the supposed witch. They were all minor figures, not of much account in that society.

The group that mattered is fairly easy to define. They were those who lived on the unearned income from inherited land. These were the men "of ancient honor and name," however recently acquired. To fall from this class, to lose one's patrimony and dissipate one's inheritance, as the Yorkshire gentleman did, is the final ruin. It is a disgrace not only to oneself but also to one's ancestors and posterity. It is for this reason that he kills his children in *A Yorkshire Tragedy*:

> My lands showed like a full moon about me, but now the moon's in the last quarter, waning, waning. And I am mad to think that moon was mine, mine and my father's and my forefathers'—generations, generations. Down goes the house of us, down, down it sinks. Now is the name a beggar; begs in me that name which hun-

dreds of years has made this shire famous. In me and my posterity runs out. . . .

My eldest beggar! Thou shalt not live to ask an usurer bread, to cry at a great man's gate or follow "good your honor" by a coach; no, nor your brother. 'Tis charity to brain you.

The gulf between the two estates was regarded as absolute, though in practice it was not quite. It is the distinction still preserved in the armed forces between the enlisted men and the commissioned officers. The one is governed, the other is the governing class. There were, however, two distinct views on the structure of the governing class, views that are clearly formulated by Fulke Greville in his account of the Queen's intervention in the quarrel between Sir Philip Sidney and the Earl of Oxford in 1579:

The Queen, who saw that by the loss or disgrace of either she could gain nothing, presently undertakes Sir Philip, and (like an excellent monarch) lays before him the difference in degree between earls and gentlemen, the respect inferiors owed to their superiors, and the necessity in princes to maintain their own creations as degrees descending between the people's licentiousness and the anointed sovereignty of crowns: how the gentleman's neglect of the nobility taught the peasant to insult both.[3]

The motivating fear in the Queen's position is fear of "the people's licentiousness," of the insulting peasant. If not structured and controlled by order and degree the irrational lower classes would destroy all order. For, says Elyot, when man "hath destroyed that wherewith he doth participate by the order of creation, he himself of necessity must then perish, whereof ensueth universal dissolution." "Imagine," says the character, Thomas More, addressing the London rioters in *Evil May Day*:

that you sit kings in your desires,
Authority quite silenced by your brawl,

And you in ruff of your opinions clothed,
What had you got? I'll tell you: you had taught
How insolence and strong hand should prevail,
How order should be quelled, and by this pattern
Not one of you should live an aged man:
For other ruffians, as their fancies wrought,
With self-same hand, self reasons, and self right,
Would shark on you, and men, like ravenous fishes,
Would feed on one another.[4]

It was a plausible fear. There was no police force, no stand-ing army. The London riot is put down by the presence of noble-men and their retainers, and by the eloquence of Thomas More. There was poverty, grievance, and there were too many root-less men, such as those described by Hythloday in More's *Uto-pia* and interviewed by Thomas Harman. To deal with this potentially disruptive situation, the means of order were, in the Queen's view, the reverence attached to "the annointed sover-eignty of crowns" and the hierarchical stepping down by de-grees of power and respect, inviting and compelling awe from inferior to superior. It was a congenial way of thinking, for the universe itself was so ordered, from the lowest element to the highest sphere, as was the celestial society that rose by de-grees through all the orders of angels to God.

On the other hand, Sidney's view that there are really only the two classes, ordered by the relationship of master and serv-ant, is perhaps more accurate of his society than the elaborate hierarchical structure that the Queen and Sir Thomas Elyot expound, though both apply. This is Greville's account of Sid-ney's position:

Whereunto Sir Philip, with such reverence as became him replied: first, that place was never intended for privilege to wrong: witness herself, who how sovereign soever she were by throne, birth, education and nature, yet was she content to cast her own affections into the same moulds her subjects did, and govern all her rights by their laws. Again, he besought Her Majesty to con-sider that, although he were a great lord by birth, alliance and grace, yet he was no lord over him: and therefore the difference of degrees between free men could not challenge any other homage than precedency. And by her father's act (to make a princely wisdom become the more familiar) he did instance the government of King Henry the Eighth, who gave the gentry free and safe appeal to his feet against the oppression of the grandees, and found it wisdom by stronger corporation in number to keep down the greater in power, inferring else that if they should unite, the overgrown might be tempted by still coveting more to fall (as the angels did) by affecting equality with their maker.[5]

The motivating fear in Sidney's position is the fear of great magnates, of such "grandees" as had in the preceding century caused the feudal chaos of the Wars of the Roses. Those that matter are the "free men," and, among these, difference in degree is only a matter of ceremony. The particular relationship among the free men is of the same sort as the general relationship between the two classes of the commonweal; it is that of master and servant. All, for example, are servants of the crown. But Oxford, though a great lord, is not to be lord over Sidney, unless there had been, as there was not, some specific feudal obligation on Sidney's part to Oxford. And what obligations do exist do not inhere in the prerogative of degree but are under and by the law. Nor was this doctrine merely of theoretical interest. Mary, Queen of Scots, like the Princes in Sidney's *Arcadia* (1593, Book 5) claimed as a "prince absolute" not to be answerable to the law of England. The claim was disallowed, though the point was not settled.

This, then, is a world quite different from ours. In our world it is not the wealthy or the great officers of state and their associates who make the principal contributions to literature and learning. We have, at the most, an occasional man of letters somewhere in the government, an Assistant Secretary of State or a scientific adviser to the President. And we have no millionaire poets. But in the world of Renaissance England, literature and learning were produced by and for the wealthy and governing class. A simple enumeration will make this clear.

The highest officer of state in England, in dignity if not necessarily in power, was the Lord Chancellor (or, with lesser prerogatives, the Lord Keeper of the Great Seal). He took precedence. Two of the most important of our authors were Lords Chancellor, Thomas More and Francis Bacon, and Bacon's father had been Lord Keeper. John Donne, until the disgrace of his clandestine marriage, had been secretary to Sir Thomas Egerton, the Lord Keeper.

The next highest officer of state was the Lord Treasurer. Thomas Sackville, cousin to Queen Elizabeth, created Earl of Dorset by James I, was Lord Treasurer. Sir Philip Sidney was the son of a Lord Deputy of Ireland, and the nephew of the Earls of Warwick and of Leicester. At the time of his early death he was Governor of Flushing. Sir Walter Ralegh, of course, was for a long time one of the Queen's favorites, Captain of the Guard, Lord Lieutenant of Cornwall, Lord Warden of the Stannaries, and Governor of Jersey. Sir Fulke Greville, later Lord Brooke, "neither sought for nor obtained any great place or preferment in court during all the time of his attendance, neither did he need it, for he came thither backed with a plentiful fortune, which, as himself was wont to say, was the better held together by a single life, wherein he lived and died a constant courtier of the ladies." Yet he became eventually Chancellor of the Exchequer and a Privy Councillor.

Sir Thomas Wyatt, who was in a position to pursue in vain one of Henry VIII's mistresses, was Ambassador to the court of Charles V, as was also Sir Thomas Elyot. John Skelton and John Palsgrave were tutors, and Gilbert and Harvey were physicians to royalty. John Heywood was court entertainer and servant to three sovereigns, Henry VIII, Edward VI, and Mary. Richard Hooker's great work was commissioned by the government. Even Shakespeare, who had legitimate pretensions to gentility, which his success confirmed, was first the Lord Chamberlain's servant and then the King's servant, and wore the King's livery on a state occasion. The popular drama of his day could not exist except by the favor of the great. Even Ben Jonson, the stepson of a master bricklayer, becomes in legal documents "gentleman" and received for many years a handsome pension from the King. And Edmund Spenser wrote almost solely for court preferment: the *Prothalamium* celebrates the betrothal of the Earl of Worcester's daughters, and has as a kind of climax a fulsome compliment to the Earl of Essex. George Gascoigne's *Woodmanship* is a begging poem to Lord Grey of Wilton, Lord Deputy of Ireland, who was also Spenser's patron.

But it is not only a literature by and for the governing class, it is also a literature in which class distinctions are literary distinctions. Tragedy, for example, is concerned only with the governing class, and usually with heads of states, with Lear, with Claudius and Hamlet, with Julius Caesar. The death of a salesman was not tragic. Even those few plays which modern historians of literature distinguish as "domestic tragedies," that is, as not primarily political, are nevertheless concerned with men of ancient honor and means, as in *A Yorkshire Tragedy*.

This will seem strange to us, but what is even more strange is that there were class distinctions in matters of sex and of love. Whoring and lust may be expected in the lower class. It is whoring and lust in the upper class, or between nobility and the citizen's wife, that is particularly the object of satiric vehemence in Wyatt, Greville, and Jonson. The worst is the corruption of the best. So it is "my lord" Stallion and his "court-bred filly," "stretched upon the rack of lust," who are the special objects of invective. And, conversely, the whole area of what we call romantic love is the prerogative only of the upper class. It is an experience open to Lady Hungerford and Darrell of Littlecote, to Lady Rich and Sir Philip Sidney, to Argalus and Parthenia and Shakespeare's Viola and Orsino. In them it may be destructive or amusing; it may even be ridiculous to the calm sight of those not in love, as in Jonson's *Lovers Made Men*; but it is proper. In their servants it is comic and ridiculous, with the ridiculousness of impropriety:

> Much ado there was, God wot;
> He would love and she would not.

There are, furthermore, class distinctions in style. By and large, in the drama the one class speaks in verse, the other in prose. This is quite clear in the early Shakespeare, and in *A Midsummer Night's Dream* there are even further refinements. The heads of state speak a dignified blank verse, the wellborn lovers blank verse and couplets; the rude mechanicals speak rudely in prose; and the extra-human characters have their class distinction: they may use lyric measures. But there are distinctions also in prose. The sustained sentence, the aureate diction, the verbal figures of repetition are proper to, are required by, the heroic world of the *Arcadia*, and furnished for a century afterward the model for courtly speech. There was a consonance between elevation in rank and an elevated style. On the contrary, the lower class character in the *Arcadia* (1590) speaks like Mrs. Quickly:

> Oh the good old woman, well may the bones rest of the good old woman! She called me to her into her house. I remember full well it stood in the lane as you go to the barber's shop, all the town knew her, there was great loss of her. She called me to her, and taking first a sup of wine to comfort her heart—it was of the same wine that comes out of Candia which we pay so dear for nowadays, and in that good world was very good cheap—she called me to her, "Minion," said she— indeed I was a pretty one those days though I say it— "I see a number of lads that love you."
>
> 2.14

In brief, it was not a democratic society.

THE OLD LEARNING AND THE NEW

Shakespeare in the sixty-sixth sonnet, enumerating the upside-downness of things in this world, how captive Good is in the service of Captain Ill, speaks of "art made tongue-tied by authority." It is an odd statement, and odd in its context, even if properly understood. For it is not, of course, as it is often taken to be, a reference to literary and dramatic censorship. His "art" is not our art. It referred, rather, to give a rough translation, to the world of learning. And what is complained of in the phrase is that the constant repetition of the old basic texts prevented the formulation of new propositions. It is as if he had been reading Bacon, or had been listening to Ben Jonson: "I know nothing can conduce more to letters than to examine the writings of the Ancients, and not to rest in their sole authority, or take all upon trust from them . . . For to all the observations of the Ancients, we have our own experience."

There was in Renaissance England what we may call the Old Learning and the New. The New Learning developed slowly and comes into prominence only toward the end of our period. It comprised a hodgepodge of recent concerns and developments: in mathematics and science, in various interests associated with the new classical philology, grammar, for example, and antiquarian research, all with a much clearer history on the continent than in England. But there were accomplishments: Gilbert's speculations, Harvey's demonstration, Bacon's intuition. There was the cold sociological interviewing of Thomas Harman. There were interesting developments in the common law, represented by Sir Edward Coke's *Reports* (1600-1615). There was the new history: Bacon's *Henry VII* (1622) and Lord Herbert's *Henry VIII*; the profound learning of John Selden; and the new antiquarian and topographical discovery of England, of which William Camden's *Britannia* (1586) and John Stow's *Survey of London* (1598) are best known. But, for the most part, the Old Learning was still dominant.

It was, essentially, the learning of the Middle Ages, and formed the matrix and texture of most of the thought and literature of the time. To understand that, we must relearn it, at least in outline. It was the common possession of everyone of the least education. It was an elementary learning, consisting largely of a series of clear and simple distinctions. There are the three souls, the four elements, the three grammatical genders, the seven deadly sins. These were learned as one learns the Catechism, and repeated again and again as one recites the Catechism. Indeed, the Catechism itself was a good part of the learning, for theology was still the principal science, as judicial astrology was still the principal experimental, that is, predictive, science.

Nor was this learning only a school matter. It was matter for well-bred conversation in the houses of the upper class. An Elizabethan musician, onetime "servant and scholar" to John Heywood, tells in his autobiography of the conversation in the household of a woman who had been to court:

I took pleasure many times to talk and discourse of such things as she by experience had had some knowledge of: as sometimes, of religions, she would argue in matters of controversy in religion; sometimes of profane matters; sometimes she would touch matters of the country, with the good husbandry and housewifery thereof . . . sometimes we should enter into talk of humors, the which of them four, bearing chiefest rule in man, should instinct incline and provoke him to follow those effects whereunto they were inclined. Then should we sometimes wade into communication and talk of the planets and the celestial signs with the constellations, and what their operations and workings were, and what effects they wrought in all things that were subject to them.[6]

It is only to be expected, then, that this system of elementary distinctions should appear everywhere in the literature of the times as allusion, as material, and as structural principle. A simple example of the latter is afforded by Donne's little epigram on Hero and Leander:

> Both robbed of air, we both lie in one ground,
> Both whom one fire had burnt, one water drowned.

The whole story of the lovers is apprehended, summarized, and enclosed in the simple scheme of the four elements, in phrases of four and six syllables, in iambic pentameter, and rhymed. It is neat, ingenious, and absolute in its own way. But it must not be thought that this is anything peculiar to Donne. Sidney, some years earlier, in one of the *Arcadia* poems, has the following two lines:

> Man oft is plagued with air, is burnt with fire,
> In water drowned, in earth his burial is.[7]

The two lines do not rhyme—the form is terza rima, not couplets—but otherwise the correspondences technically and in the structural use of the four elements are exact.

The elementary distinctions of this learning were so securely the possession of everyone who counted that a writer could jump from one to another without transition or strain. This is what Donne does in his witty conjugations. You will find in the fifth stanza of *A Valediction: Of my Name in the Window* the doctrine of the three souls: the rational, by which one understands; the sensitive, in common with animals, by which one perceives; the vegetable, in common with plants, the principle of growth and decay:

> as all my souls be
> Imparadised in you—in whom alone
> I understand and grow and see—

He passes in the next stanza to the theological doctrine of the resurrection of the body:

> Till my return, repair
> And recompact my scattered body so.

And then the principle of judicial astrology, the influence of the stars:

> As all the virtuous powers which are
> Fixed in the stars are said to flow
> Into such characters as graved be
> When these stars have supremacy.

The modern reader who needs notes and patient explanation may think of Donne as ranging in such passages through various fields of learning. To Donne it was, for the exercise of wit, a single field with interchangeable parts. They were all of a piece.

What is new in these passages from Donne is not the learning or the use of learning, though it is a little more on display than was customary. What is new is literary. The monumental quality of Donne's epigram suggests the revived classical tradition of Sannazaro rather than the brutal doggerel tradition of

John Heywood. And the world of the *Valediction* is the revived
world of Latin erotic elegy, of Propertius and Ovid, where "thy
melted maid, / Corrupted by the lover's gold, and page," lays
"His letter at thy pillow."[8]

DEATH, RELIGION, AND LOVE

People in different times and places are alike and different. If
we stress the difference we make them seem unintelligible. If
we stress the similarities we encourage ourselves to understand
them too readily, and so to misunderstand them. All men are
concerned with death and love, and hence with religion, but not
all have the same concern.

The Englishman of this period was more at home with death
than we are. He lived with it, and sometimes for it. He said
much about it, but there is not much to be said about what was
said: it is all so simple and direct. There was a preoccupation
with the fact of death; not with the subtlety of decay, as in
Thomas Mann's *Death in Venice*, but with the bareness of the
whitened skull. It was a preoccupation directed to the calm
acceptance of death. The principal art of life, in fact, was the
art of dying well. John Skelton's *Upon a Dead Man's Head* is a
meditation on a skull, and a meditation in medieval form. It
begins with the traditional syllogism, "All men are mortal," in
inverted order: the conclusion, "Die we must," followed by the
explicit major premise, "It is general to be mortal." The signs
of death are then enumerated, and we conclude with a prayer.
Again, in one of Heywood's epigrams a prisoner, awaiting hang-
ing and quartering, pauses as he searches for worms in his hand,
and meditates: in doing this I am only showing myself an enemy
to the worm and a friend to the crow who will eat me as I hang
on the gibbet. To speak here of acceptance of death is under-
statement. And so, again and again, sometimes with the assurance of salvation, "When Thou hast done that Thou hast Donne,"
the simple fact of death is looked at and embraced.

The attitude, of course, is Christian, as was the society. The
essence of Christianity was still the incomprehensible mystery
of God, the Trinity, and the historical fact that God became
man, the Incarnation, so classically stated by Hooker. "The

strength of our faith is tried by those things wherein our wits and capacities are not strong." But there were variations in Christianity, some of which are important for our purposes. For a principal fact of England at this time is the change in religion, or rather the successive changes under four monarchs: Henry VIII, Edward VI, Mary, and Elizabeth. The two poles were Rome and Geneva, the Old Religion and the Reformed, with differences of doctrine, of feeling, and with political differences. For religion was politics, and politics religion, and neither was the less sincere for that. Of our authors four were executed for treason, and in each case religion and the question of the succession of the crown were involved: More, the Lady Jane, Chidiock Tichbourne, and finally Ralegh, though in his case as pretext rather than fact.

Between Rome and Geneva or Germany there was more than a difference in politics, or the differences in doctrine clearly stated, for example, in the *Examination of Lady Jane Grey*; there were also differences in feeling. They are apparent in the attitudes of the Lady Jane and Abbott Fecknam. They are apparent in two poems, each of the highest quality, that illustrate as well as anything the emotional difference between Calvinism and Catholicism. As feeling it can only be experienced. But one can say that in Greville's *Down in the Depths* the firm conviction of absolute corruption and the equal conviction of divine election ("Even there appears this saving God of mine") march doggedly through the stanzas with an unsocial and impressive solemnity. It is an experience of simultaneous corruption and salvation; it is not a prayer. Jonson's *To Heaven*, on the other hand, is a prayer, an act of perfect contrition:

> Yet dare I not complain, or wish for death
> With holy Paul, lest it be thought the breath
> Of discontent, or that these prayers be
> For weariness of life, not love of thee.

But Rome and Geneva were not the only possibilities. We can see in Donne's *Satire: On Religion* (the *Third Satire*, line 43 to the end) the possibilities open in the 1590s to a young man in his twenties, of good family, whose patrimony has been partially dissipated. He is ambitious for service in the State, partly for itself and partly to repair his fortunes, but he is also by family, training, and temperament a Roman Catholic. As such he would be debarred from preferment. He enumerates in the satire five positions, each of which he scornfully rejects, phrasing his scorn in similies identifying the quest for the True Church with that of true love. "Seek true religion. O where?" One man seeks her at Rome because he knows she was there a thousand years ago. But this is to worship her old clothes. Another at Geneva. For this Donne has even greater contempt. The passion for Calvinism is compared to a "lecherous humor" for coarse country wenches, "contemptuous yet unhandsome." The next possibility is that true religion is to be found in the English Church. It is good that Donne's *Satires* were not printed in his lifetime; he could not quite have been hanged for what he says. The English Church, he tells us, has changed like fashions in clothes. Whatever some preachers ("vile ambitious bawds") and some laws bid us accept at the moment we are to take as perfect. We are, in fact, to take our religion as a ward in that society must take whatever wife his guardian offers, or pay the forfeit. We must accept the current religion, or pay the fines for recusancy. These three positions, Rome, Geneva, and Canterbury, we may call regional. The next two are philosophical. The skeptic argues from the diversity of churches that there is no true church; his opposite maintains on the same grounds that one is as good as another, and so any one will do.

Donne's own position, which he now proceeds to sketch out, is a curious one but sufficiently clear. He is sure there is a True Church, and only one True Church, and he seems pretty sure that it is not one of the five already enumerated. The problem is to find it. There will be required, first of all, a patient searching of tradition, for though truth and falsehood are near twins, truth is a little older. Secondly, consider that Rome, Geneva, and Canterbury on any point may all be wrong. The example he gives is that the adoration, condemnation, and depreciation of images "may all be bad." Finally, "doubt wisely," for truth is to found, as Polonius knew, by indirections and "assays of bias." But it is a wise doubting as a means to truth, which can be found and, once found, held to, not a wise doubting as a way of life. For we must find the True Church before old age, "death's twilight," "for none can work in that night." In brief he does not know the True Church, but is certain he will find it in due time by patient and supple inquiry, and he is certain it will not be a church stipulated by the State. What good will it do at the last judgment, he asks, to plead that Philip of Spain or the Pope, Henry VIII or the Puritan Martin Marprelate, taught you your doctrines? The final source of power is God and not the State.

So we come to love. There are several traditions in the depiction of love, and it may be helpful to name them and to make some simple distinctions. There is, of course, love as an Idea, the exemplar being that heavenly love that Spenser hymned, of which the lady of courtly love is sometimes a parody. Then there is the tradition of Christian preaching, of Juvenal's satires and Martial's epigrams, and this is still with us. It is ugly, realistic in detail, brutal with either a vehement or an urbane brutality. Campian's *Epigram*, "Kate can fancy only beardless husbands," illustrates the urbane. Again, there is the tradition of Latin erotic poetry, of Catullus, Tibullus, Propertius, and Ovid. To put it too briefly, for the tradition comprises a wide range of themes and sentiments, it is frankly sexual, however musingly subjective. For this reason it seems realistic to us. Jonson's "You have a husband is the just excuse / Of all that can be done him," gives the essence of the matter, and Donne's *Elegy* and Campian's *It Fell on a Summer's Day* illustrate it. Finally, there is the tradition of courtly love, or perhaps one should say of love at Court. This seems to us artificial in comparison with Donne's world, and in this we are right and wrong. It is artificial, but it is an artificiality that had been lived and experienced by a society through many generations, whereas Donne's world was a re-creation from literary Antiquity, though, perhaps, a re-creation that had contemporary validity. The society was a society of people who thought themselves important, and were, and who often had superfluous leisure. How they occupied this Campian tells us in *Now Winter Nights Enlarge*: "Though love and all his pleasures are but toys, / They shorten tedious nights." So courtly love may involve an evening's unserious pastime, a ritual flirtation, the sentimental occupation of years, or it may be the ornate setting of vulgar adultery. But its locale is the Court where it helps pass the time. It helps pass the time as befitted the atmosphere, with formality, compliment, ceremony, with precedent and by rules. Sidney's *Astrophil and Stella* and Ralegh's *The Ocean to Cynthia* illustrate the tradition.

Astrophil and Stella is the earliest sonnet sequence in English, and raises the problem of that literary form, and the allied problem of love at Court. The poet depicts in a sonnet at the beginning of the sequence the slow progress on his part of the relationship, by stages from liking through loving, to an absolute submission to the tyranny of love at a time when he had already lost the opportunity for legitimate fulfillment. His reason argues sophistically against reason in favor of passion, and he sends this clear delineation of the act of mortal sin as a compliment to the lady. (This is curious hyperbole for an earnest Christian.) Then realizing the shame of enduring such tyranny, he meets the lady and tells her, "Go to, unkind, I love you not," though he doesn't mean it. She in turn takes the first step in the dance of love, the look, and admits the lover to a chaste relationship. Then the attempted kiss, the banishment, the denial, the poems in absence, and finally the resolution: that she should authorize him to accept, as in her service, an office of state. This, plausibly, would be the governorship of Flushing, which he accepted in 1585, the year before his death.

The problem of the sonnet sequence is usually conceived in terms of the question, Is this fiction? or memoir? and is sometimes solved by denying there is a problem. The poems "should be read as poems," that is, without locating the field of experience they refer to. But this is to destroy them as poems. To return: By fiction is meant that the situation is invented; the structure, at least in part, planned out in advance; and the work as a whole responsible to the truth of human nature but not to fact. As memoir, on the other hand, the poems are evidence, their genesis private, and the reader eavesdrops. If only the two terms, fiction and memoir, were available and applicable, one would have to say that the sequence is memoir. For this is not the way Sidney thought of fiction or wrote it.

We know from his critical treatise, *Defence of Poesy*, his conception of fiction, and we know from the *Arcadia* how he wrote it. Fiction was, first of all, ideal, presenting notable images of virtue and vice. What this means we can see in the episode of Argalus and Parthenia. (1. 5 and 7) The hopeless and constant lover, offered an exact replica of his love—indeed, it is Parthenia herself, unidentified—courteously declines: "It is only happiness I refuse, since of the only happiness I could and can desire I am refused." He is in love with her identity. This is a notable image of the virtue of constancy. But the images need not be only of virtue and vice. If there is a hunt, let it be the ideal hunt, as one might write an account today of the ideal summer vacation. If one thinks of representing a young girl in love, let it be not this girl or that but the essence of a young girl in love, and then one writes Jonson's *A Nymph's Passion*.

Fiction is also an imitation of an action, that is, an interconnected series of external events of a certain size—something more than a stolen kiss or a disturbance of feeling, something with a plot in the old sense. Something with such striking and notable events as the disfigurement and the cure of Parthenia. The cure, one may remark on the side, is marvellous but not supernatural or impossible, though it was undoubtedly beyond the competence of any physician of the time. It is, in fact, an early instance of science fiction. The plot should also have, as almost necessary ingredients, a final reversal of fortune, usually as in this episode simultaneous with a recognition of identity. *Astrophil and Stella* may be, though I think not, ideal, but there is in it no imitation of an action, no striking event, no reversal of fortune, and no recognition. It is not fiction.

The poems, then, are memoir in that they record an experience in the game of love. But they are not memoir in the sense that the poet attempts to come to terms with that experience, or to delineate it for a reader or for himself. The poems are not private, though intended for a very limited audience, and are not written to be overheard, but are rhetorically addressed to an audience. It is a very small audience of those in the know. The poems are, in fact, actions in the game of love, and their locale is the Court. They are for the most part compliments to the lady, apologies, explanations, entreaties: their aim is to persuade.

The context of such poems is, interestingly enough, clearly pictured in the *Arcadia* (3. 1) as a moment in the larger structure of the story of Pamela and Musidorus. Pamela at one point pities Musidorus in his love despair and shows her pity by a look. He, presuming, offers to kiss her, and is summarily banished. It is a situation from *Astrophil and Stella*. And then we have this depiction of the lover as poet:

> Then began he only so far to wish his own good, as that Pamela might pardon him the fault, though not the punishment: and the uttermost height he aspired unto, was that after his death she might yet pity his error and know that it proceeded of love, and not of boldness. That conceit found such friendship in his thoughts, that at last he yielded, since he was banished her presence, to seek some means by writing to show his sorrow, and testify his repentance. Therefore getting him the necessary instruments of writing, he thought best to counterfeit his hand (fearing that already as she knew his, she would cast it away as soon as she saw it) and to put it in verse, hoping that would draw her on to read the more, choosing the elegiac as fittest for mourning. But never pen did more quakingly perform his office; never was paper more double moistened with ink and tears; never words more slowly married together, and never the Muses more tired than now, with changes and re-changes of his devices: fearing how to end, before he had resolved how to begin, mistrusting each word, condemning each sentence. This word was not significant; that word was too plain; this would not be conceived; the other would be ill conceived; here sorrow was not enough expressed, there he seemed too much for his own sake to be sorry; this sentence rather showed art than passion, that sentence rather foolishly passionate than forcibly moving. At last, marring with mending, and putting out better than he left, he made an end of it; being ended, was divers times ready to tear it, till his reason assuring him, the more he studied the worse it grew, he folded it up, devoutly invoking good acceptation unto it; and watching his time, when they were all gone one day to

> dinner, saving Mopsa, to the other lodge, stole up into Pamela's chamber, and in her standish (which first he kissed, and craved of it a safe and friendly keeping) left it there to be seen at her next using her ink (himself returning again to be true prisoner to desperate sorrow) leaving her standish upon her beds-head, to give her the more occasion to mark it: which also fell out.
>
> 3. 1

It is in such a context, with just a shade of the comic about it, that *Astrophil and Stella* was written and is to be read.

But there can be nothing comic about it, except, perhaps, to an unconcerned modern observer, if the lady is the Queen. The cruel mistress to whose moods the lover is completely subject, who has power of life and death over him, may in other instances be an emotional reality or a courtly fiction; in the case of the Queen and her favorites it was the plain fact. "First of all, you must consider with whom you have to deal," Sir Edward Dyer wrote to Sir Christopher Hatton on a crisis in his relationship with Elizabeth, "and what we be towards her; who, though she do descend very much in her sex as a woman, yet we may not forget her place, and the nature of it as our Sovereign." And so the offending lover did not despair in the solitariness of the woods but in the solitariness of the Tower. There, probably in 1592, Ralegh wrote the incomplete draft of the poems of the eleventh book of *The Ocean to Cynthia*.

THE REVOLUTION IN STYLE

There is toward the end of this period a consciousness of achievement, especially in literature. This first appears in the 1590s, and indeed would not have been warranted before that decade. It was the decade of the *Faerie Queene*, of the first half of Shakespeare's work, of the first edition of Bacon's *Essays*, of Donne's most memorable poetry, and of Jonson's first great plays. There was a suddenness about the achievement that seems to call for an explanation.

But history is not a predictive science. It thinks up reasons for what has already happened, or is thought to have happened. It is what we can make of what remains of the past. And what we can make of it will depend on the nature of the remains and on our own concerns. If the remains are primarily literary, and our concerns are literary, we will look for a literary answer, though it may be only a partial answer.

Let us say, then, that the achievement of the 1590s, and of the subsequent decades, is partly a consequence of a revolution in style. For only then was there at hand an adequate instrument in poetry and in the drama. The importance of this is often overlooked. Literature, however, is not written with ideas, experiences, emotions, but with a pen, with language. And not with any language, but with a particular system of inclusions and exclusions; one writes with a style, and in poetry with a meter also, which is an aspect of style. And so a new style, a new meter, is a new attitude, a new form, new subject matter, so far unexpressed detail. Styles are innovated, and imitated, and imitation establishes a tradition.

The new styles that permitted the achievements of Elizabethan literature were innovated in the 1580s and perfected in the 1590s. This is clearest in the drama. The earlier dramas had been written, with the exception of one in blank verse (1562) in which Thomas Sackville had a hand, in mediums that would have precluded *Richard III* and all that followed. One of John Heywood's plays, for instance, printed in 1533, begins with this speech:

> God speed you, masters, every one,
> Wot ye not whither my wife is gone?
> I pray God the devil take her,
> For all that I do I can not make her
> But she will go a-gadding, very much
> Like Antony pig with an old witch
> Which leadeth her about hither and thither,
> But, by our lady, I wot not whither.

This is, of course, verse in the old Germanic tradition, a four-beat accentual meter held together by rhyme instead of alliteration. It can express simple truth and simple vulgarities, but there are many things that cannot be said in this style. Another medium is illustrated by the opening of *Cambises, King of Persia* (1570):

> My Council, grave and sapient, with lords of legal train,
> Attentive ears towards me bend, and mark what shall
>   be sain.

This is the grave fourteener of the mid-sixteenth century, rhymed in couplets. It yielded a few impressive short poems, but nothing in drama. With such instruments not even Shakespeare could have been Shakespeare. He could at best have written in the octosyllabic tradition the verses inscribed on his tomb:

> Good friend, for Jesus sake forbear
> To dig the dust enclosed here!

Sometime in the late 1580s a new voice is heard on the London stage. The innovation was blank verse. It was not wholly new, of course, it had been used in some translations from the Latin, by Gascoigne in *The Steele Glas* (1576), in a play acted at the Third University of England, the Inns of Court. But it suddenly took on. We do not know who established the fashion, or how he hit on the new instrument. Some say Kyd, some Marlowe, and it may have been someone else. But it made the difference between Heywood and Shakespeare. This is the voice:

> When the eternal substance of my soul
> Did live imprisoned in my wanton flesh,
> Each in their function serving other's need,
> I was a courtier in the Spanish court.
> My name was Don Andrea.

From this, the opening of Kyd's *Spanish Tragedy*, to *Hamlet* is simply a matter of time and genius. The means are available.

And the innovation derives from the attempt to realize in English some of the qualities of the poetry of Classical Antiquity. For the most simple and obvious difference between that poetry and the poetry of this time is that the one was unrhymed and the other rhymed. This is not just a difference in effect; it is a difference in what can be said. A word to be rhymed immediately suggests its rhymes, and at the same time rules out all expressions that are not potentially rhymable. It is a notable instance of a system of inclusions and exclusions. Furthermore, unrhymed verse involves not merely a freedom from limitations. It will have its own limitations, and one of these is that, in a tradition in which rhymed verse is common, the avoidance of rhyme is a positive principle of selection.

The heroic line of blank verse was developed originally in nondramatic poetry, and with rhyme. It is, ultimately, Chaucer's line. But something had happened to Chaucer's line in the centuries after his death, partly, no doubt, because the language had changed. At all events, it is clear that at the court of Henry VIII there was no commonly agreed-upon metrical tradition, particularly for the heroic line. It was a situation similar to our own, except that the possibilities of metrical confusion have multiplied since that time. And it is a serious situation for the history of poetry, more serious than the reader may think. For, as prose is written in syntax, in phrases, clauses, sentences, so poetry has a second principle of organization concurrent with that of grammar: it is written in lines. The meter of a poem determines the line. And as an uncertainty in grammar would make it difficult to write good prose, so an uncertainty in meter makes it difficult to write good poetry.

It would be a patient and delicate task to explore the whole problem in the early sixteenth century, but a brief analysis will show the nature of the problem. Wyatt more often than not writes the traditional heroic line as Chaucer had established it:

But as for me, alas, I may no more.

But he also writes a line simply of ten syllables, sometimes counting the final unaccented syllable:

In this also see you be not idle:

or of nine syllables, unless "laughter" is trisyllabic:

It is but love; turn it to laughter.

or a ten-syllable line organized by the four-beat tune of the Germanic tradition:

From under the stall, without lands or fees.

This last was the principal problem, for the Germanic and the Chaucerian traditions cannot live together; the heavy four-beat chant which we learned in our childhood ("Jóhnny ís a stínkér") drives out the grace and subtlety of the traditional meter. To write with both tunes in mind is to produce the baffling rhythms of Heywood's epigrams. To slip from one to the other, as Sir Thomas Elyot does, is metrical chaos:

> The poet fashioneth by some pleasant mean
> The speech of children, tender and unsure,
> Pulling their earës from wordës unclean,
> Giving to them precepts that are pure,
> Rebuking envy and wrath if it dure.
> Things well done he can by example commend;
> The needy and sick he doth also his cure
> To récomfort, if aught he can amend.

So it was that the poets of the next several generations undertook to discipline the syntax of poetry to the firm iambic line, the "drumming decasyllabon." They simplified the rules: they imposed special limitations. The ten-syllable line would be phrased in units of four and six syllables, in a limited number of syntactical patterns, and often enough the accented syllables in each phrase would be bound together and pointed by some rhetorical device, usually by alliteration and syntactical repetition:

> The life is long that loathsomely doth last,
> The doleful days draw slowly to their date.

It is a style that can handle obvious subjects, uncomplicated feelings, eternal truths, and simple sin. It is the style in which one writes from the Tower on the eve of execution. It is, furthermore, at its best an impressive style, as in Tichbourne's *Elegy*, and one that even Donne recurred to when he had an obvious subject and direct feelings about it. His *A Hymn: To God the Father* is clearly in this style: let us call it the moral style.

The poem is phrased for the most part in units of four and six syllables in normal iambic pattern, and the phrasing is underlined by rhetorical repetition:

> Wilt thou forgive that sin where I begun,
> Which was my sin though it were done before?
> Wilt thou forgive

It is an impressive but not a sufficient style; it excludes too much. It cannot handle ordinary life. It cannot rise and fall. And so there developed in the 1580s, out of a good deal of experimenting in prose and verse, several new styles: the ornate style of Spenser, and the new plain style, modeled on the plain style of Latin Antiquity. In this the innovator was Sidney. It is not his consistent style; he is often ornate; he writes sometimes in the moral style. But there are many passages in *Astrophil and Stella* in a fully accomplished plain style:

> Dear, therefore be not jealous over me
> If you hear that they seem my heart to move;
> Not them, O no, but you in them I love.

It was there. It needed only to be recognized and imitated. It was recognized and imitated by Campian and Donne, and perfected by Jonson.

Campian (1591?):

> Whither thus hastes my little book so fast?
> To Paul's Churchyard. What? in those cells to stand
> With one leaf like a rider's cloak put up
> To catch a termer?

Donne (1597) on a calm at sea:

> No use of lanterns, and in one place lay
> Feathers and dust, today and yesterday.

or:

What are we then? How little more, alas,
Is man now than before he was. He was
Nothing. For us, we are for nothing fit;
Chance or ourselves still disproportion it.

Jonson (1616):

Think,
All beauty doth not last until the autumn.
You grow old while I tell you this.

It became the central style of English poetry.

Lyric Style in the 1590s

~~~~~~

Wordsworth in the Preface to the *Lyrical Ballads* speaks of the formal engagement an author makes in the act of writing verse that "he will gratify certain known habits of association . . . that certain classes of ideas and expressions will be found in his book . . . that others will be carefully excluded." Now, the inclusion and exclusion of certain classes of ideas and expressions, and in verse of certain meters and metrical practices, constitutes a style. And in any literary situation certain attitudes and experiences, "certain known habits of association," are available to a particular style, and the exploration of other attitudes and experiences requires a new and different style, for a style is itself a principle of selection and order. This is what Wordsworth implies when he says in the sentence that follows: "This exponent or symbol held forth by metrical language must in different eras of literature have excited very different expectations; for example, . . . in the age of Shakespeare and Beaumont and Fletcher, and that of Donne and Cowley. . . ." What we are concerned with here is the discrimination of certain kinds, or traditions, or styles of metrical language in a given literary situation, the 1590s in England, and the indication, so far as our clumsy means permit, of the exponent or symbol that these hold forth.

The age of Shakespeare and Beaumont and Fletcher is the age of Donne; the age of Cowley is something else again. For

311

Shakespeare and Donne, if we restrict ourselves to the evidence, appear on the literary scene at about the same time, around 1592, and Fletcher died five or six years before Donne. But the chronological dislocation that Wordsworth endorses still persists; it has distorted literary history, and consequently the interpretation of the relevant texts. In The Pelican Guide to English Literature, for example, the works of the 1590s are distributed through the first three volumes: Spenser in volume I, Shakespeare and Jonson the dramatist in volume II, Donne and Jonson the poet in volume III, and there are only seven volumes for the whole of English literature from Chaucer to the present day.

Let us imagine, then, a young man, probably of good family and possibly a younger son—Campian or Wotton or Davies or Donne—who comes to London around 1590. He has, perhaps, a small patrimony, has had a thorough grammar school education, a year or two at Oxford or Cambridge, and has now entered the Third University of England, one of the Inns of Court. He is, in brief, Lorenzo, Jr., alias Edward Knowell, of Ben Jonson's *Every Man in His Humour*.[1] And, indeed, that character is quite possibly modeled on Donne, for not only did Jonson later write a dialogue on poetry in which Donne was the principal speaker, but also Donne's *First Satire* furnishes the "invention" of the play: a scholarly young man of good family, interested in poetry, is invited by a friend and goes out on the town to observe and describe the follies of various social types. Our poet, then, is something of a wit, and is ambitious. He will write some toys in verse, partly to display his wit, and partly in the hope he will be noticed by someone in power, some official of the state who might further his ambitions—Lord Essex, let us say, or Sir Thomas Egerton. What will he write, and in what way will he write it? What styles were available? What styles could he reject?

There were notably two. The first is the one commonly associated with the Elizabethan lyric, what C. S. Lewis has called the Golden. It is, he says, a "poetry which is, so to speak, innocent or ingenuous. In a Golden Age the right thing to do is obvious; 'good is as visible as green.' . . . Men have at last learned how to write; for a few years nothing more is needed than to play out again and again the strong simple music of the uncontorted line and to load one's poem with all that is naturally delightful—with flowers and swans, with ladies' hair, hands, lips, breasts, and eyes, with silver and gold, woods and waters, the stars, the moon, and the sun."[2] It is a style I would prefer to call the sweet or pleasant style, *dulce . . . orationis genus et solutum et fluens, sententiis argutum, verbis sonans,* "sweet, fluent, and copious, with bright conceits and sounding phrases,"[3] the style of epideictic oratory. Its exemplar in its octosyllabic form is *The Passionate Shepherd to His Love*:

> Come live with me and be my love,
> And we will all the pleasures prove
> That valleys, groves, hills and fields,
> Woods, or steepy mountains yields.

It is a poetry in which one sits

> By shallow rivers to whose falls
> Melodious birds sing madrigals.

Indeed, *The Passionate Shepherd* attains the perfection of which the sweet style is capable, for that style aims at a harmonious arrangement of elements that have already a preestablished harmony. It is really an abstract style, like a Navaho rug, dependent on design, and its triumphs are quite impersonal. Such a poem is written by no man but by a tradition.

But more basic and native at this time is another style, what Lewis calls the Drab and I, the moral style. It is the style of *The Nymph's Reply to the Shepherd*, ascribed quite plausibly to Ralegh:

> Time drives the flocks from field to fold
> When rivers rage and rocks grow cold
> And Philomel becometh dumb.
> The rest complains of cares to come.

It is relentlessly iambic; the line is organized in two distinct halves, with two four-syllable phrases bound into internal unity by structural alliteration of stressed syllables, or, for variation, the flat music of

> And Philomel becometh dumb.

It is a central, a limited, and an impressive style:

> But could youth last and love still breed,
> Had joys no date and age no need.

The *locus classicus* in decasyllabic form, of course, is:

> O eyes! no eyes, but fountains fraught with tears;
> O life! no life, but lively form of death;
> O world; no world, but mass of public wrongs,
> Confused and filled with murder and misdeeds![4]

In poulter's measure it is the style of Father Southwell's *The Burning Babe*, for the old habit of vision goes comfortably with it. It is the way in which one writes in the Tower on the eve of execution, "Even such is time that takes in trust," or Tichbourne's *Elegy* (1586):

> I sought my death and found it in my womb,
> I looked for life and saw it was a shade,
> I trod the earth and knew it was my tomb,
> And now I die, and now I was but made.
> My glass is full, and now my glass is run,
> And now I live, and now my life is done.

Tichbourne's *Elegy* belongs to a particular literary kind, what I call the moral poem, which is the exemplar and pattern of the moral style. It is a small but sturdy genre that flourished in the late middle ages, and continued to thrive until the last decade of the sixteenth century: Chaucer's "Flee fro the press, and dwelle with sothfastnesse," and Dunbar's "Be mirry, man, and tak nocht far in mynd," are examples of the style. It consists of a sequence in serial order of sententiae, maxims, proverbs, or propositions of a similar kind, usually one to a line, sometimes two,

and occasionally a single *sententia* over two lines, commonly
in decasyllables and in an extended stanza, often in ballade form.
The decasyllable is normally phrased in fours and sixes in iambic pattern, though sometimes in reverse order of six and four,
and the phrases are bound by alliteration of stressed syllables:

> The life is long that loathsomely doth last,
> The doleful days draw slowly to their date,
> The present pangs and painful plagues forpast
> Yield grief aye green to stablish this estate,
> So that I feel in this great storm and strife
> The death is sweet that endeth such a life.

Thus line is piled on line in unvarying units. When successful,
as in Tichbourne's *Elegy*, the moral poem expresses a cumulative experience of serious insistence. For it is moral, in the
simple, old-fashioned meaning of that term.

Hence the exponent or symbol of this particular and quite
limited tradition is easy to describe: a heavy-handed serious-
ness, a scorn of urbanity, a deliberate rejection of that delicacy
which would discriminate shades of white and of black. It is a
morally ruthless, secure, and overpowering style. And so Sidney
in the *Astrophil* series, as he accumulates compliments, exploits
sentiment, and dallies with the potentialities of adultery, is ever
vigilant against the stable four and six structure and the firm
advancing beat of the "drumming decasyllabon":

> Dear, therefore be not jealous over me
> If you hear that they seem my heart to move.
> Not them, oh no, but you in them I love.

In contrast, when he expresses the old morality in those sonnets
that are often appended by editors at the end of *Astrophil*, he
does it in the moral style:

> Band of all evils, cradle of causeless care,
> Thou web of will whose end is never wrought,
> Desire, desire! I have too dearly bought
> With price of mangled mind thy worthless ware.

And:

> Then farewell world, thy uttermost I see.
> Eternal love, maintain thy life in me.

By the end of the decade the moral style had lost for the most part its productive vigor; only Matheo and Bobadilla of *Every Man in His Humour* in 1598 think the "O eyes! no eyes" passage "simply the best that ever you heard." Yet on an apt occasion, with an obvious subject and direct feelings about it, those who grew up with the style can return to it, as Donne did in *A Hymn to God the Father*, with verbal repetition instead of structural alliteration:

> Wilt thou forgive that sin where I begun,
> Which was my sin though it were done before?
> Wilt thou forgive those sins through which I run
> And do run still though still I do deplore?

It is a poem from an earlier age.

The sweet and the moral, then, were available to the young man in 1590; they were styles he could accept or reject, and those we are concerned with here for the most part rejected them. And the new style? It is said to be "metaphysical," and to have been innovated by Donne. Now much has been said of this style, and much that has been said is untrue. It is said to be colloquial, which it is not, except in rare passages of dialogue, as in the *First Satire*. But "colloquial" is not really a descriptive term in current criticism but a term of praise, like "subtle" and "complex," and like those terms in need of definition. By "colloquial," I take it, one means that in the sort of situation sketched or implied in the poem what is said is what could be said somewhat casually by one person to another without seeming to be affected, or indeed insane. One has only to visualize the situations in Donne's lyrics and try acting them out to have unappeasable doubts about his colloquiality:

> I wonder, by my troth, what thou and I
> Did till we loved?

This could possibly be said musingly, though hardly in reply to some remark of the partner. But what will the lady make of:

> Were we not weaned till then?
> But sucked on country pleasures childishly?
> Or snorted we in the seven sleepers' den?

No, the style is not really colloquial, for these are not dialogues. They are in part written in the familiar style of the familiar letter, as perhaps here, and in a variety of different styles. For the genuinely colloquial in the lyric you will do better with Sidney who sometimes writes a shorter poem in dialogue form:

> Take me to thee and thee to me.
> No, no, no, no, my dear, let be.

The truth is, the work of Donne that would be available to his circle at this time does not offer a consistent model of style. His answer to the *Passionate Shepherd*, for example, opens in the pleasant style:

> And we will some new pleasures prove
> Of golden sands and crystal brooks,

proceeds by way of a light line to a Petrarchan hyperbole:

> There will the river whispering run,
> Warmed by thy eyes more than the sun.

then to a Gorgianic figure of the "living sepulcher" type:

> When thou wilt swim in that live bath,

developed now by the qualification of philosophic exactness:

> Each fish which every channel hath

and ending with a juxtaposition of grammatical words which one may call colloquial but which defies the enunciation of common speech:

> Will amorously to thee swim,
> Gladder to catch thee than thou him.

Actually, this is probably an attempt to do what Latin permits and English resists. A little further on we get rather simple bad writing, the jammed-up line:

> Let coarse, bold hands from slimy nest
> The bedded fish in banks out-wrest,

And the poem concludes with an easy, and pleasing enough, urbanity:

> That fish that is not catched thereby,
> Alas, is wiser far than I.

This is not a style but a heterogeneity of styles.

A similar stylistic uncertainty can be seen in a much better poem, *The Calm*, written in 1597 during the Islands expedition, and one of the poems we have reason to believe would have been available as a model in this decade. It begins:

> Our storm is past, and that storm's tyrannous rage
> A stupid calm, but nothing it, doth swage.

The couplet is troubled by a tight idiomatic qualification, "but nothing it," which is not needed by the rationale of the poem; it is a metaphysical side-reflection, an operation on a term. There follows an allusion to an obscure fable. Then in a few lines:

> As steady as I can wish that my thoughts were,
> Smooth as thy mistress' glass, or what shines there,
> The sea is now.

This is random ingenuity. The young Donne is an improvisatory genius, an extemporal wit, a better-born Thomas Nashe. As Samuel Butler the elder put it: "Dr. Donne's writings are like Voluntary or Prelude, in which a man is not tied to any particular design of Air, but may change his Key or mode at pleasure.

So his compositions seem to have been written without any particular scope," that is, end in view.

Yet he does in another sense have an end in view. His motive is clear and explicit; it is the desire for novelty:

And we will some new pleasures prove.

Now, the charm of *The Passionate Shepherd* lies precisely in its lack of novelty; it is the almost accidental issue of an apparently stable tradition. Again, the force and weight of *The Nymph's Reply* is grounded on the age-old wisdom of her sentences. Novelty, however, is no positive principle; it stipulates only a something else. It is a principle of rejection rather than of selection. The author of *The Bait* will go neither Marlowe's way nor Ralegh's; but if he goes he must go some way, and we may ask, Where does he find it? In the detail of style, as we have seen, he goes uncertainly. And as for the invention? His shepherd is not a shepherd but a fisherman, and that is the clue. For at the end of the last century Sannazaro sought to treat the pastoral convention under a novel guise, and wrote his Latin piscatory eclogues. That is, Donne goes for his invention to that vast, once living though now dead, body of contemporary literature, the current Latin poetry of the Renaissance. And not only in this instance. The whole body of his early work, with the partial exception, and it is partial only, of the *Songs and Sonnets*, is an attempt to realize in English the contemporary forms of occasional poetry in Latin, and especially those that admitted the particularities of sexual or of disreputable experience, and the details of everyday life. He writes epigrams, not in the tradition of Heywood, but in that of Martial, and satires on the model of Horace. He uses the verse letter as the humanist poets used it. He naturalizes the subjective-erotic elegy of Propertius and Ovid, and writes an heroical epistle whose subject is lesbianism; as, also, an epithalamium which, if you compare it with Spenser's, is clearly the epithalamium of a Latinist.

But Donne was not alone in turning his interests to the erotic experience of Latin elegy and the realistic social description of satire and epigram. It is an interest that suddenly appears, and at precisely this time, in several other men of his own age, and one somewhat older, at the Inns of Court as he was. The older poet was Thomas Campian, whose elegies and epigrams in Latin were printed in 1595, but whose *Observations in the Art of English Poesy*, containing fully realized English epigrams in the Latin mode, and one elegy, may be the book entered in the Stationer's Register on October 12, 1591.[5] If the text entered in 1591 was substantially the text printed in 1602, Campian may have given the hint, though to Ben Jonson, some years later, Donne is the innovator:

> Whose every work of thy most early wit
> Came forth example, and remains so yet.

But to realize new genres, to explore hitherto unexploited areas of experience, involves the problem of style. Neither the pleasant nor the moral style would do; the material was inherently repugnant to them. What was needed was the English equivalent of the Classical plain style in Latin. This John Davies, among others, attempted to supply in his *Epigrams*, datable about 1594. It is a plain style, but it is the plainest of plain styles, the *genus humile* rather than the *genus tenue*. However, it can handle the sights and sounds and characters and place names of the streets of London, directly and without disguise:

> See yonder melancholy gentleman
> Which hoodwinked with his hat alone doth sit,
> Think what he thinks, and tell me if you can
> What great affairs trouble his little wit.
> He thinks not of the war 'twixt France and Spain ...
> But he doth seriously bethink him whether
> Of the gulled people he be more esteemed
> For his long cloak or his great black feather,
> By which each gull is now a gallant deemed.
> Or of a journey he deliberates
> To Paris Garden, Cockpit, or the play,
> Or how to steal a dog he meditates,
> Or what he shall unto his mistress say.

Here is no alliterative phrasing, or phrasing by fours and sixes. Here is nothing that is naturally delightful. It is a prosaic style; it has, in fact, the characteristics of good workaday prose, in which what interest there is is in what is being talked of. But it is workaday prose in metrical form at a time when there was little workaday prose in literary prose. It can handle any subject so long as it can be handled in its proper terms and without adornment. It is the flat style. It aims at an unassuming lack of distinction, and with appropriate material has its own rightness, as in Hoskyns' epitaph *On a Man for Doing Nothing*:

> Here lies the man was born and cried,
> Told threescore years, fell sick, and died.

But the difficulty with the flat style, of course, is that it is flat. This is what Jonson had in mind when he told Sir John Harington that his epigrams "were narrations and not epigrams," or said of Owen's that they were "bare narrations." That is, to translate the remarks into our English, Harington's epigrams and Owen's are unadorned exposition, without distinction of style. So Shakespeare in an experiment in the flat style and its attendant attitudes and subjects seeks to relieve or transform the flatness by introducing some verbal figures that might be thought congruent with the style:

> When my love swears that she is made of truth
> I do believe her though I know she lies,
> That she might think me some untutored youth
> Unlearned in the world's false subtleties.

So far all is flat, except for the slight rhetorical touch of "untutored," "unlearned." But now he introduces more pointedness:

> Thus vainly thinking that she thinks me young,
> Although she knows my days are past the best,
> Simply I credit her false-speaking tongue;
> On both sides thus is simple truth suppressed.

And concludes with an epigrammatic pun:

> Therefore I lie with her and she with me,
> And in our faults by lies we flattered be.

By such means, by a sparse use of the elementary verbal figures, together with a tightness of metrical form, there was developed what I call the English plain style. The chief technical difference between this and the Classical plain style, which I shall next discuss, is the bareness of its diction and the regular coincidence of grammatical and metrical units, whereas in the classical style, especially when written in decasyllabic couplets, the lines are often run over, or, as Jonson says, "broken like hexameters." Small masterpieces of the English plain style are Hoskyns' *Absence* and Aytoun's *Upon Love*:

> I loved thee once, I'll love no more,
> Thine be the grief as is the blame,
> Thou art not what thou wast before,
> What reason I should be the same?
> He who can love unloved again
> Hath better store of love than brain.
> God send me love my debts to pay,
> While unthrifts fool their love away.

Styles are noticeable or unnoticeable. The sweet and the moral are noticeable; the flat is unnoticeable but undistinguished. What is needed is a noticeably unnoticeable style, the style of Cicero's Attic orator, *Nam orationis subtilitas imitabalis illa videtur esse existimanti, sed nihil est experienti minus,* "a directness of speech that seems to one judging easily imitable, to one trying it nothing less so."[6] Such a style first appears in this particular literary situation scattered here and there in Sidney's *Astrophil and Stella*, as in the passage quoted earlier:

> Dear, therefore be not jealous over me
> If you hear that they seem my heart to move.
> Not them, oh no, but you in them I love.

If Campian's *The Writer to His Book* was written by 1591 there was a fully realized model in blank verse available to the poets we are concerned with:

> Whither thus hastes my little book so fast?
> To Paul's Churchyard. What? in those cells to stand

With one leaf like a rider's cloak put up
To catch a termer?

How close this is to Jonson:

Nor have my title-leaf on posts or walls
Or in cleft sticks advanced to make calls
For termers.

It is the style of Donne's early poetry at its best. A style that can
handle circumstantiality and detail, can accommodate in poetry
what we think of as the material of prose, and yet without modulation of manner can strike through to the heart of human feeling. In Donne's early poetry it appears intermittently, amid a
debris of other incongruous and indecorous manners, but when
it appears it is absolute, unrevisably right. It appears in the
verse letter, *The Calm*, to which we alluded earlier, in the couplet Jonson pointed out to Drummond of Hawthornden:

No use of lanterns, and in one place lay
Feathers and dust, today and yesterday.

a kind of exact and minute particularity almost unknown to the
poetry of the preceding decades. Or:

Whether a rotten state, and hope of gain,
Or to disuse me from the queasy pain
Of being beloved, and loving, or the thirst
Of honor or fair death out pushed me first,
I lose my end.

Or again:

What are we then? How little more, alas,
Is man now than before he was. He was
Nothing. For us, we are for nothing fit:
Chance or ourselves still disproportion it.

Where did Donne get this style? Possibly from Sidney, possibly
from Campian, but certainly from the effort to realize in En-

glish the forms of Latin poetry, and their appropriate styles. There remained only for a Ben Jonson to recognize it, perfect and establish it, and in the forms that Donne had pioneered: epigram, elegy, satire, verse letter, epithalamium, and in the same tradition of Latin learning. The relationship of Jonson and Donne is that of Horace to Lucillius, perfector to inventor.

With That Facility

False Starts and Revisions in *Love's Labour's Lost*

~~~~~~

The title page of the earliest extant edition of *Love's Labour's Lost*, the First Quarto of 1598, describes the play as "A Pleasant Conceited Comedie."[1] This is, of course, an advertisement, a blurb, and indeed we know from various allusions that title pages were struck off separately and displayed "at the recognised 'posts' throughout the town" "to catch a termer."[2] But an advertisement tells us something: it tells us what a seller thinks will be attractive to a buyer, and what it says of a product may sometimes be so. It is, I think, so in this instance. What is it a prospective buyer would anticipate who was interested in a pleasant conceited comedy? The description is not uncommon on the title pages of that time, though not routine. We have "The Old Wives Tale, a pleasant conceited Comedie . . . " in 1595; "A Pleasant Conceited Historie, called The taming of a shrew" in 1594; and the earliest text of *Romeo and Juliet*, the Bad Quarto of 1597, is "An Excellent conceited Tragedie. . . ." The term "conceit," of course, was also used to describe the striking hijinks of a comic character; the First Quarto of *1 Henry IV*, for example, promises on the title page not only the Battle of Shrewsbury but also "the humorous conceits of Sir John Falstaffe."[3] But when applied to a play as a whole, whether comedy, tragedy, or history, though it is peculiarly appropriate to comedy, "conceited" indicates that the work will be especially rhetorical in style, full of witty and ingenious turns of thought and speech.

It is interesting that whatever reputation Shakespeare had in the literary and theatrical world of London up to 1598, so far as we can recover it from the records of the time, was not a reputation for creation of character or contrivance of plot but precisely for qualities of style, and particularly for pleasant, conceited writing. The evidence is, considering the scantiness of records of this sort, surprisingly full. The first clear reference linking Shakespeare and the stage is, of course, the allusion by Greene in a pamphlet of 1592 to Shakespeare as player turned playwright; an antic, Greene says, "garnisht in our colours," that is, ornamented in those colors of rhetoric, those figures of speech, which the writer gives to the actor, and yet he now thinks "he is as well able to bombast out a blanke verse as the best of" the professional playwrights:[4] that is, to fill out "the spacious volubilitie of a drumming decasillabon,"[5] no doubt with "farre-fetcht phraise,"[6] for bombast, of course, is the foam rubber of the time, the material used to pad out fashionable clothing. Shakespeare, a mere actor, has picked up Greene's style and meter, the new style and meter that made possible the glories of the late Elizabethan stage. Chettle in a subsequent apology for Greene's attack, also of 1592, speaks particularly of Shakespeare's "facetious grace in writting, that aproues his Art"; that is, to translate the compliment into modern idiom, the witty and ingenious charm of style that ratifies his skill. For Barnfield in 1598 it is Shakespeare's "hony-flowing Vaine," his mastery of the sweet style, that pleases the world and praise obtains. In the well-known catalogues of Francis Meres, also of 1598, Shakespeare is listed with his peers, Sidney, Spenser, and others, as one by whom "The English tongue is mightiliy enriched, and gorgeouslie inuested in rare ornaments and resplendent abiliments"; again, "the Muses would speak with *Shakespeares* fine filed phrase, if they would speake English"; and, finally, "the sweete wittie soule of *Ouid* liues in mellifluous & hony-tongued *Shakespeare*."[7]

One would expect, then, from the promise of the title page

and from the reputation of the author, that *Love's Labour's Lost* would be a work replete with witty, charming, ingenious turns of thought and speech, that it would be a display of the rhetoric of the sweet, the pleasant style, the *genus amoenum* of Antiquity. And so it is.

It is, in fact, so much of a display that when the reader or viewer comes to the middle of the last scene, he will be suddenly delighted and relieved. For there the hero of the play renounces his rhetoric:

> O neuer will I trust to speaches pend,
> Nor to the motion of a Schoole-boyes tongue:
> Nor neuer come in vizard to my friend,
> Nor woo in rime like a blind harpers songue.
> Taffata phrases, silken tearmes precise,
> Three pilde Hiberboles, spruce affection:
> Figures pedanticall, these sommer flies,
> Haue blowne me full of maggot ostentation.
> I do forsweare them.
> 5. 2. 402-10

The modern lover, whose eloquence is confined to reciting what he takes to be the story of his life and who demands of love the illusions of sincerity, feels now at home. He applauds as Berowne goes on:

> and I here protest
> By this white Gloue (how white the
> hand God knowes)
> Hencefoorth my wooing minde shalbe exprest
> In russet yeas, and honest kersie noes.

And does not notice that Berowne, in renouncing rhetoric, renounces it rhetorically, crowding in one phrase the figures of exclamation, asseveration, and one of the varieties of verbal repetition. He cannot renounce it, for to speak in russet and kersey would be inappropriate to his rank in society and to Rosaline's, and inappropriate to courtly love. For russet and kersey are cheap cloths, the dress of the lowborn, and one woos only the lowborn in russet yeas and honest kersey noes. Thus, when Don Armado of the fantastic phrase woos Jacquenetta, the country wench, he says with absolute russet simplicity:

"Maide."

To which Jacquenetta replies in kersey:

"Man."

But the play deals chiefly with love at court and courtly love, and both demand witty invention and figurative language. For, as an elder contemporary of Shakespeare's tells us: "But as it hath bene always reputed a great fault to vse figuratiue speaches foolishly and indiscretly, so it is esteemed no lesse an imperfection in mans vtterance, to haue none vse of figures at all, specially in our writing and speaches publike, making them but as our ordinary talke. . . ." To make the point clear he uses the very analogy that the hero used above, and that Francis Meres used in the passage alluded to earlier where he spoke of the English tongue "gorgeouslie inuested in rare ornaments and resplendent abiliments":

And as we see in these great Madames of honour, be they for personage or otherwise neuer so comely and bewtifull, yet if they want their courtly habilements or at leastwise such other apparell as custome and ciuilitie haue ordained to couer their naked bodies, would be halfe ashamed or greatly out of countenaunce to be seen in that sort, and perchance do then thinke themselves more amiable in euery mans eye, when they be in their richest attire, suppose of silkes or tyssewes & costly embroideries, then when they go in cloth or in any other plaine and simple apparell. Even so cannot our vulgar Poesie shew it selfe either gallant or gorgious, if any lymme be left naked and bare and not clad in his kindly clothes and coulours, such as may conuey them some what out of sight, that is from the common course of ordinary speach and capacitie of the vulgar judgement.

Style, then, is an ornament, and a needed ornament, but it must also be fitting and proper. And what is fitting and proper to love at court? Or, to quote our author again, "In what forme of poesie the amorous affections and allurements were uttered." He answers: "And because loue is of all other humane affections the most puissant and passionate . . . it requireth a forme of poesie variable, inconstant, affected, curious, and most witty of any others. . . ."[8] "Variable," "inconstant," "affected," "curious," and "most witty"—the terms need explanation since, except perhaps for the last, they do not at all mean what the modern reader would take them to mean. It must be "variable," that is, there should be a copious variety of phrases, a flow and outpouring of eloquence, such as we shall see later in Berowne's display, making the worse appear the better cause. It should be "inconstant"; the style should not keep a single tenor, but rise and fall, with a mingling of styles. The violation of these two requirements in his own sonnets is the theme of Shakespeare's seventy-sixth sonnet:

> Why is my verse so barren of new pride?
> So far from variation or quicke change?

The style should also be "affected"; that is, it should show feeling. It should be "curious," or carefully, highly, finely wrought, and "most witty," with many turns and conceits of speech and thought.

It is an old theory of style, though out of fashion in our day, and clearly relevant to *Love's Labour's Lost*. The play as a whole is an illustration of the qualities of style of amorous poesy, as also at times of the foolish and indiscreet use of figurative speeches. The theory was simple: it distinguished between the naked thought nakedly expressed and the same thought decently or even gorgeously appareled. The problem in practice was to achieve, first, an ability to clothe any thought in rich and varied costume, to have "a mint of phrases in his braine" (1. 1. 166); and then to exercise discretion in choosing just what was suited to this speaker, addressing this person, on this occasion. The prior problem, of course, though usually subsequent in attainment, was to find the thought. They called this "invention," borrowing the Latin word for finding, and they especially prized an invention that was apt and peculiarly fitted to the speaker, audience, and circumstances.

Such was the theory and practice of composition in Shakespeare's day. That he wrote explicitly by it, at least at times, is clear from several passages in this play. These are passages where, with some uncertainty but also with a good deal of plausibility, we can see Shakespeare at work.

But perhaps we should dwell for a moment on this point, for the desire to find genius at work has sometimes dispensed with scrutiny of the evidence. There have been those, and there still are, who would like to see in, for example, the earliest printed texts of *Romeo and Juliet* and *Hamlet*, the Bad Quartos as they are called in modern scholarship, Shakespearean first drafts, or the inferior work of a Shakespearean predecessor, or, most commonly, some mingling of both early draft and other work. The critic can then show by comparison how the prior effort has been transformed into a Shakespearean masterpiece. But if the current view of most textual critics is correct, the process is the other way around, and the evidence is no evidence for Shakespeare at work. It is not that a prior effort has been transformed by Shakespeare, but that Shakespeare has been mercilessly transformed and corrupted by others. For there is fairly general agreement that the Bad Quartos are reconstructions from memory of the authentic text. Why it was done, and by whom, are subjects for conjecture and imaginative fiction. But surely the "To be or not to be" soliloquy in its first published form would require a more than Shakespearean genius to transform it into the form we know. It reads:

> To be, or not to be, I there's the point,
> To Die, to sleepe, is that all? I all:
> No, to sleepe, to dreame, I mary there it goes,
> For in that dreame of death, when wee awake,
> And borne before an euerlasting Judge,
> From whence no passenger euer retur'nd,
> The vndiscouered country, at whose sight
> The happly smile, and the accursed damn'd.

And so on, for fourteen more lines.

There is in this portion something that does tend to support the view that this version represents an effort to remember and record the received text:

> To Die, to sleepe, is that all? I all:
> No, to sleepe, to dreame, I mary there it goes.

The man who is trying to remember the speech is dictating to a secretary who writes down all, including "No, that's not the way it goes," and "Yes, yes, that's the way it goes."

But the texts we will deal with and the evidence for revision are of a different kind, for we will be concerned with passages where the earliest editions preserve in the same text alternate versions of the same speech. It is not a situation peculiar to *Love's Labour's Lost*; there are other instances. In *Othello*, for one, there is a passage (2. 1. 77-83) whose significance for the textual history of the play has not been appraised. There are two early editions, the Quarto of 1622, and the Folio of 1623. The passage reads in the Quarto:

> —great *Ioue Othello* guard,
> And swell his saile with thine owne powerfull breath,
> That he may blesse this Bay with his tall shippe,
> And swiftly come to *Desdemona's* armes.
>   *Enter* Desdemona, Iago, Emillia, *and* Roderigo.
> Give renewed fire,
> To our extincted spirits.
> And bring all Cypresse comfort,—O behold
> The riches of the ship is come ashore.

In the Folio:

> Great Ioue, *Othello* guard,
> And swell his Saile with thine owne powreful breath,
> That he may blesse this Bay with his tall Ship,
> Make loues quicke pants in *Desdemonaes* Armes,
> Give renew'd fire to our extincted Spirits.
>   *Enter Desdemona, Iago, Roderigo, and Aemilia.*
> Oh, behold,
> The Riches of the Ship is come on shore:

The texts are substantially identical up to line 80. There the author wrote "And swiftly come to Desdemona's arms," bringing the sentence and the speech to a close. Then, for whatever reasons, and I think we can see plausible reasons, he crossed out "And swiftly come," interlined "Make loues quicke pants," and swung the sentence over the line-end, making more vivid Othello's private life and acknowledging his public role.

What is textually interesting here is that one needs both Quarto and Folio to recover what Shakespeare wrote and what he rejected; that is, there must have been a manuscript ultimately common to both texts in which both first draft and revision indistinguishably stood. It would in this respect be like the copy for Romeo's last speech in the Good Quarto of 1599. The relevant portion reads:

> Ah deare *Iuliet*
> why art thou yet so faire? I will beleeve,
> Shall I beleeve that vnsubstantiall death is amorous,
> And that the leane abhorred monster keepes
> Thee here in the darke to be his parramour?
> For feare of that I still will staie with thee,
> And never from this pallat of dym night.
> Depart againe, come lye thou in my arme,
> Heer's to thy health, where ere thou tumblest in.
> O true Appothecarie!
> Thy drugs are quicke. Thus with a kiss I die.
> Depart againe, here, here, will I remaine,
> With wormes that are thy Chamber-maides: O here
> Will I set up my everlasting rest:
> And shake the yoke of inauspicious starres,
> From this world wearied flesh, eyes looke your last:
> Armes take your last embrace: And lips, O you
> The doores of breath, seale with a righteous kisse
> A dateless bargaine to ingrossing death:
> Come bitter conduct, come vnsauory guide,
> Thou desperate Pilot, now at once run on
> The dashing Rocks, thy seasick weary barke:
> Heeres to my Love. O true Appothecary:
> Thy drugs are quicke. Thus with a kisse I die.

There are two false starts in the passage, both lovingly preserved by the printer, and both, of course, cancelled by the subsequent revision. And we can, given the evidence, see why. This is Romeo's great aria, and so the declarative "I will believe" is immediately altered to the heightened form of a rhetorical question. What follows is adequate, but not sufficiently extended, not copious enough, and not sufficiently elevated; indeed, with "where ere thou tumblest in" it falls to vulgarity. And so Shakespeare picks up "Depart againe," getting thirteen lines for four, introducing a Gorgianic figure of the vultures-are-living sepulchres type ("With wormes that are thy Chamber-maides"), figures of verbal repetition ("here, here," "O here"), apostrophe, personification ("Come bitter conduct"), periphrasis ("And lips, O you / The doores of breath")—a speech variable, inconstant, affected, curious, and in an Elizabethan sense most witty.

The passages in *Love's Labour's Lost* are similar to the *Romeo* passage. We have the first draft and the revision, and we can see what was done to it. In each case the revised version immediately follows the first draft, and in two cases repeats with slight variation the opening line of the first draft. An eighteenth-century editor who first noted one of these passages (4. 3. 291*ff.*) explained convincingly what had happened in that instance: "penned in haste, found weak in some places, and its reasoning disjointed, it had instant correction; but wanting the proper mark of correction by rasure or otherwise, printers took what they found."[9]

There are three such passages, two of which have been noticed by previous commentators. But the third is the simplest, and we will begin with that. It reads in the earliest extant edition, 1598 (the Pedant, Holofernes, is speaking):

> PEDA. Sir, you shall present before her the Nine Worthies. Sir *Holofernes*, as concerning some entertainement of time, some show in the posterior of this day, to be rended by our assistants the Kinges commaund, and this most gallant illustrate and learned Gentleman, before the Princesse: I say none so fit as to present the nine Worthies.
>
> 5. 1. 124-30

There is a minor point to be noted in this passage before we come to the major one. The passage is reprinted in the first collected edition of Shakespeare's plays, 1623, with one correction: "rendered" for "rended." This could be right, for certainly the Pedant intended to say "rendered." But it is more likely that Shakespeare intended him to mistake the word and say "rended" instead. For the rendering of the Nine Worthies, when we come to it a little later, is certainly "rended," limb from limb. It is a habit of Shakespeare's comic characters to say the unselfconsciously obvious thing, to "mistake the word"[10] to their own derogation. For instance, the clown in *Love's Labour's Lost* says of a letter, "Sir the contempts thereof are as touching me." (1. 1. 191)

We come now to the major point. The Pedant, of course, is Holofernes, and so he would seem in the second sentence to be addressing himself. This is obviously wrong. One could perhaps justify it by some exquisite psychological construction but such subtlety would be out of place in a broadly comic speech. Besides, the Pedant is not entitled to be called "Sir," and Elizabethans were very finicky on such details. On the other hand, Nathaniel, the Curate, is entitled to "Sir" by virtue of his office, and editors usually correct "Holofernes" to "Nathaniel," so that the first sentence is addressed in direct reply to Armado, the second to Sir Nathaniel. But this is clumsy. Furthermore, both sentences say exactly the same thing, the first straightforwardly, the second in the Pedant's own style. The first is the naked thought; the second is clothed in figures pedantical.

The traces of what happened are clear on the printed page. Shakespeare wrote the speech prefix "Peda." and put down in a straightforward sentence what he wanted him to say. Then, perhaps after a warm beer, he started over, writing the speech prefix "Holofernes," and recast what he wanted him to say in pedantical style. Either he neglected to mark the first sentence for deletion or the printer missed the mark. In the second sentence the printer corrected "Holofernes Sir" to the more plausible "Sir Holofernes." If this reconstruction is correct the passage should begin:

HOLOFERNES: Sir, as concerning some
        entertainment

And how does Shakespeare go about recasting the original sentence? First, he turns it into a suspended, a periodic, sentence, sending out an extended flanker movement before bringing up the main clause. This tends to elevation of style, and recognizes the social gulf between Armado, who is addressed, and the Pedant. Second, the notion in "you shall present" is expanded into two phrases, the second employing the phrase he had a moment before collected for his own phrase-book from Armado's jeweled speech: "The *posterior* of the day, most generous sir, is liable, congruent, and measurable for the after noone: the worde is well culd, chose, sweete, & apt I do assure you sir, I do assure." And finally, he finds a Latinate, an aureate term, "illustrate," to go with the other two complimentary epithets by which Armado is addressed. It is like "peregrinate," earlier in the scene, which Sir Nathaniel wrote down in his notebook for future use, "A most singuler and choyce Epithat."

The second passage comes toward the end of the last scene of the play. The princess has imposed a year's penance on the king, at the end of which he may claim her in marriage. After this, in the earliest edition, Berowne says to Rosaline, "And what to me my Loue? and what to me?" And she replies:

> You must be purged to, your sinnes are rackt.
> You are attaint with faultes and periurie:
> Therefore if you my fauour meane to get,
> A tweluemonth shall you spende and neuer rest,
> But seeke the weery beddes of people sicke.
> 5. 2. 827-32

Whereupon Dumaine says to Katherine, almost echoing the words of Berowne, "But what to me my Loue? but what to me?" And after she has put him off for a year, and Maria has put Longaville off for the same period, Berowne again addresses Rosaline, and she again imposes the same sentence on him, but with a significant addition:

> Oft haue I heard of you my Lord *Berowne*,
> Before I saw you: and the worldes large tongue
> Proclaymes you for a man repleat with mockes,
> Full of comparisons and wounding floutes:

Which you on all estetes will execute,
That lie within the mercie of your wit:
To weede this wormewood from your fructfull braine,
And therewithal to winne me, yf you please,
Without the which I am not to be won:
You shall this tweluemonth terme from day to day,
Visite the speachless sicke, and still conuerse,
With groning wretches: and your taske shall be,
With all the fierce endeuour of your wit,
To enforce the pained impotent to smile.
5. 2. 851-63

It is generally agreed that here too the printer set up an un-
revised version followed by the revised version. In writing this
final scene Shakespeare knew that by all laws of precedence the
king's exchange with the princess must come first. He then went
on with Berowne and Rosaline, who perhaps interested him as
they interest us, but soon saw that by all the laws of interest
these two must come last. So he started over, gave Berowne's
speech to Dumaine with the change of "And" to "But," and after
taking care of the other lovers returned to the hero and heroine.
He must have seen that Rosaline's original speech was not only
much too short for the purpose but also pretty flat in the writing. Furthermore, the penance imposed on the hero had no special ingenuity to it, no exact fitting of the punishment to the
crime. What he needs, then, is a notion, a gimmick, an invention,
and this will yield the detail to amplify the passage and give it
the requisite bulk. He keeps, then, only the idea of "purged" and
develops it in the line "To weede this wormewood from your
fructfull braine."

And for penance? Berowne's sin has been wit. He has been

a man repleat with mockes,
Full of comparisons and wounding floutes:
Which you on all estetes will execute,
That lie within the mercie of your wit.

And so the original idea of sentencing him to tending the sick for twelve months is given an apt and decorous twist:

> You shall this tweluemonth terme from day to day,
> Visite the speachless sicke, and still conuerse,
> With groaning wretches: and your taske shall be,
> With all the fierce endeuour of your wit,
> To enforce the pained impotent to smile.

The description of Berowne as a wit and the description of his penitential expense of that wit furnish the material for amplification.

In the first passage we found Shakespeare writing down what he wanted to say, and then saying it as he wanted to say it. The problem is one of clothing the thought. In the second passage the proper management of the ending led him to cancel the lines, and the flatness of style and of the climactic idea forced him to develop new lines and an ingenious twist of the old idea. It was a question of invention.

The third passage is the most extensive, and the one in which the reconstruction of the process of composition is the most conjectural. This is the first draft:

> Haue at you then affections men at armes,
> Consider what you first did sweare vnto:
> To fast, to study, and to see no woman:
> Flat treason gainst the kingly state of youth.
> Say, Can you fast? your stomacks are too young:
> And abstinence ingenders maladies.
> And where that you haue vowd to Studie (Lordes)
> In that each of you haue forsworne his Booke.
> Can you still dreame and poare and thereon looke.
> For when would you my Lord, or you, or you,
> Haue found the ground of Studies excellence,
> Without the beautie of a womans face?
> From womens eyes this doctrine I deriue,
> They are the Ground, the Bookes, the Achadems,
> From whence doth spring the true *Promethean* fire.
> Why vniuersall plodding poysons vp
> The nimble spirites in the arteries,

As motion and long during action tyres
The sinnowy vigour of the trauayler.
Now for not looking on a womans face,
You haue in that forsworne the vse of eyes:
And studie too, the causer of your vow.
For where is any Authour in the worlde,
Teaches such beautie as a womans eye:
Learning is but an adiunct to our selfe,
And where we are, our Learning likewise is.
Then when our selues we see in Ladies eyes,
With our selues.
Do we not likewise see our learning there?

                                   4. 3. 290-317

There is no question of invention here. Berowne has already used at the beginning of the play (1. 1. 59*ff.*) the line of argument by which he will make the worse appear the better cause, and used it in a similar context. It is an extemporal display of wit, like the display of a fencing master: "Com'on then" in the earlier passage, and "Haue at you then" here. And it employs the same commonplace of the vanity of learning: "continuall plodders" in the first act, and "vniuersall plodding" here. It is a display in the tradition of Nashe, and perhaps of Tarleton: "but giue me the man whose extemporall veine in any humour will excell our greatest Art-maisters deliberate thoughts; whose inuentions, quicker than his eye, will challenge the prowdest Rhetoritian to the contention of like perfection with like expedition."[11]

There are some indications at the beginning and end of this first draft that Shakespeare was getting down something to say, as he did in the Holofernes passage. The line, "In that each of you haue forsworne his Booke," lacks metrical and rhetorical shape; it is a line that belongs to another style, a consequence of rhetorically unsuccessful exactness. In the next line he overcorrects by introducing rhyme in a line that is too easily and obviously shaped: "Can you still dreame and poare and thereon looke." There is a similar unsuccessful exactness at the end of the passage where he is trying out a new line of argument. Here the separate line "With our selues" has puzzled editors, and they have tended simply to omit it. But the argument is drawn from metaphysics—it is a development of the proposition "Learning is but an adiunct to our selfe"—and Shakespeare is trying to get it down exactly. He wrote, "Then when our selues we see in Ladies eyes, with our selues do we not likewise see our learning there?" He moved from verse to the exactness of prose; it was more reason than rhyme. But since metrical composition involves a habit of forming sentences simultaneously grammatical and metrical, the last ten syllables come in a syntactical unit metrically acceptable, and the printer set it up as verse. At this point Shakespeare abandons the thought, and the first start, and starts over again:

> O we haue made a Vow to studie, Lordes,
> And in that Vow we haue forsworne our Bookes:
> For when would you (my Leedge) or you, or you?
> In leaden contemplation haue found out
> Such fierie Numbers as the prompting eyes,
> Of beautis tutors haue inritcht you with:
> Other slow Artes intirely keepe the braine:
> And therefore finding barraine practizers,
> Scarce shew a haruest of their heauie toyle.
> But Loue first learned in a ladies eyes,
> Liues not alone emured in the braine:
> But with the motion of all elamentes,
> Courses as swift as thought in euery power,
> And giues to euery power a double power,
> Aboue their functions and their offices.
> It addes a precious seeing to the eye:
> A Louers eyes will gaze an Eagle blinde.
> A Louers eare will heare the lowest sound,
> When the suspitious head of theft is stopt.
> Loues feeling is more soft and sensible,
> Then are the tender hornes of Cockled Snayles.
> Loues tongue proues daintie, *Bachus* grosse in taste,
> For Valoure, is not Loue a *Hercules*?
> Still clyming trees in the *Hesperides*.
> Subtil as *Sphinx*, as sweete and musicall,
> As bright *Appolos* Lute, strung with his haire.

And when Loue speakes, the voyce of all the Goddes,
Make heauen drowsie with the harmonie.
Neuer durst Poet touch a pen to write,
Vntill his Incke were tempred with Loues sighes:
O then his lines would rauish sauage eares,
And plant in Tyrants milde humilitie.
From womens eyes this doctrine I deriue,
They sparcle still the right promethean fier,
They are the bookes, the Arts, the Achademes,
That shew, containe, and nourish all the worlde.
Els none at all in ought proues excellent.
Then fooles you were, these women to forsweare:
Or keeping what is sworne, you will proue fooles,
For Wisedomes sake, a worde that all men loue:
Or for Loues sake, a worde that loues all men.
Or for Mens sake, the authour of these Women:
Or Womens sake, by whom we Men are Men.
Let vs once loose our othes to finde our selues,
Or els we loose our selues, to keep our othes:
It is Religion to be thus forsworne.
For Charitie it selfe fulfilles the Law:
And who can seuer Loue from Charitie.
                                        4. 3. 318-65

Shakespeare had two problems, a problem of order and of amplification; the speech had to have size and to move. He had begun in the earlier wit display by dividing his subjects; he will take up the three vows in order. But the line of argument is that the second vow, "to study," entails rejection of the third vow, "to see no woman," and hence part three of the speech, which is clearly indicated by the transitional "now for not looking on a womans face," must in effect simply repeat in other words the content of part two. He needs, then, a new principle of order, and suddenly finds it. He fuses the two vows, treats them together as inherently they demand to be treated, and fuses at the same time much of the detail of the draft. The notion of women as teachers becomes "beauty's tutors" who teach love poetry. The earlier "vniuersall plodding" suggests "leaden contemplation," as also the distinction of "Other slow arts." Out of the same sentence, dropping the inapt simile of the traveler, he picks up the physiological notion of "The nimble spirites in the arteries," which perform in Elizabethan science the functions of our modern "nervous system"; this is now identified with love, which "Courses as swift as thought in euery power" and increases each faculty. He proceeds to amplify, as the textbooks suggest he should, by division. The five senses are faculties, and so he enumerates four of them.

And why not five? Partly because the fifth would complete a pattern and might bring the fluent facility to a stop, and partly because he has suddenly found another principle of order that will keep the eloquence flowing. He will now move from new material to new material by clear and simple associative links. "Love's tongue proues daintie, *Bachus* grosse in taste" suggests a richer field of amplification, mythological comparisons, culminating in "the voyce of all the Goddes." This suggests poetry and the effects of music. When this flags, he has at hand the salvaged lines on the true Promethean fire, and brings the argument to a conclusion, summarizing in a pointed couplet:

> Then fooles you were, these women to forsweare:
> Or keeping what is sworne, you will proue fooles.

But the impetus persists; he is not willing to quit. The pointed couplet with its repetitions suggests a passage of verbal repetition: for, as a contemporary says, "the eares of men are not onlie delighted with store & exchange of divers words, but feele great delight in repeticion of the same. . . ."[12] And now he finally concludes with what is really conclusive, and plucked out of nowhere, a Scriptual text: "For Charitie it selfe fulfilles the Law."

One sympathizes with the judgment of his colleague, Ben Jonson: "Hee . . . had an excellent *Phantsie*; brave notions, and gentle expressions: wherein hee flow'd with that facility, that sometimes it was necessary he should be stop'd. . . . His wit was in his owne power; would the rule of it had been so too."[13]

In Shakespeare's Day

~~~~~~

There is Shakespeare experienced and Shakespeare explained. I remember as a boy reading the plays without introduction or notes in individual volumes bound in an imitation leather that smelled awful. It was an almost uncued experience, and I think I can remember something of the freshness and distance of that reading. Now, if the purpose of dramatic art, in Shakespeare's day and in ours, is "to hold the mirror up to nature," there must be a communicable constant, open to boy and scholar; else it would not be the mirror and it would not be nature. But if what is shown there—and there are other mirrors —are the features of virtue and images of scorn, these vary throughout our own world; they have changed in my own society in my lifetime. And if they are shown implicated in "the age and body of the time," abstracted in brief chronicle, some sense of the time must be intuited or acquired. Otherwise, the given is not given, and the "form" the poet impresses on the time, as a seal on wax, is for us impressed on water.

Much of the given—mirror, nature, the time—is given in the text if we will believe it, including the theory of drama just abstracted from *Hamlet*. If we will believe it. But we departmentalize art, especially canonized art, confine it to aesthetic

This essay was originally the Introduction for an anthology edited by J. V. Cunningham, *In Shakespeare's Day*, a collection of over a hundred selections.

patterns, and process the experience. We are told why the family warns Ophelia not to get involved with Hamlet, but we take the warnings as characterizing the warners and not as the facts of high political life at the time. We read as "character" what Aristotle calls "thought." But to be told is one thing, to perceive is another, for that involves the persuasion of actuality. And so one needs not only the text but some such book as this, a book to browse in, thumb through, perhaps to read. A book of evidence, not of conclusions. A book of implicit answers looking for questions.

If it is not quite clear what to look for, it is partly because looking is thwarted by premature clarity. Begin, first, with simple, unfocused curiosity, and then with absorption there will come an ambience, an unreferred feel for the time, acquaintance seeking familiarity. Go with a German tourist to the Court of Queen Elizabeth and observe government by ceremony and magnificence, then cross the Thames by water taxi and see *Julius Caesar* at the Globe. Soon you will find that your experience of a play, of *Hamlet*, is invaded by a certain literalness. There were traveling players who turned up at provincial courts, pirates were not storybook, and the "same strict and most observant watch" of the first scene was an experience of 1599. On the other hand, the ghost does not wear the "ghost suit" and "ghost bodice" listed in another company's theatrical inventory of 1598, but appears in "complete steel" and in his dressing gown, "in his habit as he lived." And so the texture of your experience of the play little by little becomes dense.

So far small detail, now for the large. The next step is cross-reference, and first on disguise. We regard it as a story element, something that happens in fiction, as in the source for *Measure for Measure*. For, if the best kind of plot, as Aristotle says, involves "discovery," "a change from unknown to known, happening between those characters whose happiness or unhappiness forms the catastrophe of the drama," then disguise and mistaken identity are obvious means. It is the disguise of Viola that ties the knot of *Twelfth Night*, and the revelation of her identity and sex that unlooses it. But disguise also happened in real life. There is Moll Cutpurse, "a notorious baggage that used to go in men's apparel and challenged the field of divers gallants," and there is the disguise of make-believe in the game of courtly sex, as with the French king and his bride.

Again, at the end of *King Lear* Regan is murdered, Goneril commits suicide, Cordelia is executed, Edmund killed in trial by combat, Gloucester's death is reported, and Lear himself "is gone indeed." But in the sources for the story, France and Cordelia are victorious, Lear is restored to the throne, and all the principals, except Albany and Cornwall, are alive. The change deeply distressed Dr. Johnson. Yet, "the movement of events in tragedy," according to Diomedes, "is almost always from happy circumstances to bitter deaths, accompanied at the end with the perception that the fortunes of the house involved have gone to ruin." The House of Lear is destroyed, as was the House of Hamlet, and succeeded by the House of Gloucester. The story is seen in a "tragic glass." Nevertheless, *The Tragedy of Cymbeline* has a happy ending.

This suggests the need for negative capabilities, for a parsimony with generalizations and with value judgments, both useful and necessary but not idly to be employed. To start a sentence "Tragedy is" or "The Elizabethans thought" is to preclude the claims of variety and the hesitations of ignorance. The Elizabethans thought many, and sometimes contradictory, things, though it is true they did not think some things we do. However, Marlowe was thought to be an atheist, "daring God out of heaven with that atheist Tamburlaine." We read both "Bloodshed by bloodshed still is nourished" and "for empire and greatness it importeth most that a nation do profess arms as their principal honor, study, and occupation." The first points to Macbeth, the second to Henry V and, perhaps, Fortinbras. Plays were divided into five acts on Horace's authority, and Gloucester is blinded on stage despite Horace. So also with value judgments. To compare the Shakespearean passage with Plutarch's description of Cleopatra and ascribe the differences to Shakespeare's genius is to bet on a race after it is official, and to miss the race.

Finally, each of us has his own interests, his own competencies, and one or other of these may be relevant to Shakespeare. I am an old hand with the iambic pentameter and the perception of style, and am interested also in realizing the literary situation as it was when Shakespeare entered it. So I look at the testimony. The first reference to him in that connection is as a player turned poet, one of "those antics garnished in our colors," that is, in our livery (players are the poet's servants), but also in our colors of rhetoric, our figures of speech, our new style. And this jack-of-all-trades "supposes he is as well able to bombast out a blank verse as the best of" the new poets. Perhaps by writing bombast, but that meaning is a little later and derived from such passages as this. The metaphor here is new. Bombast was the foam rubber of the time with which you padded out the fashionable parts of the body. Now the obvious way to stuff out a blank verse line is with disyllabic possessives and adjectives, epithets that adorn, with the accent on the first syllable: "O tiger's heart wrapped in a women's hide!" (*1 Henry VI*, 1. 4. 137) or "From jigging veins of rhyming mother wits." (Prologue to *1 Tamburlaine*) It is to write "a bombast circumstance / Horribly stuffed with epithets of war." (*Othello*, 1. 1. 13-14) This yields what Nashe calls "the spacious volubility of a drumming decasyllabon."

Enough: These are instances. Let not "my anticipation prevent your discovery."

The Heart of His Mystery

~~~~~~

Fulke Greville comments on what I am about to do:

> Yet not asham'd these Verbalists still are,
> From youth, till age and study dimme their eyes,
> To engage the *Grammar* rules in civill warre,
> For some small sentence that they patronize.[1]

I shall begin with a "small sentence" and observe that a classic in time becomes a palimpsest, where interpretation blots the text, both in the local context and in the large. The task, then, becomes one of subtraction and recovery. My example is trivial, if anything is trivial that has been read, rephrased, written out, set, proofread, and glanced at in the study in edition after edition since Pope's, where it first appeared.

You will recall that the Ghost at his first meeting with Hamlet says: "But that I am forbid / To tell the secrets of my prison house / I could a tale unfold" that, among other phenomena, would make "each particular hair to stand an end / Like quills upon the fearful [or F, fretful] porpentine." (1. 5. 13-15, 19-20) And at the second meeting the Queen observes this phenomenon in Hamlet and likewise describes it by similes: "And, as the sleeping soldiers in th' alarm, / Your bedded hair . . . / Starts up, and stands an end." Vivid enough. But she also uses a parallel simile, "Your bedded hair, like life in excrements, / Starts up. . . ." (3. 4. 120-22) The usual gloss (I have seen only one

346

deviation[2]) equates "excrements" with hairs—a piece of scientific lore, that hair is excremental, with presumably the meaning "like life in hairs," "as if it had life in it." But so understood it is no simile. To recover the comparison one needs another piece of scientific lore. Your hair starts up as flies and such-like do from a pile of manure in spontaneous generation. A simile, and vivid enough.

Now to less trivial matters. I should like to pluck the mystery out of Hamlet's "you would pluck out the heart of my mystery" (3.2.382) and erase even more of time's palimpsest. There is no note on the passage in the many editions I have looked at—it is taken to be self-evident—yet the phrase has become central in the interpretation of the play, which for most consists in the interpretation of Hamlet's character, on the premise formulated by A. C. Bradley "that the whole story turns on the peculiar character of the hero."[3] We look in Dover Wilson's *What Happens in Hamlet* and find in the Index under "Hamlet" the subheading, "his mystery." Harley Granville-Barker in the final pages of his Preface writes: "Here, for me, is the master-clue to Hamlet's 'mystery.' . . . He does not pluck out the heart of it himself. Neither are we meant to. For his trouble is rooted in the fact that it is a mystery."[4] Another critic says: Hamlet is "the greatest riddle of all—a mystery, he warns Rosencrantz and Guildenstern, from which he will not have the heart plucked out." And this is later generalized to "the haunting mystery of life itself that Hamlet's speeches point to,"[5] giving, as it were, the moral of the play. But you are all familiar with this, and with its premise: "In a play's world, each part implies the other parts, and each lives, each means, with the life and meaning of the rest," a descendant—to show my bias I will say a bastard descendant—of organic form. That is, the passage functions not in its local context but rather in a solution in which are suspended phrases, images, aspects of character, some actions, soliloquies, the interpretive tradition, the personal concerns of the critic, together with some principle or, perhaps, intuition of unity, all subsumed under what we call character in discussing fiction, as distinguished from experiencing it. But in its local context our passage is something else.

The King's response to the play has confirmed his guilt.

"I'll take the ghost's word for a thousand pound! Didst perceive?" "Very well, my lord." "Upon the talk of the poisoning." I note in passing that in the renaissance tradition, in that rhetorical age, it is the word, "the talk of poisoning," and not the action in pantomime, that strikes the heart. It is Hamlet's speeches to his mother that strike her. To return: He then calls for music, "the recorders," and enter Rosencrantz and Guildenstern to report the King's "distemper" and to summon Hamlet to his mother's sitting room, as had been planned. He asks: "Have you any further trade with us?" *Trade*, a common figure for business. They have. They try to find out, as they had been instructed, what Hamlet is up to—in brief, *his* business. In reply he mingles, as in the ultimate sources of the play, "craft and candor."[6] For candor, he "lacks advancement"; he is only heir designate to the throne. He then takes them aside, borrowing one of the musician's recorders, and asks Guildenstern: "Will you play upon this pipe?" He replies he cannot; in effect, though not in these words, he doesn't know how: he doesn't have the trade, he is not competent in the mystery, the skill, the occupation of recorder playing. Yet, says Hamlet, you would play me, as indeed they were trying to, as one might play a recorder, to learn my occupation, my business, my mystery, to find out what essentially it is that I do. For there are two *mysteries* in Shakespeare's language, one from *mysterium*, whose provenance is theological, though also used more generally in our sense of the mysterious. The other is from *ministerium* and is a common word, as is *quality*, for craft, skill, trade, occupation. There is, for instance, the mystery of being a bawd, about which there is in the other sense no mystery. In brief, the Hamlet of this passage corresponds to the Hamlet of Belleforest, who "pretending extreme madness" yet "spoke so aptly."[7] What he says is precisely responsive to the immediate situation, to the local context. In context, if you take the phrase as the commentators take it, he is saying to Guildenstern: "You are trying to find out why I have not already killed the King," or "You are trying to use me as a resource person to gather material for the definitive MLA paper on the mystery of my character."

There is a similar mildly figurative use of the synonym *quality* in Portia's "The quality of mercy is not strained" (*Mer.*

Ven. 4. 1. 184), in which "quality" is rarely glossed by editors, though Dover Wilson gives "trait, human characteristic." That is, he glosses "quality" by "mercy." "Strained," however, is normally glossed, and usually as aphetic for "constrained," in direct answer to Shylock's "On what compulsion must I" be merciful? But an aphetic form of "*cons*trained" seems odd, of "*re*strained" common, and I take "restrain" in the legal sense. Portia, recognizing that mercy cannot be compelled, turns the question upside down and says: There is no legal injunction, no restraint, against mercy being one's occupation, against "the quality of mercy." "It droppeth," and so on.

But to return to *mystery*. In *Henry VIII* "our travelled gallants" have returned from France fully Frenchified, and the Lord Chamberlain asks: "Is't possible the spells of France should juggle / Men unto such strange mysteries?" (1. 3. 1-2), into acting like foreigners, for *strange*, as you know, means "foreign," and *mysteries* are what they do.

Finally, in this sort, a passage in *Lear*: "And take upon 's the mystery of things / As if we were God's spies." (5. 3. 16-17) Johnson's note is sufficiently close, though in the final clause *mystery* in the modern sense misleads him: "As if we were angels commissioned to survey and report the lives of men, and were subsequently endowed with the power of prying into the original motives of action and the mysteries of conduct." But now that *Lear* has displaced *Hamlet* as a source of literary religious texts, academic unitarianism, we find such notes as these: "i.e. contemplate the wonder of existence as if with divine insight, seek eternal rather than temporal truths"; or, "profess to read the riddle of existence, as if endowed with divine omniscience."[8] We are back to the mystery at the heart of things.

What Lear says he and Cordelia will do in prison is presumptuous, as he indicates, but it is much less presumptuous than this. He says that in prison they will "tell old tales, and laugh / At gilded butterflies," that is, affected courtiers, "and hear poor rogues / Talk of court news; and we'll talk with them too, / Who loses and who wins, who's in, who's out"—then our passage, followed by "and we'll wear out, / In a walled prison, packs and sects of great ones / That ebb and flow by the moon." (5. 3. 12-19) The context is clearly court news, and great ones are the politically powerful, as in Bacon's *Of Great Place*, or Macbeth on Duncan: "So clear in his great office" (1. 7. 18)— not "so blameless," as glossed, but so distinguished a king, as in *viri clarissimi*, or perhaps *personae clarissimae*. Or Claudius on Hamlet: "Madness in great ones must not unwatched go" (3. 1. 196), or Hamlet himself: "Rightly to be great." (4. 4. 53) He is not talking—the Hamlet legend again—of "true nobility of soul," as Kittredge and others would have it, but of being the true prince. Lear and Cordelia, then, will take it upon themselves to relate court doings, to write John Chamberlain's letters to Dudley Carleton, as if they really knew, "As if we were God's spies."

In the preceding I may or may not have plucked the mystery out of some phrases, yet there still remains the question of why men act as they do, and, more narrowly, how Shakespeare perceived this, and, more narrowly still, how some of his characters perceived it. First, sometimes they do not know. "Why yet I live to say 'This thing's to do,' " says Hamlet, "I do not know." (4. 4. 44, 43) And Aufidius on Coriolanus gives three explanations—pride, defect of judgment, or a natural moral habit (what Hamlet calls "nature's livery"): "nature / Not to be other than one thing," "commanding peace / Even with the same austerity and garb [habit] / As he controlled the war;" concluding "but one of these— / As he has spices of them all— not all, / For I dare so far free him. . . ." (*Cor.* 4. 7. 36-47) He does not know which is the determining factor. Ignorance, I may add, is not mystery, or we would all be mysterious. Finally, Hamlet, in a passage that is not in the Folio, categorizes how men go wrong. He is not speaking of himself, but of men. It is a condensed monograph, which rhetoricians would have called thought, διάνοια, not character, 'ἐθos:

> This heavy-headed revel east and west
> Makes us traduced and tax'd of other nations:
> They clepe us drunkards, and with swinish phrase
> Soil our addition: and indeed it takes
> From our achievements, though perform'd at height,
> The pith and marrow of our attribute.
> So, oft it chances in particular men,

That for some vicious mole of nature in them,
As in their birth—wherein they are not guilty,
Since nature cannot choose his origin—
By the o'ergrowth of some complexion,
Oft breaking down the pales and forts of reason,
Or by some habit that too much o'er-leavens
The form of plausive manners, that these men,
Carrying, I say, the stamp of one defect,
Being nature's livery, or fortune's star,—
Their virtues else, be they as pure as grace,
As infinite as man may undergo,
Shall in the general censure take corruption
From that particular fault: the dram of eale
Doth all the noble substance of a doubt
To his own scandal.

1. 4. 17-38

The Danes as a nation have soiled "their addition," their title of honor, by drunkenness. So men, individually, may carry "the stamp of one defect," impressing its form on the soul. This may be "some vicious mole of nature in them, / As in their birth"— he begins with an exception, "wherein they are not guilty." He is thinking not of inborn moral habit, that comes later, but of status, for instance bastardy, as with Don John or Edmund. Next, it may be a consequence of an imbalance of humors, or, again, of a dominant moral habit, in the Aristotelian sense: "some habit that too much o'er-leavens / The form of plausive manners." "Carrying, I say, the stamp of one defect," and then he throws in extra both natural habit, "nature's livery," and the external determinations of Fortune and "skyey influences," here identified: "fortune's star." To what end? The commentators say "The dram of evil" will "damn a man's whole reputation." I say, and I think Shakespeare said, will damn his immortal soul:

> Their virtues else, be they as pure as grace,
> As infinite as man may undergo,

The associations are theological, as also with "corruption" in the next line:

Shall in the general censure take corruption
From that particular fault.

On a national fault he spoke of reputation. On the particular faults of particular men he speaks of damnation: they shall in the General Censure, *iudicium generale*, the Last Judgment, take corruption. For the contrary case: Psalm 16:10: "For thou wilt not leave my soul in hell; neither wilt thou suffer thine Holy One to see corruption." To return: It takes just one mortal sin: "The dram of evil / Doth all the noble substance of ['em]," the immortal soul, "do out"—in our language "do in"—"To his [its] own scandal" (*Ham.*, 1. 4. 36-38),[9] to its moral ruination. For "scandal," though it had our current meaning at the time, had also a special meaning, technical and theological. It is by word or deed to be the occasion of moral or spiritual ruination to someone else. So St. Thomas.[10] And Hooker: "Men are scandalized when they are moved, led, and provoked unto sin."[11] But in this case the noble substance is done in, not to someone else's but to its own moral ruination. So in conclusion, for myself, and for you, I say out of context, "Angels and ministers of grace defend us," and God have mercy on our souls.

I add: The question of damnation is recurrent in *Hamlet* and, of course, implied in the moral problem of revenge, especially in a dynastic context. The principal references are Laertes: "To hell allegiance, vows to the blackest devil"—feudal allegiance and religious commitment—"I dare damnation." (4. 5. 131, 133) Hamlet resolves to kill the king when he is clearly engaged in an act of mortal sin "that his soul may be as damned and black / As hell, whereto he goes." (3. 3. 94-95) And does: "Here, thou incestuous, murd'rous, damned Dane"—the order of adjectives is climactic—"Drink off this potion." (5. 2. 336-37)

Sorting Out
The Case of Dickinson

∿∿∿∿∿∿∿∿∿∿∿∿∿∿∿∿∿∿∿∿∿∿∿∿∿∿∿∿∿∿∿∿∿∿∿∿

I

I am a renegade Irish Catholic from the plains of Montana, upper lower class, a onetime scholar in Latin and in the English Renaissance. Consequently, I speak without authority on a nineteenth-century New England spinster, of the American governing class, schooled in the feelings and expectations of revivalistic Calvinism, and an admirer of Emily Brontë and Elizabeth Barrett Browning. That I have anything new to say seems unlikely at this date in Dickinson studies; even a new untruth—but we shall see. I shall at least be novel in what is not said.

My topic is sorting out. This is, of course, an element in all experience; we do it as we enter a room, we do it consciously at the laundromat. We do it as occasion and need require, and as motive directs. The particular occasion is this essay. The larger occasion is the publication in 1955 of an authoritative diplomatic text of the poems, and in 1958 of the letters, so that there has been, as it were, a starting over in Dickinson studies. It is a starting over that, despite much hard work and more publication, is still somewhat in confusion.

We have no authoritative normalized text. The more or less firm canon of better poems, established in the twenties and thirties, is no longer firm; poems of merit and poems that at-

353

tract attention are mingled in the anthologies. The kinds of poems and the kinds of experience their abstractions allude to are incompletely and sometimes erroneously discriminated. There are, of course, reasons for this inherent in the situation. We have almost 1,800 items in the collected poems, all of them short, one after the other, with no apparent principle of order. It is easier to hold in mind and sort out the plays of Shakespeare or the novels of George Eliot, for they have scope and structure. So we come to motive. My motive is exasperation. I have become entangled with this woman, and I must get her in hand or get out.

But explicit sorting is a final stage. There is always an antecedent and implicit sorting given in the history of the text, of the commentary, and of our own involvement with them, and most unnoticeable of all, in the attitudes we bring to the task. In what cues our attention, our concerns precede us, and these may well have been handed us on the sly.

I should like, then, to deal briefly with two attitudes and one presupposition that affect the reconsideration of Dickinson; and, first, our attitude toward the striking. We tend to reject the striking phrase. The Gorgianic sobriquet for vultures, "living sepulchres," has been praised by some and rejected by most in the long history of sophistic rhetoric. We are uneasy with the striking, and tend to rephrase the matter harmlessly, to say in response to "The soul has bandaged moments," (512)[1] "Don't you mean we sometimes feel hurt?" But we can be cued to prefer the striking, and then not only the notable but every deviation from the ordinary or from propriety has inherent value. The off-rhymes, the wayward lineation, the colloquialisms, the bad grammar, indeed the pidgin English, that distressed the original editors and their public in the 1890s are now praised as triumphs over correctness.

But to return to matters of substance. Dickinson is sometimes striking in thought:

> It might be lonelier
> Without the loneliness. (405)

where the personification of a state of mind becomes a companion; more often in diction. And she achieves the effect commonly by a single device, by what rhetoricians call metonymy and I call the device of the proximate or neighboring word. "Bandaged," for instance, is in the neighborhood of "hurt." The device may be extended to the idea and the detail of a whole poem, especially if sufficiently short. In *A clock stopped, not the mantel's* (287) death is figured as a stopped clock, for to die is to quit time. And the detail is likewise neighboring: "Geneva's farthest skill / Can't put the puppet bowing," for the Swiss are famous for clockwork and "utmost" is "farthest." Then, "The figures . . . quivered out of decimals / Into degreeless noon," though duodecimals would be more correct; and "This pendulum of snow," this person cold in death.

The unusual has its virtues as has the usual. The proximate word may be striking, and so both memorable and satisfying to the occasional desire for novelty. It may also suggest a further and converging meaning. The stillness when she dies "Was like the stillness in the air / Between the heaves of storm," (465) "heaves" instead of "gusts," as with a horse or with the dying. It may, however, be only an alternative, an elegant variation: "Would not the jest / Have crawled too far!" (338) instead of the harmless "gone too far." Or, as we shall later see, it may suggest irrelevant frayed meanings. Finally, sometimes the apparently proximate word is not the proximate but proper; in "the distance / On the look of death," (258) "look" is more proper than "face."

In the poem, *A clock stopped*, the unusual is only novelty, the inferences from clock to person being immediately apparent, unless one judges that the analogy permits and protects the unexpected implication of the conclusion:

> The Shopman importunes it,
> While cool, concernless No
> Nods from the gilded pointers,
> Nods from the seconds slim;
> Decades of arrogance between
> The dial life and Him.

The Shopman can only be God, whose solicitation to immortal

life the dead coolly, concernlessly rejects, superior through eternity. Nevertheless, contrast this relentless metonymy with the dry, unassaulting style of:

> The last night that she lived,
> It was a common night
> Except the dying, this to us
> Made Nature different. (1100)

I turn now to our attitude toward the finished. We think we approve of it, and sometimes we do, but in confrontation we often disapprove, for the finished has a precluding effect. It seems to shut us out. It invites only our admiration, not our participation; there is nothing to finish. So the mass and mess of the collected poems, with many items literally unfinished and most not subjected to finality, has advantaged her reputation, as has the diplomatic text, presenting as accurately as typography permits the authoritative copy with its eccentric lineation and its plentiful dashes, sometimes for punctuation, more often the squiggles of a nervous tic: poetry neither adorned nor nude and bare, but in disheveled undress, so that even the finished looks unfinished.

But what is the finished? It is, of course, the complete. The beginning will be a given, but the end must be an apparent end. Furthermore, no word, phrase, aspect shall challenge alteration; the choices have been made and are not to be reopened. It is, however private its origin, public in expression, in idiom common. It must be correct, though not necessarily of a schoolmarm's correctness. There must be no sense of strain, but an accomplished easiness. The ingenious and the virtuoso, though locked tight in completeness, are not the finished. In brief, it must give an unanalyzed conviction of just-rightness, and it must be something somewhat better than good.

Hence formality is an indispensable element in the finished. Symmetrical pattern, exact meter and rhyme lay claim to it; they are by nature clinchers. It follows that if there is a taste for the unfinished, inexactness may become in itself a virtue, or it may suggest the value of the open as opposed to the closed, freedom instead of constraint, or finally the variations may be linked with other aspects and found significant. So it is thought to be with Dickinson, but it is not so. In one poem, *Because I could not stop for death* (712), she rhymes "me" and "immortality," "away" and "civility," "ring" and "sun," "chill" and "tulle," "ground" and "ground," "day" and "eternity." Yet in another, *There's a certain slant of light* (258), the rhymes are "afternoons" and "tunes," "scar" and "are," "despair" and "air," "breath" and "death." It is clear that in the economy of the poem there is no difference between the two sets. In her phonetic world identical, full, vowel with vowel, and terminal consonantal rhyme, including rhyming of cognate consonants, have the same status. There is no difference between them, and hence no significance in the difference; there is not even the piquancy of inexactness. Only in the larger economy of the English language and of poetic tradition are the variations noticeable.

The case is similar with some instances of inexact meter. She writes for the most part in the traditional measures of the hymn book, and of much of the poetry in English, in common (8686) and short (6686) meters, and it is in these that the inexactitude occurs. The lines are regularly iambic—except, of course, that there are some poems in the trochaic analogue—but, especially in the first and third lines, the nonrhyming lines, a 6 or a 7 may replace the schematic 8, or a 7 or an 8 the schematic 6. In brief, under certain restrictions, trimeter and tetrameter, like full and off-rhyme, are prosodic equivalents whose phonetic difference has no aesthetic significance.

This is puzzling but, I think, explicable. One finds in her letters again and again passages in these meters incorporated in prose, and sometimes several bridged by prose links. She apparently went around the house with scraps of paper in her pocket on which she jotted metrical snatches to be later salvaged for poem or letter (or both), or to be thrown away. She had a habit of phrasing incomplete fragments of quatrains in common or short meter—it was a way of talking to herself—so that, unless she directed her attention to the matter, the choice of which form was accidental.

The situation can be further defined by contrast with her practice in other meters, particularly in tetrameter and what is called common particular meter on the one hand, and in iambic pentameter on the other. I find sixteen poems in iambic tetrameter, two in trochaic tetrameter catalectic. They are all unfailingly exact in meter except for one line, the last line, in one poem: it is iambic trimeter. Again, in the 886886 stanza, common particular meter, the situation is similar. Of thirty-four poems twenty-nine are exact, two begin with three eights, three conclude with a quatrain, but these exceptions are otherwise exact.

The contrast is clear, yet there is no difference in the kind and quality of poem between those in the four measures discussed or those in exact and in inexact meter. Common particular, for instance, is suited to the light as are the others, and to the plangent:

> These are the days when birds come back,
> A very few, a bird or two,
> To take a backward look.
>
> These are the days when skies resume
> The old, old sophistries of June,
> A blue and gold mistake.
>
> Oh; fraud that cannot cheat the bee,
> Almost thy plausibility
> Induces my belief,
>
> Till ranks of seed their witness bear,
> And softly through the altered air
> Hurries a timid leaf.
>
> Oh, sacrament of summer days,
> Oh, last communion in the haze,
> Permit a child to join,
>
> Thy sacred emblems to partake,
> Thy consecrated bread to take,
> And thine immortal wine! (130)

This is the central style and manner of women's poetry, a particular genre, from Emily Brontë through Christina Rosetti and Alice Meynell to Louise Bogan. Yet she writes it also in inexact meter:

> As imperceptively as grief
> The summer lapsed away,
> Too imperceptible at last
> To seem like perfidy (1540)

which begins in common and continues in short meter.

Iambic pentameter, however, is another matter. In this she is in effect, though not, I think, in explicit intention, experimental in our more recent sense. The experimental, though it borrows prestige from science, is not experiment, except that when genuine it is risk. To be experimental is to undertake the formally deviant, hoping to elicit a kind of thing not hitherto said. The experimental is exploratory in unforeseen contingency, and when it succeeds it is no longer experimental. One can be experimental, then, not only with respect to the tradition as a whole, but also with respect to the norm of one's own work, and it is in this sense that Dickinson is experimental in pentameter.

I find at most thirty poems containing that measure. In some she essays uncharacteristic styles; for instance, the poetic:

> Unto guessed crests my moaning fancy leads me (295)

or:

> And shade is all that devastates the stillness (1441)

or an idiomatic simplicity:

> I cannot see my soul but know 'tis there (1262)

or:

> I know some lonely houses off the road. (289)

In others she tries out the traditionally eloquent:

> Next time to stay! Next time, the things to see
> By ear unheard, unscrutinized by eye (160)

or:

> 'Tis compound vision, light enabling light,
> The finite furnished with the infinite,
> Convex and concave witness back toward time,
> And forward toward the God of him. (906)

The last line is tetrameter, and in it the eloquent falls on its face. In brief, if she begins with pentameter she does not sustain it— there are two exceptions, both of four lines; in other poems pentameter comes and goes, a mixed meter in the general tradition of the English Pindaric. What's more, and this is curious, the nine-syllable iambic line—"Safe in their alabaster chambers"—which in most English poetry is an alternative tetrameter, seems rather to be for Dickinson, both in the line quoted and elsewhere, equivalent to the pentameter:

> Safe in their alabaster chambers,
> Untouched by morning and untouched by noon,
> Sleep the meek members of the resurrection,
> Rafter of satin and roof of stone. (216)

The middle lines are conventional pentameters—conventional is not a value judgment—in conventional high style, but in the fourth the meter breaks down, or is thrown away: it is a swinging four-beat line. In the three efforts she made at a second stanza she continues in the four-beat line, her all-out cadence:

> Light laughs the breeze in her castle above them,
> Babbles the bee in a stolid ear

In this case when pentameter broke down she had nowhere to go. Perhaps because the claimed enthusiasm of the cadence concealed a lack of belief.

In brief, there was a different and more varied poet, though not necessarily a better one, hidden in iambic pentameter that never quite got out.

II

But the ordering, interpretation, and evelution of the poems has been from the first publication more openly dominated by pre-suppositions of biographical relevance: by the legend of Emily on the one hand, and by the responsible attempt on the other to locate the reference of the poems, and to order at least some of them by a reconstructed history of the poet's emotional life. This last, if it could be done, would give us a partial whole in-stead of splintered fragments and brief realizations. It would, in effect, arrange some poems in the form of a sequence.

But biography, as historical discipline, and literary inter-pretation have, though at times concurrent, ultimately divergent ends. History would destroy the text to attain the fact. Inter-pretation takes the poet at his word; it seeks only to realize the text, and to this end asks, What area of experience is here re-ferred to? What kind of poem is this? We have already in pass-ing distinguished one kind, what Ruskin calls the poem of will-ful fancy: *A clock stopped, not the mantel's.* Such "cheating of the fancy" pleases, he says, because it "involves no real ex-pectation that it will be believed." Hence, such poems are not biographically relevant, except insofar as one's poems are events in his life. And so it is amusing that one of the best known of these, *I taste a liquor never brewed* (214), has been until quite recently read as a self-portrait of Legendary Emily, that "De-bauchee of dew," that "little tippler / Leaning against the sun." But it seems more likely that the speaker is not Emily at all, but a hummingbird; that the poem is, as many similar nature poems are, a riddle; and we have long missed the answer, not knowing *Guess Who?* was being asked.

Other poems, and a few of the best, are general: I call them thoughts. They are definitions concerned with "The difference between despair / And fear," (305) or gnomic conclusions on life and pain:

> The heart asks blessing first;
> And then excuse from pain;
> And then those little anodynes
> That deaden suffering;
>
> And then to go to sleep;
> And then if it should be
> The will of its Inquisitor
> The privilege to die. (536)

To read these with particularity of reference, though indeed they may apply to her life as perhaps to ours, is to misread, to take an impersonal poem as a personal one. It is the difference between "Women are bitches" and "My wife is a bitch." So, too, in *My life closed twice* (1732), to be concerned with the identity of the two the poet lost by death, to attempt to narrow the reference by biographical constructs, is to give a false particularity and to distort the text:

> My life closed twice before its close;
> It yet remains to see
> If immortality unveil
> A third event to me
>
> So huge, so hopeless to conceive,
> As these that twice befell:
> Parting is all we know of heaven,
> And all we need of hell.

The subject is immortality considered as parting; the literary form, a gnomic epigram concluded with the antithesis of Heaven and Hell, and structured internally by two to make ready and three to go, a structure given in childhood, not elicited from experience. If she had had only one such loss, or many, she still needed two for the poem.

But even this poem, of course, is not a mathematical theorem; it is not so general as to be of all time. The concern with personal immortality, and especially the open-endedness of the feeling, is of Dickinson's time and place, and peculiarly a Dickinson concern. It is relevant, then, to ask how the poem fits in, to locate it in time and place, and in that biography in which the events are her poems.

III

We know of that biography that she lived in a Christian family, in a religious town, in a time of revivals. We know from her own statements that she was once converted, or almost, and that she immediately fell away. At fifteen she writes a friend: "I have had the same feelings myself Dear A. I was almost persuaded to be a christian—and I can say I never enjoyed such perfect peace and happiness as the short time in which I felt I had found my savior. But . . . One by one my old habits returned to me and I cared less for religion than ever. . . . I feel I shall never be happy without I love Christ." (*L*: I, 27)[2] To such an experience a later poem alludes:

> If I'm lost now, that I was found
> Shall still my transport be,
> That once on me those jasper gates
> Blazed open suddenly . . .
>
> I'm banished now, you know it.
> How foreign that can be
> You'll know, sir, when the Savior's face
> Turns so away from you. (256)

She has lost salvation.

What, then, can we say of her attitude toward the orthodox religion of her youth and her time? The question has naturally been discussed in the commentary, but the form of the question has stipulated a kind of answer, however qualified, that misrepresents the evidence. The question implies an answer, but the evidence gives many answers. In fact, her attitudes cover the full range of possibilities, now this, now that, including, as we shall see, those current attractions, Taylorism and Perfectionism. Nor is there any clear sequence of development, no unfolding religious change, except that we may presume faith was given in childhood and only later became subject to diversity.

At one extreme there is a marching evangelical fervor, feeling in excess of belief:

> Given in marriage unto Thee,
> O Thou Celestial Host!
> Bride of the Father and the Son,
> Bride of the Holy Ghost! (817)

There is pious effusion, a little dialogue with Jesus:

> "Unto Me?" I do not know you;
> Where may be your house?
> "I am Jesus, late of Judea,
> Now of Paradise." (964)

But seldom simple belief and never the simple simple belief of a Herbert or a Jonson, as in Jonson's *To Heaven*:

> As Thou art all, so be Thou all to me,
> First, midst, and last, converted one, and three,
> My faith, my hope, my love, and in this state
> My judge, my witness, and my advocate.

And yet at times God is a living presence; she stays home, for God is her visitor. (674)

On the other hand, there are four lines of flippant doggerel on Faith versus Science, in favor of Science. (185) And there is irreverence; the mediation of the Son for the Father is compared to that of John Alden for Myles Standish. (357) And more than irreverence. She apologizes to the Heavenly Father "For Thine own duplicity." (1461) There are also complaints against God, perhaps in the spirit of Job:

> Of course I prayed, and did God care?
> He cared as much as on the air
> A bird had stamped her foot. (376)

Of this we may say it is still Christianity, though perhaps not commendably pious; but is it Christianity to assert, in the verses already cited, that life is a Spanish Inquisition, and the Inquisitor is God, of whom one asks only the privilege, or if you will the luxury, of dying, with the implication that death is final?

Hence, in other poems she professes substitute religions. In one, a religion of Nature, of the garden: "Some keep the Sabbath going to church; / I keep it . . . / With a bobolink for a chorister." (324) In another, the human consciousness is God; if they differ

> they do
> As syllable from sound (632)

as specification from ground. Indeed, the poet represents herself as acting as a predestinating god:

> The soul selects her own society,
> Then shuts the door;
> To her divine majority
> Present no more. (303)

For *majority* is "election," a neighboring word, and hers is divine.

So in "that religion / That doubts as fervently as it believes," (1144) disbelief and threatened belief recur. To lose one's faith is more than loss of an estate, for "estates can be / Replenished, faith cannot." (377) And yet we need it:

> Infinitude, hadst thou no face
> That I might look on Thee? (564)

Those who died in the past knew where they went:

> They went to God's Right Hand.
> That Hand is amputated now,
> And God cannot be found.

As a consequence we are trivialized:

> The abdication of belief
> Makes the behavior small.
> Better an ignis fatuus
> Than no illume at all. (1551)

And so at times she expresses not this or that note in the gamut of possibilities, but rather the dissonant chord of mixed feelings. She writes to her cousins toward the end of her life: "When we think of the lone effort to live, and its bleak reward, the mind turns to the myth 'for His mercy endureth forever,' with confiding revulsion." (*L*: III, 711)

Yet even this does not exhaust the range of possibilities. There is also Satanism: ". . . though in that last day, the Jesus Christ you love, remark he does not know me there is a darker spirit will not disown his child." An internalized Satanism of the divided self, as in the loaded gun poem. (754)

In brief, the poems that express her attitudes toward religion do not support one another, do not converge on an attitude. They must be sorted out. They must be taken one by one, and, indeed, sometimes the variants within a poem must be taken one by one. On the critical point of Immortality, for instance, there is a poem, extant in two copies, with alternate lines. In one, the attar of the rose, though roses decay, will make summer in the lady's dresser drawer when she lies "In ceaseless rosemary," immortality affirmed; in the other, "In spiceless sepulchre," immortality denied. (675)

IV

Is this simply whimsical whirlygig? Or spiritual crisis? It is, in fact, a prolongation of that adolescent crisis, already referred to, of incomplete conversion, in a context of emotional Christianity yet open to all the destructive anti-Christianity of nineteenth-century thought: "The Bible is an antique volume / Written by faded men / At the suggestion of Holy Spectres." (1545) It is a tale of Election, of Salvation and Perdition; of the rebirth of a Second Baptism; of Celestial Marriage to God, to someone, or simply in itself, by which one becomes a spiritual wife, "Sealed to eternity," and at the same time puts on maturity and puts away the child. It is a tale in which fantasies of dying are spiritual exercises, for death is the premise of immortality. It is also a tale of the failure to break through, to give up the world and self-will, to achieve election, with the subsequent conviction of being lost, of perdition, but it is not a perdition of hellfire. It is the perdition of death as final, or of the horror of stopless life. So one gives up hope, that last stage before conversion, gives up the enterprise and with it the fear. But it is not a tale, so far as the chronological evidence permits inference, of moving through successive positions to a final conclusion; rather, these are elements in a matrix of experience, reexperienced again and again in whole and in part, and concluded only by the poet's death.

Let us look into it:

> Soul, wilt thou toss again?
> By just such a hazard
> Hundreds have lost indeed,
> But tens have won an all. (139)

Election is at hazard, angels and devils witnessing, the odds ten to one against ever winning, favorable odds for a Calvinist. But notice: one may choose to play; one may provoke conversion; the attempt is a willed activity, and a repeatable one. It follows by emotional proximity that, if one can venture at will on conversion, one can succeed by willed assertion. One can succeed since the power of election has passed from God to man, or, perhaps, woman.

"Mine," she says, "by the right of the white election!" (528) What is mine? Clearly salvation, for white is the color of salvation, and, indeed, in one instance of perdition, "And that white sustenance, / Despair" (640), and hence of immortality: "Mine by the grave's repeal!" "Mine long as ages steal!" But there are two curious aspects to this poem, both contained in the line: "Mine here in vision and in veto!" It is salvation and immortality attained here, in this life, and hence Perfectionism:

> Eternity obtained in time,
> Reversed divinity! (800)

And it is election at the discretion of the elect, "in vision and in veto," and hence Taylorism; indeed, the phrase is a translation of Taylor's maxim: "Certainty with the power to the contrary." In brief, God proposes, and man disposes.

But these poems are not doctrinal in reference; they refer to experiences, the decision to try again, the assertion of accomplishment. At this remove from Christianity they are experiences available to most of us only by imaginative empathy, and to that end the experience in prose, avowedly autobiographical with its claim to fact, may restore a legitimate vividness and a sense of actuality. We have such an account by John Humphrey Noyes, the founder of the Oneida Community, twenty years older than Dickinson but of the same region and social origins. He grew up in Brattleboro, in the Connecticut Valley, within fifty miles of Amherst. His father, as was Dickinson's, had been a Congressman. The religious setting for both was New England Congregationalism and revivalism. He writes— the date of the experience is 1834:

> The first results of the act of faith which I have described—[*it was*: If I pass through the form of dying, yet in fact I shall never die]—were delightful. I passed one night in unspeakable happiness. I felt I had burst through the shroud of death into the heavenly places. But I soon found that the spiritual transition which I had made had placed me in new relations to evil spirits as well as good, that I had entered a region where the powers of darkness were to be encountered face to face as I had never encountered them before.
>
> In the course of the following day a strange, murky spiritual atmosphere began to gather around me. . . . The multitude of involuntary thoughts which fermented in my mind finally settled into a strong impression that I was about to part with flesh and blood either by ordinary death or by an instantaneous change. Nor was it merely an impression that seemed to summon me away. Ere long I began actually to feel a suffocating pressure on my lungs. This was not the effect of physical disease, for my organs of respiration were

healthy before and afterward. Nor was it the effect of
excitement, for I had no fear of death and was entirely
calm in heart. I put my room in decent order, and lay
down to die. The pressure increased till my breathing
stopped, and my soul seemed to turn inward for its
flight. At this crisis, when I had resigned myself wholly
to the consciousness of dying, the pressure was instantly
removed, and I arose with the joy of victory in my heart.
To my imagination the transaction was as if I had been
enclosed in a net, and dragged down to the very borders
of Hades, and then in the last agony had burst the net
and returned to life. This transaction was repeated
several times.

After this I went through a protracted process of
involuntary thought and feeling, which I can describe
by no better name than a spiritual crucifixion. All the
events of Christ's death were vividly realized in my feelings. I went through them not as a spectator, but as a
victim. At length came the resurrection, and for a time
I was released from suffering. . . .

After the spiritual crucifixion which has been described I received a baptism of that spirit which has
since manifested itself extensively in the form of Mil-
lerism.[3]

And now Dickinson; it is an experience of the same ilk,
though the outcome is opposite:

> Just lost when I was saved,
> Just felt the world go by,
> Just girt me for the onset with Eternity
> When breath blew back and on the other side
> I heard recede the disappointed tide! (160)

In the hazard of election, at the point of salvation she is lost.
Is she sealed to Perdition? At the point of giving up the world,
literally in some sort of spiritual suicide, breath returned—had
she been holding it?—and the overwhelming tide missed its ap-
pointment. So far this is report of experience; she concludes with

comment and anticipation. She has come back with intuitions of the novel and awful secrets of Revelation, and resolves next time to stay, to attain immortality. We have already seen that she claims to have done so. But the nature and structure of the experience are more fully detailed in another poem.

"Title divine is mine," she says (1072), and certainly the title she claims is divine, "Empress of Calvary." She is the bride of Christ, of suffering and Redemption. It is "Acute degree," that is, by the device of the proximate word, high rank. But she is "The wife without the sign," "Royal, all but the crown." Now *sign, seal, crown* are technical terms in the theology of Revelation. She is without "an appearance or occurrence indicative of the divine presence, and authenticating a message or messenger." And she lacks the crown of life: "Be thou faithful unto death, and I will give thee a crown of life." (Rev. 2:10) In brief, she is self-elected. She has, in fact, become married without the ordinary accompaniments of earthly marriage:

> Betrothed without the swoon
> God sends us women when you hold
> Garnet to garnet, gold to gold.

She has been "Born, bridalled, shrouded in a day, / Trivictory!" Reborn, as depicted in other poems, by a second baptism: "except a man be born again, he cannot see the kingdom of God." (John 3:3) She has been bridalled, and the heavenly bridal suggests the earthly:

> "My husband," women say,
> Stroking the melody.
> Is this the way?

Is this experience of mine, she asks, of the same kind as ordinary marriage? Nor is the transition surprising, for as we all know, as John Humphrey Noyes knew, "Religious love is very near neighbor to sexual love. . . . The next thing a man wants, after he has found the salvation of his soul, is to find his Eve and his Paradise," and to find them in terms of the theology of Revelation. So "There came a day at summer's full" when "Each was to each the sealed church," each was the saved and the source of salvation to the other, bound by exchange of crucifixes, which I take figuratively:

> Sufficient troth that we shall rise,
> Deposed at length the grave,
> To that new marriage justified
> Through Calvaries of love. (322)

The marriage is new; that is, the marriages of this world are cancelled. The two are spiritual spouses, "sealed to eternity" not through the mediation of the Son, but through each other's private love and suffering—a strange doctrine of Justification! We do not know what other person was involved: the name, as elsewhere in Dickinson, may be *N*. What was involved, however, is clear.

Hence in another poem she asserts, "I'm wife." (199) There is here no theological reference, and indeed no other person: "I'm wife. Stop there!" This is spiritual marriage, that curious phenomenon of nineteenth-century revivalism, in a special form, and deprived of spouse. Noyes will again instruct us as to the nature of the experience. He writes to Abagail Merwin, an early disciple and early defector:

> Let it be distinctly understood at the outset, that I intend no interference with any earthly engagement. . . . At length in the midst of another series of sufferings at Prospect I saw you again clothed in white robes, and by the word of the Lord you were given to me. . . . I know now that my love for you is the gift of God, pure and free, above all jealousy and above all fear. I can say of you to my Father: "She was thine, and thou gavest her to me; all mine are thine, and thine are mine." Nothing can shake my assurance that in a coming time you will be my joy and crown—"a diadem of glory from the land of the Lord."

"Born, bridalled, shrouded in a day, / Tri-victory!" The experience, I think, is simultaneous, not successive—in another poem (473) she is "Baptized this day a bride"—and the crucial element is "shrouded." Attempted conversion involves, in Dickinson it is willfully provoked by, a fantasy of dying, what Noyes calls "the consciousness of dying." The poems that issue from this spiritual exercise are among her most impressive. In one she heard a fly buzz when she died:

> and then it was
> There interposed a fly
>
> With blue, uncertain, stumbling buzz
> Between the light and me,
> And then the windows failed, and then
> I could not see to see. (465)

In another she presides at her own funeral:

> I felt a funeral in my brain,
> And mourners to and fro
> Kept treading, treading, till it seemed
> That sense was breaking through.
>
> And when they all were seated
> A service, like a drum,
> Kept beating, beating, till I thought
> My mind was going numb.
>
> And then I heard them lift a box
> And creak across my soul
> With those same boots of lead again,
> Then Space began to toll
>
> As all the Heavens were a bell
> And Being but an ear,
> And I and Silence some strange race
> Wrecked, solitary here.
>
> And then a plank in reason broke
> And I dropped down and down,

> And hit a world at every plunge,
> And finished knowing then. (280)

Toward the close the experience expands into that of a double divided self; on the one hand, the total engrossment of being in the universe; on the other, personal identity and Silence, non-being, alienated and outcast. Lost. And to be lost is to lose all. So she passes out; it is a psychotic episode.

In other poems she gives up the enterprise, gives up hope, the preparatory stage, and with it the fear:

> When I hoped, I feared.
> Since I hoped I dared
> Everywhere alone
> As a church remain. (1181)

"As a church"? This is a peculiarly Dickinson idiom, as in "I wish I was a hay!" Thus, to remain a church, everywhere alone, is to be one of a Church Triumphant whose membership is one. Personal religion with a vengeance? Or the necessity of despair?

So she can finally view the consequences with acceptance, even with spiritual snobbery:

> The missing All prevented me
> From missing minor things.
> If nothing larger than a world's
> Departure from a hinge,
> Or sun's extinction, be observed,
> 'Twas not so large that I
> Could lift my forehead from my work
> For curiosity. (985)

Only loss of salvation justifies such hyperbole.

V

Some of the poems that have been cited are good, some indifferent, and some really bad, but all in the service of understanding and realization. Let us conclude, then, by bringing our inquiries to bear on a poem universally acknowledged to be of her best. We find, not the fallacy of willful fancy, but Ruskin's other pathetic fallacy, "shadows hold their breath." The odd-numbered lines vary from six to eight syllables with no significance in the variation. In kind, it is a report of a repetitive and involuntary experience, "None may teach it any"; it is not to be argued with; a nature experience yet theological in form, "heavenly hurt"; it is the intimation that one is sealed to Perdition: "'Tis the Seal, Despair!'":

> There's a certain slant of light,
> Winter afternoons,
> That oppresses like the heft
> Of cathedral tunes.
>
> Heavenly hurt it gives us;
> We can find no scar,
> But internal difference
> Where the meanings are.
>
> None may teach it any;
> 'Tis the Seal, Despair!
> An imperial affliction
> Sent us of the air.
>
> When it comes, the landscape listens,
> Shadows hold their breath;
> When it goes, 'tis like the distance
> On the look of death. (258)

Edwin Arlington Robinson
A Brief Biography

~~~~~~

Robinson was a man almost without biography who became a legend to his friends. He was decent, reticent, likable, and contrary—he himself called it selfish. He was not going to work for a living. He would do nothing but write poetry, except at times prose fiction or drama for their economic potentialities. But in this he failed; prose was not his language. And unsuccessful prose he ultimately transmuted to poetry. The prose sketch of 1894, "in a lighter vein," "of a philosophic tramp . . . looking for rest" becomes in a few years *Captain Craig*.

To think of oneself as a poet has serious consequences, even if one's dignity precludes the dionysiac role of a Hart Crane. The professed poet must keep writing, "scrivening to the end against his fate," for it is the justification of his life. So he wrote too much, and when written out he could not swear off. Again, the role is jealous of all other roles. Without an independent income and a secure place in society loneliness, dispossession, chronic indigence follow. Finally, the role is vatic; the poet must intuit and communicate a meaning in the universe. So he kept asking the inadmissable question, What is it all about? especially considering the pain. That it was unanswerable he thought guaranteed the question. He spoke again and again of the Light,

which was now the Grail, now a woman, now "The light behind
the stars," and always something that blurs "man's finite vision
with misty glimmerings of the infinite." He believed in love and
in belief with "a kind of optimistic desperation."

Tobacco, alcohol, and Wagner were his passions and his
stay. The first he occasionally, but never seriously, gave up.
The second, apparently under the persuasion of friends, he did
for long periods, which is remarkable, for he drank whisky
straight by the tumblerful. The last he never wearied of.

At twelve or thirteen he came under the influence of a local
osteopath who had forsaken all else to write sonnets and the
French forms. Now, metrical speech is a language which, like
any language, must be learned young or never. And as a language it must have an audience; this the doctor and a cultivated local poetic circle provided so that in his later career he
never faltered in meter, and at his most involved and obscure
is still speaking to an audience.

At twenty-one, after three years of helping around the home
place and doggedly writing, he entered Harvard College, "the
object of almost the only patriotism I possess," as a special
student. It was the making of the poet; for there is an educated
ease with ideas and experience and a breadth that is denied to
the self-tutored. It is interesting that later in the decade Frost
and Stevens were also special students at Harvard.

After two years he returned home, the family dead, dying,
or physical and spiritual wrecks. Four years later, at twenty-
seven, he left home, finally settling in New York. The dissipation
of the family fortune—he had tacitly expected to live on a
modest patrimony—and a stubborn worldly incompetence reduced him at the age of thirty to absolute poverty, a life of
cadging, and ten months' employment as a timekeeper on a
construction job. The job finished, he was supported until his
fiftieth year by public and private patronage: by a sinecure at
the New York Customs House, arranged by President Theodore
Roosevelt, by the contributions of his friends, ultimately made
systematic, and by summer residence at the MacDowell Colony.
At fifty-one, when the *Collected Poems* was awarded the first of
his three Pulitzer prizes, he could finally live on what his poetry
made, and with the extraordinary success of *Tristram* in 1927

he was able to repay many of his debts and remain financially secure. Thereafter he wrote long poems, one a year until his death, which were bought primarily by public libraries and gave him a steady income. The principal other event of these years was the First World War and the destruction of the world he had known, which he translated into the Arthurian legend, "And there was darkness over Camelot."

He lived during his mature life among the moderately wealthy and cultured and with the outcast and miscast. He belonged to the former by breeding, to the latter by experience, imagination, and compassion. And he wrote of both. Yet little that he wrote was a direct transcription of experience. He had a life of fantasy in which Tilbury Town was and was not Gardiner, Maine, and those who come no more to Calverly's had their own existence, transpositions or opposites of himself and his friends. Though celibate he wrote with insight and some tedium of sexual passion. And he knew we do not really know about others; we do not know about him.

Toward the end of his life he concluded: "As lives go, my own life would be called, and properly, a rather fortunate one." Most commentators have not thought so, but it seems true. He died of cancer at sixty-five.[1]

Though he wrote too much, he wrote much that was distinctive and good, and even in the dull wastes there are fragments. He commanded from the beginning the full range of late Victorian styles, from the flat naturalistic prose line (and his own special roundabout pentameter) through incantatory jingle and the tightly rhymed stanzas of the light verse tradition to the full diapason of Romantic rhetoric: "Something of ships and sunlight, streets and singing, / Troy falling, and the ages coming back, / And ages coming forward." He had a gift for simile, "The stillness of October gold / Went out like beauty from a face," and especially for the abstract simile: the recurrent cadger "Familiar as an old mistake, / And futile as regret." He could secure the commonplace with the right epithet: "At someone's tinkling afternoon at home." He could manage unobtrusive profundity: "Love builds of what Time takes away, / Till Death itself is less than Change," and mark the quiet defeat of a life:

nor was there anything
To make a daily meaning for her life . . .
But the blank taste of time.[2]

The Styles and Procedures
of Wallace Stevens

~~~~~~

Shortly before the last war it became apparent· that Wallace
Stevens was about to displace T. S. Eliot as the exemplar of
American poetry, as the object of devotion, of imitation and
explication by younger poets, critics, and academics. His own
comments at that time on his predecessor in prestige will set
our problem:

> I don't know what there is any longer to say about
> Eliot. His prodigious reputation is a great difficulty.
> While that sort of thing: more or less complete ac-
> ceptance of it, helps to create the poetry of any poet,
> it also helps to destroy it.[1]

I should like to rescue the poetry of Wallace Stevens from
himself and from his friends. I feel it is worth rescuing, and I
am sure it needs it. I speak, then, for the estate of poetry, of
which I am the impersonal, and by definition imperfect, spokesman. The situation is this: there are over twelve thousand lines
of poetry, almost four hundred separate titles, and much of this
is junk, and most is repetitious. There is, furthermore, an immense body of commentary which is, with some notable exceptions, scandalously wrong, irrelevant, and confusing, much of it

consisting of centos of phrases from the poetry. The problem, then, is to sort out the poetry of Wallace Stevens, and to understand it. But, first, to understand it.

Anyone who reads through this mass of material will feel as one does who reads through the *Complete Poems* of Emily Dickinson and the attendant commentary, that he has gotten his hands inextricably involved in the taffy—oversaturated, bewildered, unable to tell the good from the bad, snatching at this poem and that, this passage and that, to save something from the confusion. And, I think, for much the same reasons. They were both amateurs in poetry in all but one sense. Now, an amateur does things for his own sake, for the sake of doing them. A professional does things for the thing's sake.[2] The professional poet as a writer of poems may not like to write—he may, as Thomas Mann said, be a man who finds writing more difficult than most people do—but once engaged in a poem his single aim is to perfect the poem. The amateur, on the other hand, likes to write poems, and may perfect them or not. He doesn't mind botching the job. Stevens in one of his best poems begins a stanza with a parable, "A red bird flies across the golden floor," but after four lines, interesting in themselves, he discovers he has been carried away; he doesn't really know what the parable is about, and so muses, "Shall I uncrumple this much crumpled thing?"

Instead, he begins again, precisely and magnificently:

> I am a man of fortune greeting heirs;
> For it has come that thus I greet the spring.
> These choirs of welcome choir for me farewell. (13)[3]

and he leaves the unsuccessful attempt standing in the text. It is still there.

Again, not only was he an amateur in the writing of poetry, he was not in his public life professionally a poet; he was an insurance executive, as Dickinson was, professionally, a New England spinster, a maiden aunt. Only in his very private life, as Dickinson in hers, did he see himself as a poet, and this cherished fantasy was not to the good; it had to be validated again and again by the production of poems of whatever quality.

For he needed to see himself as a poet, as poetry itself, not only because he was a man possessed by a genius for a prodigality of phrasing that was not to be denied, but also just to keep alive within the commonplaceness, the horror, the wantingness of American business civilization:

> Am I a man that is dead
>
> At a table on which the food is cold?
> Is my thought a memory, not alive?
>
> Is the spot on the floor, there, wine or blood
> And whichever it may be, is it mine? (173)

He was a man who must get up and go back to work on Monday morning, "in Monday's dirty light," where employer and employee contend while the pheasant sleeps late. "There is no place, / Here, for the lark fixed in the mind," for an absolute or imaginative conception of nature; the cock will serve only to waken them for work. "Morning is not sun, / It is this posture of the nerves" in which a poet blunted by business civilization holds tight to the nuances of poetry: "It must be this rhapsody or none." And so, in the winter of 1936-37, as the Depression dragged on:

> Here is the bread of time to come,
>
> Here is its actual stone. The bread
> Will be our bread, the stone will be
>
> Our bed and we shall sleep by night.
> We shall forget by day, except
>
> The moments when we choose to play
> The imagined pine, the imagined jay. (182-84)

The moments are preserved in the collected poems. He might have taken to drink; he took to poems, instead, to too many rot-gut poems.

Finally, he had, like Dickinson, only a few subjects, a group of rather simpleminded ideas and procedures, repetitive ways of getting started with a poem, and getting on with it. These have never been adequately discriminated and described, and it will be the novelty of this essay that they are discriminated and described. For a somewhat clearer understanding of them than Stevens had himself, as witnessed by his prose, is necessary to the understanding and evaluation of his work.

Let us begin with his recurrent concerns. There is, first of all, the loss of an implicit belief in the Christian God, or in any God—"The death of one god is the death of all" (381)—and hence of any belief in personal immortality, or, indeed in any structuring of the universe or of experience:

> This structure of ideas, these ghostly sequences
> Of the mind, result only in disaster. (326)

or, again:

> There is order in neither sea nor sun. (122)

But he had not lost the need to believe, to believe as one's grandfather had believed:

> Is it ideas that I believe?
> Good air, my only friend, believe,
>
> Believe would be a brother full
> Of love, believe would be a friend,
>
> Friendlier than my only friend,
> Good air . . .

He argues, if the old traditions are untrue, then they are fictitious, myths, and we as poets can construct our own myths: "A substitute for all the gods." (175-76) And we are driven to this because whatever we are, whatever we attain—say a "complete simplicity" that

> Stripped one of all his torments, concealed
> The evilly compounded, vital I
> And made it fresh in a world of white,
> A world of clear water, brilliant-edged,
> Still one would want more, one would need more . . .
>
> There would still remain the never-resting mind,
> So that one would want to escape.

But not only to escape, also to

>   come back
> To what had been so long composed.
> The imperfect is our paradise.

And so he is driven from pole to pole of experience, and in this process, delight is in the writing of poems:

> Note that, in this bitterness, delight,
> Since the imperfect is so hot in us,
> Lies in flawed words and stubborn sounds. (193-94)

Yet there is also a desire for rest, for stasis, for fulfilling peace:

> Is it I then that keep saying there is an hour
> Filled with expressible bliss, in which I have
>
> No need, am happy, forget need's golden hand,
> Am satisfied without solacing majesty,
> And if there is an hour there is a day,
>
> There is a month, a year, there is a time
> In which majesty is a mirror of the self:
> I have not but I am and as I am, I am. (404-05)

Allied to these concerns, which may be thought of as theological, is a preoccupation with philosophizing. Now, perhaps the most elementary thing one can think of in a philosophical way is that there is oneself and there is something other than oneself, and that the other exists for us insofar as we are aware of it, and that what we are aware of conditions our awareness. Subjective and objective. The terms can be distinguished and can be identified, and in this elementary occupation of distinguishing and identifying Stevens spent much of this mature life. One is his environment, his environment is him: "Nota: man is the intelligence of his soil" (27) and later: "his soil is man's intelligence." (36) The procedure is dialectical; a position is stated and then its opposite or contradictory; sometimes there intervenes a resolution, and then the terms or positions are again set free. These are the transformations of a Hartford Hegel. It is the residue of the teaching of Royce, William James, and Santayana, of Harvard College in the late 1890s, as his original style we will see is not to be distinguished from that of his immediate predecessors there, Robinson in his romantic mode, Trumbull Stickney, and Cabot Lodge.

The poles of subjective and objective are treated by Stevens under the rubrics of imagination and reality, sometimes distinguished, sometimes identified by the axiom that opposites are one, and the conjugation of these terms forms a meditation, or a system of meditation, which he sometimes feels is an imitation of, or a part of, or identified with, the essential meditation of the universe in its transformations from day to night, winter to summer. But we will never understand Stevens' poetry until we perceive that these ideas, except when he is being routine, are not ideas as such but rather specific kinds of experiences, just as in his better poetry what are sometimes thought of as the symbols of sun and moon, winter and summer, are really sun and moon, winter and summer, and their appropriate sun and winter experiences. Furthermore, the rubrics of imagination and reality refer now to one kind of experience and now to another, and hence we must describe and discriminate the quite different areas of experience alluded to by these terms.

We may distinguish under the rubrics of imagination at least six areas. First, it is the romantic as opposed to the realistic, in the ordinary high school sense of those terms—James Branch Cabell as opposed to Theodore Dreiser:

> O thin men of Haddam
> Why do you imagine golden birds?

> Do you not see how the blackbird
> Walks around the feet
> Of the women about you? (93)

Second, it is the kind of fantasy associated in Stevens with a high-spirited nonsense, by which one imagines "At night an Arabian in my room, / With his damned hoobla-hoobla-hoobla-how." (383), or by which "an old sailor, / Drunk and asleep in his boots, / Catches tigers / In red weather." (66) Something no proper housewife in a white nightgown would think of, and so in that way related to the first. Third, it is the distortion of feeling, the affective elements qualifying plain fact, the Imagistic enterprise:

> He rode over Connecticut
> In a glass coach.
> Once, a fear pierced him,
> In that he mistook
> The shadow of his equipage
> For blackbirds. (94)

I suspect, by the way, that the glass coach was in plain fact not Cinderella's equipage but the New York, New Haven, and Hartford Railroad. Fourth, it is the perception of resemblances, a perception between diverse phenomena by which we may intuit a oneness in the universe in which the intuiter may partake. It is an instrument of the monistic experience:

> The river is moving.
> The blackbird must be flying. (94)

The procedure can be consciously induced and pursued. One looks at a pineapple on the table and imagines:

> 1. The hut stands by itself beneath the palms.
> 2. Out of their bottle the green genii come. (*NA* 86)

It is "Not that which is but that which is apprehended," so that a mirror becomes "a lake of reflections in a room," and then "A glassy ocean lying at the door." (468) Fifth, it is a process of abstraction, a furious negative exclusion of all associations with the object, especially those of Christianity, but also of the trite and cliché, in order to intuit an inherent, a bare reality. To perceive "The inconceivable idea of the sun"

> You must become an ignorant man again
> And see the sun again with an ignorant eye
> And see it clearly in the idea of it.
>
> Never suppose an inventing mind as source
> Of this idea nor for that mind compose
> A voluminous master folded in his fire . . .
>
>   The sun
> Must bear no name, gold flourisher, but be
> In the difficulty of what it is to be. (380-81)

But it is a reality of which ultimately nothing can be said, hence we must find it to be nothingness, or body it forth. And so, sixth, imagination is the act of constructing and projecting a myth, analogous to the Christian myth, that will represent the intuited reality. The myth may be of two sorts, a) grandiose, "a hero's head" (165), a giant, an immense rock or mountain, the bedrock of reality, the analogue of Mt. Olympus, or b) whimsical, trivial, ordinary, and antihero, the modern successor and parody of the heroic age: "The major abstraction is the idea of man / And major man is its exponent . . ."

>   Who is it?
> What rabbi, grown furious with human wish . . .
>
> Does not see these separate figures one by one,
> And yet see only one, in his old coat,
> His slouching pantaloons, beyond the town,
>
> Looking for what was where it used to be?
> Cloudless the morning. It is he. The man
> In that old coat, those sagging pantaloons . . . (388-89)

But it is a fiction in which we do not believe; it isn't there. So we come full circle, we come back to plain fact, to reality.

Reality itself is also manifold. It is, first of all, things as we ordinarily see and describe them, external reality:

> The eye's plain version is a thing apart,
> The vulgate of experience. (465)

Of this there are two subdivisions, a) plain fact, and b) the fuller exact descriptive statement but without intrusion of feeling or illusion. It is, secondly, the humdrum of ordinary life in this civilization, to which one may be adjusted or not. The Canon Aspirin's sister in *Notes Toward a Supreme Fiction* is completely adjusted. She lived in her house in a sensible ecstasy, dressed her children in the poverty that became them:

> She held
> Them closelier to her by rejecting dreams.
>
> The words they spoke were voices that she heard.
> She looked at them and saw them as they were
> And what she felt fought off the barest phrase. (402)

It is a life without imagination, and hence to the unadjusted an alien life, a life of horror and boredom, in which "The time of year has grown indifferent" (96), in which "A little less returned for him each spring":

> Only last year he said that the naked moon
> Was not the moon he used to see, to feel
>
> (In the pale coherences of moon and mood
> When he was young), naked and alien,
> More leanly shining from a lankier sky. (148-49)

It is defined by the absence of imagination. But there is also real reality, ultimate reality, beyond or behind appearance, significance defeating boredom, to be attained by the procedures of imagination, monism at the heart of things. And finally, there is the discovery that there is no reality behind appearance, no significance in triviality; reality is nothingness. Such, then, is the machinery of much of Stevens' poetry.

How does it work out in the poems? A good deal that Stevens wrote, especially in his later years, was in the form of sequences of short poems. These are sometimes only a miscellany of items, numbered consecutively, and headed by an irrelevant title. (252-59) At other times they are a group of poems, more or less related to each other, especially at the beginning and end, but also intermittently in between. Of such sort, of course, are *Sunday Morning* and the monocle poem, but the sequences I have in mind now differ from those in that they make a more explicit, a more systematic though not finally systematic, use of the procedures I have enumerated under the rubrics of imagination and reality, which are at their extremes solipsism and monism. The skeleton of the method can be seen in an early poem, *Metaphors of a Magnifico*:

> Twenty men crossing a bridge,
> Into a village,
> Are twenty men crossing twenty bridges,
> Into twenty villages,

That is, each consciousness creates a separate world; it is solipsism:

> Or one man
> Crossing a single bridge into a village.

Or all participate in a central consciousness, a single world; it is monism. Then follows an arpeggio, an affective comment, a deviation on the principle: "The acquisitions of poetry are fortuitous; *trouvailles*. (Hence its disorder.)" (*OP* 169), though this is a very mild instance:

> This is old song
> That will not declare itself.

Then:

> Twenty men crossing a bridge,
> Into a village,
> Are
> Twenty men crossing a bridge
> Into a village.

Or, it is just a fact:

> That will not declare itself
> Yet is certain as meaning . . .
> The boots of the men clump
> On the boards of the bridge.
> The first white wall of the village
> Rises through fruit-trees.

As fact it is subject to more extended description. And now follows a third arpeggio, and the repetition of part of the preceding two lines as a kind of dying cadence:

> Of what was it I was thinking?
> So the meaning escapes.

> The first white wall of the village . . .
> The fruit-trees. (19)

It is not much of a poem, but it shows in brief the procedures, the movement from one position to the next, the irrelevancies to the argument, the final messing it up. And the subjects are solipsism, monism, plain fact. Another early poem, *Thirteen Ways of Looking at a Blackbird*—had it been twelve or fourteen, would the poem have so caught the fancy of readers?—displays, along with a few purely imagistic sections, in a wholly unsystematic form the same procedures; in fact, I have already quoted three of the sections in illustration of the different aspects of imagination and reality, and now add one more:

> A man and a woman
> Are one
> A man and a woman and a blackbird
> Are one. (93)

There are two propositions: opposites involve each other; reality is monistic.

Let us look, now, briefly at some of the later and longer sequences. *The Man with the Blue Guitar* begins by posing explicitly the problem of imagination and reality and its relationship to writing poetry:

> The man bent over his guitar,
> A shearsman of sorts. The day was green.
>
> They said, "You have a blue guitar,
> You do not play things as they are."
>
> The man replied, "Things as they are
> Are changed upon the blue guitar."
>
> And they said then, "But play, you must,
> A tune beyond us, yet ourselves,
>
> A tune upon the blue guitar
> Of things exactly as they are." (165)

The day, of course, was green by the natural association of sunlight and greenery, and is rendered falsely in the blue of illusion. The problem is to get it exactly and at the same time to strike through to the reality beyond reality. In the next section the poet cannot quite strike through to an idea of man that would yet be a man; in the third section, Ah, if he could; in the fourth, attempting to get "A million people on one string," mankind and man at once, feeling suddenly breaks through

> The feelings crazily, craftily call,
> Like a buzzing of flies in autumn air. (166)

the distortion of feeling. So far, and for the next two, the sections pretty much develop out of each other, but soon they become somewhat more miscellaneous. This is an improvisatory poetry, but improvisation for the most part within the unsystematic system I have analyzed, yet permitting those intrusions from the mood and fact of the depression that were quoted at the beginning of this essay. And the sequence ends with a return to ordinary reality and the escapist imagination:

The bread
Will be our bread, the stone will be

Our bed and we shall sleep by night.
We shall forget by day, except

The moments when we choose to play
The imagined pine, the imagined jay. (184)

Notes Toward a Supreme Fiction, which many now say is Stevens' greatest poem, and which I regard as a failure, on the whole a mess with intermittent successful passages, employs the same general method. It, too, begins with an injunction: to perceive the idea of the world, as, for example, of the sun, the reality behind reality, to perceive it by a process of furious abstraction, by becoming "an ignorant man again," by negating traditional theological, mythological associations. (380-81) And at the end of the sequence we come back to ordinary reality, to the "Fat girl"—no doubt, one's wife—whom one thinks of "as strong or tired, / Bent over work, anxious, content, alone," and yet who also remains "the more than natural figure," "the soft-footed phantom, the irrational / Distortion," "The fiction that results from feeling." (406) Humdrum reality and the something more.

It is clear, then, that Stevens had a homemade machine for the endless production of poems. And so he could never come to a final belief about experience or the universe, for

If ever the search for a tranquil belief should end,
The future might stop emerging out of the past . . . (151)

there would be no more poems. But he could never come to a final belief for a deeper reason: because he did not believe, and because he terribly wanted to believe; this kept him trying, that destroyed each attempt.

And now to sort out the poems. They are in one of four styles, and sometimes in a mixture of styles. The first is the imagistic style, whose characteristic instrument is the cadenced meter of the late 1910s. The coach passage I have quoted from the blackbird poem will illustrate the style. It is not a style of much interest, though some nice little things have been done in it.

The second is the mannered style. I observe in passing, since it is worth observation, how much of the literature of prestige in our time is mannered in the extreme: the prose of Gertrude Stein and *Finnegans Wake*, the *Cantos* of Ezra Pound, the poetry of Hart Crane and Dylan Thomas, surely there has not been such a collection of artificial languages in esteem since the latter days of the Roman Empire, and this among readers who believe they believe in the absolute virtue of the accents of real speech. But to return: Stevens' mannerism consists of a whole system of what I call hijinks: nonsense cries, exotic names of persons and places, extraordinarily rare words, ostentatious alliteration, and vulgarity in internal rhyming. It is the style of a man with no taste at all, of a man who regards poetry simply, in the words of Eliot's preface to *The Sacred Wood*, as "superior amusement," and by *superior* is also meant that the poet is being superior. The poems, or parts of poems, in this style are occasionally amusing, but usually merely tiresome. Yet occasionally amusing, as in *Bantams in Pine-Woods*, in which, curiously enough, both the banty cock and the poet are being superior. As the banty struts it is obvious he feels he is a ten-foot-tall poet, cock of the universe, and the poet an inchling. The poet replies, we both live in our own solipsistic grandeur. And the poet struts back, himself now taller than the pines:

> Chieftain Iffucan of Azcan in caftan
> Of tan with henna hackles, halt!
>
> Damned universal cock, as if the sun
> Was blackamoor to bear your blazing tail.
>
> Fat! Fat! Fat! Fat! I am the personal.
> Your world is you. I am my world.

You ten-foot poet among inchlings. Fat!
Begone! An inchling bristles in these pines,

Bristles, and points their Appalachian tangs,
And fears not portly Azcan nor his hoos. (75-76)

He is a chieftain If-you-can in a world where one lives as-can.
And the style is a conglomerate of mannerisms. We have the
nonsense cries, the "hoos," the vulgar internal rhyming, the
flaunting alliteration, the apparently exotic names, and the ex-
tremely rare word *tang*, "projection," for the height of the
pines. Yet there is gusto to it, and fun, control, a brilliant conceit
("As if the sun / Was blackamoor to bear your blazing tail"),
and strut for strut is a human reaction. It is a good little poem.
But, at the best, you can do no more than little things in this
manner.

The third style is another matter. This is the nineteenth-
century rhetorical style of *Sunday Morning*, the style of Wordsworth's *Prelude*, Keats' *Ode to Autumn*, Tennyson's *Ulysses*; it
was the style, as I indicated earlier, of his near contemporaries
at Harvard, and of his own undergraduate verse, though now
more sinewy. It is the style that his early education made available to him, as it is not available to a young man now. It is associated in his practice with the Christianity of his youth and
with an erotic sentimentality. He corrupts it with the superiority of mannerism in the address *A High-Toned Old Christian
Woman*; he alternates it with mannerism in *The Comedian as
the Letter C*; and keeps a little distance between himself and its
implicated feelings by touches of mannerism in the great poems
of the style—a little in *Sunday Morning*, a good deal more in the
monocle poem. When he uses it without protection, he writes
with an almost persuasive badness, as in the idealistic sentimentality of *To One of Fictive Music*, or, with a less sustained rhetoric, the adolescent vision of the Nanzia Nunzio section of *Notes
Toward a Supreme Fiction*.

Sunday Morning is the triumph of the style, and one of the
great poems in the language. However, I have dealt with it at
length elsewhere, and have nothing new to say. I shall illustrate
the style, then, by a poem in the *Sunday Morning* stanza, and

written apparently out of the same impulse, *Of Heaven Considered as a Tomb*, in which the very metaphor of heaven as a tomb signals the loss of belief in Christian, or any, immortality:

> What word have you, interpreters, of men
> Who in the tomb of heaven walk by night,
> The darkened ghosts of our old comedy?
> Do they believe they range the gusty cold,
> With lanterns borne aloft to light the way,
> Freemen of death, about and still about
> To find whatever it is they seek? Or does
> That burial, pillared up each day as porte
> And spiritous passage into nothingness,
> Foretell each night the one abysmal night,
> When the host shall no more wander, nor the light
> Of the steadfast lanterns creep across the dark?
> Make hue among the dark comedians,
> Halloo them in the topmost distances
> For answer from their icy Elysée. (56)

This is the eloquent style, his native inheritance.

But in some of the earlier poems, and in most of the later poems, he writes in a plain style, a style at its best unflavored by mannerisms or rhetoric, except for the rhetoric of simple repetition, as in *The Death of a Soldier*:

> Death is absolute and without memorial
> As in a season of autumn
> When the wind stops,
> When the wind stops and, over the heavens,
> The clouds go, nevertheless,
> In their direction. (97)

It is characteristic of the plain style that it is difficult to describe, for it is describable chiefly by negation. Styles are noticeable or unnoticeable, and what does one say of the unnoticeable? The mannerism of *Bantams in Pine-Woods* is obvious and obtrusive; it is more immediately noticeable than what is said in the poem. The rhetoric of *Sunday Morning*, though neither obvious nor obtrusive, is yet noticeable; there is a sustained and elevated eloquence that is in itself striking. But a poem in the plain style has no such effect; it is scrupulously unmannered, and studiously uneloquent. It may be flat, humdrum, and dull; it may be relaxed, somewhat careless, undistinguished; or, as in the best of Stevens, apart from the great poems in the rhetorical style, it may be noticeably unnoticeable, a quietness so apt it is heard. One of the triumphs in this style, in what I may call the quiet plain style, is *The House was Quiet and the World was Calm*; another in what one might call the cold plain style is *The Snow Man*:

> One must have a mind of winter
> To regard the frost and the boughs
> Of the pine-trees crusted with snow;
>
> And have been cold a long time
> To behold the junipers shagged with ice,
> The spruces rough in the distant glitter
>
> Of the January sun; and not to think
> Of any misery in the sound of the wind,
> In the sound of a few leaves,
>
> Which is the sound of the land
> Full of the same wind
> That is blowing in the same bare place
>
> For the listener, who listens in the snow,
> And, nothing himself, beholds
> Nothing that is not there and the nothing that is. (9-10)

It is a poem of bleak acceptance of rejections. It takes a special kind of mind, a winter mind—and, clearly, this is the experience of becoming one's environment—to look coldly on a winter landscape, and to reject the ascription of anthropomorphic feeling or monistic intimation to the sound of the wind and a few leaves. Become depersonalized, one perceives only appearance, and that there is no reality behind appearance. Yet winter in this poem is not just a symbol, though it is the natural symbol for the experience; it is initially a New England winter, and Stevens took his winters hard, as I do.

Toward the end of his life he rewrote the poem at least twice: once in *The Course of a Particular* developing the theme of the "Nothing that is not there and the nothing that is":

> Today the leaves cry, hanging on branches swept by wind,
> Yet the nothingness of winter becomes a little less.
> It is still full of icy shades and shapen snow.
>
> The leaves cry . . . One holds off and merely hears the cry.
> It is a busy cry, concerning someone else.
> And though one says that one is part of everything,
>
> There is a conflict, there is a resistance involved;
> And being part is an exertion that declines:
> One feels the life of that which gives life as it is.
>
> The leaves cry. It is not a cry of divine attention,
> Nor the smoke-drift of puffed-out heroes, nor human cry.
> It is the cry of leaves that do not transcend themselves,
>
> In the absence of fantasia, without meaning more
> Than they are in the final finding of the ear,[4] in the thing
> Itself, until, at last, the cry concerns no one at all.
>
> (*OP* 96-97)

The poem, in a relaxed plain style, depicts not only the acceptance of rejections, but something of the process of acceptance. The cry of the leaves seeks for the moment to diminish the nothingness of winter, but winter persists, and one merely hears the cry as not concerning him. For though one tries to believe one is part of a universal monistic whole, it is an effort, and one gradually gives up. There is only that that gives things as they are, without divine solicitude or human, without imagination, meaning only what it is, a sound, in the final finding of the ear, of concern to no one at all.

The third version of this poem, written some ten years earlier, is on the theme of "nothing himself." It is now not January but early April, at the end of winter, when one is just beginning, if only in anticipation, to come back. It is written in what I would call a prose plain style:

> On an early Sunday in April, a feeble day,
> He felt curious about the winter hills
> And wondered about the water in the lake.
> It had been cold since December. Snow fell, first,
> At New Year and, from then until April, lay
> On everything. Now it had melted, leaving
> The gray grass like a pallet, closely pressed;
> And dirt. The wind blew in the empty place.
> The winter wind blew in an empty place—
> There was that difference between the and an,
> The difference between himself and no man,
> No man that heard a wind in an empty place.
> It was time to be himself again, to see
> If the place, in spite of its witheredness, was still
> Within the difference. He felt curious
> Whether the water was black and lashed about
> Or whether the ice still covered the lake. There was still
> Snow under the trees and on the northern rocks,
> The dead rocks, not the green rocks, the live rocks. If,
> When he looked, the water ran up the air or grew white
> Against the edge of the ice, the abstraction would
> Be broken and winter would be broken and done,
> And being would be being himself again,
> Being, becoming seeing and feeling and self,
> Black water breaking into reality. (254-55)

And with spring and the spring sun comes hope, hope, for example, that Ulysses will finally come to Penelope:

> But was it Ulysses? Or was it only the warmth of the sun
> On her pillow? The thought kept beating in her like
>   her heart.
> The two kept beating together. It was only day.

It was Ulysses and it was not. Yet they had met,
Friend and dear friend and a planet's encouragement.
The barbarous strength within her would never fail.
(521)

And though he never comes, yet there is something, something that gives meaning, though not a personal, not a consoling meaning. It is, whatever it is, "the life of that which gives life as it is." (*OP* 96) Call it, if you will, *The River of Rivers in Connecticut,* "The river that flows nowhere, like a sea," the river this side of the river Styx. (533)

T. S. Eliot
on Poetry and Poets

T. S. Eliot's short pieces of criticism, *On Poetry and Poets*,[1] supplements the earlier *Selected Essays*. The pieces are for the most part written for delivery on a public occasion and for delivery by a poet of recognized distinction. They are the utterances of a public figure and have on the whole the ease and authority that this circumstance permits. He speaks of the social function of poetry, of Vergil, Dr. Johnson, Byron, and one feels that what is said is what should have been said. To read this volume is to know that poetry is worthwhile, and to know it without demonstration.

It is, then, an impressive book, and yet it is a troubling one, troubling in an accumulation of small and gradually larger ways. For ease and authority sometimes mislead the author, and may mislead his audience. I give for the moment a small instance, an instance in which the imprecision of an amateur scholarship is given the appearance of care and precision. Mr. Eliot speaks in one sentence of George Herbert and "certain other poets his contemporaries—Donne, Vaughan and Traherne" and two sentences later discriminates between Herbert and a poet "a little senior to him," Herrick. This seems harmless enough, seems even to display a scholarly conscientiousness, yet Herrick was only a year or two older than Herbert, while Donne was over twenty years his senior, Vaughan about twenty-five years his junior, and Traherne was unborn at Herbert's death. A small instance, no doubt, though not perhaps to one interested in the history of English poetry. But if small, yet troubling, for it raises the suspicion that the speaker is more persuasive than is desirable.

The persuasiveness is soundly founded in rhetoric, in the employment of commonplaces and in the character of the speaker. These pieces rehearse with a dry restatement the rubrics of modern criticism. We are, for instance, again and again tantalized with the common distinction between poetry and verse, and feel at home in the difficulties it provokes. If the speaker at one point confesses with respect to this distinction that "the critical tools we are accustomed to use in analysing and criticising poetry do not seem to work," we are won by the unassuming honesty of the declaration. For the speaker is not merely a public figure with a dignity imputed to him by his reputation. He is a carefully delineated personality, solidly placed in the literary history of his time, and with many engaging traits. He has even his fleeting moment of vanity, remarking of a translated work, "when I read it in French." But he is most engaging, and most conciliating, in the many statements of disavowal and recantation. Some are personal, as in the disavowal of "a few notorious phrases which had had a truly embarrassing success in the world," or in the account of the ingenuous origin of the notes to the *Waste Land*. Others are disavowals for his generation and tradition: of *Finnegans Wake* we may say "one book like this is enough." Such statements will be of great consolation to the common reader, and will relieve him of a burden of irritable guilt.

But the most valuable parts of the book, and the most convincing in delineating the character of the speaker, are the many passages of literary autobiography, some brief and in passing, some fairly extensive. These passages are peculiarly appropriate to the form of public address, and could not have been done better. There is no lapse of taste. But more than this. From these passages one could realize, one could relive if he had not lived it himself, the experience of the literary revolution of our times.

This is what it is to have been in the center of literary achievement. And so the voice of the speaker is located in circumstance. It is a voice of dry charm, distinguished, attractive, human, agile. It is the voice of an elderly revolutionary, of an usurper whose forces have long since conquered the kingdom of letters. He speaks now with the assurance of a de facto legitimacy. He sees no need for further revolution. Our task is to consolidate the position, to develop and exploit the tradition which he and his peers established: "If the poetry of the rest of this century takes the line of development which seems to me, reviewing the progress of poetry through the last three centuries, the right course, it will discover new and more elaborate patterns of a diction now established."

This is the issue. Can the tradition be developed, and should it? I do not myself believe that Mr. Eliot understands the nature of the revolution he was engaged in. He depicts it as a return to the colloquial and the particular, and this is both too general and surely untrue of a good deal even of his own work. But taking the tradition as we have it, what can we do with it? A tradition is a collection of models for imitation and an associated set of principles for the production of works. It is the task of criticism to provide the principles. Are Mr. Eliot's fruitful?

The principle he most commonly recurs to, and the only one he exemplifies at length, is what he calls the principle of musical structure. He is, of course, quite aware of the dangers of analogy, and protects himself and the reader from any illegitimate confusion of poetry and music. But he does feel we can speak legitimately of "the musical pattern of emotional overtones," of "a rhythm of fluctuating emotion essential to the musical structure of the whole," and he shows us in some detail how such structure operates by an analysis of the opening lines of *Hamlet*. I quote the passage entire, excising only the denomination of particular characters and actions and the extensive quotations: "From the short, brusque ejaculations at the beginning . . . the verse glides into a slower movement . . . and the movement changes again . . . into the solemn and sonorous. . . . There is an abrupt change to staccato . . . this rhythm changes again. . . . The scene reaches a resolution with the words. . . .

There emerges, when we analyse it, a kind of musical design."

The method consists in characterizing successive passages by appropriate adjectives, and in asserting that change and resolution occur. With this paradigm one could analyze the whole of recorded literature, needing only a store of adjectives and, for variety, synonyms for "change." By this method whatever one wrote himself in whatever sequence could be shown to have structure, "and structure," Mr. Eliot affirms, "I hold to be an important element of poetic composition."

We need a counter-revolution.

V

The Quest of the Opal

A Commentary on *The Helmsman*

There is little to say of the imaginative figure to whom I ascribe these jottings except that he was a frequenter of small coffee shops where for a nickel or a dime one used to be able to sit undisturbed for as much as half an hour. There, particularly on a dark or rainy day, he would pen these notes, originally in verse and now in prose, on old sheets of paper or backs of envelopes amid shopping lists, algebraic formulæ, and odd quotations from detective stories. They were what one could do in that time and under those conditions, but the circumstances should not be thought of merely as hindrances since they became like most hindrances a method. The notes were at first a way of saving some fragments from his ruminations, but in time his ruminations became a way of achieving notes. Consequence and implication, order and outline, the devices by which insight is aggravated into sufficient bulk and extended to the decent solemnity of prose became at last only ways of prospecting for what otherwise would have lain hidden. Hence, if he anticipated a time and place for coffee, he would fall into a meditative melancholy out of which when the occasion arrived he would begin to write as if he had not intended to. His notes were no longer memoranda for a work; the essays he spoke to himself in meditation were rather memoranda for notes. He became an epigrammatist.

What he then wrote in verse he later put in prose, for verse is obscure of its very nature since few are persuaded it can mean what it says, and sometimes what his verse said was itself obscure. Not that he claimed for himself the privileges of vatic exaltation; he had trifled with this attitude once under the pressure of the modern tradition in poetry and from a desire not to be found wanting in the dark pretensions of his early associates who were almost without exception congenital romantics, however classical their creed; but this was accidental. Substantially, he viewed himself rather as a professional writer, however laconic, one to whom poetry was verse.

For the generally received distinction between poetry and verse, he said in *For My Contemporaries*,[1] derives from a widely and deeply felt discrimination not merely between the products of writing but also between the attitudes with which the act of writing is approached and between the kinds of life which surround and supplement it. Verse is a professional activity, social and objective, and its methods and standards are those of craftsmanship. It is a concern of the ordinary human self, and is on the whole within a man's power to do well or not. Its virtues are the civic virtues. If it lacks much, what it does have is ascertainable and can be judged. But poetry is amateurish, religious, and eminently unsociable. It dwells in the spiritual life, in the private haunts of theology or voodoo. It is passive to the powers it cannot evoke. It is the accidental issue, the plain bastard, of grace and inspiration, or of the demons of anxiety—even of somatic irritation, for indigestion may be your angel. In that region the elected of God and the elected of themselves are scarcely distinguishable, and if the true oracle is nonsense to sense, so nonsense is often taken for oracle.

But the earlier verses in his book were nothing but constructions that offered to the reader certain schemes of experience, certain progressions of thought and feeling from the first line to the last. The later ones were direct statements of something he had to say, given form and definitiveness by the technique of verse. But what he had to say was often in the legitimate sense of that term original, and the common expectation of the reader is that the idea of a poem should be commonplace or given, its expression original. Hence the reader is often baffled since his expectation is foiled, and a man will sooner change anything than his expectations.

Again, the lyric especially—that is, the short poem—is commonly thought to be of general application. It should be such that the reader can appropriate it as his own, can regard himself as speaking in his own circumstances the words of the poet. He usually intended to disappoint the reader in this expectation also. He wanted him to know that this was his poem, not yours; these were his circumstances, not yours; and these were the structures of thought by which he had penetrated them. He attempted to enforce this by a recurring exactitude of qualification. If the reader persists in regarding the poem as of general application—that is, as an utterance of the indiscriminate I who is anyone—the recurrent qualifications can only perplex him. The poem is impenetrable since he has missed the point of penetration. The author, in fact, was only satisfied with a poem when qualification complicated qualification and yet the whole contrivance seemed to achieve stability and absoluteness by a coincidence with some given and simple external form.

To these sources of difficulty or obscurity must be added some of less dignity: the use, especially in the earlier poems, of special learning and uncommon reference, certain failures in expression, and a few miserably ingenious turns or conceits which can only be characterized as mistakes. There were many more of these in poems excluded from *The Helmsman* or discarded completely; what remained were kept for the virtues of the rest of the poem and they were such as seemed ineradicable in revision without destroying the whole.

The poems in *The Helmsman* were arranged roughly in chronological order, and hence there was in the successive poems of the book a story; but it was not any reader's story, and it was not the conventional novel that some knowledge of the external events might prompt the reader to reconstruct. It could be told as well in technical terms as in dramatic; it could be regarded as the history of a style.

His native style was dry, abstract, tightly formal. It derived its texture from a chastity of diction and a crispness of technique, and its inner structure from some odd turn and complication of thought. It was a style without softness, downright, somewhat angular, more assured than it should have been. It was a style that, though capable of poetic effects, was essentially in the current sense unpoetic and certainly unlyrical. It got its drive from a white passion for exactitude of statement, and filled its lines with the residues of a mind that was too nimble—not, he hoped, tangled and confused, but crisscrossed and webbed with subtlety and distinctions and fragments of special learning.

Hence the history of the style in general was the history of an endeavor to attain, on the one hand, what may be called a poetic surface, with its attendant mastery of imagery, of human irrationality, of associative rhetoric, and of the full line in which sound and the choice of diction implicate feeling. This was the pursuit of what was then called sensibility. To this end he contrived poems that were schemes of experience. On the other hand, it was the history of the pursuit of simplicity. But the simplicity sought was not that which comes from an ignorance or rejection of the prolific complexity of thought or of thought's duty to approximate the wrinkled lineaments of experience and truth. It was a simplicity that would fix with an air of easiness and a lack of strain all the qualifications and hesitations that shade the vulgar outline of thought into a simulacrum of honesty and life. It was an attempt by this or that slight translation of the axes of reference, by some sharp attack from an untraditional center, though with all the appearance of tradition—for only thus does simplicity seem to be simple—to define the nimble and compounded lattice of qualification and distinction and the inescapable novelty of point of view to which time and logic had driven him. He returned at last to direct statement.

Perhaps the clearest example in this book of his native style and of the special difficulties inherent in it was *Lector Aere Perennior*. It was angular, dry, fairly lacking in poetic grace or adornment. What the poem says was somewhat original, and the gadgets used to say it were dependent on technical terms and not too common learning. The title referred to the famous ode in which Horace claimed that in his poems he had built a monument more enduring than bronze, a variant of the classical commonplace that furnished the first line: "Poets survive in fame." The poem was developed by means of the scholastic concepts of substance, matter, and form, a philological pun on breath, spirit, and inspiration, the theological notion of imputation, and by the metaphorical use of the Pythagorean doctrine of the transmigration or metamorphosis of souls. Yet, however gadgety, it was all statement.

One could hardly blame a reader for finding the poem difficult or obscure. Yet in this case the difficulty was perhaps legitimate. The special terms and knowledge employed were sufficiently commonplace to those few readers who had studied the Latin tradition so that there was a real, though small, audience to whom the poem was directly addressed. Furthermore, none of the details was used simply for its own sake or for ornamental or extraneous reasons. And finally, the poem though difficult was figurable; explanation will add nothing to the poem that is not implicit in the text.

The sense of the Latin epigraph (*Perire constat auctores, ruere monumenta, lectorem manere aere perenniorem*) was: "The writer dies, his bust crumbles on the shelf, the reader only remains."

The poem said: We are told that the immortality of a writer consists in the fact that his name lives. Yet this is no immortality that relates to him, for he was as a man an integrated substance of body and spirit and his work as a writer was a similarly integrated substance of text and meaning, whereas a reputation is a mere name. Insofar as he continues in a recurrent existence he lives as the text of his writings. This is the inert clay which a sympathetic reader can inform with the breath of existence if he has the irrational trick of assuming the spirit of the author, of inviting a kind of transmigration of soul. The text only is constant, but in this reader or that it may come to life again with the soul of its original meaning. Hence a writer's immortality as such lies in the possibility of his work's being realized again by some reader or other. The author dies; his text is inert; the reader is his life.

But the earliest poems in the book, *The Wandering Scholar's Prayer to St. Catherine of Egypt* and *The Dogdays*, were ones in which his native style was breaking down of itself, the unsimplified elements becoming refractory to plain statement, and in which, at the same time, it was being somewhat deliberately shattered and reformed in pursuit of modern feeling, of shadows and blunted light. Hence the alteration of tradition which in *The Dogdays* predicated "unachieved intent" of the full light of noon. He was becoming a little lost in the post-romantic chiaroscuro. He had said in an earlier poem (*Distinctions at Dusk*): Reason is light which distinguishes reality into shapes and shadows, but there are times and conditions in which all is shaded or light so diffused that nothing is distinguishable. Such are the obscure regions of spiritual pride where the sharp edge of reason cannot penetrate, yet such regions can in their own terms and by their own methods be mapped and charted. Similarly the dusk in a later poem (*Coffee*) represented the same area of engrossing irrational experience, one that did not respect the distinction between subjective and objective ("That no glass can oppose"), and hence was similar to the pantheistic experience, though different in quality. You cannot take these by the throat and throttle them, for there is nothing to get your hands on; you must outwait and outwit them; you must distract yourself and them by some odd device or other. Yet there were values there, curious accessions of insight and energy, intimations beyond the routine, and an ordering of all by an adjustment to the consistent grayness of a mood. But there was also waste and the perception of waste.

The Dogdays, then, was the first issue of what he called privately the quest of the opal: the attempt to court and possess, and at the same time disinterestedly to understand, roughly what was then called sensibility: the province of modern art, the deep well of creativity, the secret and sacred recesses of personality, the Gothic chamber of modern psychology, and the fall of light among the teacups. But an opal, particularly the deep fire opal, derives its color and attraction from flaws in the stone. If this were all, the flaws would be virtues. But any accidental sharp knock, as on the side of a basin while one is washing his hands, may cause the stone to crack; and though it remain in its setting for a while, in some unguarded moment the pieces will fall out, and one will have the ring without the jewel, the promise without the fulfillment. Yet he was not wholly at the mercy of magic and chance; he had his own sources, his unornamented being, and could return to them enriched by what he had lost. Hence it was a quest in which he succeeded for his own purposes and failed to all appearances, and need no longer feel any need of.

The whole course of this quest, so far at least as it was implicated in personal relationships, was clearly anticipated in *The Dogdays*, though it preceded by nine and a half years the conclusion. Yet it may be regarded not only as anticipatory of the undetermined future, but almost as an epilogue, a summary after the event, detailing the plot. So one may reflect that if there be an element of determinism in human personality, other than the mechanical determinism of flesh and nerve or the impingement of external event, of necessity and chance, this determinism may very well reside in that awareness in the individual which from the beginning supplies the lines of approach and of action, and which will, as it were quite unnoticed, demand the fulfillment in event, the artistic resolution in the real world, of its early perception. One's awareness conditions him, and conditions the response of others. That which he saw must be coped with will actualize itself because he saw it, and hence in the obvious sense cannot be coped with. We are determined by awareness, and we live only to accept and to adjust ourselves to the brutal fulfillment in the outer world of our insight. Premonition is destiny. Such at least will be the case when the attitude toward the situation is from the beginning adjusted to its necessary issue, though the full predication of necessity can only unfold in time.

The poems which followed in this sequence were not written after the event to illustrate a story or to develop a judgment, but were contrived from time to time out of the context of circumstance and idea. *All Choice is Error*, though it was overdecorated in the first half, contained in the middle an outrageous conceit, and was in fact the forced yoking together of two attempts, originally addressed to two quite different young women, nevertheless stated in the latter half an idea of the greatest importance, if not generally, at least for the author. It was not an idea that would have come to him, as we say, naturally, from his training and his associates, nor was it one that intrigued him and that he found pleasant to play with. In fact, he did not know how it came or how it developed, except that it issued from the frame of experience: it was impersonal in that he could not evade it. It was the notion of particularity and of choice, and especially the formula which has shocked everyone that ever stopped to look at it, as it shocked him: "All choice is error." For choice implies exclusion, rejection, restriction, limitation. To choose *this* is not only to prefer one thing to something else, but rather to prefer it to everything else.

The doctrine was developed in a later poem, *Haecceity*. The subject of that poem was metaphysical evil, evil as a defect of being. Any realized particular, anything which is this and not that and that, is by the very fact evil. For to be this is to exclude not only any other alternative but to exclude all else in the universe. Perfection is in possibility, in the idea, but that which is realized, specific, determined, has no possibilities. It is precisely this and nothing else at all. It is lacking in all the being of the universe other than its own particularity. The more realized a thing is the greater its defect of being; hence any particular choice is as such evil though morally it may be the best choice.

It follows that the fundamental compulsion of one's life (*Epigram 36*) is not love, lust, gregariousness, the will to live, or any of the emotions or instincts assigned to man. It is that to live is at every moment to be and to do some particularity: in this respect *what* does not matter, only it must be something. The void must be specified. Loneliness is an intimation of the void which we attempt to defeat by some more notable specification. Haecceity, or thisness, is the primal and ultimate compulsion of one's life; it is the principle of insufficient reason. But there is considerable human danger in too sharp an awareness of this truth. For if choice is purely arbitrary, as essentially it is, there is no reason we should not be purely arbitrary in choosing. Hence one's choices may have in them a good deal of the precipitancy and doggedness of despair.

The problem is certainly central, and very likely insoluble. For it is not merely philosophy but one's life. If he accepts the classic solution in which choice is thought of as the inevitable result in action of reasoned and considered judgment, then choice is completely determined in such fashion that the moral agent may be assured he has inescapably moved toward the best. Hence what he moves toward will be best, hence reasonable, and appetite is confounded with judgment. It is true that in classical ethics the rightness of right reason is considered to be constantly imperiled by passion, against which one must be unremittingly and warily on guard. But the consequence of this position is to enforce an absolute dualism of reason and passion, unmanageable except, perhaps, by religious and ritual means. And when such means must be invoked they tend insensibly to take primacy over reason, until through the dualism of reason and passion they come ultimately to be identified with passion, and with a passion that now, under the pseudo-authority of its impersonal source, delivers the personality to the absolute dictates of passion: called God, or that parody of God in the courtly tradition, Love.

He attempted to outwit this problem by the nature of his choice and the way in which he construed it. Hence, the central poem in this series was *The Beacon*, which seemed to be but was not at all Platonic. Its theme was commonplace. It was the problem of identity and difference in the special context of love. We identify ourselves with the object insofar as it is our own construction to which we can impute our own feelings; we distinguish it as object insofar as it is distinct from us, and as such it is ground for reflection and judgment. But this is commonplace in the sense of being ordinary only if the distinction does not in our special circumstances strike us, only if the problem is not a problem.

The point here is one of more general application. A good many arguments are over whether to take a proposition as an organizing insight into experience or as a truism. It is a question of concern: the subsidence of concern about an idea is its reduction to a truism. In this case the problem was really a problem: the distinction proved in time to be an ineradicable difficulty.

The poem said, in brief: Men give their hearts away but cannot pass judgment on this act so long as they construct the object of love according to their desires, for the will takes pleasure in begetting its own image. I on the contrary choose an object other and distant, a cold landmark toward which contemplation looks. The object remains apart, but let us hope that in time it may be possessed.

Or again, at greater length: The allegiances of the heart are absolute—our early loyalties are given and the later ones of reverence, of friendship, or of love are as emotional commitments unavoidable, and as such beyond our control. But if we give allegiance merely to allegiance, if the object is regarded merely as the shape of our needs or as the arbitrary name we give to our emotional life, there is no room for reason, reflection, or judgment. There is no otherness involved, for the will is delighted to beget itself. Hence we must reserve prestige for the external and the distant, the distinct and the remote. By this contrivance the will is deceived—its allegiance is no less committed but the impossibility of identifying itself with the object leaves the judgment free to contemplate and to assess. Yet this is a desperate situation and certainly not to be enjoyed for itself. Let us hope that before death revokes the possibility of fulfillment we may possess the object in its immediacy without sacrificing the distinctions of judgment. The desire to accomplish this in this life removes the poem from a Platonic or a Christian context.

But once allegiance has been assigned (*Choice*) and its irrevocability sealed in the Absolute, once it has been as possessed as things are in this world, how shall one live? Only by protecting himself against the consequences of his extravagance in the daily routine of society. That such a program did not in this instance work out too well, or that its working out entailed a disproportionate cost, may be conjectured from the lethargic resignation of *Summer Idyll*, the rather terrible inertia of a late June afternoon when the ripe apricots fall in the sullen orchard with a foreboding sound. In the poem the scenery of the immediate occasion, the Santa Clara valley in California, is transposed into imagery derived from his early life on the Montana plains. Though for many years he had scarcely recalled, and certainly never meditated on, any image or experience of his early life, he found that the patterns of his deepest feelings were most often clothed in the landscapes of that time.

By "ecstacy" in the first line of the original version of this poem he meant that standing apart from oneself, so that the personality, separate, retired, remote, and apparently inert, rip-

ens and comes to fulfillment in its own internal term, a fulfillment of so absolute a value that it need never be manifested—
the apparent unconsciousness of ripening may pass without a
sigh into the unconsciousness of death. It is not precisely that
"emotional maturity" which we use so handily on others, but
rather an inner ripening through whatever quiet or hectic experiences, from which issues in time of trial, certainly not mastery or wisdom or insensibility, but a central poise arising from
a boredom almost with one's own most primary concerns.

The poems that conclude this series were written almost on
successive days: *August Hail*, *This Tower of Sun*, and *Autumn*.
The first issued from a context similar to that of *Summer Idyll*.
Its subject was the sudden incidence of passion, which comes
like an impersonal force and apparently from the outside; and
it had a moral: "Who shall revenge unreason?" though it destroy
all. The meter of the poem was accentual: four, three, four, and
two accents a line.

But what shall one do with passion? He wrote at this time
a poem on the subject (*Passion*) in which he developed a pun
on the word, on passion in the ordinary sense as an aspect of
love and passion as the philosophic complement of act. The
pun is taken as implying reality. Passion in the ordinary sense
is here said to involve all that is unrealized in any particular
act of love. By definition, then, it is unrealizable in terms of act.
But in its own terms, as involving all the potentialities of love,
surmised or rejected, it is latent in each act, surrounds it and
gives resonance to it. The act is the tone of which passion is
all the overtones. By this device he found a place for all those
possible experiences that haunted his appetite and for which
circumstance or morality afforded no actual place.

In *This Tower of Sun* he represented a decision on the alternatives suggested by the incidence of passion. The romantic experience of stillness and light, occurring in some solitary natural
surrounding, with its quasi-mystical intimation of a vague absolute beyond, other than, or above the realized entelechy, he said,
is an illusory experience. As illusion, of course, it has a certain
existence, for an illusion is a reality which we prefer to disregard
or to disvalue. It is a discriminated part of reality, marked off
from what we normally call the real by applying the ancient dis-

tinction between Appearance and Reality, though both are real.

But to return to the poem: The quiet of this glade into which he suddenly emerges is merely relative; the illusion of absolute quiet is imported into the scene by the willful inattention of the observer. And the sudden almost palpable sunlight which strikes him as he comes out into such a clearing in the woods reveals at the same time the surrounding trees which are the instruments of the illusion. The feeling of absolute light derives from the contrasting shade which the light itself makes clearly visible.

The experience of romantic love is analogous, and its phantom object is contrived as willfully as the romantic object of such quasi-mystical experiences. But only a realized particular embodies the concept of love, the true ideal. What might be conjectured from such an experience as this—a romantic, higher, unrealized love—is precisely the absence of the Absolute; it is the undifferentiated many, realizable in no particular one, for if realized it would no longer have its characteristic property of being unspecific. This is a later application of the doctrine of choice, and represents in manner a return to the abstract and dry, to a poetry of statement.

The series was concluded in *Autumn*, a poem just short of successful, in which the whole manner of the quest was devoted to acquiescence in what amounted to its abandonment. Here experience has ripened for the harvest, the time of falling leaves, the time of acceptance—even of indifference—when grief is subdued to the resignation of the season. For the mellowing of the heart and the parallel dispersal of hope—like leaves flying in an autumn storm—is only what should be expected from the passing of time, and it should be accepted without rebellion. This is, if you will, a manifestation of tiredness of spirit, an embracing of fatigue. And so you may object that no sound moralist should retire and live sufficient to himself, seeking, as it were, a cloistered virtue. He answered that this is but the necessary act of the man of experience, the tried. He cannot keep the occasions of adventure or of hope far *from* his heart—he is not so much *The Scarecrow*—but he may and will keep them hidden far *in* his heart. He is acquainted with the occasions of adventure whose symbol is the passing train, but he will not heed their persuasions for he knows there is in them no abiding rest.

This in effect concluded the quest. Beyond this there was only the unraveling, the protracted dissipation of anger, and the return to himself and the lean winds of his own country. On the publication of his book he revived that final crisis in memory, and recorded the vision in an epigram (*Epigram 17*) that wore a deliberate air of obscurity, having a dark elevation consonant with its tone. But only the air of obscurity made it seem obscure. He interrogated an image of experience as if he would fix it by name and dispel the fears of spirit that came with its apparition. But he knew very well who it was and what were the fears. It was a ghost he had laid and, as a man will, had conjured again, whose values were an envisaged, though rejected, way of life, still happily unstayed by the voice of desire, still escaping though called, and escaping because dismayed by the intrinsic fears for which it had been previously rejected. The ghost was not the person—no ghost is—but the experience the person evoked: the temptation to the continued pursuit of the quest but transposed now into the vagrant way of life of *The Wandering Scholar*.

For concurrent with this series of poems was another, the poems that deal with those early experiences out of which his aptitude for the abstract and dry had been formed and corrupted. The earliest of this series, *The Wandering Scholar*, in which the passing train first occurs, attempts like the earliest and latest of the other, *The Dogdays* and *Autumn*, to apprehend and order those experiences by one of the recurrent schemes of irrationality in modern poetry: This is the scheme in which a scene is presented by details which implicate a personal situation and a mood, out of which a comment is struck that narrows the application of the scene, and then the poem curves off like the curve of an hyperbola into some more general image of, perhaps, sunset or light, and leaves the reader, if he cooperates in the journey, soaring off into the vast or the remote. But this scheme was not native to him, who lived rather with the consecutive propositions of thought: it pressed on him with the urgency of experience demanding notice and evasion.

The details of *The Wandering Scholar* were in part realistic details from his year of wandering during the depression, apprehended as poetic lines through the structure of a rather irrespon-

sible wit ("Clicking their heels"), through a Hart Crane-ish violence of epithet ("the ravelled faces of the park" are unshaven),
and especially through that forced association, though it seemed
natural at the time, of fragments of special learning with quite
other aspects of life and feeling which it is now fashionable to
call metaphysical. There was certainly a good deal of similarity
between the kind of detail in this poem and in the dedicatory
poem, but the material was more personal, the references less
integrated in consecutive syntax, and the feeling not so subdued
to the firmness of thought. The structure of the poem was in part
a device for alluding to jagged bits of experience, and only in
part itself a structure of experience. Yet on the far edge of one's
nerves the poem held together.

For, if a man goes down at night to see the freight trains
rumble into an unspecified distance, and if he is homeless and
desperate, with tags of Latin learning and an inherited tradition of Catholicism that is as homeless as he is himself, he may
well conceive that Catherine, the patron saint of scholars who
was martyred by being racked on a wheel, is racked on these.
At least at that age and in those circumstances the conceit will
serve the purpose of stiffening some discordant experience into
a few lines of verse. But the subject of the poem is the loss or
betrayal of all one's early loyalties; hence the central comment,
"Not unabsolved do they grow rude," for though one is never
absolved by his associates, he is so absolutely.

The range of experiences which this poem refers to were
handled again in *The Helmsman: An Ode*, *A Moral Poem*, and
Montana Pastoral. The last was a curt autobiography, written
seven years after the others, in which the details of fear, thirst,
hunger, and the desperation of this huddled chill were hardly
a just summary of his first twenty years but rather an epigrammatic presentation of the salient motives those years communicated to his later life.

The Helmsman: An Ode was more ambitious in dealing
with the same material. It was in the first place an attempt to
imitate the Horatian ode, in external form and in internal structure. The meter of the poem was intended to achieve in English
the effect of the Alcaic strophe. It consisted of four lines, each
of a different metrical pattern, so that the strophe stood out as

a unit without the use of rhyme, though rhyme was admitted here and there as a figure of diction. The line consisted, to use the ordinary terminology, of a combination of disyllabic and trisyllabic feet, with the unaccented syllable at the end of the first two lines combining with the unaccented syllable at the beginning of the following line to give a further suggestion of trisyllabic feet. But the trisyllabics were so arranged that whenever they began to gallop off with the poem they were pulled up short with disyllabics. The lines, however, admitted the ordinary substitutions and variations of standard meter, except that extra syllables were not admitted. The pattern, then, differed essentially from the ordinary patterns of standard meter in that the various feet occur at predetermined places and not as free variations. The *Elegy for a Cricket* employed the same kind of meter, in this case an imitation of the Catullan hendescasyllabics.

There were three other examples of metrical experiment in his book: the accentual meter of *August Hail*, and of *Fancy* in which the principle was that each line should have four accents and that there should be no regular pattern of feet; and the syllabic meter of *A Moral Poem*, in which the principle was that each line should consist of five syllables and that there should be no regular pattern of feet.

Helmsman was also an imitation of Horace in its method. The qualities he then saw in the Horatian ode were conceived of in contrast with the medieval Latin lyric, with which he identified, not wholly correctly, his native style. The latter he found uncompromisingly rational and logical in structure and detail. In the former he discerned a unity of sensibility which exhibited the vagaries and unpredictability of experience and resisted an abstract, logical, or classificatory form. Its unity resided in the unformulable feeling that, as the poem unfolded, its length and the arrangement of parts were proper and inevitable: "that just now is said what just now ought to be said." He found that the progression from detail to detail was by a kind of imagic shift or transformation image which, like a train through a tunnel, brings one to a new prospect on the other side of the divide. Under this persuasion he tried the wasp in *The Dogdays* and especially the outrageous root of the tree in *All Choice is Error*. But as he read on in Horace he came to see that the point of the method lay in the transitions from concrete detail to detail: that the transitions were not elliptical in the sense that the poet had merely omitted a chain of thought which the reader was to supply, and that the details themselves did not imply an abstraction that connected them. The meaning lay in the transitions themselves, in a certain balance of sensibility, a nice adjustment between imagery and statement which met the insoluble problems of life with a controlled use of distraction and irrelevance.

He analyzed the famous Soracte ode (1. 9) which begins with an extended description of a midwinter scene and closes with an extended, but in no way parallel, description of a summer love scene. By a relative clause, and in an unemphatic manner, a description of the equinoctial storms is worked in. The sequence of images gives by implication, but by implication only, the theme: that season follows season, and that time is fleeting. The transitions from image to image are effected by generalized statements that are related to but never state the central theme, so that the point of the poem is qualified by images, whole and concrete in themselves, which cannot be said to illustrate the point. They are not subsumed under it as examples; they are rather digressions that prove to be developments.

He attempted to order the experience of his tradition by this method, and wrote his own ode. The poem said: The normal course of a man's life, we are told, is through experience to maturity—to poise, assurance, mastery. The traditional term is wisdom. But such mastery, if in fact it visit us, is only accidental to the process of living, and is at the best casual, fitful, and dependent upon some source of illumination external to the inner personality. Furthermore, it presupposes normal, comfortable, easy circumstances; it is a consequence of good weather. But time may fail us, the loves that render such accomplishment possible may die or disappoint us, so that the very idea of fulfillment is only a childhood memory. There is a certain degree of want and loss, varying with circumstance, that destroys a man's self-respect. So he goes his own way, though the vision of what might have been intrudes from time to time like an importunate panhandler. He cuts free of the past—Ajax and the Grecian isles—putting out his last reserves for a special dinner and a pint of bootleg, and sets forth on his travels. If ever he should feel secure, he will drowse and fall from the wheel like Aeneas' helmsman, Palinurus, whose unburied bones will finally wash up on some unknown shore.

The latter half of the poem was stolen from Horace, *Odes* 1. 7. 21-32, and the *Aeneid* 5. 870-71.

A good deal of the experiences that lay behind these particular poems were bound up with his family, and much that bewildered him was sanctioned by family legend and, though disapproved of, had been ascribed to various of his direct and collateral ancestors. The tradition that surrounded him and formed much of the texture of his early years was the tradition of Irish Catholics along the railroads of the West. To this he finally bade such farewell as one can to his past in *A Moral Poem*. So far as a man's traditions are himself they cannot be altered but they need not be exploited. He who is inured to the past is at liberty to be what he becomes.

He dealt with the specific problem of his religious inheritance in *Timor Dei*. He was a Catholic by tradition, training, and deep feeling, but the Absolute is greedy, as pervasive and as destructively absorbent as sensation or passion or sympathy. Hence his own identity he fenced off, and though it formed part of the terrain it had its property lines. Yet he could look back to the smoke of burning leaves and grass, of the swinging censers, and of breath in the chill northern air of his boyhood and almost acquiesce: for though he would not regret the loss of what he would not have, the traditional patterns of feeling still had power to dominate him.

In brief, by one process or another, through experiences of the kind alluded to in these poems, he had lost almost all his loyalties, though loyalty was his predominant passion. But there still remained the structures of experience which those had satisfied, names calling for an object. In this very formulation of the problem he found the way to solution. He returned to himself, to his own talent for the abstract and dry; he decided he was not a man of sensibility and gave up the quest. He undertook the pursuit of simplicity. He said (in *L'Esprit*): So far as I am—and perhaps it is a matter of temperament—I am the idea that informs my experience; it is the Idea by whose evil eye I am held as men were by the legendary basilisk. He found himself maintaining that the devices of discourse, such notions as identity and diversity, essence and accident, out of which the traditional Absolute had been inferred into existence and dowered with all that its definition denied, so that its light supported all the realms of darkness and the plentitude of its being overflowed into the defect of being—all these were fictions though no less real than the specific which could not become real until apprehended in the form of such fictions.

He applied his doctrine to the quest, and dealt with the problem of universals in *The Metaphysical Amorist*. The idea was there regarded as method, having its own reality as method and having a guarded applicability to social phenomena. There is, for instance, the idea of Love and the situation one finds himself in. These are separate and distinct orders of reality, and yet relatable to each other, as the man who sees is distinct from what he sees and yet his way of seeing determines what it is he sees. The attempt to regard Idea as Phenomenon (Platonic realism), or Phenomenon as Idea (pragmatic nominalism), or to hold a mid-position between these terms (conceptualism) is a mistake. The terms are distinct. The Idea is the method by which we apprehend and order phenomena, yet the phenomena are amenable to various methods. One may have beer bottles and a method for counting them, yet the bottles are distinct from the method and the method from the bottles, and there are different methods.

He expounded his doctrine again in an expository poem, *Reason and Nature*, written a few days after the concluding poems of the other series. The subject was again the relation of method and material, thought and sensation, reason and nature. He said: The pool in a pure frame is the projection of reason in which reason can only see its own construction, and one's notion of his identity is such a construction. The unchanging, unalterable pool, therefore, is a fiction, a device of method. But what we call the real pool, the pool of sensation and experience where we may find a willow or two, is not unrippled. Though the alterations in its surface be as minute as the slight waves caused by skimming flies, these results of chaos and change will exemplify no given rule, will be the realization of no definable method. Nor will any isolatable part of change be a microcosm containing implicitly the whole, nor will it be a calculable curve from which the whole may be inferred. Our experience does not validate induction, just as our postulates have as such no reference.

In brief, he characterized the Idealist as one whose Ideals reflect merely their postulation. He now characterized the Sensationalist as a Narcissus who cannot possibly see his identity on the irrational surface of experience. But if he cannot find it in appearance he can even less find it in the annihilation of immediacy, for an engrossed fusion with experience destroys that distance by which alone any predication can be affirmed.

He asserted that he was both Sensationalist and Idealist, both change and constancy, both material and method. He knew both what he saw and what he thought, confusion and clarity, and though these were distinct and separate the one was applicable to the other, method to material, and applicable only because they were distinct. In this he developed the doctrine of *The Beacon*, but generalized and abstracted it from the special circumstances of that poem. He argued that to say one thing is another (A is A) is to affirm that they are different and yet that their identity is valid and constructible. A man is distinct from his experience or he could not speak of it, yet he is his experience or it would not be his. He must be both disinterested and engrossed.

He saw now that the pursuit of sensibility had been the pursuit of an engrossment in immediacy of experience, but immediacy by definition cannot be talked about, cannot yield a line of verse. Perhaps one sees himself immediately, which is as much as to say that the self is the self. But from this point of view, from the point of view of the concentrated duration of consciousness, all one's thoughts and actions are in an ultimate sense unreal. They are mistakes, if you will, since they are objectifications of the self and as such are other than the self; hence they have not the self's immediate validity except insofar as this is imputed to them by the customary psychic sleight of hand.

The appeal to immediacy of experience is always a recourse. It is always an apology and a defense of some thoughts and actions, for these are objectifications of the self, and only these need apology. On the level of immediacy, of the purely subjective (if it exist), no one needs apology or can offer it. What is is, and even this is to say too much. But one's thoughts and actions must either be sufficiently integrated in themselves so that for the most part they form a satisfactory structure of personality; or this failing, either because of the refractory nature of the materials or because of some failure in persistency and comprehensiveness of insight, the objectifications must be confused with the self by a desperate or innocent ambiguity so that these may then draw validity from the unassailable validity of the immediate.

Thus whenever one speaks in a critical situation of the immediate and the unique, whenever one invokes the primary self as an ultimate source of appeal, this is only a device, and sometimes a dodge, for denying the existing, available, obtruding categories of integration for the purpose of discovering or substituting others. The appeal to the self is obviously an objectification in the sense defined and not an immediacy, for on the level of immediacy no one acts or thinks; there everything is absolute simply because it undifferentiatedly is. In fine, immediacy is a methodological fiction, but a fiction is an Idea and not an immediacy. Hence the applicability of method to material, reason to nature, Idea to immediacy, is the necessary and irreducible postulate, and neither term can be sacrificed to the other.

Finally he observed that judgment and sympathy were terms of the same order and he wrote another book in which this was the theme.

The Journal of John Cardan

~~~~~~

I

When I began writing some years ago I had a shocking amount
of assurance. I knew right and wrong, truth and error, and it
all formed much of a system—what holes there were in it I knew
could be worked out. But I feel quite differently now. It isn't
that I've become anything so innocent as a sceptic or so crude
as disillusioned; it is that I am left with limited insights, the
plain implications of experience but restricted in generality,
and cold assumptions whose systematic development unfolds
as one lives them. These you might say constitute a group of
points of whose location I am fairly assured; the curve that embraces them and the equation that generates the curve I trust
are figurable. But there is all that paper that the curve will not
enclose, if it be a closed curve, all those propositions that I used
to make or that I now read in others' books but can make no
sense of, can find nothing to refer them to. So perhaps the frag-
mentary form of these notes is not merely the result of exigency
but rather proper to the form of my thought and experience.

II

To what extent does scandal reside in the dissemination of specific circumstances, of realistic detail, which invite the hearer

to reenact the scene and at the same time offer to his attention those items of commonness and vulgarity which qualify the generalities of passion, evil, or social mischance that were the basis of scandal? In these latter some dignity is to be found, at least in the generality of application to others, and in private surmise to the hearer's self. But realistic detail impedes this effect, localizes the general in the particular places, times, and persons concerned, and makes it difficult for one to conceive that this could happen to him who is not those persons nor was in those times and places. So the foundation for sympathy is displaced and there is left chiefly the malice of discomfort at this disturbance of one's social security; the threat to oneself, being suppressed, grows malignant, and the arrogance of spiritual superiority is given full scope.

III

Where the issue of our commitments denies even a reasonable fulfillment to our desires we must act in accordance with the commitment, even to the extent of effectively pretending that we enjoy what cannot be altered. We can do this without in the least denying the existence, or the validity, or even the power of desire. So we save ourselves from the sentimental death of the heart, and at the same time protect ourselves from engrossment in our wayward wishes. For a man must live divided against himself: only the selfishly insane can integrate experience to the heart's desire, and only the emotionally sterile would not wish to.

IV

The current attitude toward love usually ignores the element of want or need, for it spreads from the protected children of the middle class who have never seen want face to face and whose needs wander among the luxuries, since they are provided with the necessities, of life. But need is more important than sentiment, for it simply is while the latter comes and goes and enjoys its own ambiguities. Hence another's need lays obligations upon us which we cannot reject without moral damage to ourselves, while another's sentiment is merely an invitation to share in the exploitation of his leisure.

V

No one will deny, what is overwhelmingly obvious, the immediacy and absoluteness in itself of one's primary experience. But this is by definition self-sealed, isolated, and incommunicable, whether this be its glory or its defect. To speak or to think or to write is to go beyond this, and even to risk—to put to the wager—this. For to write is to confront one's primary experience with the externally objective: first, with the facts of experience and with the norms of possibility and probability of experience; secondly, with the objective commonality of language and literary forms. To be successful in this enterprise is to integrate the subjectively primary, the immediate, with the objectively communicable, the mediate, to the alteration of both by their conformation to each other, by their connexity with and their immanence in each other. It is the conquest of solipsism, the dramatic conflict of self with, on the one hand, reality in all its objectivity and potentiality, and, on the other, with philology in its old and general sense: or, with private and with public history.

VI

No dignity, except in silence; no virtue, except in sinuous exacting speech. So a scrupulosity toward experience promotes scandal, and a scrupulosity toward scandal invites inertia, or dignity devoid of quickness and virtue.

VII

I have been reflecting on the common notions about intellectualism. I have observed that the intellectual, unless it be a fraud, derives its content and its vitality from emotion and experience.

An intellectual distinction is both an emotional experience in itself, in the perception of it, and a realignment of the emotional experiences which are the content of the distinction. Hence the history of a man's thought is memoir as well as the history of his emotional life; and each of these, together with the other elements that could be distinguished, furnishes content and form to the other.

VIII

Contradictions are not to be put down side by side and gaily dismissed, as if this testified to a profundity that embraced the complexity of human nature. Nor are they to be admitted as a debater's device, to show how broadminded, even how humble, one is, for this is really to be so confident of one's conclusions that he can dispose of all difficulties by cheerfully admitting them. But this is not to say that contradictions are to be resolved by some dialectical agility: they are rather where the problem lies, and a sign that one's methods are unapt.

IX

The operations of logic, at least as far as regards the mind in its effort to grasp a logical method or distinction, are not so much subtle as massive. When we reflect on the process involved we feel that it cannot be expressed by the figures of thrusting and penetrating, of cutting and biting: what seems perhaps to others to be in effect a fine distinction has to the mind that achieved it no quality of thinness or edge. For logical apprehension seems rather to involve the moving of large blocks until—it may be suddenly—they settle deeply into place. We know they are in place because they settle, and though we test them they will not move.

X

In connection with Rilke one might develop, among other ideas,

two that now occur to me: 1) the hierophantic style which issues
from the concept of the poet-priest, an elevated obscurity whose
most notable stylistic device is the rhetorical question; and 2),
the Rilkean ideal involved in his notion of love, of death, of angels, and all the religious apparatus of surrender and goblin-
chasing—an ideal whose pragmatic basis seems to be that state
of feeling, that disturbed somatic exaltation which characterizes
a woman in love, together with her active desire for passivity
and surrender. But it is the state of feeling as such which is held
valuable, and the effort is bent toward sustaining and prolonging
that state by a skillful romantic excitation while denying to it
any release either in the gross physical discharge of some sexual
act, in the integration of that feeling into the social world by
associating it with some person, or by directing its reference
toward a theological structure of some definite content. It remains in Rilke both erotic and religious, but the eroticism is
directed toward nubile and shadowy objects, and the theological structure is consciously emptied of as much content as possible, what is left being deliberately rendered ambiguous and
confused.

XI

One recognizes with the misgivings of experience the imminence
of the state of passion, of engrossed choice of an object to love.
But the state of passion is an emanation of the indeterminable
sources of personal identity, the void region of possibilities
where dwells the promise of multiple and unrestricted fulfill-
ments. The realm of history, personal or public, where particular acts occur in particular times and places is something else
again. Hence love, the allegiance of passion to a given external
object, betrays this inner void whose principle of being is to be
neither this nor that, to be pregnant with every possible future,
because not committed to any particular one. But choice turns
the unconditioned idea into a conditioned process, into a succession of acts whose ultimate intention gives structure to each
as it happens, while the feeling that surrounds each act hurries
it on to its successor. So intimation falls away into fact.

XII

The premises of a logical or nonhistorical system are: 1) the causes determine the effect; 2) the fact, which is an effect, is an instance of the general, and hence the effect as a realized fact involves no element of radical novelty; and usually 3), the process is reversible, that is, nontemporal. The principles of order are therefore causal result and subsumption of instance under rule. But the premises of historical systems, on the other hand, are: 1) the effect determines the causes, or the principle of *post hoc, ergo propter hoc*, as qualified by some particular doctrine of relevance; 2) the specific fact is something other than an instance of the general, and in truth the general is only a methodological device for distinguishing those aspects of the specific which relate to the particular doctrine of relevance entertained. Hence, 3) the historical process is irreversible in time, since the subsequent effect alters the nature and relationship of the precedent effects which are its cause. But the premises of a historical system are inherently contradictory, since the doctrine of relevance which must be invoked if there is to be any order at all implies the premises of a nonhistorical system. The problem is yet to be solved.

Briefly, then: in nonhistorical systems the cause determines the effect; in historical systems the effect determines the cause.

Balboa and Palo Alto
1942-44

Several Kinds of Short Poem

Poetry may be thought of in various ways, and the way one habitually thinks of it will qualify the poetry he writes. For definition is not subsequent to action but precedes it; it is not gathered from the result but shapes the result. I do not, for example, ordinarily think of poetry as vision, although I know it sometimes is, and so I have no vision. I have no intuition into the heart of things; I have no special way of seeing. I think of poetry as a way of speaking, a special way of speaking. As a poet I speak in meter, and sometimes in rhyme; I speak in lines. It follows naturally that I am a formalist and that anything that can be said in metrical lines is subject for poetry, even vision, and that anything worth saying should sometime be said. This last adds a principle of value, the principle of what is worth saying as distinguished from what is not. And to this, formalism adds another principle of value, for the aim of the formal is the definitive. A poem, then, on this view is metrical speech, and a good poem is the definitive statement in meter of something worth saying.

Such a view of poetry, if we do not take it too loosely, will somewhat narrow the kinds of poetry one writes. Some poems, for instance, are not in any ordinary sense of the term statements. They are constructs, fiction, things made up. I have writ-

431

ten a few such—one, for example, on that mythical bird, *The Phoenix*:

> More than the ash stays you from nothingness!
> Nor here nor there is a consuming pyre!
> Your essence is in infinite regress
> That burns with varying consistent fire,
> Mythical bird that bears in burying!
>
> I have not found you in exhausted breath
> That carves its image on the Northern air,
> I have not found you on the glass of death
> Though I am told that I shall find you there,
> Imperturbable in the final cold,
>
> There where the North wind shapes white cenotaphs,
> There where snowdrifts cover the fathers' mound,
> Unmarked but for these wintry epitaphs,
> Still are you singing there without sound,
> Your mute voice on the crystal embers flinging.

But this is not my characteristic mode. Of such a poem one does not say that it is definitive or not, but that it is just right or it is not.

Other poems aim at recording a real or imagined personal experience; they are memoir. In such poems, if one has a partiality toward the definitive, the attitude is directed not so much toward the statement as toward the experience. The aim becomes not so much definitive statement as the asseveration under oath that this is exactly the way it was, in fact and feeling. The poems toward the end of this essay illustrate this aim, if not its accomplishment.

The characteristic poem motivated by a concern for definitive statement, however, will be the poem that explains—an expository poem, a statement in the ordinary sense of that word. And it will be short, for the concern for definitiveness is a prejudice for brevity. If one has said something definitively he will not be impelled to amplify, to say it again undefinitively. So the poet who holds this view becomes an epigrammatist. He writes:

When I shall be without regret
And shall mortality forget,
When I shall die who lived for this,
I shall not miss the things I miss.
And you who notice where I lie
Ask not my name. It is not I.

or:

In whose will is our peace? Thou happiness,
Thou ghostly promise, to thee I confess
Neither in thine nor love's nor in that form
Disquiet hints at have I yet been warm;
And if I rest not till I rest in thee
Cold as thy grace, whose hand shall comfort me?

or:

And what is love? Misunderstanding, pain,
Delusion, or retreat? It is in truth
Like an old brandy after a long rain,
Distinguished, and familiar, and aloof.

But the short poem in isolation has the defect of brevity; it comes naked to the reader without a locating context. It cannot build its own world, as *The Faerie Queene* and *The Prelude* do. And so one thinks, if he is committed by temperament and habit to the shorter poem, how he can make it longer.

There are two ways—perhaps there are more, but two I shall speak of here—by which a group of shorter poems can be aggrandized into a work of greater length. Length, however, is only a means; what one wants is a situation in which the several items can lend each other context, reference, and resonance, in which this short poem will be something more than it would be in isolation by belonging to a whole. The first method is an ancient one, invented, we are told, in Rome at the time of Vergil: one sets the poems in a matrix of relevant prose. The most famous, and most influential, work exemplifying this method is Boethius' *The Consolation of Philosophy*. It is the method of Dante's *The New Life*. And in both these works the poems gain stature from the surrounding prose. And, indeed, it is a matter of common observation that the poem we encounter in the course of reading a novel or an essay is more likely to stay in our memory than one read among other poems, for we come to it in a relevant context. Some fifteen to twenty years ago I used this method myself in a little work called *The Quest of the Opal*. There I surrounded a group of my early poems with prose commentary and paraphrase.

There is, however, a problem in the marriage of prose and verse that arises from an ambiguity of attitude on the part of audiences. On the one hand, the audience for poetry is willing, and sometimes eager, to hear the poet speak of his own work, as I am doing now, especially if he can adjoin to the work some anecdotal richness or give some hints of insight into the creative process. Yet the same audience on another occasion will feel, and sometimes strongly, that the poem should not need prose, that it should stand by itself unexplained, that the intrusion of commentary is a confession of failure. There is, then, both an appetite for commentary and a superiority to it, and what at one time is gratefully welcomed, at another is regarded with embarrassment.

There is an alternative way of aggrandizing a group of shorter poems into a work of greater length, and that is the poetic sequence. The sequence is a series of short poems in whose succession there is an implicit structure—in the case I have in mind, a narrative structure. The ancient precedent for the poetic sequence is the *Cynthia* of Propertius, a contemporary of Vergil. It consists of twenty-two or so elegies, what the Germans have called subjective erotic elegies, but though there are narrative elements in that sequence there is no story-line; the several poems are merely related to an established narrative context, and this is also the case with such a Renaissance sonnet sequence as Sir Philip Sidney's *Astrophil and Stella*. The particular form of sequence I have here in mind was invented, I believe, by Tennyson. It is likely that he discovered the form in the process of composing *In Memoriam*, for that sequence began apparently as a series of journal entries, acts of memoir, and was then developed within a structure of ideas and an implicit narrative structure, the Christmas poems marking off the years. Subsequently, he wrote *Maud*, a fictional narrative with primary attention to the emotional aspects, in which the narrative is implicit in the sequence of lyrics. It is an interesting form, though *Maud* is a bad poem.

An interest in a form is an invitation to attempt to realize it. I had entertained the general notion of such a sequence for many years and had designated the areas of experience that would be involved. The poems would deal with the American West, that vast spiritual region from Great Falls, Montana, to El Paso, Texas; from Fort Riley, Kansas, to the sinks of Nevada; and with the California Coast, another and perhaps less spiritual region. And the poems would relate some sort of illicit and finally terminated love affair. And there would be a fusion of the feeling in the personal relationship and the feeling for the West and the Coast. But nothing happened for eight or nine years until a few years ago, driving west through the Dakotas to Sheridan, Wyoming, I composed in memory these four lines:

> I drive Westward. Tumble and loco weed
> Persist. And in the vacancies of need,
> The leisure of desire, whirlwinds a face
> As luminous as love, lost as this place.

This was clearly the beginning of the sequence.

I turn now to the sequence in its final form, and say no more of the accidents of composition. It is entitled *To What Strangers, What Welcome*, and consists of an epigraph and fifteen poems. They are of various sorts, in the tradition of *Maud*: epigram, lyric, discourse; construct, memoir or purported memoir, and statement. They are in various formal patterns, some traditional and some as untraditional as octosyllabic blank verse and syllabic meters. Consequently, the unity of the sequence, if it has unity, will not depend on a formal consistency, as in a sonnet sequence, but on the story that is implied. It is, as it must be, a simple story, so common that any audience can supply what must be said between one poem and the next. A traveler drives west; he falls in love; he comes home. The conclusion is anticipated by the epigraph, which consists of some lines from Edwin Arlington Robinson's long Arthurian poem, *Merlin*. It is one of

Robinson's finest passages. Merlin is speaking, having just returned to Camelot after three years in Broceliande with the Lady
Vivian; he says if he does not go back to her the Lady Vivian
will remember him, and say:

> "I knew him when his heart was young,
> Though I have lost him now. Time called him home,
> And that was as it was. . . . "

The sequence proper opens with "I drive Westward," with
its intimation of a face "As luminous as love, lost as this place."
There follows:

> On either side of the white line
> The emblems of a life appear
> In turn: purpose like lodgepole pine
> Competitive and thin, and fear
>
> Agile as aspen in a storm.
> And then the twilit harboring
> In a small park. The room is warm.
> And by the ache of traveling
>
> Removed from all immediacy,
> From all time, I as time grows late
> Sense in disordered fantasy
> The sound and smell of love and hate.

And then an unsent letter, meditated at midnight, to no one at
all, of which this is the central stanza:

> I'll not summon you, or feel
> In the alert dream the give
> And stay of flesh, the tactile
> Conspiracy.
>   **The snow falls**
> With its inveterate meaning,
> And I follow the barbed wire

To trough, to barn, to the house,
To what strangers, what welcome
In the late blizzard of time.

After certain unrewarding adventures, a pick-up at one time, at
another a stripper in Las Vegas, the traveler comes to the Pacific:

> the surf breaking,
> Repetitive and varied as love
> Enacted, and inevitably
> The last rim of sunset on the sea.

He has an apartment on the beach:

> The night is still. The unfailing surf
> In passion and subsidence moves
> As at a distance. The glass walls,
> And redwood, are my utmost being.
> And is there there in the last shadow,
> There in the final privacies
> Of unaccosted grace,—is there,
> Gracing the tedium to death,
> An intimation? Something much
> Like love, like loneliness adrowse
> In states more primitive than peace,
> In the warm wonder of winter sun.

The intimation becomes reality:

> A half hour for coffee, and at night
> An hour or so of unspoken speech,
> Hemming a summer dress as the tide
> Turns at the right time.
>   Must it be sin
> This consummation of who knows what?
> This sharp cry at entrance, once, and twice?
> This unfulfilled fulfillment?

                              Something
         That happens because it must happen.
         We live in the given. Consequence,
         And lack of consequence, both fail us.
         Good is what we can do with evil.

At this point "Time called him home, And that was as it was":

         I drive Eastward. The ethics of return,
         Like the night sound of coyotes on a hill
         Heard in eroded canyons of concern,
         Disposes what has happened, and what will.

There is the long drive back across the continent, over the high
desert, through the central plains, to the stone walls of New
England:

         Absence, my angel, presence at my side,
         I know you as an article of faith
         By desert, prairie, and this stonewalled road—
         As much my own as is the thought of death.

There in the last warmth of a New England autumn the story
comes to an end, and the traveler addresses himself:

         Identity, that spectator
         Of what he calls himself, that net
         And aggregate of energies
         In transient combination—some
         So marginal are they mine? Or is
         There mine? I sit in the last warmth
         Of a New England fall, and I?
         A premise of identity
         Where the lost hurries to be lost,
         Both in its own best interests
         And in the interests of life.

Technology and Poetry

~~~~~~

Over the past ten years I have been told by eight persons on eight occasions at cocktail parties, and I go very seldom to cocktail parties, that they had photocopied my first book in Iowa City. I have been told also of unauthorized broadcasts of taped poetry readings. Technology has made one's property freely available, with payment only to Xerox and Wollensak. But such mundane, practical matters are not here the object of concern. I will comment only that with the invention and diffusion of sound recording, we have not only an oral poetry and a written poetry, but also a written oral poetry, not written down from dictation but reproducible as spoken.

But the concern here is rather with those figures of our imagination, the epic heroes of our despair, Technological Man in his Technocratic Society, whether already realized or about to come into being. What will they do to the arts? What will the arts do with them?

Certainly there are relations between what we call the arts and what we call society. I am in one of my roles a historian. I observe that in *Midsummer Night's Dream* the head of state speaks in weighty blank verse, the highborn lovers in blank verse and rhymed couplets, the otherworldly characters may use lyric measures, and Bottom and company speak prose. In *As You Like It* what we would call romantic love is appropriate only to the high born; in them it may be amusing, but in the low born it is ridiculous. The class structure of society is a principle of order in the plays, even in the style.

But there is not only a sociology of the literary work, there is also a sociology of literary men. All the great figures of Elizabethan literature were related directly to the Court. Sir Thomas More and Sir Francis Bacon were Lords Chancellor of England, the highest office of state in precedence if not in power. Sir Philip Sidney was the nephew of two earls, the brother of a countess, and Governor of Flushing. Jonson had a state pension, and Shakespeare was servant to the Lord Chamberlain, later to the King, and on one attested State occasion wore the King's livery.

There are also relationships between my poetry, myself as poet, and the society in which I live and which in part structures my experience. But is that society a technological one? My role and its product, certainly, is premised on print, and on an education in which print is important. But this is too factual for the spirit of this occasion.

For the Idea of Technological Society has nothing to do with fact, much to do with feeling and with fears. It is an invention of rhetoric. It is instant history in the service of other causes. It expresses the fears of a managed society on the part of those who would manage society themselves, who speak of propaganda as if rhetoric and lying were new arts. It is the anti-image of the pastoral myth, or the mad scientist's dream of utopia. In one's name computerized, one's identity an assemblage of bits, is symbolized the rage of the unimportant that they are in fact unimportant. Indeed, the importance of the unimportant is immanent in much modern literature, as in Chekhov or in Williams: "so much depends / on a red wheelbarrow / full of rainwater / beside the white chickens." So much depends. And, above all, the Technological Society comes with the light of Never Before, *Novus ordo saeculorum*. But new orders, new dispensations, new testaments are quite old. There is a history of Apocalypse: "and, lo, there was a great earthquake, and the sun became black as sackcloth of hair, and the moon became as blood, and the stars of heaven fell unto the earth. . . . For the great day of his wrath is come, and who shall be able to stand." It is apocalyptic vision in the service of that recurrent American phenomenon, Revivalism, which recently possessed the educated classes—a revivalism, however, without Christianity, without established places to put and to structure our irrationalities, that range from astrology and witchcraft to the science-fiction revelation of Technology. This vision has affected some poems but none I know of merit.

But there have been changes in society that do deeply affect poetry. The role of poet as professor or poet as dropout was not available to me when I was young; had they been, my life and poetry would have been different. Indeed, a few years earlier the role itself would not have been available. The class I grew up in, the upper lower class, did not write poetry. The art of compliment, which motivated so many love lyrics, has been lost; and sight-reading has something to do with the breakdown of meter. But let me conclude with two extraordinary changes and their effect on the art of poetry.

Consider the social act of death. This has so changed in my lifetime that any competent anthropologist would be forced to conclude that a whole society had been destroyed and replaced by invaders. Death is no longer ritualized. Men no longer train themselves to die a good death. We have no *Ars Bene Moriendi*. And when did you last see the black armband, the purple wreath? Formal mourning is out of style. This with the dissipation of Christianity, also in my lifetime, has profoundly affected poetry. One may come to the consequence sparely as in this epitaph for oneself:

> When I shall be without regret
> And shall mortality forget,
> When I shall die who lived for this,
> I shall not miss the things I miss.
> And you who notice where I lie
> Ask not my name. It is not I.

One may come to it through the traditional eloquence of blank verse, as in this modern consolation, *Consolatio Nova*, on the death of my friend and publisher Alan Swallow:

> To speak of death is to deny it, is
> To give unpredicated substance phrase

And being. So the discontinuous,
The present instant absent finally
Without future or past, is yet in time
For we are time, monads of purposes
Beyond ourselves that are not purposes,
A causeless all of momentary somes.
And in such fiction we can think of death.

One may come to it through the casualness of syllabic meter, as in *Think*:

Let us forget praise and blame,
Speak only of quietness
And survival. Mad toadstools
Grow in the dampness, englobed
Enormities, inherited
Treachery of all our pasts.
Forget. What was day is night.
In curtained sufficiency
Rest in the living silence,
Rest in arrogant sleep. Think
What houseflies have died in time.

But one must come to it somehow. Technology has not yet repealed death, and, if it did, who could live with the horror of immortality.

Notes

~~~~~~

Most Shakespeare citations throughout this book are from George Lyman Kittredge, ed., *The Complete Works of Shakespeare* (Boston, 1936). I have generally modernized texts.

I
Woe or Wonder: The Emotional Effect of Shakespearean Tragedy

Woe or Wonder was completed in 1945. I have since cut, rearranged, and rephrased parts of it but have made no substantial alterations.

~~~~~~

Ripeness is All

1 G. B. Harrison, *Shakespeare: 23 Plays and the Sonnets* (New York, 1948), 3. Similarly O. J. Campbell, *The Living Shakespeare* (New York, 1949), 1: "In his plays we constantly meet our own experiences; in his poetry we constantly find our inmost thoughts and feelings expressed with an eloquence and a precision far beyond our reach."
2 T. S. Eliot, *Selected Essays* (New York, 1950), 231.
3 Robert Bechtold Heilman, *This Great Stage* (Baton Rouge, 1948), 112. The correct interpretation is given in passing by Alfred Harbage, *As They Liked It* (New York, 1947), 56.
4 Hugh Latimer, *Sermons* (Everyman's Library, London, 1906), 352-53.
5 Thomas Wilson, *Art of Rhetoric*, ed. G. H. Mair (Oxford, 1909), 83. *Cf.* John Bruce, ed., *Diary of John Manningham* (Camden Society Publication, XCIX, Westminster, 1868), 146, under March 24, 1602 [1603]: "This morning about three at clock her Majesty departed this life, mildly like a lamb, like a ripe apple from the tree."

Aught of Woe or Wonder

1 "De ratione studii," *Opera Omnia* (Leyden, 1703), I, 528C-D. There is a paraphrastic translation of the treatise in William Harrison Woodward, *Desiderius*

443

Erasmus concerning the Aim and Method of Education (Cambridge, 1904), 162-78.

2 *If This be not a Good Play, the Devil is in It* in *The Dramatic Works of Thomas Dekker* (London, 1873), III, 265.

3 John Burnet, ed., *Platonis Opera* (Oxford, 1903), III.

4 Ingram Bywater, ed., tr., *Aristotle on the Art of Poetry* (Oxford, 1909), ad 1452a4, 60a11, 60a18.

5 The classic formulation, cited from the index, *s.v.*, *casus*, of the Vives edition (Paris, 1862 and 1861) of Thomas Aquinas, *Summa Theologica*. Hereafter referred to as *ST*.

6 C. F. Tucker Brooke, ed., *The Shakespeare Apocrypha* (Oxford, 1908), 44.

7 "tristitia namque tragoediae proprium." Diomedes, *Ars Grammatica* in Heinrich Keil, ed., *Grammatici Latini* (Leipzig, 1857), I, 488.

8 Thomas Dekker, *The Magnificent Entertainment* . . . (London, 1604) in *Dramatic Works, op. cit.*, I, 269. Sir Philip Sidney, *Works*, ed. Albert Feuillerat (Cambridge, 1923), III, 23.

9 Hardin Craig, *The Enchanted Glass* (New York, 1936), 27; Hardin Craig, *Shakespeare* (Chicago, 1932), 804.

10 Richard Hooker, *Works*, ed. John Keble (7th ed., Oxford, 1888). Hereafter referred to as *EP*.

11 However, for a generalized argument see John Marston's *Sophonisba*.

12 Julius Caesar Scaliger, *Poetice*, 3. 97 in F. M. Padelford, tr., *Select Translations from Scaliger's Poetics* (New York, 1905), 57. John Jewel, *The Defence of the Apology* (Publications of the Parker Society, XXV, Cambridge, 1848), 249-50.

The Donatan Tradition

1 The material in the following pages is vulgate: Wilhelm Cloetta, *Beiträge zur Litteraturgeschichte des Mittelalters und der Renaissance* (Halle, 1890-92); Joel E. Spingarn, *A History of Literary Criticism in the Renaissance* (2nd ed., New York, 1908); John W. Cunliffe, ed., *Early English Classical Tragedies* (Oxford, 1912); L. E. Kastner and H. B. Charlton, eds., *The Poetical Works of Sir William Alexander* (Manchester, 1921); A. Philip McMahon, "Seven Questions on Aristotelian Definitions of Tragedy and Comedy," *Harvard Studies in Classical Philology*, XL (1929), 97-198.

2 "Inter tragoediam autem et comoediam cum multa tum inprimis hoc distat, quod in comoedia mediocres fortunae hominum, parvi impetus periculorum, laetique sunt exitus actionum, at in tragoedia omnia contra, ingentes personae, magni timores, exitus funesti habentur; et illic prima turbulenta, tranquilla ultima, in tragoedia contrario ordine res aguntur; tum quod in tragoedia fugienda vita, in comoedia capessenda exprimitur; postremo quod omnis comoedia de fictis est argumentis, tragoedia saepe de historia fide petitur." Cited from McMahon, *op. cit.*, 128-29. The text is apparently by Evanthius, whose treatise on comedy is included in the Donatan commentary.

3 A Renaissance commonplace: see Justus Lipsius, *Two Bookes of Constancie*, tr. Sir John Stradling, ed. Rudolph Kirk (New Brunswick, N.J., 1939), 85-86.

4 Jacobus Zabarella, *Opera Logica* (Venice, 1586), 81: "Quod Rhetorica et Poetica solius civilis disciplinae instrumenta sint, et quomodo."

5 Sidney, *Works, op. cit.*, III, 23.

6 McMahon, *op. cit.*; A. Philip McMahon, "On the Second Book of Aristotle's Poetics and the Source of Theophrastus' Definition of Tragedy," *Harvard Studies in Classical Philology*, XXVIII (1917), 1-46.

7 "Tragoedia est heroicae fortunae in adversis conprehensio. a Theophrasto ita definita est, *tragoidia estin eroikes tuches peristasis*. . . . Comoedia est privatae civilisque fortunae sine periculo vitae conprehensio, apud Graecos ita definita, *komoidia estin idiotikon pragmaton akindunos perioche* . . . in ea viculorum, id est humilium domuum, fortunae conprehendantur, non ut in tragoedia publicarum regiarumque . . . comoedia a tragoedia differt, quod in tragoedia introducuntur heroes duces reges, in comoedia humiles atque privatae personae; in illa luctus exilia caedes, in hac amores, virginum raptus: deinde quod in illa frequenter et paene semper laetis rebus exitus tristes et liberorum fortunarumque priorum in peius adgnitio. quare varia definitione discretae sunt. altera enim *akindunos perioche*, altera *tuches peristasis* dicta est. tristitia namque tragoediae proprium." Keil, *op. cit.*

8 Cited from Cunliffe, *op. cit.*, xvi*ff.*

9 Frederick S. Boas, ed., *The Works of Thomas Kyd* (Oxford, 1901), 164.

10 Richard Simpson, ed., *The School of Shakespeare* (London, 1878), II, 241*ff.*

11 Brooke, *op. cit.*, 35.

Wonder

1 Sidney, *Works, op. cit.*, III, 23.

2 For fuller discussion and citation with respect to the history of wonder as an aesthetic term, see my unpublished Ph.D. dissertation, "Tragic Effect and Tragic Process . . ." (Stanford, 1945); Richard Heinze, *Virgils Epische Technik* (Leipzig, 1903), 454*ff.*; Marvin Herrick, "Some Neglected Sources of *Admiratio*," *Modern Language Notes*, LXII (1947), 222-26. The historians of Renaissance criticism, until Herrick's note, had regarded the concept as introduced in the middle of the sixteenth century by Minturno and without effective influence on the drama until Corneille: Gregory Smith, *Elizabethan Critical Essays* (Oxford, 1904), I, 392; Spingarn, *op. cit.*, 52-53, 72, 78-79, 285; René Bray, *La Formation de la Doctrine Classique en France* (Paris, 1927), 213*ff.* and 319; Allan H. Gilbert, *Literary Criticism: Plato to Dryden* (New York, 1940), 461 and index, *s.v.*, "admiration."

3 Bywater, *op. cit.* For the relationship of wonder (*to thaumaston*) and astonishment (*ekplexis*), see Aristotle, *Topics*, 4. 5. 126b13*ff.*

4 Gorgias, *Helena*, 9, ed. Otto Immisch (Berlin, 1927), though the text seems untrustworthy; E. E. Sikes, *The Greek View of Poetry* (London, 1931); Max Pohlenz, "Die Anfänge der griechischen Poetik," *Nachr. d. Gott. Ges. d. Wiss.* (1920), 167*ff.*

5 Gilbert, *op. cit.*, 15.

6 Leonhard Spengel, ed., *Rhetores Graeci* (Leipzig, 1853-56), II, 455.

7 Plotinus, *Enneades*, ed. Emile Bréhier (Collection Bude, Paris, 1924); translation revised from Stephen McKenna, *The Ethical Treatises* (London, 1926).

8 Horace Leonard Jones, ed., tr., *The Geography of Strabo* (Loeb Library, London, 1917), I, 23.

9 Polybius, *The Histories*, ed., tr. W. R. Paton (Loeb Library, London, 1922), I, 377, 379.

10 Plutarch, *Moralia*, ed., tr. Frank Cole Babbitt (Loeb Library, London, 1927), I.

11 Cited by Sikes, *op. cit.*, 112.

12 Aristotle, *Rhetorica*, tr. W. Rhys Roberts in W. D. Ross, ed., *The Works of Aristotle* (Oxford, 1946), XI. I have revised the second sentence.

13 Cited and translated by G. L. Hendrickson, "The Origin and Meaning of the Ancient Characters of Style," *American Journal of Philology*, XXVI (1905), 255-56. I have substituted "astonished" for "moved" toward the end of the

next-to-last sentence. Text, Augustus Mayer, ed., *Theophrasti Peri Lexeos Libri Fragmenta* (Leipzig, 1910), 14-15.

14   T. H. Moxon, tr., *Aristotle's Poetics, Demetrius on Style* (London, 1934); I have made some revisions. Text, W. Rhys Roberts, ed. (Cambridge, 1902).

15   [Longinus,] *On the Sublime*, ed., tr. W. Rhys Roberts (Cambridge, 1907). There is an excellent translation by Benedict Einarson (Chicago, 1945).

16   Cicero, *De Oratore . . . De Partitione Oratoria*, ed. H. Rackham (Loeb Library, London, 1942), II, 329, 337, 355, 365.

17   Quintilian, *Institutes of Oratory*, tr. John Selby Watson (London, 1909-10), II, 78, 87. I have substituted "wonder" for "admiration" in the last two sentences. L. Rademacher, ed. (Leipzig, 1935).

18   *Patrologia Latina*, XLII, 90.

19   *Opera Omnia*, ed. Augustus Borgnet (Paris, 1890), VI, 30a-31a. My translation.

20   My translation.

21   The relevant passages are reprinted and translated by Ruth Kelso, "Girolamo Fracastoro, *Naugerius sive De Poetica Dialogus*," *University of Illinois Studies in Language and Literature*, IX (1924), 75ff.

22   *Ibid.*, 58-59.

23   My translation. The texts are cited in Bernard Weinberg, "The Poetic Theories of Minturno," *Studies in Honor of Frederick W. Shipley* (St. Louis, 1942), 104n6(1), 110n17.

24   E. K. Chambers, *William Shakespeare* (Oxford, 1930), I, 412 and II, 188.

25   Brooke, *op. cit.*

26   J. Churton Collins, ed., *The Plays and Poems of Robert Greene* (Oxford, 1905), I, 264.

27   Henry Harvey Wood, ed., *The Plays of John Marston* (Edinburgh, 1934-39), I.

28   Brooke, *op. cit.*

29   Ben Jonson, *Works*, ed. C. H. Herford, Percy Simpson, and Evelyn Simpson (Oxford, 1925-52), IV.

30   A. H. Bullen, ed., *The Works of Thomas Middleton* (Boston, 1885-86), VI, 370-71.

Reason Panders Will

For the interpretation of Hamlet's phrase, "reason panders will," I am deeply indebted to Lily B. Campbell, *Shakespeare's Tragic Heroes* (Cambridge, 1930), 146.

 1   "Definitio . . . est imitatio actionis illustris, voluntarie perfectae, cui inest vis universalis circa res praestantiores, non autem particularis de singula re praestanti: qua quidem imitatione animi recta afficiuntur affectione per misericordiam atque terrorem in eis orta." *Voluntarie* can also be construed as an adjective without significant change of meaning. "Paraphrasis in librum Poeticae Aristotelis," tr. Jacobus Mantinus, ed. Fridericus Heidenhain, *Jahrbücher für classische Philologie*, 17th Supplementband (1890), 359. For Renaissance editions see Lane Cooper and Alfred Gudeman. *A Bibliography of the Poetics of Aristotle* (Cornell Studies in English, XI, New Haven, 1928), *s.n.* Averroes.

 2   A medieval commonplace: see Alexander of Hales, *Summa*, 1. 1. 1. ad 1 and ad 2 (Quaracchi, 1924), I.

 3   Charles R. S. Harris, *Duns Scotus* (Oxford, 1927), II, 288ff.; see also Arthur C. McGiffert, *History of Christian Thought* (New York, 1932-35), II, 299ff.; D. E. Sharp, *Franciscan Philosophy at Oxford* (Oxford, 1930), 336-41. *ST*, 1-2, 8. 1. For St. Thomas' doctrine, see Michael Wittmann, *Die Ethik des Hl. Thomas von Aquin* (Munich, 1933); Etienne Gilson, *Moral Values and the Moral Life*, tr. Leo R. Ward (London, 1931).

4 *Phaedra*, 177*ff*.; *Metamorphoses*, 7. 20-21. These passages are cited by Melanch-thon in his refutation of Stoic fatalism, *Corpus Reformatorm* XVI, 42-50, 189-201, 336-46.

5 Craig, *Enchanted Glass, op. cit.*, 116.

6 Ludwig Schutz, *Thomas-Lexicon* (Paderborn, 1895), *s.vv.*

7 C. F. Tucker Brooke and Nathaniel Burton Paradise, eds., *English Drama: 1580-1642* (Boston, 1933).

8 A. W. Verity, ed., *Thomas Heywood* (London, n.d.).

9 The punctuation is from Q1.

10 G. W. Kitchin, ed., *Bacon's "Advancement of Learning"* (Everyman's Library, London, 1930), 132.

11 Lancelot Andrewes, *Lectures* (London, 1657), 256.

12 Elmer E. Stoll, *Othello* (Minneapolis, 1915); Elmer E. Stoll, *Art and Artifice in Shakespeare* (Cambridge, 1933), 6*ff*.; Craig, *Shakespeare, op. cit.*, 715-16.

13 Jewel, *op. cit.*, 70.

14 In the following analysis I obviously owe a good deal to Walter Clyde Curry's *Shakespeare's Philosophical Patterns* (Baton Rouge, 1937).

15 Kitchin, *op. cit.*, 146.

16 Simpson, *op. cit.*

Appendix I: The Ancient Quarrel Between History and Poetry

1 Curry, *op. cit.*, xi-xii.

II
Tradition and Poetic Structure

Poetry, Structure, and Tradition

1 Archibald MacLeish, *Collected Poems: 1917-1952* (Boston, 1952), 41.

2 *Shorter Oxford English Dictionary* (Oxford, 1933), *s.v.* See also James Craig La Driere, "Poetry and Prose" in Joseph T. Shipley, ed., *Dictionary of World Literature* (New York, 1943).

3 Aristotle, *Poetics*, 1. See Gerald Else, *Aristotle's Poetics: The Argument* (Cambridge, Mass., 1957), *ad loc.*

4 St. Petersburg, April 21, 1914.

5 The theory and point of view here developed closely parallels that of Wellek in René Wellek and Austin Warren, *Theory of Literature* (New York, 1949), Chapter 12.

6 St. Augustine, *Confessions*, tr. E. B. Pusey (Everyman's Library, London, 1907), 274-75.

Classical and Medieval

1 Statius, *Silvae*, 5. 4, ed. Henri Frère, tr. H. H. Izaac (Paris, 1944), 205.

2 J. W. Mackail, *Latin Literature* (New York, 1895), 189-90.

3 Robert Yelverton Tyrrell, *Anthology of Latin Poetry* (London, 1901), 302-03; D. A. Slater, *The Silvae of Statius* (Oxford, 1908), 22-23; H. W. Garrod, ed., *The Oxford Book of Latin Verse* (Oxford, 1912), 495-500; E. E. Sikes, *Roman Poetry* (London, 1923), 86-88; J. H. Mozley, ed., tr , *Statius* (London, New York,

1928), xii; J. Wight Duff, *Literary History of Rome in the Silver Age* (London, 1927), 492; Philip Schuyler Allen, *The Romanesque Lyric* (Chapel Hill, 1928), 76-77. In this last the Latin text is printed in an appendix (321) with the Argus passage excised.

4   H. W. Garrod, ed., *The Poetical Works of John Keats* (Oxford, 1939), 460, 533.

5   John W. Cunliffe, ed., *The Complete Works of George Gascoigne* (Cambridge, 1907-10), II, 143; Frank Allen Patterson, ed., *The Student's Milton* (New York, 1931), 160.

6   This is deliberate with Gascoigne: "Certayne notes of Instruction," *Works*, I, 465*ff*.

7   Patterson, *op. cit.*, 159.

8   Whether there is any such playing of accent against quantity in classical Latin is still under dispute.

9   W. H. Fyfe, in fact, reduces the four lines to one—"But my sad eyes their nightly vigil keep"—and expands the second line into two in order to achieve a sonnet. Garrod, *The Oxford Book of Latin Verse*, 495. Slater, *op. cit.*, 23.

10   E. de Selincourt and Helen Darbshire, eds., *Works* (Oxford, 1946), III, 8-9.

11   *Silvae*, 5. 1. 34-35; Ovid, *Metamorphoses*, 14. 708.

12   Friedrich Vollmer, ed., *Silvae* (Leipzig, 1898), 10; *Silvae*, 3. 5. 37-42.

Logic and Lyric

1   Richard von Mises, *Positivism* (Cambridge, Mass., 1951), 289.

2   Harold R. Walley and J. Harold Wilson, *The Anatomy of Literature* (New York, 1934), 143, 144.

3   Scholiast cited in Otto Bird, "The Seven Liberal Arts" in Shipley, *op. cit.*, 55; Joel E. Spingarn, *A History of Literary Criticism in the Renaissance* (2nd ed., New York, 1908), 24-27; David Hume, *Philosophical Works* (Boston, Edinburgh, 1854), III, 264; von Mises, *op. cit.*

4   H. M. Margouliouth, ed., *The Poems and Letters* (Oxford, 1927), II.

5   T. S. Eliot, *Selected Essays* (new ed., New York, 1950), 254; Helen C. White, Ruth C. Wallerstein, and Ricardo Quintana, eds., *Seventeenth Century Verse and Prose* (New York, 1951), I, 454.

6   Eliot, *op. cit.*, 253-54, 255.

7   John M. Berdan, ed., *The Poems of John Cleveland* (New Haven, 1911), 80-81.

8   Wright Thomas and Stuart Gerry Brown, eds., *Reading Poems* (New York, 1941), 702; Douglas Bush, *English Literature in the Earlier Seventeenth Century* (Oxford, 1945), 163.

9   My translation, except for "the brief sum of life forbids our opening a long account with hope," which is Gildersleeve's; see Paul Shorey and Gordon J. Lang, eds., *Horace: Odes and Epodes* (rev. ed., Chicago, 1910), *ad loc.*

10   W. Mackay Mackenzie, ed., *The Poems of William Dunbar* (Edinburgh, 1932), 20-23.

11   Ronald B. McKerrow, ed., *The Works of Thomas Nashe* (London, 1904-10), III, 283.

12   *Contra Gentiles*, 3. 27, 29-31, 36, 48, in *Opera Omnia* (Rome, 1882-1948), XIV; Anton C. Pegis, ed., *Basic Writings of Saint Thomas Aquinas* (New York, 1945), II.

13   James Joyce, *A Portrait of the Artist as a Young Man* (Modern Library, New York, 1928), 273-75.

14   McKerrow, *op. cit.*, IV, 440.

15   This essay has been refuted by Frank Towne, "Logic, Lyric, and Drama," *Modern Philology*, LI (1953-54), 265-68.

Convention as Structure

1 Fred N. Robinson, ed., *The Complete Works of Geoffrey Chaucer* (Boston, 1933), 2; John Livingston Lowes, *Geoffrey Chaucer* (Boston, 1934), 198; Robert Dudley French, *A Chaucer Handbook* (2nd ed., New York, 1947), 203.
2 French, *op. cit.*, 203.
3 Robinson, *op. cit.*, 2-3.
4 William Witherle Lawrence, *Chaucer and the Canterbury Tales* (New York, 1950), 38.
5 Robert Armstrong Pratt and Karl Young, "The Literary Framework of the Canterbury Tales" in W. F. Bryan and Germaine Dempster, eds., *Sources and Analogues of Chaucer's "Canterbury Tales"* (Chicago, 1941), 2.
6 George Lyman Kittredge, *Chaucer and His Poetry* (Cambridge, Mass., 1915), 149: "There is not one chance in a hundred that he had not gone on a Canterbury pilgrimage himself."
7 Robinson, *op. cit.*, 663.
8 *Ibid.*, 315.
9 4. 1245*ff.* G. C. Macaulay, ed., *The Complete Works of John Gower* (Oxford, 1901), II. 335*ff.*
10 Suggested by Emile Legouis, *Geoffrey Chaucer*, tr. L. Lailavoix (London, 1928), 85-86.
11 Howard R. Patch, "Characters in Medieval Literature," *Modern Language Notes*, XL (1925), 1-14.
12 Lines 812-16 in the Middle English version; 796-800 in the original. Ernest Langlois, ed., *Le Roman de la Rose* (Société des Anciens Textes Français, CXII, Paris, 1920), II.
13 M.E., 160-61, original, 150-51; M.E., 220-21, original, 208-09.
14 Kittredge, *Chaucer*, 166; Lawrence, *op. cit.*, 30.

Idea as Structure

1 William Oldys and Thomas Birch, eds., *The Works of Sir Walter Ralegh* (Oxford, 1829), II, xlvi.
2 Richard Hooker, *Laws of Ecclesiastical Polity* in *Works*, ed. John Keble (7th ed., Oxford, 1888), II, 247-48.
3 St. Thomas Aquinas, *Summa Theologica* in *Opera Omnia* (Leonine ed., Rome, 1882-1948). Hereafter *ST*.
4 Some details of the following interpretations have been anticipated by other scholars, particularly by the Indian scholar, Ranjee. See William Shakespeare, *The Poems*, ed. Hyder Edward Rollins (The New Variorum, Philadelphia, 1938), 323-31, 559-83.
5 Alexander B. Grosart, ed., *Robert Chester's "Loves Martyr"* (London, 1878), 169 (top pagination).
6 John Gerard, *The Autobiography of an Elizabethan*, tr. Philip Caraman (London, 1951), 48: "I must not forget to mention a certain lady and her husband (they were gentlefolk) who made a vow of chastity. . . . I kept in touch with them for many years afterward and I can say that during all that time they remained faithful to their vow." See also on Mrs. Line: ". . . she made a vow of chastity, a virtue she practiced in her married life." (86) Father Gerard was a noted Jesuit; the events described occurred in the 1590s.
  The only testimony relating to the circumstances of this poem, if it does relate to this poem, is the remark made in passing by Fr. Henry More, S.J. (1660) about Ann, Lady Stourton: "a daughter of Edward, Earl of Derby, and sister to the Stanley whose epitaph Shakespeare wrote." (Rollins, *op. cit.*,

578) There were five sisters (John Seacome, *The History of the House of Stanley* [Preston, 1793], 130-31), but none of them seems to fit the apparent specifications of the poem. Sir John Salusbury's wife, of course, was a natural daughter of the fourth Earl of Derby, and hence a niece of Lady Stourton's, as was Dorothy Halsall, her sister, with whom Sir John seems to have been in love. (Carleton Brown, ed., *Poems by Sir John Salusbury and Robert Chester* [E.E.T.S., e.s. cxiii: London, 1914], xxxviii*ff.*). I add, for the fun of it, that Salusbury's motto, "posse et nolle nobile" (Brown, xxix) is the theme of Shakespeare's Sonnet 94.

7 Grosart, *op. cit.*, 177, 181-86 (top pagination).

8 The last line of the *Epode* appears in *England's Parnassus* (1600).

9 A. J. Denomy, "An Inquiry into the Origins of Courtly Love," *Medieval Studies*, Pontifical Institute of Medieval Studies, Toronto, VI (1944), 175-260, especially 209.

10 Robert Ellrodt in *Shakespeare Survey* 15 (1962) offers new material on the Phoenix tradition. However, further investigation of that tradition is unlikely to yield useful results. The symbolism of *The Phoenix and Turtle*, except for the bare idea of the Phoenix, is sufficiently explicated in the poem, as it is in the following epigram on Queen Jane and Edward VI:

> Phaenix Jana jacet nate Phaenice: dolendum est
> Saecula Phaenices nulla tulesse duas.

The Phoenix as Phoenix offers no problem.

But there are problems to be investigated. 1) We need a history of married chastity, particularly in the decade before 1601. It involved a mutual vow to cohabit without intercourse, as in the case of the Virgin Mary. (*ST*, 3. 28. 4) According to Father Gerard it was practiced by at least two couples in this decade. 2) We need a few paragraphs on the customary order of funerals. 3) We need to classify the poem. It is hyperbolical compliment of a conventional sort: the lovers are the Ideas. 4) We would like to know the occasion of the poem. What are the referents, real or supposititious? And what occasioned Shakespeare to write of them? The latter question can be partially answered from context. The "new compositions" appended to *Loves Martyr* were commissioned (see Jonson's *Praeludium*), and Shakespeare's poem was available to Marston and hence may have been the starting point for the others. But Marston's poem has different referents, for his birds have issue. As for the identity of the birds, I have been unable to find any gold in the only clue I know, the statement that Shakespeare wrote an epitaph for a daughter of Edward, Earl of Derby (*supra*, note 6). Finally, there are the two important problems 5) of the stylistic tradition and 6) of the value of the poem.

Plots and Errors

1 A. C. Bradley, *Shakespearean Tragedy* (London, 1912), 89; Allardyce Nicoll, *Studies in Shakespeare* (London, 1927), 43.

2 E. M. Forster, *Aspects of the Novel* (New York, 1927), 144: "The plot, then, is the novel in its logical intellectual aspect."

3 Henry James, *The Ambassadors* (New York, 1909), II, 200-01 (Bk. X, ch. 3).

4 Mark Twain, *The Adventures of Huckleberry Finn*, introductory Notice; André Gide, *Journal of "The Counterfeiters"* (New York, 1951), July 11, 1919 entry; Forster, *op. cit.*, 152; Sherwood Anderson in Robert E. Spiller, et. al., eds., *Literary History of the United States* (New York, 1948), II, 1230-31; Elizabeth Bowen, *Collected Impressions* (London, 1950), 249; Edwin Muir, *The Structure of the Novel* (London, 1928), 38, 39, 40, 43, 47-48.

5 Ben Jonson, *Masque of Blackness*, line 6 in *Works*, ed. C. H. Hereford, Percy Simpson, and Evelyn Simpson (Oxford, 1925-52).

6 *Discoveries*, 2747-49: "For the episodes and digressions in a fable are the same that household stuff and other furniture are in a house."

7 Samuel T. Coleridge, *Lectures and Notes on Shakespeare* (London, 1897), 472.

8 T. W. Baldwin, *Shakespeare's Five-Act Structure* (Urbana, 1947); Marvin Theodore Herrick, *Comic Theory in the Sixteenth Century* (Urbana, 1950); Madeleine Doran, *Endeavors of Art* (Madison, 1954).

9 Kittredge, *ad loc.*

10 Iodocus Willichius, ed. (Cologne, 1567), on *Andria*, 1. 1.: "Quod autem actus fabularum partimur in scenas, aliamque primam, aliam secundam, et sic deinceps dicimus, quam perite et intelligenter id fiat, quaerendum puto. Equidem libere ut dicam, grammaticorum hanc, non poetarum, esse partitionem arbitror." *Orationes, Epistolae, et Poemata* (Leipzig, 1698), 696: "omnino autem illam inutilem et supervacaneam, et a stultis literatoribus excogitatum actuum in scenas divisionem, quaeso te, ut tollas." Baldwin, *op. cit.*, cites these passages and the Jonson. (277)

11 Quintilian, 3. 5. 5.

12 Allan H. Gilbert, *Literary Criticism: Plato to Dryden* (New York, 1940), 511.

13 Baldwin, *op. cit.*, ch. 2; text, ed. Paul Wessner (Leipzig, 1902), 2 vols.

14 5. 4. 255-56.

15 *Discoveries*, 2625.

16 Giraldi Cinthio in Gilbert, *op. cit.*, 254.

17 Gilbert, 528-29.

Tradition and Modernity

1 References to Stevens' *Collected Poems* (New York, 1954) are by page number in parentheses.

2 *The Necessary Angel* (New York, 1951), 26.

3 *Prelude*, 1. 337-44.

4 Lines 126-33 and 800-08.

5 *Life on a Battleship* in *Opus Posthumus*, ed. Samuel French Morse (New York, 1957), 79.

6 *The Necessary Angel*, 86.

III

The Problem of Form

1 William A. Ringler, Jr., ed., *The Poems of Sir Philip Sidney* (Oxford, 1962), 105, lines, 67-68.

The Problem of Style

1 Hart Crane, *Atlantis*.

2 Emily Dickinson, *There's a certain slant of light* (258).

3 There have been many attempts to describe the rhythms of English prose, and how successful they have been becomes clear when we notice that scarcely anyone builds on the work of his predecessors. Yet, the ancients write clearly

and securely about prose rhythm, and there is much evidence that not only did speakers consciously employ certain rhythms but also that their audiences explicitly recognized them. Such an open employment of recognizable rhythmical patterns is not in our tradition, certainly not in prose, and it is becoming somewhat rare in poetry. This discrepancy between ancient and contemporary experience calls for explanation.

4 Diodorus Siculus, 12. 53. 2-4, tr. C. H. Oldfather (London, 1950).

How Shall the Poem be Written?

1 John Donne, *Elegy*, 10. 14.
2 Sir Philip Sidney, *Astrophil and Stella*, 91. 13.
3 *The Collected Poems and Epigrams of J. V. Cunningham* (Chicago, 1971), 84.
4 *Ibid.*, Epigram 90.
5 *Ibid.*, Epigram 83.
6 *Ibid.*, "To What Strangers, What Welcome," Poem 8 (sometimes entitled *Miramar Beach*).
7 This paragraph and several sentences on page 267 are from my essay "The Problem of Form."

IV

~~~~~~

Ideal Fiction

1 *Ars Poetica*, 128-35.
2 Chaucer, *The Knight's Tale*, 1668-69.
3 Aristotle, *Rhetoric*, 2. 24. 1402a.
4 Cicero, *Rhetorica ad Herennium*, 1. 8. 13.

The Renaissance in England

1 Thomas Campian, *Observations in the Art of English Poesy*.
2 Francis Bacon, *Of the Advancement of Learning*, I.
3 *The Life of the Renowned Sir Philip Sidney*, cited from Mona Wilson, *Sir Philip Sidney* (New York, 1932), 100.
4 *Evil May Day* is the anthology title for the scene in *The Book of Sir Thomas More*, often ascribed to Shakespeare.
5 Wilson, *op. cit.*, 100-01.
6 *The Autobiography of Thomas Whythorne*, ed. James M. Osborn (London, 1962), 80, 82.
7 See my essay "The Problem of Form," 249.
8 For the relationship of Campian and Donne to the Latin elegiac tradition, see my "Campian and Propertius," *Philological Quarterly* XXXI (January 1951), 96; Donne's *Canonization* has the same internal form.

Lyric Style in the 1590s

1 The character is called Lorenzo, Jr. in the 1601 edition of the play (produced 1598), Edward Knowell in the revised 1616 edition.

2 C. S. Lewis, *English Literature in the Sixteenth Century* (Oxford, 1954), 64-65.
3 Cicero, *Orator*, 42.
4 Thomas Kyd, *The Spanish Tragedy*, 3. 2. 1-4.
5 I owe this date to Professor Walter R. Davis of the University of Notre Dame.
6 Cicero, *Orator*, 76.

With That Facility

1 *Love's Labour's Lost, 1598.* Shakespeare Quarto Facsimiles, No. 10 (Oxford, 1957). All quotations are from this text.
2 R. B. McKerrow, "Booksellers, Printers, and the Stationers' Trade" in *Shakespeare's England: An Account of the Life & Manners of His Age* (Oxford, 1932), II, 231. Percival Vivian, ed., *Campion's Works* (Oxford, 1909), 34.
3 E. K. Chambers, *The Elizabethan Stage* (Oxford, 1923), III, 461; IV, 48; III, 483, 485.
4 E. K. Chambers, *William Shakespeare: A Study of Facts and Problems* (Oxford, 1930), II, 188.
5 "Preface to R. Greene's 'Menaphon' " in Ronald B. McKerrow, ed., *The Works of Thomas Nashe* (Oxford, 1958), III, 312.
6 *The Collected Poems of Joseph Hall*, ed. A. Davenport (Liverpool, 1949), 16.
7 Chambers, *Shakespeare*, II, 189, 195, 194.
8 *The Arte of English Poesie* (London, 1589; Kent, Ohio, 1970, facsimile ed.) 3. 2, p. 115; 3. 1, p. 114-15; 1. 22, p. 36.
9 Capell in Variorum (Philadelphia, n.d.), 4th impression, ad 4. 3. 317-22 and 330-38, p. 193.
10 *The Two Gentlemen of Verona*, 3. 1. 283.
11 McKerrow, *Works of Nashe*, III, 312.
12 Louise Brown Osborn, *The Life, Letters, and Writings of John Hoskyns* (New Haven, 1937), 125.
13 Ben Jonson, *Works*, ed. C. H. Herford, Percy Simpson, and Evelyn Simpson (Oxford, 1925-52), VIII, 584.

The Heart of His Mystery

1 Fulke Greville, *Poems and Dramas*, ed. Geoffrey Bullough (Oxford, 1945), I, 161.
2 Joseph Quincy Adams, ed., *Hamlet* (Boston, 1929), *ad loc.*
3 A. C. Bradley, *Shakespearean Tragedy* (New York, 1955), 79.
4 Harley Granville-Barker, *Prefaces to Shakespeare: Hamlet* (Princeton, 1946), 258.
5 Maynard Mack, "The World of Hamlet," *Yale Review* XLI (1952), 506, 522.
6 Saxo Grammaticus, *Danish History* in Joseph Satin, ed., *Shakespeare and His Sources* (Boston, 1966), 387.
7 Francois de Belleforest, *Tragic Stories* in Satin, *ibid.*, 399.
8 Pelican and Signet editions, *ad loc.* Maynard Mack says of *Lear* that "it is peculiarly the play of [Shakespeare's] that speaks with urgency to our time." " 'We Came Crying Hither': An Essay on Some Characteristics of *King Lear*" in Gerald W. Chapman, ed., *Essays on Shakespeare* (Princeton, 1965), 138.
9 *Hamlet,* 1. 4. 37 reads in Quarto "of a doubt," but a pronoun is needed, either "it" or " 'em."
10 St. Thomas Aquinas, *Summa Theologica*, 2-2. 43.
11 Richard Hooker, *Of the Laws of Ecclesiastical Polity*, 4. 12. 2 (Everyman's Library, London, 1907), I, 406.

Sorting Out

1 The poem numbers in parentheses are those in Thomas H. Johnson, ed., *The Poems of Emily Dickinson* (Cambridge, Mass., 1955). Texts have been normalized.
2 *L*, followed by volume and page, refers to Thomas H. Johnson, ed., *The Letters of Emily Dickinson* (Cambridge, Mass., 1958).
3 George W. Noyes, comp., *The Religious Experience of John Humphrey Noyes* (New York, 1923), 138-40, 143, 353.

Edwin Arlington Robinson

1 The poem numbers in parentheses are those in Thomas H. Johnson, ed., *The York, 1940), 101; hereafter *SL*. *Untriangulated Stars*, ed. Denham Sutcliffe (Cambridge, Mass., 1947), 150; hereafter *US*. *SL*, 90. *US*, 124. *Collected Poems* (New York, 1928), 24; hereafter *CP*. *SL*, 75. *CP*, 177, 178. *Selections from the Letters of Thomas Sergeant Perry*, ed. E. A. Robinson (New York, 1929), 6. *US*, 155, 244, 246. *SL*, 137, 75. *US*, 216, 24 (September 13, 1891). *CP*, 314. *SL*, 32, 103. *US*, 119, 161. *SL*, 163 (September 18, 1931).
2 *CP*, 178, 52, 56, 544, 17, 188.

The Styles and Procedures of Wallace Stevens

1 *The Harvard Advocate*, CXXV (Dec. 1938), 41-42, cited from Daniel Fuchs, *The Comic Spirit of Wallace Stevens* (Durham, N.C., 1963), 26-27n20.
2 "It was William James, I think, who defined the difference between the professional and the amateur by saying that the latter interests himself especially in the result obtained, the former in the way in which he obtains it." Henri Bergson, *Mind-Energy: Lectures and Essays* (New York, 1920), 78.
3 References to Stevens' *Collected Poems* (New York, 1954) are by page number in parentheses, to *The Necessary Angel* (New York, 1951) by page number preceded by *NA*, to *Opus Posthumous* (New York, 1957) by page number preceded by *OP*.
4 In *The Course of a Particular* I read, with Yvor Winters, "ear" for "air," as originally printed in the *Hudson Review*, Spring 1951.

T. S. Eliot on Poetry and Poets

1 T. S. Eliot, *On Poetry and Poets* (New York, 1957).

V

~~~~~~

The Quest of the Opal

1 The poems referred to in this essay can be found in *The Collected Poems and Epigrams of J. V. Cunningham* (Chicago, 1971).

Acknowledgments

~~~~~~

Pages 455-56 constitute an extension of the copyright page.

I

My Ph.D. dissertation, "Tragic Effect and Tragic Process . . . ." (Stanford University, 1945), was cut and revised and published as *Woe or Wonder* in 1951 by the University of Denver Press; by Alan Swallow, Denver, in 1960; Appendix I was published in *Poetry*, September 1949; and Appendix II in *Tradition and Poetic Structure*, 1960.

II

Tradition and Poetic Structure was published by Alan Swallow, Denver, in 1960. These essays, except for the ones on Statius and Stevens, were public lectures at the University of Chicago, Spring 1952. The Statius in earlier form was read at the Stanford Philological Society about 1938, and published in *Philological Quarterly*, October 1948; the Stevens was a public lecture at the University of Michigan, Spring 1949, and published in *Poetry*, December 1949. "Logic and Lyric," *Modern Philology*, August 1953. "Convention as Structure," *Modern Philology*, February 1952. "Idea as Structure," *ELH*, December 1952.

III

"The Problem of Form," read at Library of Congress, October 24, 1962; *Shenandoah*, Winter 1963. "The Problem of Style," Introduction to *The Problem of Style*, Fawcett, New York, 1966. "How Shall the Poem be Written?" read at University of Denver, November 17, 1966; *Denver Quarterly*, Spring 1967. "Graduate Training in English," *Carleton Miscellany*, Winter 1964.

IV

"Ideal Fiction," read at MLA, Chicago, 1967; *Shenandoah*, Winter 1968. "The Renaissance in England," Introduction to *The Renaissance in England*, Harcourt,

Brace and World, New York, 1966. "Lyric Style in the 1590s," read in earlier form at Brandeis University, 1961; read in present form at English Institute, 1965; *Folio*, Brandeis, Spring 1966. "With That Facility," read at University of Denver, Spring 1964; in present form in *Essays on Shakespeare*, ed. Gerald W. Chapman, Princeton University Press, 1965; in shorter form in *Love's Labour's Lost*, Dell, New York, 1965. "In Shakespeare's Day," Introduction to *In Shakespeare's Day*, Fawcett, New York, 1970. "The Heart of His Mystery," read at MLA, Chicago, 1973. "Sorting Out," read at Mt. Holyoke College, November 14, 1967; at University of California, Berkeley, January 17, 1968; *The Southern Review*, Spring 1969. "Edwin Arlington Robinson," *Denver Quarterly*, Spring 1968; in *Atlantic Brief Lives*, ed. Louis Kronenberger, Little, Brown, Boston, 1971. "The Styles and Procedures of Wallace Stevens," read in earlier form at University of Virginia, March 4, 1964; in present form at Bennington College, March 17, 1965, and at University of Denver, April 7, 1966; *Denver Quarterly*, Spring 1966. "T. S. Eliot on Poetry and Poets," *Virginia Quarterly*, Winter 1958.

V

The Quest of the Opal, Alan Swallow, Denver, 1950. "The Journal of John Cardan," *Sequoia*, Stanford, Winter 1961; in *The Journal of John Cardan*, Alan Swallow, Denver, 1964. "Several Kinds of Short Poem," read on Voice of America broadcast, September 21 and 24, 1964; in *Poets on Poetry*, ed. Howard Nemerov, Basic Books, New York, 1966. "Technology and Poetry," read at Seton Hall University, April 16, 1970; *Modern Occasions*, Spring 1972.

Index

457